Cases in Financial Management

Fourth Edition

Stephen Foerster
Craig Dunbar
James Hatch
David Shaw
Larry Wynant

Richard Ivey School of Business, The University of Western Ontario

Prentice
Hall

Toronto

Canadian Cataloguing in Publication Data

Main entry under title:

Cases in Financial Management

4th ed.
Previous eds. had title: Canadian Cases in Financial Management
ISBN 0-13-086049-2

1. Business enterprises – Canada – Finance – Case studies.
2. Business enterprises – Finance – Case studies. I. Foerster,
Stephen R. II. Title: Canadian cases in financial management.

HG4015.5.C35 2003   658.15'2'0971   C2002-900827-1

ISBN 0-13-086049-2

Vice President, Editorial Director: Michael J. Young
Executive Editor: Dave Ward
Marketing Manager: Deborah Meredith
Associate Editor: Susanne Marshall
Production Editor: Judith Scott
Copy Editor: David Handelsman
Production Coordinator: Andrea Falkenberg
Page Layout: Bill Renaud
Cover and Interior Design: Lisa Lapointe
Cover Image: Photodisc

To order copies or request permission to reproduce Ivey materials, contact Ivey Publishing, Ivey Management Services, c/o Richard Ivey School of Business, The University of Western Ontario, London, Ontario, Canada N6A3K7; phone (519) 661 – 3208, fax (519) 661 – 3882, e-mail cases@ivey.uwo.ca

One time permission to reproduce granted by Ivey Management Services on December 1, 2001.

Statistics Canada information is used with the permission of the Minister of Industry, as Minister responsible for Statistics Canada. Information on the availability of the wide range of data from Statistics Canada can be obtained from Statistic Canada's Regional Offices, its World Wide Web site at http://www.statcan.ca, and its toll-free access number 1-800-263-1136.

14 15 16 CP 13 12 11
Printed in Canada

contents

preface

This book presents students with a variety of decisions typically faced by financial managers. The cases are drawn from a broad range of industries and reflect the various economic, market, corporate, and behavioural factors that affect financial decision making. The decision maker is usually the senior financial officer in the firm, but may be a potential investor in or a lender to the company. In each case the student must adopt the role of the decision maker, define the problem and the alternatives, consider the objectives for the company as they apply to the situation, analyze the relevant data for each alternative according to the objectives, and reach a decision.

The topics covered in this casebook are intended to complement an introductory course in corporate finance. We have taught these courses in our undergraduate and MBA programs and in programs for executives.

The fourth edition includes 29 cases, of which 14 are new cases and two are significantly revised. The fourth edition incorporates more of an international emphasis with four of the new cases reflecting this thrust.

A complete set of teaching notes is available to adopters of this book. The notes provide a thorough analysis of each of the cases plus suggestions for case sequencing, assignments, teaching approach, and supplementary readings and references.

We are indebted to many persons for this book. First we wish to thank the many business executives who provided the material for the cases. Their generosity with time and data, some of which was confidential and controversial, was very much appreciated and critical to the success of each case.

Second, several colleagues have provided case materials and assistance in teaching and revising the cases in this book. The late Professors Samuel Martin and James Taylor contributed in many ways to this book, but especially by writing original versions of cases we regard as "chestnuts." Professors Paul Bishop and John Humphrey contributed through writing earlier versions and providing teaching feedback. We appreciate the efforts of our colleagues, past and present, for establishing and maintaining an environment of cooperation for developing and testing new materials.

A number of case research assistants contributed to the development of this fourth edition. We are indebted to and wish to thank Ahmed Arif, Rob Barbara, Arati Chervu, Steve Cox, Geoff Crum, Sandra Galli, David Goldberg, Chris Lounds, John Manning, John McCartney, J.J. McHale, Richard Nason, John Siambanopoulos, Peter Yuan, Blair Zilkey, Gabriel Vinizki, and Jerry White for their efforts. Over the four editions we have had a dedicated group of casewriters, all of whom have contributed to the development of the book.

We owe special thanks to our dedicated assistants and those in Ivey Publishing: Elaine Carson, Sheryl Gregson, Shirley Koenig, Sherri Moore, Karen Pepers, Marg Reffle, Pegg Saunders, and Jeannette Weston. Their assistance in typing the various drafts, setting the formats and making corrections, always offered in a cheerful and cooperative way, was invaluable.

The deans and associate deans of the Richard Ivey School of Business, who have provided us with grant support over the years for our casewriting activities and encouraged us to publish this casebook, deserve special commendation. Funds and assistance provided by the school contributed greatly to the development of this textbook. The Richard Ivey School of Business is supported by a large number of corporations, foundations and alumni who are committed to excellence in management education. This support has been invaluable to our completing the fourth edition. Thank you.

Stephen Foerster
Craig Dunbar
James Hatch
David Shaw
Larry Wynant
2002

part one

An Assessment of the Firm and Its Cash Needs

NATIONAL FABRICATORS INC.

On July 20, 1994, Mr. Jim Kasmar, manager of the Confederation Bank of Canada main branch in Winnipeg, Manitoba, was reviewing the credit file of National Fabricators Inc. The president of National Fabricators, Mr. Tom Kruger, had telephoned that morning with a request that the bank continue to extend a temporary line of credit of $1,000,000 for a further period of sixty days. "In two months' time, we should be pretty well out of the woods as far as our cash bind is concerned," said Mr. Kruger. "We've had some delays in collecting our holdbacks, but I'm expecting payment for sure about the middle of September. Then you can cut our line back to the normal $800,000 and we should be able to operate perfectly well within that limit from then on."

The regional credit office of the bank had extended National Fabricators a 30-day temporary line of $1,000,000 on June 20, 1994, when the company experienced difficulty in collecting $216,000 in hold-backs from a contract for two large school locker-room installations in Regina (the capital city of Saskatchewan with a population of 180,000). Mr. Kasmar knew that the regional office of the bank had granted the 30-day extension reluctantly; in fact, the regional office made it crystal clear to Mr. Kasmar that it was relying entirely on the strong endorsement which he had given National Fabricators' new young president.

On paper, nothing in the application warrants the extension of further credit; in fact, we are concerned about the safety of our existing line with the company. However, because of the confidence you have expressed in the new president of the company, your closeness to the situation, and the importance of National Fabricators to the community, we will authorize a 30-day credit line to a maximum of $1,000,000 . . .

Richard Ivey School of Business
The University of Western Ontario

IVEY

Rob Barbara prepared this case under the supervision of Professor Larry Wynant solely to provide material for class discussion. The authors do not intend to illustrate either effective or ineffective handling of a managerial situation. The authors may have disguised certain names and other identifying information to protect confidentiality.

Mr. Kasmar knew that to convince the regional office to grant an extension of a further 60 days, it would be necessary to submit a comprehensive and compelling application to the senior credit officers in Winnipeg. In view of the responsibility he already carried for the first extension, he wanted to do so only if he himself was entirely convinced that National Fabricators, under Mr. Kruger's direction, was capable of overcoming the financial problems which had plagued it for almost 10 years.

With these thoughts in mind, Mr. Kasmar proceeded to review all the information which he had accumulated in the file of the company.

BACKGROUND

National Fabricators Inc. was reorganized under its present name after the bankruptcy of Canadian Metal Fabricators Limited in 1936. Canadian Metal Fabricators Limited had been the outgrowth of a blacksmith shop founded by the Blackwell family of Winnipeg in 1868, and later incorporated as the Blackwell Wire and Iron Works Limited. By the early 1980s, control of National Fabricators Inc. had passed through five generations of the Blackwell family. At this time, none of the twenty-seven family shareholders expressed a keen desire to take an active role in the management of the company, and operating results deteriorated for a period of almost 10 years.

In November 1992, Mr. Tom Kruger convinced a group of influential National Fabricators shareholders to sell him their shares in National Fabricators Inc. For a cash payment of approximately $75,000 (and a complicated agreement of payment of the balance), Mr. Kruger acquired control of the company and assumed the position of president of the company on November 15, 1992.

Mr. Kruger, a native of Montreal, had earned the degrees of B.Com. (McGill, 1982) and MBA (Harvard, 1986), and was a Certified Management Accountant. From 1987 to 1989, he worked for two management consulting firms in Montreal, where he gained experience in organizational problems, production control, office and plant layout, and salary and wage incentives. In 1989 he joined the firm of Rodricks Associates, management consultants in Toronto; and from 1989 to 1992, he held the position of accountant, office manager, assistant to the secretary-treasurer and general manager of that firm. Mr. Kruger had told Mr. Kasmar that his personal savings had been used up in acquiring control of National Fabricators.

Upon gaining control of National Fabricators in 1992, Mr. Kruger immediately applied himself to the problem of putting the company back on a profit-making basis. Although he was not completely satisfied with the performance of certain key employees, Mr. Kruger decided not to replace any of the senior management for the first year, in order to "preserve morale and build up good will." Mr. Charles Wilkes, a long-time employee of the organization, continued as vice president and general manager in charge of production. The positions of secretary-treasurer and office manager were entrusted to Mrs. Ethyl Samson, another employee of long standing.

OPERATIONS

National Fabricators manufactured lockers, school furniture, toilet partitions, and steel shelving. Cold rolled sheets were purchased from warehouses located in Winnipeg, in varying gauges and quality. Mr. Kruger stated that delivery could be obtained on a day's notice from these sources, compared to three months' delivery by large steel producers. Also, warehouse credit terms were much more favorable—60 to 90 days were common—whereas the large producers demanded payment within 30 days. Prices from the warehouse averaged about 12 to 15 per cent higher than purchase of similar quantities directly from steel producers.

The manufacturing cycle, comprising seven operations in the case of a locker, required 44 minutes to complete. First, the correct gauge of steel was selected, prime sheets being used for locker doors and seconds for locker backs. Shearing and cutting to size preceded the notching of the corners and the punching operations. Then the different pieces were bent for fitting so that they could be bolted or welded into place. At last, the lockers were ready for painting. Similar procedures were followed in manufacturing school furniture and toilet partitions.

The number of direct production workers at National Fabricators varied between 20 and 25. Most of these employees were semi-skilled, but there were a few skilled mechanics who did the layout work. The production workers were organized by the United Steel Workers. Mr. Kruger commented that "this union was no worse than any other union." In addition, there were eight to 10 office workers and manufacturing supervisors employed by the firm.

According to Mr. Kruger, the steel fabricating industry was plagued with several problems. Scheduling was tied closely to the construction industry which, in turn, was very dependent on the general economic climate. In mid-1994, the Canadian economy appeared to be on the road to recovery from the severe recession of the early 1990s, fueled largely by a substantial growth in exports. However, recent increases in long-term interest rates and a sluggish level of consumer confidence caused many economic forecasters to predict minimal growth in gross domestic product and some to warn of another round of economic decline. Mr. Kruger shared these concerns and was particularly concerned about the impact of widespread provincial and federal government cutbacks on medical and educational spending.[1] He felt that these combined factors could cause National Fabricators' sales to fall as much as 10 per cent during fiscal 1994 or to a level of about $3.6 million.

Lags caused by numerous die changes presented the industry with another headache. Because of the number of cuts to be made, the number and size of corners to be notched, and the varying shapes to be bent, the dies had to be altered fairly often, particularly when production runs were short. In addition, the industry was very competitive, with "anybody and their uncle" being able to manufacture lockers.

Rapid modernization had taken place in the industry as a result of mechanization. In 1993, National Fabricators spent nearly $120,000 on equipment. National Fabricators' punching and stamping equipment overall was rather old, but not obsolete by industry standards.

Production was divided equally among the three major items produced. Lockers, school furniture and toilet partitions each accounted for about 30 per cent of total production, while the specialty items such as steel shelving provided the remaining 10 per cent.

COMPETITION

Competition in the steel fabricating industry was very intense. Rising costs and severe price cutting minimized returns and demanded efficient operations for survival. The three large conglomerates, National Manufacturers, Shanahan Ltd. and General Storage Systems, that were dominant players in the field were investing substantial amounts for new tooling and upgrading of facilities in an effort to become more efficient and to gain market share. One of these had recently stated in a trade magazine:

> We have begun the difficult process of rationalizing our Building Products business, which continues to suffer from under-utilized facilities and some weak markets. This is our main area of concern for 1994.

The three larger firms served all of Canada and controlled close to 65 per cent of the market. The remaining 35 per cent was served by numerous regional firms. While the large firms were not able to control prices, they were able to control industry specifications. By offering full product lines, large firms forced smaller firms to copy their product specifications.

MARKETING

Most companies distributed their products coast to coast because of the small Canadian market, but the majority of the business was carried out in large centres such as Winnipeg, Calgary, Vancouver, Montreal and Toronto. Recently, a number of Canadian fabricators were beginning to market their products in the U.S. National Fabricators had successfully sold lockers to one school project in Wisconsin, and Kruger was optimistic that other contracts would follow in the future.

As previously stated, National Fabricators' main product lines were lockers, school furnishings and toilet partitions. Locker production was the most competitive, and Mr. Kruger commented that lockers were produced mainly as a contribution to overhead, with little realizable profit margin; they were a necessary product to carry in order to "round out the line."

---

[1] Non-residential construction was forecasted to decrease by 0.9 per cent in 1994 after decreasing by 9.1 per cent in 1993.

National Fabricators' potential market was in schools, hospitals, motels, hotels, shopping centres, offices and sports clubs. Normally, the architect for a particular building would determine the specifications, and the construction company would do the actual purchasing. However, in the school furnishings line, some school boards were doing the buying themselves, thus eliminating the commissions to the construction contractors.

Service and delivery were very important factors for National Fabricators. Most of the installations were subcontracted to local construction crews. In one case, National Fabricators had bid on installation in Edmonton and lost it to a competitor. The competitor was unable to deliver in the allotted time, and the contract was, therefore, reassigned to National Fabricators (at the National Fabricators' bid price) under the condition that delivery be made in one week. National Fabricators had been able to deliver the order and arrange installation in six days.

Pricing for National Fabricators and its competitors was crucial. When asked how some of the competitors bid, Mr. Kruger stated:

> It depends on what kind of a crazy mood they are in. First a bid is sent in, but the first bid rarely brings any results. The purchaser, when he has received all the bids, usually plays one supplier against another, shaving the price down. In other words, you bid and then haggle.

Personal contact with the architect in some cases proved to be an influential factor, although price was the primary determinant.

Promotion and advertising were minimal. Catalogues were delivered personally by sales agents to architects, but little advertising was carried in trade magazines and commercial papers. Mr. Kruger referred to a recent advertisement by one of his competitors in a trade magazine as "a waste of money."

Selling was handled through fifteen sales agents across Canada. Mr. Kruger was not able to provide Mr. Kasmar with precise sales figures for each agent, although he indicated that sales per agent averaged $260,000. Recently, one of National Fabricators' leading agents had been made sales manager; and Mr. Kruger had released one, and intended to release another. One salesman was reassigned to cover the industrial aspect of the market. Mr. Kruger planned to visit his agents at least twice a year. National Fabricators' agents were paid on a straight commission basis.

FINANCIAL POSITION

National Fabricators was facing a tight working capital situation propagated by losses totaling $480,315 over the four-year period, 1990 to 1993. These losses had caused a heavy cash drain on the company with a resultant decrease in the current ratio from 2.3 to 1.1. Operations were being financed exclusively on bank credit with the company maintaining a cash fund of only $3,200. At the end of December 1993, outstanding bank loans of $784,000 exceeded the previous year's total by $248,000. Comparative balance sheets, income statements and financial ratios are shown in Exhibits 1 to 3.

In 1993, a profit of $1,000 was earned. Mr. Kruger told Mr. Kasmar that he was expecting to break even or incur a small loss in 1994 because of the decline in new school and hospital construction, which he felt would be somewhat less than offset by an increase in office and sport club construction. He anticipated sales of approximately $3.6 million. Mr. Kruger attributed the improved operating picture of the company primarily to a new plant layout, which enabled production time and the number of production workers to be decreased. Three major contracts had pushed National Fabricators' sales above the break-even point in 1993.

Since taking over the company, Mr. Kruger had been working on a job cost system intended to give him the profit on each job and the contribution of each line. No standards had been developed within the plant; however the president considered them no more useful than actual data, and proposed to use the latter in his cost control system. The company had been operating at between 50 per cent and 70 per cent of capacity over the last few years.

National Fabricators constantly operated under the threat of increasing steel prices and wage rates. Competition and contract bargaining forced sales prices down and depressed profit margins. In August 1993, National Fabricators' employees received a two per cent increase in pay. This one-year contract was comparable to that negotiated by some of the larger competitors. In addition, sales fluctuated considerably following the cyclical trends in that sector of the construction industry which steel fabricators serviced. Since fixed costs constituted a large part of total costs, capacity operations were extremely important to the profitability of the company. Details of operations for the year ended December 31, 1993 are shown in Exhibit 4.

The age of receivables increased in December 1993 to 101 days over 77 days the previous year. Mr. Kruger attributed the increase to holdbacks on large accounts. The nature of the company's business was such that the supplying firm was not paid until the contractor had settled with the institution for which a building was erected. Government accounts were generally slow in payment and very little could be done to force settlement of an account. Mr. Kruger considered the receivable problem so important that he gave it his own personal attention. This required constant badgering of the contractor until payment was received. Although payments were slow, bad debts had not been significantly large. Ninety-five per cent of National Fabricators' business was of the contract and holdback nature. On June 30, 1994 receivables stood as follows:

Less than 30 days	$264,000
30 to 60 days	208,000
60 to 90 days	80,000
Over 90 days	44,000
Holdbacks*	216,000
Liens and Legal*	36,000
Total	$848,000

* Information pertinent to Liens and Holdbacks may be found in Exhibit 5. Legislation similar to The Builders' Lien Act of Manitoba is in place in other provinces.

Inventories in mid-1994 stood at approximately $500,000, of which $100,000 was raw materials, $200,000 work-in-process and $200,000 finished goods. The company produced primarily on a job basis, but also manufactured items for stock. A fairly large inventory of finished goods was required to service orders that requested immediate delivery. Because of the poor working capital position of the company, management was unable to speculate on the purchase of steel. Usually just enough sheet steel was purchased to take advantage of quantity discounts. This practice caused inventories of raw materials to fluctuate considerably throughout the year.

The lack of scheduling and status reporting allowed work-in-process to be controlled only by visual inspection. Mr. Kruger indicated that he recognized this problem, and expressed a desire to improve his inventory control procedures. Previously, physical inventories had been taken once per year; however, the inventory of paint had been checked twice in 1994 and Mr. Kruger was in the process of developing records which would enable him to exercise greater control over raw steel. Also planned for the near future were more detailed perpetual inventory records.

Mr. Kruger's statement, "we pay when they holler," generally reflected the company's policy in making payments to suppliers. In order to minimize the need for bank credit and to keep this line open as a future source of funds, National Fabricators held back payments as long as possible. In Mr. Kruger's opinion, this practice was typical of everyone in the industry. Steel mills, however, did not allow such practices. With a three-month lead time, they would not even accept orders from a customer with accounts over 30 days. As a result, many of National Fabricators' competitors purchased from warehouses.

Land was carried on the books at $45,200; however, Mr. Kruger conservatively estimated its present value at over $500,000, since it was in downtown Winnipeg in a location of historical significance to the city. On the other hand, the buildings were in poor repair.

Kruger considered factoring to be too expensive as a method of financing, especially since he had been able to obtain bank loans on his accounts receivable and fixed assets at considerably lower rate of prime plus two per cent.[2] Factors' rates reflected their traditional distaste for service accounts because of installation damage claims.

Because of the poor performance of the company over the past ten years and the present questionable

---

[2]The prime rate was currently 7.5 per cent.

financial position, Mr. Kasmar realized that sale of common or preferred stock was either impractical or impossible at this time. Furthermore, Mr. Kruger in no way wanted to jeopardize his control and ownership of the firm through a stock issue. The aim of the president was to improve the profit position of the company through stricter cost control and better marketing strategy. Mr. Kruger hoped that the bank would increase National Fabricators' loan until profits had improved and funds could be generated internally.

Exhibit 1				
BALANCE SHEET AS AT DECEMBER 31, 1990-1993				
	1993	**1992**	**1991**	**1990**
Assets				
Current Assets:				
Cash	3,200	1,600	1,600	2,700
Accounts Receivable (net)	1,114,584	672,968	871,260	791,928
Inventories	662,620	541,017	564,692	674,248
Prepaid Expenses	2,265	5,632	18,128	24,792
Deposits	0	0	1,500	1,000
Total Current Assets	1,782,669	1,221,217	1,457,180	1,494,668
Fixed Assets (net of accumulated depreciation):				
Land	45,200	45,200	45,200	45,200
Buildings	163,060	138,408	147,744	157,620
Machinery and Dies	115,140	25,556	29,460	36,824
Trucks and Auto	884	1,264	4,864	6,948
Total Fixed Assets	324,284	210,428	227,268	246,592
Total Assets	2,106,953	1,431,645	1,684,448	1,741,260
Liabilities				
Current Liabilities:				
Bank Overdraft[1]	143,852	0	332,744	162,616
Bank Loans[1]	640,000	536,000	588,000	560,000
Accounts Payable	751,980	86,968	94,376	159,148
Accrued Expenses	0	82,388	86,952	64,556
Cheques Outstanding	0	209,040	0	0
Taxes Payable	57,744	0	0	0
Total Current Liabilities	1,593,576	914,396	1,107,072	946,320
Mortgage Payable	0	4,852	6,388	7,864
Shareholders' Equity:				
Preferred A (Issued 5,250 shares @ $40)	210,000	210,000	210,000	210,000
Common (Issued 66,808 shares @ NPV)	34,020	34,020	34,020	34,020
Capital Surplus	13,344	13,344	13,444	13,344
Retained Earnings	256,013	255,033	313,624	529,712
Total Liabilities & Equity	2,106,953	1,431,645	1,684,448	1,741,260

[1] Amounts due to the bank are secured by:
a) Collateral mortgage on company's premises of $500,000.
b) A general assignment of receivables.
c) An assignment of inventories.

	Exhibit 2			
	STATEMENT OF PROFIT & LOSS **FOR THE YEARS ENDED DECEMBER 31, 1990-1993**			
	1993	**1992**	**1991**	**1990**
Sales	4,027,852	3,205,452	3,892,168	3,401,448
Cost of Goods Sold	3,639,820	2,861,588	3,621,056	3,163,380
Gross Profit	388,032	343,864	271,112	238,068
Expenses:				
Administration	190,112	235,588	269,692	243,864
Selling	145,960	114,372	161,724	181,812
Interest & Bank Charges	66,700	77,015	64,860	53,184
Total Expenses	402,772	426,975	496,276	478,860
Operating Profit (Loss)	(14,740)	(83,111)	(225,164)	(240,792)
Other Income	15,720	24,520	9,076	34,176
Net Profit (Loss)	980	(58,591)	(216,088)	(206,616)

Exhibit 3

FINANCIAL RATIOS

	1993	1992	1991	1990	1989	1988	1987	1986	1985	1984
Current Ratio	1.12	1.34	1.32	1.58	2.33	2.40	1.64	2.09	2.38	2.07
Acid Test	0.70	0.74	0.79	0.84	1.05	1.35	0.97	1.15	1.32	1.23
Inventory Turnover (days)	66	69	57	78	N/A	N/A	62	N/A	52	52
Age of Receivables (days)	101	77	82	85	59	69	83	N/A	72	81
Earnings/Share	0.015	(0.88)	(3.23)	(3.09)	(1.07)	0.91	(0.82)	(0.62)	0.90	0.99
CGS/Sales	90.4	89.3	93.0	93.0	87.1	96.0	99.5	101.0	96.0	97.0
Gross Profit/Sales	9.6	10.7	7.0	7.0	12.9	4.0	0.5	(1.0)	4.0	3.0
Admin. Exp./Sales	4.7	7.3	6.9	7.2	8.1	6.7	6.6	7.5	7.0	6.8
Selling Exp./Sales	3.6	3.6	4.2	5.3	5.9	4.8	5.0	6.5	5.3	5.1
Interest Exp./Sales	1.7	2.4	1.7	1.6	1.5	2.9	1.6	0.5	2.4	1.2
Net Profit/Sales	0.0	(1.8)	(5.6)	(6.1)	(2.3)	1.3	(1.2)	(1.2)	1.4	1.6
Equity/Assets	24.4	35.8	33.9	45.2	63.0	64.5	46.8	58.5	62.8	57.5
Debt/Assets	75.6	64.2	66.1	54.8	37.0	35.5	53.2	41.5	37.2	42.5
Sales ($000s)	4,028	3,205	3,892	3,401	3,132	4,800	4,416	3,592	4,232	4,184
Equity ($000s)	513	512	571	787	988	1,064	1,012	1,072	1,124	1,092
Profit After Taxes ($000s)	1.0	(58.6)	(216.1)	(206.6)	(71.2)	61.2	(54.8)	(41.6)	60.4	66.4

Exhibit 4		
INCOME STATEMENT INCORPORATING FIXED AND VARIABLE EXPENSE ESTIMATES **FOR THE YEAR ENDED DECEMBER 31, 1993**		

Sales		$4,027,852
Variable Expenses:		
Commissions	$ 102,000	
Heat, Light and Power	70,592	
Materials	2,607,576	
Direct Labor	616,000	
Repairs and Maintenance	62,572	
Miscellaneous and General	22,408	
	$3,481,148	
Less: Inventory Adjustment	21,276	
	$3,459,872	
Contribution Margin		567,980
Fixed Expenses:		
Salaries	$ 313,492	
Telephone	800	
Supplies	6,400	
Depreciation	27,560	
Heat, Light and Power	1,200	
Insurance	19,552	
Taxes	81,456	
Repairs and Maintenance	60,000	
Interest	64,060	
Miscellaneous	8,200	
	$ 582,720	
Operating Profit (Loss)		(14,740)
Other Income		15,720
Net Income		$ 980

Exhibit 5

**SUMMARY OF PERTINENT SECTIONS OF THE
BUILDERS' LIEN ACT OF THE PROVINCE OF MANITOBA**

Section 2(1): Substantial Performance

For the Purpose of this Act, a contract or sub-contract shall be conclusively deemed to be substantially performed when:

- (a) the structure to be constructed under the contract or sub-contract or a substantial part thereof is ready for use or is being used for the purpose intended or, where the contract or sub-contract relates solely to improving land, the improved land or a substantial part thereof is ready for use or is being used for the purpose intended; and

- (b) the work to be done under the contract or sub-contract is capable of completion or correction at a cost of no more than
  - (i) 3% of the first $250,000 of the contract price,
  - (ii) 2% of the next $250,000 of the contract price, and
  - (iii) 1% of the balance of the contract price.

Section 13: Creation of a Lien

Any person who:

- (a) does any work; or
- (b) provides any services; or
- (c) supplies any material to be used;

in performance of a contract or sub-contract for any owner, contractor or sub-contractor has, by virtue thereof, a lien for the value of the work, services or materials which, subject to section 16, attaches upon the estate or interest of the owner in the land or structure upon or in respect of which the work was done or the services were provided or the materials were supplied, and the land occupied thereby or enjoyed therewith.

Section 24(1): Holdback

The person primarily liable for payment under or by virtue of which a lien may arise shall, as the work is done or the services are provided or the materials are supplied under the contract, deduct 7.5% of each payment to be made by him in respect of the contract, and retain that amount for at least 40 days after:

- (a) a certificate of substantial performance is given under section 46; or
- (b) the work to be done under contract has been completed, the services to be provided under the contract have been completely provided and the materials to be supplied under the contract have been completely supplied; or
- (c) the work to be done under the contract, the services to be provided under the contract and the supplying of materials to be supplied under the contract have been abandoned;

whichever first occurs, so that the total holdback shall be equal to 7.5% of the contract price for the whole contract, or if there is no specific contract price, 7.5% of the total value of the work, services and materials done, provided or supplied in the performance of the contract.

FINANCIAL PERFORMANCE OF DELL COMPUTER[1]

INTRODUCTION

Anya Grand was working as a financial analyst at Dell Computer Corporation. She had graduated from a well-known business school the year prior and had been working at Dell, as a special assistant to the treasurer. In the afternoon on March 1, 2001, the treasurer had returned from a meeting with Dell's founder and chief executive officer (CEO), Michael Dell. The company's stock was on a slide and was currently less than 50 per cent of its value from one year ago. Many of the key shareholders, as well as Michael Dell, had expressed concern for this slide and were wondering about its cause. The treasurer called Grand into his office and discussed what occurred at the meeting. He asked her to provide him with some analysis by morning so that he could report his findings to Michael Dell the next day. Grand decided that she would gather relevant data and investigate some of Dell's competitors to identify whether this slide in stock performance was unique to Dell or was industry-wide.

DELL COMPUTER CORPORATION

Headquartered in Austin, Texas, Dell was the world's number one computer systems company. Dell's business model was centred on delivering the best possible customer experience by directly selling computing products and services. This direct model allowed the company to build every system to order

Richard Ivey School of Business
The University of Western Ontario

David Goldberg prepared this case under the supervision of Professor Craig Dunbar solely to provide material for class discussion. The authors do not intend to illustrate either effective or ineffective handling of a managerial situation. The authors may have disguised certain names and other identifying information to protect confidentiality.

[1] This case has been written on the basis of published sources only. Consequently, the interpretation and perspectives presented in this case are not necessarily those of Dell Computer Corporation or any of its employees.

and offer custom configured systems for customers at competitive prices. Since being founded in 1984, the company had grown to more than 34,000 employees with revenues of $31.8 billion.

INDUSTRY AND ECONOMIC CONDITIONS

The computer industry as a whole was projected to grow at less than 17 per cent in 2001. While this growth rate appeared to be strong, it was less than the 20 per cent average annual growth rate experienced over the last decade. The global computer industry was projected to face continued price pressure due to overcapacity and competition over the next few years. This was coupled with increasing household penetration of desktop computers.

As the market for desktop computers was to slow, computer manufacturers were targeting higher margin, higher growth segments. A few examples of these new segments were: servers, storage devices, hand-held computers and MP3 players. These segments were projected to grow more than 30 per cent in 2001.

Global equity markets had begun to pull back in March of 2000. In March 2001, talk of a recession was beginning to circulate among economists. U.S. gross domestic product (GDP) was projected to grow by only 1.4 per cent in 2001 and it was expected that the third quarter and fourth quarter would be negative. This compared to GDP growth of more than five per cent in both 1999 and 2000. This economic information affected the entire economy as consumer confidence and overall spending dropped substantially.

THE COMPETITORS

To begin her analysis, Grand identified Dell's main competitors. In 2001, Compaq Computer Corporation, Hewlett-Packard Company, Gateway Incorporated and International Business Machines Corporation were four companies in the computers industry that competed directly with Dell.

Compaq Computer Corporation (which traded on the New York Stock Exchange with ticker symbol CPQ), an information technology company, developed and marketed hardware, software, solutions and services. The company's products and solutions included enterprise computing solutions, fault-tolerant business-critical solutions, networking and communication products, commercial desktop and portable products, and consumer personal computers.

Hewlett-Packard Company (which traded on the New York Stock Exchange with ticker symbol HWP) provided imaging and printing systems, computing systems, and information services for business and home. The company's products included laser and inkjet printers, scanners, copiers and faxes, personal computers, workstations, storage solutions, and other computing and printing systems. Hewlett-Packard sold its products worldwide.

Gateway Incorporated (which traded on the New York Stock Exchange with ticker symbol GTW) marketed personal computers (PCs) and related products and services. The company developed, manufactured, marketed and supported a line of desktop and portable PCs, digital media PCs, servers, workstations and PC-related products. Gateway's customers included individuals, families, businesses, government agencies and educational institutions.

International Business Machines Corporation (which traded on the New York Stock Exchange with ticker symbol IBM) provided customer solutions by using advanced information technology. The company's solutions included technologies, systems, products, services, software and financing. IBM offered its products through its global sales and distribution organization, as well as through a variety of third party distributors and resellers.

THE ANALYSIS

Grand attempted to gather as much information as possible. She began her analysis by collecting the financial statements (balance sheet, income statement and statement of cash flow) for Dell and its competitors (see Exhibits 1 to 3).[2] Although this analysis was useful, she found it difficult to come up with any meaningful

---

[2]Note that some items in the financial statements have been combined by the case writer to facilitate case analysis and discussion.

comparisons, as these companies were all different sizes. To better compare the companies, Grand decided to create common size balance sheets and income statements (see Exhibits 4 and 5). A common size balance sheet relates line items to total assets, which better enables comparison of companies of different sizes. A common size income statement relates each line item to revenues, similarly making it easier to compare companies with different scales of operation. Grand gathered stock data for Dell and its competitors, as well as selected market and economic data (see Exhibit 6). To gauge the relative performance of Dell's stock compared to its competitors, Grand generated comparative stock price charts (see Exhibits 7 to 9).

Grand then began to compute financial ratios to gain a better perspective on each company's relative performance. Her preliminary calculations are presented in Exhibit 10 (the definition of each ratio is provided in Exhibit 11). It was now midnight and Grand was just about to compute Dell and IBM's financial ratios. After completing her calculations, Grand could begin her final and most challenging task: interpreting the numbers.

Exhibit 1

BALANCE SHEETS FOR DELL COMPUTERS AND ITS COMPETITORS
(in millions of U.S. dollars)

	Compaq Computer		HP		Gateway Computers		IBM		Dell Computers	
	Dec. 2000	Dec. 1999	Dec. 2000	Dec. 1999	Dec. 2000	Dec. 1999	Dec. 2000	Dec. 1999	Feb. 2001	Feb. 2000
ASSETS										
Cash & Marketable Securities	2,569	3,302	4,007	5,590	614	1,337	3,722	5,831	5,438	4,132
Accounts Receivable	8,392	6,685	8,568	7,847	906	769	30,726	27,618	2,895	2,608
Inventories	2,161	2,008	5,699	4,863	315	192	4,765	4,868	400	391
Prepaid Expenses & Other Current Assets	1,989	1,854	4,970	3,342	432	400	4,667	4,838	758	550
Total Current Assets	15,111	13,849	23,244	21,642	2,267	2,698	43,880	43,155	9,491	7,681
Gross Plant, Property & Equipment	7,048	6,051	-	-	1,309	1,092	38,455	39,616	-	-
Less: Accumulated Depreciation	(3,617)	(2,802)	-	-	(411)	(346)	(21,741)	(22,026)	-	-
Net Plant, Property & Equipment	3,431	3,249	4,500	4,333	898	746	16,714	17,590	996	765
Investments	864	6,617	1,900	1,400	339	213	14,447	13,672	2,418	2,721
Deferred Income Taxes	1,604	342	-	-	291	212	-	-	-	-
Other Assets	3,846	3,220	4,365	7,922	358	87	13,308	13,078	530	304
Total Assets	24,856	27,277	34,009	35,297	4,153	3,956	88,349	87,495	13,435	11,471
LIABILITIES										
Short-Term Borrowings & Notes Payable	711	453	1,555	3,105	-	-	10,205	14,230	-	-
Accounts Payable	4,233	4,380	5,049	3,517	785	898	8,192	6,400	4,286	3,538
Employee Compensation and Benefits	-	-	1,584	1,287	-	-	3,801	3,840	-	-
Taxes Payable	-	-	2,046	2,152	-	-	4,827	4,792	-	-
Other Current Liabilities	6,605	7,005	4,963	4,260	846	912	9,381	10,316	2,257	1,654
Total Current Liabilities	11,549	11,838	15,197	14,321	1,631	1,810	36,406	39,578	6,543	5,192
Long-Term Debt	575	-	3,402	1,764	-	-	18,371	14,124	509	508
Other Liabilities	652	605	1,201	917	141	128	12,948	13,282	761	463
Total Liabilities	12,776	12,443	19,800	17,002	1,772	1,938	67,725	66,984	7,813	6,163
EQUITY										
Preferred Stock	-	-	-	-	-	-	247	247	-	-
Common Equity	12,080	14,834	14,209	18,295	2,381	2,018	20,377	20,264	5,622	5,308
Total Equity	12,080	14,834	14,209	18,295	2,381	2,018	20,624	20,511	5,622	5,308
Total Liabilities & Equity	24,856	27,277	34,009	35,297	4,153	3,956	88,349	87,495	13,435	11,471

Source: Company SEC filings.

Exhibit 2

INCOME STATEMENTS FOR DELL COMPUTERS AND ITS COMPETITORS
(in millions of U.S. dollars except per share amounts)

	Compaq Computer		HP		Gateway Computers		IBM		Dell Computers	
	Dec. 2000	Dec. 1999	Dec. 2000	Dec. 1999	Dec. 2000	Dec. 1999	Dec. 2000	Dec. 1999	Feb. 2001	Feb. 2000
Revenue	42,383	38,525	48,782	42,370	9,601	8,965	88,396	87,548	31,888	25,265
Cost of Goods Sold	32,417	29,798	34,864	29,720	7,542	7,128	55,972	55,619	25,445	20,047
Gross Profit	9,966	8,727	13,918	12,650	2,059	1,837	32,424	31,929	6,443	5,218
Selling, General & Administrative	4,637	4,939	7,383	6,522	1,359	1,108	15,639	14,729	3,193	2,387
Other Operating Expenses	1,383	2,528	1,278	1,124	-	-	156	(1,312)	300	378
Operating Income, Before Depreciation	3,946	1,260	5,257	5,004	700	729	16,629	18,512	2,950	2,453
Depreciation & Amortization	1,407	1,402	1,368	1,316	189	134	4,995	6,585	240	156
Operating Income	2,539	(142)	3,889	3,688	511	595	11,634	11,927	2,710	2,297
Interest Expense	273	211	257	202			717	727	47	34
Non-Operating Expense/(Income)	1,417	(1,287)	(1,129)	(1,095)	115	(68)	(597)	(537)	(472)	(188)
Pretax Income	849	934	4,761	4,581	396	663	11,514	11,737	3,135	2,451
Income Tax	280	365	1,064	1,090	155	236	3,441	4,045	958	785
Net Income(Loss)	569	569	3,697	3,491	241	427	8,073	7,692	2,177	1,666
Earnings Per Common Share	0.33	0.34	1.87	1.73	0.75	1.36	4.58	4.25	0.84	0.66

Source: Company SEC Filings.

Exhibit 3

STATEMENTS OF CASH FLOWS FOR DELL COMPUTERS AND ITS COMPETITORS
(in millions of U.S. dollars)

	Compaq Computer		HP		Gateway Computers		IBM		Dell Computers	
	Dec. 2000	Dec. 1999	Dec. 2000	Dec. 1999	Dec. 2000	Dec. 1999	Dec. 2000	Dec. 1999	Feb. 2001	Feb. 2000
Cash Flows from Operating Activities										
Net Income (loss)	569	569	3,697	3,491	241	427	8,073	7,692	2,177	1,666
Adjustments:										
Depreciation and Amortization	1,407	1,402	1,368	1,316	189	134	4,995	6,585	240	156
Investment Impairment	1,756	-	-	-	152	-			-	-
Gain on Sale of Businesses/Assets	-	(1,182)	(212)	-	-	-	(792)	(4,791)	(307)	(80)
Restructuring Related Activities	(86)	868								
Deferred Income Taxes and Other	(26)	21	(194)	118	(40)	-	29	(713)	1,143	1,290
Changes in Assets and Liabilities										
Receivables	(1,920)	185	(1,312)	(1,637)	76	(116)	(4,720)	(1,677)	(346)	(394)
Inventories	(72)	(97)	(845)	(171)	(123)	(24)	(55)	301	(7)	(123)
Accounts Payable	(228)	135	1,544	751	(114)	182	2,245	(3)	748	988
Other Assets and Liabilities	(835)	(598)	(450)	(385)	(92)	128	(521)	2,697	547	423
Net Cash Provided by Operating Activities	565	1,303	3,596	3,483	289	731	9,254	10,091	4,195	3,926
Cash Flows From Investing Activities										
Capital Expenditures, net	(1,133)	(1,185)	(1,317)	(592)	(315)	(338)	(3,997)	(4,752)	(482)	(401)
(Increase) / Decrease in ST Investments	636	(636)	(127)	48	79	(50)	314	(1,333)		
(Increase) / Decrease in LT Investments					(247)	(127)				
Sale / (Acquisition) of Businesses, net of cash	(370)	(517)	829	(449)			—	4,880		
Other Investing Activities	(364)	(131)	318	(84)	(471)	(317)	(565)	(464)	(275)	(782)
Net Cash used in Investing Activities	(1,231)	(2,469)	(297)	(1,077)	(954)	(832)	(4,248)	(1,669)	(757)	(1,183)
Cash Flows from Financing Activities										
Increase in short-term borrowings	258	453	(1,297)	2,399	3		(1,400)	276		
Issuance (repayment) of long-term debt	575	-	1,462	(807)	(9)	(6)	2,043	(1,377)	20	
Common stock transaction, net	(365)	(93)	(4,822)	(1,983)	26	61	(6,073)	(6,645)	(2,296)	(772)
Dividends to stockholders	(170)	(136)	(638)	(650)	-	-	(929)	(879)	-	-
Other financing activities	-	(400)							(9)	57
Net Cash Provided by (used in) financing	298	(176)	(5,295)	(1,041)	20	55	(6,359)	(8,625)	(2,305)	(695)
Effect of Exchange Rate Changes	271	(83)			1	4	(147)	(149)	(32)	35
Net Increase / (Decrease)	(97)	(1,425)	(1,996)	1,365	(644)	(42)	(1,500)	(352)	1,101	2,083
Cash and Equivalents at the Beginning of the Year	2,666	4,091	5,411	4,046	1,128	1,170	5,043	5,375	3,809	1,726
Cash and Equivalents at the End of the Year	2,559	2,666	3,415	5,411	484	1,128	3,543	5,023	4,910	3,809

Source: Company SEC filings.

Exhibit 4

COMMON SIZE BALANCE SHEETS FOR DELL COMPUTERS AND ITS COMPETITORS

	Compaq Computer		HP		Gateway Computers		IBM		Dell Computers	
	Dec. 2000	Dec. 1999	Dec. 2000	Dec. 1999	Dec. 2000	Dec. 1999	Dec. 2000	Dec. 1999	Feb. 2001	Feb. 2000
ASSETS										
Cash & Marketable Securities	10.34%	12.11%	11.78%	15.84%	14.79%	33.60%	4.21%	6.66%	40.48%	36.02%
Accounts Receivable	33.76%	24.51%	25.19%	22.23%	21.81%	19.44%	34.78%	31.57%	21.55%	22.74%
Inventories	8.69%	7.36%	16.76%	13.78%	7.59%	4.85%	5.39%	5.56%	2.98%	3.41%
Prepaid Expenses & Other Current Assets	8.00%	6.80%	14.61%	9.47%	10.40%	10.11%	5.28%	5.53%	5.64%	4.79%
Total Current Assets	60.79%	50.77%	68.35%	61.31%	54.58%	68.20%	49.67%	49.32%	70.64%	66.95%
Gross Plant, Property & Equipment	28.36%	22.18%	0.00%	0.00%	31.52%	27.60%	43.53%	45.28%	0.00%	0.00%
Less: Accumulated Depreciation	14.55%	10.27%	0.00%	0.00%	9.90%	8.75%	24.61%	25.17%	0.00%	0.00%
Net Plant, Property & Equipment	13.80%	11.91%	13.23%	12.28%	21.62%	18.86%	18.92%	20.10%	7.41%	6.67%
Investments	3.48%	24.26%	5.59%	3.97%	8.16%	5.38%	16.35%	15.63%	18.00%	23.72%
Deferred Income Taxes	6.45%	1.25%	0.00%	0.00%	7.01%	5.36%	0.00%	0.00%	0.00%	0.00%
Other Assets	15.47%	11.80%	12.83%	22.44%	8.62%	2.20%	15.06%	14.95%	3.94%	2.65%
Total Assets	100.00%	100.00%	100.00%	100.00%	100.00%	100.00%	100.00%	100.00%	100.00%	100.00%
LIABILITIES										
Short-Term Borrowings & Notes Payable	2.86%	1.66%	4.57%	8.80%	0.00%	0.00%	11.55%	16.26%	0.00%	0.00%
Accounts Payable	17.03%	16.06%	14.85%	9.96%	18.90%	22.70%	9.27%	7.31%	31.90%	30.84%
Employee Compensation and Benefits	0.00%	0.00%	4.66%	3.65%	0.00%	0.00%	4.30%	4.39%	0.00%	0.00%
Taxes Payable	0.00%	0.00%	6.02%	6.10%	0.00%	0.00%	5.46%	5.48%	0.00%	0.00%
Other Current Liabilities	26.57%	25.68%	14.59%	12.07%	20.37%	23.05%	10.62%	11.79%	16.80%	14.42%
Total Current Liabilities	46.46%	43.40%	44.69%	40.57%	39.28%	45.75%	41.21%	45.23%	48.70%	45.26%
Long-Term Debt	2.31%	0.00%	10.00%	5.00%	0.00%	0.00%	20.79%	16.14%	3.79%	4.43%
Other Liabilities	2.62%	2.22%	3.53%	2.60%	3.40%	3.24%	14.66%	15.18%	5.66%	4.04%
Total Liabilities	51.40%	45.62%	58.22%	48.17%	42.67%	48.99%	76.66%	76.56%	58.15%	53.73%
EQUITY										
Preferred Stock	0.00%	0.00%	0.00%	0.00%	0.00%	0.00%	0.00%	0.00%	0.00%	0.00%
Common Equity	48.60%	54.38%	41.78%	51.83%	57.34%	51.01%	0.28%	0.28%	0.00%	0.00%
Total Equity	48.60%	54.38%	41.78%	51.83%	57.34%	51.01%	23.06%	23.16%	41.85%	46.27%
							23.34%	23.44%	41.85%	46.27%
Total Liabilities & Equity	100.00%	100.00%	100.00%	100.00%	100.01%	100.00%	100.00%	100.00%	100.00%	100.00%

Exhibit 5

COMMON SIZE INCOME STATEMENTS FOR DELL COMPUTERS AND ITS COMPETITORS

	Compaq Computer		HP		Gateway Computers		IBM		Dell Computers	
	Dec. 2000	Dec. 1999	Dec. 2000	Dec. 1999	Dec. 2000	Dec. 1999	Dec. 2000	Dec. 1999	Feb. 2001	Feb. 2000
Revenue	100.00%	100.00%	100.00%	100.00%	100.00%	100.00%	100.00%	100.00%	100.00%	100.00%
Cost of Goods Sold	76.49%	77.35%	71.47%	70.14%	78.55%	79.51%	63.32%	63.53%	79.79%	79.35%
Gross Profit	23.51%	22.65%	28.53%	29.86%	21.45%	20.49%	36.68%	36.47%	20.21%	20.65%
Selling, General & Administrative	10.94%	12.82%	15.13%	15.39%	14.15%	12.36%	17.69%	16.82%	10.01%	9.45%
Other Operating Expenses	3.26%	6.56%	2.62%	2.65%	0.00%	0.00%	0.18%	-1.50%	0.94%	1.50%
Operating Income, Before Depreciation	9.31%	3.27%	10.78%	11.81%.	7.29%	8.13%	18.81%	21.14%	9.25%	9.71%
Depreciation & Amortization	3.32%	3.64%	2.80%	3.11%	1.97%	1.49%	5.65%	7.52%	0.75%	0.62%
Operating Income	5.99%	-0.37%	7.97%	8.70%	5.32%	6.64%	13.16%	13.62%	8.50%	9.09%
Interest Expense	0.64%	0.55%	0.53%	0.48%	0.00%	0.00%	0.81%	0.83%	0.15%	0.13%
Non-Operating Expense/(Income)	3.34%	-3.34%	-2.31%	-2.58%	1.20%	-0.76%	-0.68%	-0.61%	-1.48%	-0.74%
Pretax Income	2.00%	2.42%	9.76%	10.81%	4.12%	7.40%	13.03%	13.41%	9.83%	9.70%
Income Tax	0.66%	0.95%	2.18%	2.57%	1.61%	2.63%	3.89%	4.62%	3.00%	3.11%
Net Income/(Loss)	1.34%	1.48%	7.58%	8.24%	2.51%	4.77%	9.13%	8.79%	6.83%	6.59%

Exhibit 6

VALUATION METRICS AND ECONOMIC DATA FOR DELL COMPUTERS AND ITS COMPETITORS

Source: *Datastream*

	Compaq Computer		HP		Gateway Computers		IBM		Dell Computers	
	12/29/00	12/31/99	12/29/00	12/31/99	12/29/00	12/31/99	12/29/00	12/31/99	12/29/00	12/31/99
Share Price (US$)	$ 15.05	$ 27.06	$ 31.56	$ 44.51	$ 17.99	$ 72.06	$ 85.00	$ 107.88	$ 17.50	$ 51.00
Earnings Per Share	0.33	0.34	1.87	1.73	0.75	1.36	4.58	4.25	0.84	0.66
Price to Earnings	45.61	79.59	16.88	25.73	23.99	52.99	18.56	25.38	20.83	77.27
Common Shares Outstanding (millions)	1,702	1,693	1,979	2,018	322	314	1,763	1,809	2,582	2,536
Market Value of Equity (billions)	$ 25.62	$ 45.81	$ 62.46	$ 89.82	$ 5.79	$ 22.63	$ 149.86	$ 195.15	$ 45.19	$ 129.34
Book Value of Equity (billions)	$ 12.08	$ 14.83	$ 14.21	$ 18.30	$ 2.38	$ 2.02	$ 20.62	$ 20.51	$ 5.62	$ 5.31
Market to Book Ratio	2.12	3.09	4.40	4.91	2.43	11.21	7.27	9.51	8.04	24.37

	12/29/00	12/31/99
3 Month Treasury Bill	5.66%	4.66%
6 Month Treasury Bill	5.85%	4.76%
12 Month Treasury Bill	5.85%	4.78%
US GDP Growth	5.31%	5.99%
S&P 500	1,320.28	1,469.25
NASDAQ Composite	2,470.52	4,069.31

Exhibit 7
DELL STOCK PERFORMANCE **January 1, 1996 to March 9, 2001**

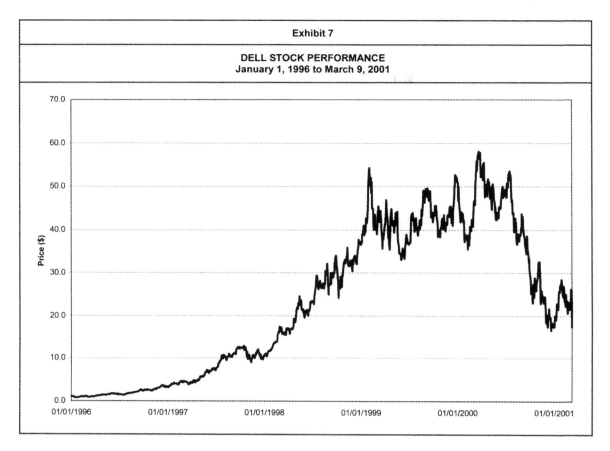

Exhibit 8
COMPETITORS STOCK PERFORMANCES **January 1, 1996 to March 9, 2001**

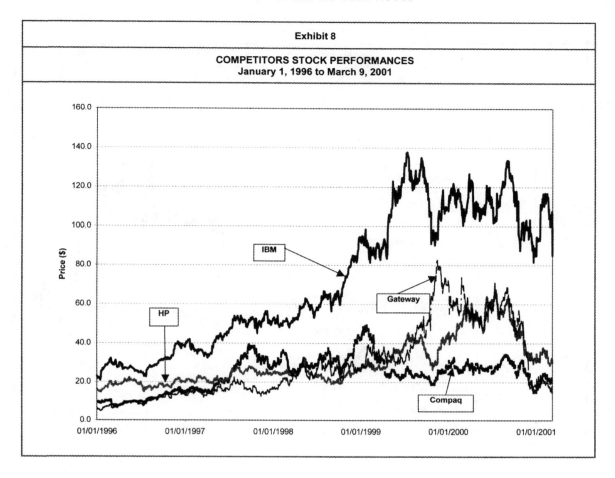

Exhibit 9

INDEXED PERFORMANCE SINCE 1996
Dell versus S&P 500 and IBM

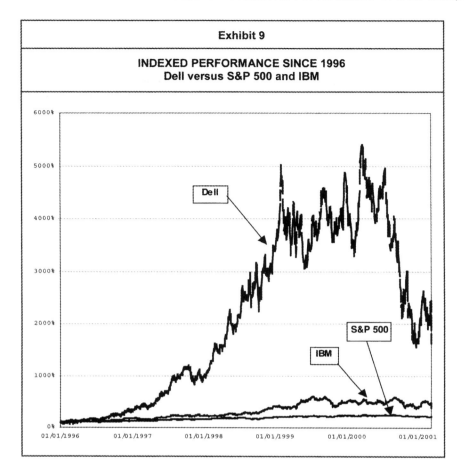

	Compaq Computer		HP		Gateway Computers	
Exhibit 10						
RATIOS						
	Dec. 2000	Dec. 1999	Dec. 2000	Dec. 1999	Dec. 2000	Dec. 1999
LIQUIDITY RATIOS						
Cash & Market Sec. To Total Assets	0.10x	0.12x	0.12x	0.16x	0.15x	0.34x
Acid Test Ratio	0.95x	0.84x	0.83x	0.94x	0.93x	1.16x
Current Ratio	1.31x	1.17x	1.53x	1.51x	1.39x	1.49x
Working Capital/Sales	0.08	0.05	0.16	0.17	0.07	0.10
EFFICIENCY						
Days of Inventory	24.33	24.60	59.66	59.72	15.24	9.83
Days Receivables	72.27	63.34	64.11	67.60	34.44	31.31
Days Payables	47.66	53.65	52.86	43.19	37.99	45.99
FINANCIAL LEVERAGE						
Debt to Total Assets	0.05	0.02	0.15	0.14	-	-
Debt to Common Equity	0.11	0.03	0.35	0.27	-	-
Long-Term Debt to Common Equity	0.05	-	0.24	0.10	-	-
Total Debt to EBITDA	0.33x	0.36x	0.94x	0.97x	0.00x	0.00x
EBITDA / Interest	14.45x	5.97x	20.46x	24.77x	N/A	N/A
EBIT / Interest	9.30x	-0.67x	15.13x	18.26x	N/A	N/A
PROFITABILITY						
Return on Common Equity	4.71%	3.84%	26.02%	19.08%	10.12%	21.17%
Return on Assets	2.29%	2.09%	10.87%	9.89%	5.80%	10.80%
GROWTH						
Sales	10.01%		15.13%		7.10%	
Operating Income	N/A		5.45%		(14.15%)	
Net Income	0.00%		5.90%		(43.59%)	
ROE DECOMPOSITION (DUPONT FORMULA)						
Return on Equity	4.71%	3.84%	26.02%	19.08%	10.12%	21.17%
Return on Sales	1.34%	1.48%	7.58%	8.24%	2.51%	4.77%
Asset Turnover	1.71x	1.41x	1.43x	1.20x	2.31x	2.27x
Leverage	2.06x	1.84x	2.39x	1.93x	1.74x	1.96x

Exhibit 11

RATIO DEFINITIONS

LIQUIDITY RATIOS
Cash & Market Sec. To Total Assets = (Cash + Marketable Securities) / Total Assets
Acid Test Ratio = (Cash + Marketable Securities + Accounts Receivable) / Total Current Liabilities
Current Ratio = Total Current Assets / Total Current Liabilities
Working Capital/Sales = (Total Current Assets - Total Current Liabilities) / Revenue

EFFICIENCY
Days Receivables = Accounts Receivable / (Revenue / 365)
Days Payables = Accounts Payable / (Cost of Goods Sold / 365)
Days of Inventory = Inventories / (Cost of Goods Sold / 365)

FINANCIAL LEVERAGE
Debt to Total Assets = (Short-Term Borrowings & Notes Payable + Long-Term Debt) / Total Assets
Debt to Common Equity = (Short-Term Borrowings & Notes Payable + Long-Term Debt) / Common Equity
Long-Term Debt to Common Equity = Long-Term Debt / Common Equity
Total Debt to EBITDA = (Short-Term Borrowings & Notes Payable + Long-Term Debt) / Operating Income, Before Depreciation
EBITDA / Interest = Operating Income, Before Depreciation / Interest Expense
EBIT / Interest = Operating Income / Interest Expense

PROFITABILITY
Return on Common Equity = Net Income (Loss) / Common Equity
Return on Assets = Net Income / Total Assets

ROE DECOMPOSITION (DUPONT FORMULA)
Return on Equity = Return on Sales x Asset Turnover x Leverage
Return on Sales = Net Income / Revenue
Asset Turnover = Revenue / Total Assets
Leverage = Total Assets / Total Equity

CHEF'S TOOLKIT INC.

Peter Jeffery, president of Chef's Toolkit Inc. (Chef's Toolkit), required funding to start manufacturing and marketing a new invention of his, a pasta server. He was uncertain how much funding he would need since the amount was dependent on sales. He wanted to start production in two weeks, on August 1, 1994. Since his distribution system was already arranged, he believed he could start selling as soon as the units were produced. He approached several venture capitalists after being turned down by the Metropolitan Bank, a Canadian chartered bank, but was reluctant to agree to what he considered excessive demands for their capital investment. He had just returned from a meeting with Dale Reid, a private investor from Toronto, who had expressed an interest in the firm. In order that he could evaluate his potential investment, Mr. Reid asked Jeffery to produce projected income statements, balance sheets, and cash flow statements for Chef's Toolkit Inc. up to July 31, 1995.

HISTORY

Chef's Toolkit Inc., founded in May 1994, was owned jointly by Peter and Sally Jeffery. The company was formed to design, develop, manufacture and to market a unique household utensil, a pasta server. The specially curved patented plastic apparatus, to be sold retail for $4.30, could be used to stir, pick up and to serve all varieties of pasta.

Richard Ivey School of Business, The University of Western Ontario. **IVEY**. Blair Zilkey prepared this case under the supervision of Professors John Humphrey and David Shaw solely to provide material for class discussion. This case is a revision of "Gourmet Gadgets Inc." (9A89B035). The authors do not intend to illustrate either effective or ineffective handling of a managerial situation. The authors may have disguised certain names and other identifying information to protect confidentiality.

Peter, who was 35, had conceived the idea for the device while working for the Food Research Institute of Agriculture Canada as a research biologist. As a recent MBA graduate, he was confident that he could bring his idea to fruition. His enthusiasm was echoed by his wife, Sally, aged 30, who, after having worked as a professional teacher, was to enter an MBA program in September. In addition to her studies, she planned to act as vice-president and secretary of Chef's Toolkit Inc., while Peter would be President and Treasurer.

The Jefferys had already spent $13,800 before incorporation on obtaining patent approval for their invention in Canada and the United States. Patents were also being processed in Italy, Germany, France and the United Kingdom. With initial capital of $20,700 raised from personal loans of $12,000 from the Metropolitan Bank and $8,700 from Best Finance Ltd., the Jefferys had established an office at their home in Kitchener and had purchased production equipment. Capital expenditures consisted of $865 for office equipment, $23,300 for a single cavity production mold, $4,200 for tools and dies and $4,430 for a blister pack mold. Development costs incurred on the molds were included in these amounts.

By July, Chef's Toolkit Inc. was ready to begin production. An agreement was made with Perfect Plastics, Inc. in Cambridge to manufacture the utensil under contract, using Chef's Toolkit Inc. molds, at a cost of $0.70 per unit. Packaging arrangements were concluded with B. Crawford & Sons Lithographic Ltd. of Kitchener to package the products the same month as produced. Distribution agreements were made with Household Ware Sales, Inc., Cooker Ltd., and Firenzo Sales Ltd.

Unfortunately, by this time, initial funds had been exhausted on capital expenditures and the final payment of $12,075 was due in August on the production mold. Cash was also required for monthly administrative expenses of $4,315 for salaries, office expenses, insurance, telephone, utilities, automobile expenses, and miscellaneous supplies once production started. Perfect Plastics would not begin production without a 50 per cent deposit and the remainder was due before any units would be released for sale. The packaging company also required cash payments on delivery. Without additional funding, the Jefferys could not start production or distribution.

PRODUCTION

The pasta server would be manufactured by an injection molding process. The process made possible the rapid production of highly finished and detailed plastic units. Plastic was melted and then injected under thousands of kilograms of pressure into a mold which was held closed by a clamping mechanism. The devices were formed into a cavity, the two halves of the mold separated allowing the formed part to fall free. In injection molding, parts could be formed in either single or multiple cavity molds, depending on total production, production rate, size and weight of the part, size of machine available and the mold cost. Chef's Toolkit Inc. initially planned to use a single cavity production mold (one device per cycle). Since four cycles could be completed per minute, monthly production capacity was about 40,000 units.

Peter feared a stock-out and planned an initial production run of 40,000 units. His production strategy was to order sufficient units to replace units sold, and to maintain a minimum of 10,000 units inventory. Perfect Plastics required production runs of at least 5,000 units. Peter planned, initially, to store inventory in the basement and garage of his home, but if inventory exceeded 10,000 units he would have to rent warehouse space at a cost of $230 per month. The warehouse space, with a capacity of 35,000 units, could be leased on a monthly basis as needed and no annual lease was required. Lease payments were due the month following.

Peter had also discussed with his accountant the problem of depreciation of the production mold. The life of a mold depended on the type of steel used, the number of cycles, the type of material to be molded and the complexity of the part to be manufactured. Handled properly, molds used to manufacture devices similar to the pasta server lasted for millions of units. However, from a practical viewpoint, Peter recognized that his single cavity mold could be obsolete after producing only 162,000 units if he decided to buy the new two cavity mold. His accountant suggested that a depreciation charge of $0.145 per unit be used in pro-forma statements to account for wear and tear and obsolescence of the mold. A combined depreciation charge of $0.017 per unit was recommended for the package mold and tool and dies. In addition, $10 per month was allowed for depreciation of office equipment, which was to be considered as an administrative expense.

The products would be blister packaged on an attractive backing which would clearly show the consumer various applications for the device. Products would be packaged the same month as they were produced. Packaging costs for the product were $0.43 per unit. Material costs were included in these prices. Chef's Toolkit Inc. would pay for shipping expenses of $0.085 per unit, incurred when units were sold.

MARKETING

The Jefferys suggested that every family in North America was a potential purchaser, since they believed all families ate some variety of pasta. The Canadian population consisted of 10.02 million families (1991 Census data, Exhibit 1). Similar data is provided for Ontario, Toronto and Kitchener. The United States market was about 10 times larger.

Household Ware Sales, Inc. would handle the accounts of the Hudson's Bay Company, Wal-Mart and Safeway. Cooker Ltd. was to handle Eaton's, Sears and independent boutiques. Firenzo Sales Ltd. would handle grocery outlets such as I.G.A., Loblaws and A & P.

The wholesale price by Chef's Toolkit Inc. to the distributors was $1.82 per unit, net 30 days. Peter believed 50 per cent of receipts would be paid the month following the sale and the remainder within the second month. Wholesalers would sell the product to retail outlets for $2.15. Chef's Toolkit Inc. was also considering expanding distribution to the United States and, once patents were approved, to Europe.

Although no identical products used specifically for pasta were on the market, similar plastic kitchen utensils were occasionally used for pasta serving. These devices sold for $3.45 to $5.15, with retailers generally receiving a 100 per cent markup.

Promotion by Chef's Toolkit Inc. would consist of an attractive blister package for the product and free guest appearances on television talk and cooking shows such as "Canada A.M." and "Celebrity Cooks." Free press exposure was anticipated through editorial statements and consumer goods articles. Retail stores would be encouraged to conduct in-store promotions and to display the device with pasta products. Consumer questionnaires would be made available to ascertain public reaction.

Considerable reliance was placed on the distributors to promote the product. The Jefferys anticipated that 500 units would be given away monthly for the first four months for promotional purposes. Peter's accountant suggested that these should be counted as sales expenses at their cost of $1.292 per unit ($0.70 for mold manufacturing, $0.43 for packaging, plus $0.162 for depreciation), the same amount as would be used to value inventory. The other suggestion was to delay amortization of the patent until Chef's Toolkit Inc. had two profitable years.

FINANCIAL IMPLICATIONS

Exhibit 2 shows the balance sheet for Chef's Toolkit Inc. as of July 15, 1994. Dale Reid was considering investing up to $85,000 for a 50 per cent share of the equity and profits of the new company. Reid stated that he may be willing to settle for a smaller ownership stake but his investment would be disproportionately lower. He would not consider investing an amount greater than $85,000 unless the Jefferys increased their investment in the company significantly. However, before he made any commitments, he wanted to examine, very carefully, a set of pro-forma statements for the venture. Reid suggested that the Jefferys calculate the total amount of financing required each month and from those calculations determine the total amount of financing that he would need to invest.

The Jefferys did not believe that they could invest any more personal funds in the company since their personal assets were tied up in the business, their home and personal possessions (Exhibit 3).

Monthly sales of the pasta serving devices were difficult to project. Peter's reasonable expectation was 10,000 units and he had prepared a production schedule based on this sales level (Exhibit 4). His most pessimistic and optimistic monthly sales forecasts were 5,000 units and 30,000 units respectively. If sales were 30,000 units or more per month, for two consecutive months, he planned to order a larger two-cavity production mold (two devices per cycle). The capital cost, including development, would be $62,000, payable in three monthly instalments, starting the month the equipment was ordered. A three month lead time, from the time of ordering, was required before this mold would be operational. When operational, the mold would not only double production capacity, but also cut costs in half to $0.35 per unit. Peter's accountant suggested a depreciation allowance of $0.062 per unit for the two cavity mold. With the reduction in material and depreciation costs, inventory would be costed at $0.848 per unit.

Peter believed that the first fiscal year's results ending July 31, 1995 were critical for the success of Chef's Toolkit Inc. He required forecasted cash flow, income statements, and balance sheets for his three different sales projections. Peter planned to use a 20 per cent tax rate. If taxes were payable, they would be due 45 days after Chef's Toolkit Inc. year end of July 31, 1995.

The Jefferys wished to limit the amount of money required from Mr. Reid. They wanted to retain as much control over the business as possible. However they recognized the danger of being under-financed. Once they decided what amount they would request from Mr. Reid, they would complete a formal information package and drop in to see Mr. Reid with their completed pro-forma financial statements.

Exhibit 1

COMPOSITION OF CANADIAN HOUSEHOLDS (1991 CENSUS DATA)

Area	Number of Members						Mother Tongue			
	1	2	3	4 – 5	6+	English	French	Italian	German
Canada 10,018,265 households Average number of people per household = 2.7	2,297,055 23%	3,144,185 31%	1,743,605 17%	2,500,245 25%	333,135 3%	17,198,282 63%	6,824,715 25%	545,977 2%	491,379 2%
Ontario 3,638,365 households Average number of people per household = 2.7	79,110 22%	1,130,965 31%	634,460 17%	948,125 26%	132,700 4%	8,399,735 80%	513,911 5%	350,622 3%	181,682 2%
Toronto 1,366,700 households Average number of people per household = 2.7	297,345 22%	391,640 29%	241,355 18%	370,420 27%	65,935 5%	2,898,132 74%	53,052 1%	233,784 6%	63,870 2%
Kitchener 128,110 households Average number of people per household = 2.7	26,315 21%	39,965 31%	23,135 18%	34,590 27%	4,105 3%	301,478 83%	4,489 1%	1,894 1%	20,298 6%

Exhibit 2

BALANCE SHEET **As of July 15, 1994**

Assets

Current	$	-
Total Current Assets		0
Equipment		
Single Cavity Mold		23,300
Tools and Dies		4,200
Blister Package Mold		4,430
Office Equipment		865
		32,795
Other		
Patent		13,800
	$	46,595

Liabilities

Current		
Accounts Payable		12,075
Equity		
Common Stock		34,520
	$	46,595

Exhibit 3

JEFFERYS PERSONAL BALANCE SHEET **As of July 15, 1994**

Assets		
Cash	$	345
Real Estate		69,000
Automobile		12,075
Stocks, Bonds, Etc.		0
Household & Personal Effects		43,125
Invested In Chef's Toolkit Inc.		34,520
Total Assets	$	159,065
Liabilities		
Bank & Finance Co. Loans		20,700
Mortgages		51,750
Other Liabilities		6,900
		79,350
Net Worth		79,715
Total Liabilities & Net Worth	$	159,065

Exhibit 4

PRODUCTION SCHEDULE IN UNITS Based on 10,000 Units/Month Sales

| Month | Production | | Sales | Promotion | Inventory | |
	Molded	Packaged			Home	Warehouse
August	40,000	40,000	10,000	500	10,000	19,500
September	0	0	10,000	500	10,000	9,000
October	5,000	5,000	10,000	500	10,000	3,500
November	7,000	7,000	10,000	500	10,000	0
December	10,000	10,000	10,000	0	10,000	0
January	10,000	10,000	10,000	0	10,000	0
February	10,000	10,000	10,000	0	10,000	0
March	10,000	10,000	10,000	0	10,000	0
April	10,000	10,000	10,000	0	10,000	0
May	10,000	10,000	10,000	0	10,000	0
June	10,000	10,000	10,000	0	10,000	0
July	10,000	10,000	10,000	0	10,000	0

PALMER LIMITED

Ms. Nancy Harris, the accountant for Palmer Limited (PL), a commercial and industrial mechanical building contractor in Saskatoon, received a request from Michel Palmer on January 6, 1999, to prepare monthly cash-flow projections for the next year, as well as a year-end projected income statement and balance sheet for the firm. The two Palmer brothers were to meet soon for their annual review with Mr. Bill Melnyk, the branch manager of the Confederation Bank. Mr. Melnyk had noted in a brief phone conversation that the bank faced a growing commitment to PL, currently $368,600.

In its past association with the bank, PL had negotiated its loan needs by outlining the cash requirements of specific contracts and by posting collateral as requested. A recent schedule of net worth that the brothers had completed for the bank valued their net personal assets, excluding the business, at $162,500. This amount consisted almost entirely of the brothers' homes and personal effects after deducting $200,000 in outstanding mortgage loans obtained from the Confederation Bank.

Their discussions with Mr. Melnyk now made it clear to the Palmer brothers that they would have to accurately assess financial needs to maintain the bank's continued support. As a starting point, they visited Ms. Harris to talk about preparation of the financial reports and the cash-flow projection.

COMPANY HISTORY

PL was founded by Michel and Andre Palmer in 1986. Before creating the firm, both Michel and Andre studied metal working in technical school and worked for several years as apprentices. Using their

Richard Ivey School of Business
The University of Western Ontario

IVEY

Professor Stephen R. Foerster revised this case (originally prepared by Professors James E. Hatch and John Humphrey) solely to provide material for class discussion. The author does not intend to illustrate either effective or ineffective handling of a managerial situation. The author may have disguised certain names and other identifying information to protect confidentiality.

accumulated savings of $25,000, they decided to go into business for themselves. Since neither brother had any experience in running a business at the time of incorporation, they decided to undertake only small construction contract jobs.

Initially, PL specialized in sheet-metal work. As business proved profitable, they expanded activities to include contracts for the installation of plumbing and heating. PL grew rapidly along with the Saskatchewan economy. However, problems in the Saskatchewan economy were compounded by the Canada-wide recession of 1990-1991. With some belt-tightening and careful management, PL was able to survive the recession. By 1998, the firm had expanded to 32 production employees (10 in the metal shop and 22 in the field), plus two administrative personnel in addition to the brothers. This expansion necessitated a new plant, which PL leased, with a floor area of 10,000 square feet—9,500 square feet for the manufacturing operation and storage, and 500 square feet for the office. The major fixed asset investments of the company were the basic tools of the manufacturing operation (small tools, welding equipment, and an immovable metal-bending press), three trucks, and the two cars used by the Palmer brothers.

Michel Palmer, 46 years old, and Andre Palmer, 49, believed that with hard work the company would continue to be the success it had always been. Both brothers were considered workaholics by their business associates. As PL's business expanded, the Palmer brothers spent more time administering the company and less time working at their trades. In 1998, with rare exceptions, they spent all of their time in administration. Michel Palmer supervised the manufacturing operations and a small portion of the outside work, while Andre quoted on jobs and supervised the major portion of the outside work. This re-organization, a larger equity base, and an expanded workforce enabled the company to undertake larger contracts. The first major contract, begun in late 1996, and worth approximately $1.6 million, involved 18-20 months of work, on a large commercial development. Such a large contract was a substantial departure for the company, and it had been a major factor in gaining the increased financial support from the Confederation Bank.

BILLINGS AND COLLECTION PROCEDURE

Most of PL's revenue came from acting as a subcontractor on construction projects. This typically involved the submission of a bid for the plumbing, heating, and sheet metal work in a commercial or industrial construction project being undertaken by a contractor. If the PL bid was successful, PL would do the bulk of the work but would subcontract parts of the job such as the installation of control devices. In the construction trade, once a bid has been accepted, the contractor and subcontractor are expected to meet all specifications for the price quoted. If the materials, labour or overhead costs vary, the contractor or subcontractors bear the loss or enjoy the extra profit. Each subcontractor submits monthly billings to the contractor, outlining materials, labour and overhead allocated to the construction project in the past month. The general contractor in turn submits an estimate of total costs to the client. The architect, in consultation with the general contractor, approves, varies, or disapproves the billings, based on his estimate of the work done to date. The architect then submits the vetted billings to the client, who then pays the general contractor the amount of the approved monthly billings, less a statutory holdback (10 per cent in the case of all contracts undertaken by PL in 1998). The purpose of such holdbacks is to protect the client against mechanics' liens which could be applied against the job by subcontractors and trades people. Once the general contractor receives its billings (less the holdback), the subcontractors are each paid subject to the same 10 per cent holdback provision. Thus PL expected 90 per cent of each month's billings to be paid 30 days later, while the 10 per cent holdbacks were expected to be paid four months after all billings were submitted.

COMPETITIVE CONDITIONS

The city of Saskatoon acted as a transportation and servicing hub for a variety of industries in northern Saskatchewan, including government, farming, oil, potash, uranium and light manufacturing. The Saskatoon economy was closely tied to the resource sector. As a result, building activity in Saskatoon varied greatly from year to year. Residential construction in 1998 was down modestly from 1997 levels, but had shown a slight upward trend in the last quarter of 1998. Commercial construction was down as well in 1998 from 1997. However, overall the Canada economy had shown strong growth over the past year. As well, the consumer price index (CPI) inflation rate had remained low, below 1.5 per cent over the past year. The prime interest rate had increased slightly to 7.00 per cent, 0.75 per cent higher than a year earlier. On the positive side, in December, the Saskatoon area had a heavy snowfall, making farmers more optimistic about the coming farm season.

In order to gain a foothold in the mechanical contracting business, PL had bid aggressively for jobs in 1996. The net result of this aggressive bidding was that gross margins previously averaging 20 per cent were reduced. Flat business activity and a decline in house construction were causing the chartered banks to carefully review all of their construction loans.

CURRENT FINANCIAL POSITION

At their meeting, Ms. Harris and the Palmer brothers discussed business prospects and future plans for the firm. Ms. Harris presented the Palmer brothers with preliminary financial statements for the fiscal year ending December 31, 1998, as well as comparative statements for 1993 to 1997 (see Exhibits 1 and 2).

All three were especially bothered by the extraordinary expenses of $164,200. Of this amount, $44,600 arose from a 1995 investment in Blue Water Limited, a family business that retailed boats and motors. The company declared bankruptcy in the fall of 1997, and the investment was written off. Another $111,800 resulted from the bankruptcy of a major customer. And the remaining $7,800 arose from other minor bad debt losses.

FORECASTING FOR 1999

Ms. Harris noted that she had no information regarding future manufacturing overhead or selling and administrative expenses. The brothers told Ms. Harris that manufacturing overhead included shop supplies, rent, utilities, vehicle expenses, business and unemployment insurance, maintenance and fringe benefits. Their selling and administrative expenses encompassed owners' compensation, life insurance, office salaries, car expenses, legal and audit expenses, stationery, telephone, fax and courier. Over the next twelve months, they forecasted their expenses (excluding interest) as follows (to be paid within that month):

**Monthly Forecasts of Manufacturing Overhead
and Selling & Administrative Expenses**

Month	Manufacturing Overhead	Selling/ Administrative Expenses	TOTAL
January 1999	$13,650	$19,500	$33,150
February	9,100	22,425	31,525
March	8,775	18,850	27,625
April	13,365	17,060	30,425
May	8,240	18,200	26,440
June	12,500	16,770	29,270
July	6,825	16,770	23,595
August	6,825	21,890	28,715
September	6,825	16,495	23,320
October	6,260	17,055	23,315
November	6,260	18,200	24,460
December	11,660	19,900	31,560

Ms. Harris next moved to a review of PL's current contracts (see Exhibits 3 to 5). The brothers noted that their estimates were highly speculative since there were many uncertainties in their line of business. For example, they pointed out that all the firms involved in one project had incurred costs higher than expected in meeting the original specifications, because of insufficient detail in the architect's original drawings. However, he had already incorporated such cost overruns in budgets presented in Exhibit 5. Michel Palmer estimated that $97,000 of the budgeted material expenses for January would likely be supplied by drawing down the available inventories (this was also the only expected change in inventory during the year). For current contracts, Palmer expected to pay its suppliers in 90 days (see Exhibits 4 and 5), while for any new contracts, Palmer expected to pay suppliers in 60 days.

The conversation turned to consideration of future prospects for the firm. Ms. Harris observed that their current contracts would be substantially completed by the end of March 1999 and asked about the type of business that could be expected in the coming year, especially in light of the uncertain local economy. Andre responded that the firm expected to return to smaller contracts with a greater emphasis on metal working and higher profit margins. He also anticipated substantial cuts in their workforce, probably down to a crew of 12 to 20. While the volume of such contracts was uncertain, they expected to generate $115,000 of billings per month, starting in April. It was difficult to estimate labour and material expenses for the new jobs; however, the brothers expected that material and labour costs would each be 37.5 per cent of billings (thus a total of 75 per cent). Ms. Harris asked about their billings expectations with this new business. Michel Palmer replied that future billings would be made when their part of the contract was essentially complete, and that the normal trade terms were net 30 days (i.e., with Palmer getting 90 per cent of billings in the next month). Holdbacks of 10 per cent on this new business were expected to be collected in four months. Reviewing their past experience, neither brother expected to return to the large contract field unless they could obtain a substantial gross margin, in the area of 20 per cent. They did not expect this to happen in the near future, but were interested in Ms. Harris' opinion. Although the firm expected to earn profits in the coming year, there would be no tax payments due to tax loss carry forwards from previous years.

The brothers closed the discussion by asking Ms. Harris to review their financial situation and prepare projected financial statements. They expected her to have the financial projections for the bank by the end of the week.

	Exhibit 1					
	BALANCE SHEETS FOR YEARS ENDING DECEMBER 31 **($000)**					
	1998 **(prelim.)**	**1997**	**1996**	**1995**	**1994**	**1993**
ASSETS						
Cash	$ -	$ -	$ 106.3	$ -	$ 16.3	$ 2.0
Accounts Receivable, Net	544.7	349.7	715.0	314.3	189.2	401.7
Inventory	141.7	50.7	103.4	36.7	25.1	16.9
Prepaid Expenses	58.5	87.8	40.3	14.3	20.4	6.4
Total Current Assets	744.9	488.2	965.0	365.3	251.0	427.0
Investments	22.1	65.4	54.9	48.1	35.1	29.5
Fixed Assets, Net	204.5	210.6	144.0	78.7	83.6	77.7
Other Assets	1.6	1.6	1.6	1.7	1.6	1.6
TOTAL ASSETS	$ 973.1	$ 765.8	$ 1,165.5	$ 493.8	$ 371.3	$ 535.8
LIABILITIES & EQUITY						
Bank Loan	368.6	199.3	286.0	95.6	65.0	97.5
Accounts Payable	314.6	253.5	487.2	148.2	103.9	257.4
Other Current Liabilities	89.1	81.1	113.8	60.8	59.3	50.7
Total Current Liabilities	772.3	533.9	887.0	304.6	228.2	405.6
Long Term Debt Due to Officers **	87.1	9.1	4.8	-	7.8	30.3
TOTAL LIABILITIES	859.4	543.0	891.8	304.6	236.0	435.9
Preferred Stock	39.0	39.0	39.0	39.0	39.0	39.0
Common Stock	8.1	8.1	8.1	8.1	8.1	8.1
Retained Earnings	66.6	175.7	226.6	142.1	88.2	52.8
TOTAL EQUITY	113.7	222.8	273.7	189.2	135.3	99.9
TOTAL LIABILITIES & EQUITY	$ 973.1	$ 765.8	$ 1,165.5	$ 493.8	$ 371.3	$ 535.8

** *No interest on Long Term Debt to Officers*

Exhibit 2

INCOME STATEMENTS FOR THE YEARS ENDED DECEMBER 31
($000)

	1998 (prelim.)	1997	1996	1995	1994	1993
Sales	$ 2,427.1	$ 1,822.6	$ 1,735.2	$ 1,404.4	$ 1,136.9	$ 1,211.0
Cost of Goods Sold:						
Materials	1,043.0	770.0	522.3	351.0	363.7	492.7
Labour	987.0	759.0	806.9	666.9	433.2	399.8
Depreciation	24.1	27.6	24.4	12.4	13.3	9.8
Overhead (Manufacturing)	32.5	39.0	35.8	118.3	117.7	78.7
Total Cost of Goods Sold	2,086.6	1,595.6	1,389.4	1,148.6	927.9	981.0
Gross Margin	340.5	227.0	345.8	255.8	209.0	230.0
Selling & Admin. Expenses:						
Management - Compensation	153.4	164.1	134.9	102.4	75.0	78.7
Other (including interest)	132.0	118.3	105.6	84.9	88.1	72.8
Total Selling & Admin Expenses	285.4	282.4	240.5	187.3	163.1	151.5
Net Operating Income	55.1	(55.4)	105.3	68.5	45.9	78.5
Plus: Other Income	-	-	5.2	1.7	0.4	-
Less: Other Expenses	164.2	11.1	-	-	-	44.9
Net Income Before Taxes	(109.1)	(66.5)	110.5	70.2	46.3	33.6
Taxes (see Note 1 Below)	-	(15.6)	26.0	16.3	10.9	7.8
Net Income After Taxes	$ (109.1)	$ (50.9)	$ 84.5	$ 53.9	$ 35.4	$ 25.8

Note 1: Given 1997 and 1998 losses, no taxes were expected to be paid for several years.

Exhibit 3	
CURRENT CONTRACTS POSITION AS OF **DECEMBER 31, 1998 AND EXPECTED BILLINGS TO MARCH 31, 1999** **($000)**	

Contract Position as of Dec. 31/98 (Total)

Past Billings (Amount Billed as of Dec. 31/98)	$ 1,788.3
Expected Billings (Amount Not Billed as of Dec. 31/98)	1,022.2
Total Current Contract Positions	2,810.5

Past Billings Details

Previously Collected During 1998	1,243.5
Holdbacks (to be received in March 1999)	178.8
December 1998 Billings (see Note 1 below)	366.0
	1,788.3

Expected Billings (for January 1999 to March 1999) Details

January 1999	436.6
February 1999	308.5
March 1999	277.3
	$ 1,022.4

Note 1: 90 per cent of this amount to be received in January 1999; 10 per cent of this amount (holdback) to be received in April 1999.

Exhibit 4

ACCOUNTS PAYABLE AGING AS OF DECEMBER 31, 1998 **($000)**

Month of Purchase	Amount	% of Total Accounts Payable
December 1998	$ 69.1	22.0
November 1998	44.5	14.0
October 1998	201.0	64.0
Total Accounts Payable December 31, 1998	$ 314.6	100.0

Exhibit 5

BUDGETED MATERIALS AND LABOUR EXPENSES **FOR COMPLETION OF CURRENT CONTRACTS** **($000)**

	Totals
Budgeted Material Expenses	
January 1999 (see Note 1 below)	$ 252.4
February 1999	137.9
Total	390.4
Budgeted Labour Expenses	
January 1999	189.0
February 1999	104.7
March 1999	96.0
Total	$ 389.7

Note 1: *$97.0 was to come from existing inventory.*

COW'S LONDON

In September 1994, James and Serena Udderlie were preparing a loan application to a London, Ontario branch of the Confederation Bank of Canada. The Udderlies were requesting a $160,000 term loan, in addition to an operating loan, for the potential opening of a Cow's ice cream and clothing franchise in London. The Udderlies had a considerable amount of marketing research and cost estimates, and in order to complete the application, they needed to develop proforma income statements and balance sheets for the store's first two years of operation. They also planned to review carefully the qualitative characteristics of their idea in order to assess the chances of success of a Cow's franchise in London. The Udderlies also wondered what collateral, if any, they would be able to provide the bank to secure against a loan, and what other terms the bank might deem necessary.

HISTORY OF COW'S

Cow's began in 1983 on Prince Edward Island (P.E.I.), Canada, as a single outlet producing and selling ice cream made from a time-honoured family recipe. However, the clothing with whimsical cow imagery that the staff wore as uniforms began attracting attention and the company soon expanded to include a retail line, which was 75 to 80 items deep by 1995. The retail line, which included such items as t-shirts, sweatshirts, pins and mooing cookie jars, was subsequently offered by mail order in 1991. Cow's began

Richard Ivey School of Business
The University of Western Ontario **IVEY**   Rob Barbara prepared this case under the supervision of Professor Steve Foerster solely to provide material for class discussion. The author does not intend to illustrate either effective or ineffective handling of a managerial situation. The author may have disguised certain names and other identifying information to protect confidentiality.

franchising with the opening of a store in Vancouver, British Columbia in 1993, and later opened stores in Park City, Utah and Whistler, British Columbia.

Cow's sold only premium ice cream, with ingredients that included dairy fresh cream, sugar, fresh eggs and pure vanilla. Also, the ice cream included very little of the air found in most commercial ice creams to increase volume. All ice cream was served in a fresh waffle cone made at the ice cream counter in full view of the customers. When customers ordered their cone, they often selected from colourful names such as Wowie Cowie, Moo Crunch and Cowrispy Crunch.

Customers were treated to a complete experience at Cow's. The staff were very friendly and were willing to give customers a sample before they decided on an ice cream flavour. All stores were innovatively decorated to include clocks displaying both the local and P.E.I. time, as well as an ice cream menu shaped as a cow with a swinging tongue. But most important to the experience were the clothing items with witty satirical designs and captions.

Cow's founder, Cobie Gable, still managed the company in July 1994. The company's creative director, Marc Gallant, a well-known P.E.I. artist, had recently passed away. While Gable was responsible for most of the business decisions that had brought Cow's its success, Gallant was the creative person behind the art work on the whimsical clothing. Gallant's creativity, inspired by his fascination with cows, was preserved by saving many of his preliminary designs in a manner that could easily be manipulated by his creative team to develop new designs.

JAMES AND SERENA UDDERLIE

James Udderlie was the Director of Market Development in the Employee Benefits Division of the Provincial Life Insurance Company. He completed his MBA from the Western Business School in 1983 and joined Provincial in the same year. Although successful and happy in his current position, as James noted, "being an entrepreneur is in the back of the mind of most business school graduates." Serena Udderlie was a special education teacher who was currently volunteering one day a week while managing their three children full-time, including the youngest child who had not yet entered public school. Serena planned on returning to work full-time once their youngest child was in school. She received a Bachelor of Arts, Bachelor of Education and a Master of Education from the University of Western Ontario, and was the gold medalist while earning the Master's degree. Serena, like her husband, was excited to open up a family business.

The Udderlies required that any business they started would neither affect James' commitment to Provincial Life nor their commitment to their family. While James and Serena accepted that changes would be necessary to the family routine, they did not want their children to suffer because of the business and discussed it with them before making a final decision. The Udderlies were under no illusions about the commitment they would have to make to the venture, but they anticipated that if they were to hire a full-time person to manage their "investment," then the time requirement could be kept to a manageable level. They felt that their requirements could be met in London since the three locations, the tentative location of the store, Provincial Life and home, would only be a short distance from each other.

James and Serena planned to incorporate, with each owning 50 per cent of the business. James would be responsible for strategic planning, finance and general management. Serena would take care of hiring the staff and marketing. They would both take turns meeting with their manager on a weekly basis to keep tabs on their "investment," by reviewing results, setting store policy and planning promotions.

THE IDEA

The idea for the Cow's franchise came about when the Udderlie family was camping on P.E.I. in the summer of 1992. At that time, James saw a magazine advertisement for Cow's ice cream that caught his attention. What struck James was the "wholesomeness" of the layout that depicted a young boy wearing clothing with the distinctive Cow's motif and having fun eating ice cream. Later, their neighbours at the campsite said they enjoyed the Cow's store they visited, and after the Udderlies visited the store themselves, they were greatly impressed with their Cow's experience. In particular, they noticed the interesting clothing and its displays, the store's layout, the friendliness of the staff and, most importantly, the delicious ice cream. After the Udderlies inquired about franchising, a company representative told them that the first company franchise was to open later that summer in Vancouver, British Columbia and that no other franchises were being considered. The representative advised the Udderlies that if they were to write a letter outlining their desire to own a franchise, the company would get back to them. The Udderlies had a strong conviction that the Cow's concept would work in London.

The first decision the Udderlies had to make was whether or not to invest time examining the feasibility of a Cow's franchise before taking the idea to a financial institution for possible financing. It was not until the summer of 1994 that the Udderlies decided to write to Cow's representatives, at which time they received a favourable response inviting them to visit the company in P.E.I. James traveled alone to P.E.I. in July 1994 and spent three days meeting with the franchiser and learning more about the company. During this time, it became obvious to James that while Cow's was a profitable business, a franchisee had to want more than just profit from owning a store. The company's core values included a strong persuasion for quality and creativity that made owning a store an expensive proposition. It was believed that only by following these values would a store have all the elements necessary for it to be successful.

MARKET RESEARCH

James brought with him to P.E.I. some preliminary market research that he had gathered from Statistics Canada, the Conference Board of Canada and the Convention Bureau of London. He felt that it was in this area that his MBA helped him most; he knew how to differentiate the important information from the irrelevant as well as how to deal with incomplete market information. From the research, he gathered two key pieces of information: aggregate spending on take-out food in the London area and an estimate of the annual number of visitors to London. The information in Exhibit 1 was meant to give James a sense of how many potential Cow's customers existed and the extent of their buying power. He focused on the counties around London.

James figured that his target segment would include tourists, local employed families, and local non-married, employed individuals over the age of 16. He believed that employment was an important characteristic of his target segment since the Cow's price point would be greater than the average price in the industry.

The population of London in 1994 was approximately 300,000. Using information he received from the franchiser, James figured that local monthly visits would be the product of both the specific month and the degree of local awareness of the store. For example, in the store's first month of operation, targeted for April 1995, he predicted that the "seasonality" factor would be 70 per cent, versus a high of 100 per cent in July, and the "awareness" factor 10 per cent, versus a high of 80 per cent by November. Since the product of these was seven per cent, he figured that seven per cent of 300,000, or 21,000 people, would be included in the predisposed base for the month of April. He then predicted that, of this base, one in twenty would visit the store. Hence, in the month of April, 1,050 individuals from the local population would visit Cow's. In addition, James estimated that 120 tourists would visit the store each month. The predicted "seasonality" factor, the "awareness" factor and projected monthly sales are listed in Exhibit 2.

The franchiser also provided the Udderlies with frequency of purchase data, broken down by product, based on the experience in P.E.I. and Vancouver. Only 10 per cent of all individuals that entered the store left without making any purchase. Of the remaining 90 per cent, 65 per cent purchased only ice cream, 10 per cent purchased only a retail product, and 25 per cent purchased both. James estimated that the average expenditures per customer would be two dollars for ice cream and $20 for retail. Using this methodology, James estimated year one (April 1, 1995 to March 31, 1996) and year two (April 1, 1996 to March 31, 1997) retail sales to be $320,450 and $542,052, respectively. Ice cream sales were projected to be $82,400 and $139,384 in the first two years.

FRANCHISE REQUIREMENTS

The franchiser had well developed store design standards and specifications, which included what items were sold and how the items were sold. For example, the franchiser prescribed that a specific Toronto-based interior design firm draw the store plans according to Cow's standards. Also, all retail merchandise and ice cream product had to be sourced through the franchiser, and the ice cream had to be served in a certain way, including weighing each cone before it was served. James considered Gable very open-minded about any suggestion and always willing to negotiate in good faith. The restrictions were meant as quality control on the products that bore the Cow's name.

James was assured that the franchiser would be very supportive throughout the start-up process. Besides supplying James with market information, the franchiser would also equip him with manuals and systems that proved to be effective at the other locations, plus source equipment and fixtures for the store. Also, a team from P.E.I. would help set up the store, train the staff and solve any initial problems.

The franchise fee was $60,000 due upon signing the agreement. James knew that this fee, an asset, could be amortized on a straight-line basis over 10 years. The agreement also stipulated a royalty of eight per cent of sales, as well as a requirement that the Udderlies spend at least two per cent of sales on local advertising.

FINANCING

The Udderlies used their first meeting with Paul MacNeil, an account manager with the Confederation Bank, to build support for the Cow's concept. They presented MacNeil with the preliminary market research, their revenue projections, photos of the store in P.E.I., and a mail-order catalogue. MacNeil was generally optimistic about both the idea and his ability to work with the Udderlies. MacNeil was also cognizant that the Confederation Bank had yet to build a strong customer base in the London area and was looking to secure more clients to establish a better presence.

At the second meeting, the Udderlies informed MacNeil that they had received a verbal offer from the franchiser to negotiate a deal. In addition, they had chosen a site for the store and had begun negotiating a lease with the owner. The chosen location was on Richmond Row, on the corner of Richmond Street and Central Avenue, across from Victoria Park. Richmond Row contained a number of unique upscale retail stores just north of the downtown area. Victoria Park featured a number of free concerts in the summer and a popular outdoor skating rink open to the public in the winter. James expressed his concern that timing was critical since the whole deal was contingent on the financing, and he would soon be receiving written offers from both his prospective landlord and the franchiser.

At this second meeting, James also provided MacNeil with costs estimates. Start-up costs would include $160,000 for equipment and leasehold improvements which would be depreciated on a straight line basis over 10 years. Opening inventory, including ice cream, would be $100,000 and all payables were due to the franchiser on a net 30-day basis. James estimated average inventory, for the next two years, to be about the same amount. Other start-up costs, such as training and other administrative costs, would total $25,000 and could be expensed in the first year. Projected variable costs were 54 per cent of sales for ice cream and 68 per cent of retail sales and included labour. Operating costs, including the manager's salary and rent, would be $7,000 per month and the Udderlies would receive a management fee of $500 per month. Operating costs would likely increase with inflation, which was estimated to be three per cent, but Cow's prices would not. The tax rate was projected to be 23 per cent. James anticipated maintaining a minimum cash balance of approximately $5,000.

MacNeil outlined his initial thoughts to the Udderlies. The Udderlies would have to provide a significant amount of collateral and he would need to include several loan covenants in any agreement. However, the Udderlies would likely qualify for a federal program which encouraged small business start-ups while limiting down-side risk. Specifically, the Canadian Federal Government made loans to start up small businesses, under the Small Business Loans Act, as part of its mandate to encourage entrepreneurs to develop enterprises. The Ontario Provincial Government had a new ventures loan program which tended to offer smaller amounts of funding. According to MacNeil, the advantages of using these programs were that there would be fewer collateral and covenant requirements, and the interest rate on these loans was typically in the prime plus 1.75 per cent range. Currently, the prime rate, the rate at which the Bank's best customers could borrow, was seven per cent. Principal re-payment would take 10 years, with one-tenth of the original loan paid off each year starting at the end of the first year. MacNeil could manage the whole loan process for the

Udderlies, including any term facility secured from the two levels of government, and any operating line of credit received from the Confederation Bank.

The Udderlies felt that, given their life-cycle stage, they could invest all of their liquid assets, about $150,000, but had to limit the collateral. Given the various start-up costs and initial inventory requirements, the Udderlies estimated the need for $160,000 in term loan financing, as well as an operating loan to meet seasonal and other short-term needs. It was anticipated that peak seasonal financing needs would occur between January and March.

ECONOMIC OUTLOOK

The province of Quebec was scheduled to have a general election in the fall of 1994. The Parti Québécois, a political party whose platform centered on Quebec's secession from Canada, was ahead in the popularity polls. This, along with the fact that Canada had the highest per capita debt levels among the major industrialized countries, had made foreigners leery of investing in Canada. The result was a Canadian dollar that was experiencing increased volatility relative to other currencies and that required intervention by the Bank of Canada to protect its value by increasing short-term interest rates. The effect on the bond market was a noticeable widening of the Canada-U.S. interest rates spread to about 1.50 per cent from 1.15 per cent in April 1994.

Canadian economic indicators were showing increasing strength on the domestic front as retail sales were up 1.3 per cent in both February and March of 1994 over the previous month. These results were partly offset by a weaker trade performance. Nevertheless, real gross domestic product (GDP) increased by 0.5 per cent in March and by three per cent in the first quarter of 1994 over the same period a year previously. The inflation environment remained very good with the annual consumer price index (CPI) increasing only by 0.2 per cent and wage settlements averaging up 0.5 per cent during the first three months of the year over the same period a year earlier.

DECISION

The Udderlies were passionate about the franchising idea. They both loved ice cream and found Cow's to be unique and exciting. They considered the consequence if Cow's turned out to be simply a fad. The costs that the Udderlies would incur to start up the store were significant, and the store would need to generate income over a number of years to guarantee that the loans were covered. They were confident that Cow's was not simply a fad since the ice cream was of very good quality and the retail line was a social satire and was, therefore, perpetually renewable.

The Udderlies knew that the ice cream might be moderately cyclical and was certainly seasonal, despite the franchiser's active development of products aimed at smoothing revenue flow, and wondered how that would affect their ability to repay any loans. In order to prepare for his next meeting with MacNeil, James needed to calculate their cash needs and sat down to develop proforma financial statements.

Exhibit 1

SELECTED MARKET RESEARCH **1993**

	Population	**Ave. Annual Growth Rate**	**Per Capita Income**	**Per Capita Retail Sales**
Huron County	60,200	1.03%	$ 14,600	$ 5,200
Perth County	71,200	0.95%	16,100	5,700
Oxford County	95,600	1.62%	16,400	5,800
Middlesex County (includes London)	387,300	2.21%	19,000	6,700
Elgin County	77,300	1.36%	15,700	5,600
Lambton County	130,400	0.65%	18,200	6,500

Number of Individuals in the Labour Force, Ontario, 1991 5,511,235
Number of Individuals in the Labour Force, London, 1991 169,245
Families in Private Households, Total, London, 1993... 102,935
Total Supermarkets and Grocery Retail Sales, Canada, 1993 .... $14.4 billion
Tourism Expenditure on Food and Beverage, London, 1989 .... $59.4 million
Estimated Number of Tourists, London, 1993.. 300,000

Sources: The London Visitors and Convention Bureau, The Financial Post, Statistics Canada

Exhibit 2

ESTIMATED SEASONALITY AND AWARENESS FACTORS
AND FORECASTED MONTHLY SALES

Month	Seasonality	Awareness	Sales
April 1995	0.70	0.1	$ 9,266
May	0.85	0.2	21,146
June	0.95	0.3	34,808
July	1.00	0.4	48,470
August	1.00	0.5	60,350
September	0.60	0.6	43,718
October	0.50	0.7	42,530
November	0.30	0.8	29,462
December	0.30	0.8	29,462
January 1996	0.25	0.8	24,710
February	0.25	0.8	24,710
March	0.35	0.8	34,214
Total (fiscal year 1995-96)			$402,850
April 1996	0.70	0.8	67,478
May	0.85	0.8	81,734
June	0.95	0.8	91,238
July	1.00	0.8	95,990
August	1.00	0.8	95,990
September	0.60	0.8	57,974
October	0.50	0.8	48,470
November	0.30	0.8	29,462
December	0.30	0.8	29,462
January 1997	0.25	0.8	24,710
February	0.25	0.8	24,710
March	0.35	0.8	34,214
Total (fiscal year 1996-97)			$681,436

SOPHISTICATED PETITES

On February 24, 1990, Ann Moore, an account manager in a London, Ontario branch of the Confederation Bank of Canada, was considering the account file of Betty and Edwin Wong. Having just completed her Account Manager Training Course, she was determined to use the skills she had learned to provide a thorough analysis for her manager.

The Wongs had just asked to increase their loan by $70,000, from $43,750 to $113,750, in order to finance the opening of a third store in London. Excited by the improved profitability in their existing stores, they were anxious to have the new store operating in time for the spring season. The money would be used to finance leasehold improvements and furniture purchases.

COMPANY BACKGROUND

The idea for Sophisticated Petites came to Betty Wong in 1986 after one of many frustrating shopping trips. Most boutiques and department stores catered to women between 5'5" and 5'10" tall. Women not in this size range had either of two choices: have their clothes custom-made or pay for extensive re-tailoring of off-the-rack clothes. The few stores that specialized in petite clothing[1] seemed to

---

[1] Petite refers to the length of the garment and the bodice; not the general sizing. A petite woman is one who is quite short but could range from a small size to a large size. In an ordinary store the sizes may range from 4-16. Petite stores have a similar size range.

Richard Ivey School of Business
The University of Western Ontario

IVEY

Arati Chervu prepared this case under the supervision of Professor Jim Hatch solely to provide material for class discussion. The authors do not intend to illustrate either effective or ineffective handling of a managerial situation. The authors may have disguised certain names and other identifying information to protect confidentiality.

concentrate on the price conscious segment of the market, emphasizing clothes for women over 50 years of age. Betty felt that there was untapped market potential for a line of medium to high priced off-the-rack petite casual and professional clothing for women executives.

Although neither of the Wongs had owned businesses before, they had always planned to do so and Sophisticated Petites seemed like an ideal opportunity to capitalize on their skills. Both Betty and Edwin had university degrees: Betty in Science and Edwin in Fine Arts. Edwin had worked for five years as a buyer of men's fashion merchandise at a major national department store chain after receiving his degree and before his current position as Assistant Advertising Manager at the same firm. Betty's job as a senior supervisor for a major credit card company gave her valuable experience at managing a substantial staff of full-time and part-time employees.

After deciding that the market potential was strong in London, they scouted out suitable locations for the boutique. The clientele that they targeted was women between the ages of 25 and 55 earning incomes above $30,000. Since field research showed that a large proportion of these women shopped on Richmond Row (an upscale downtown shopping area in London), Sophisticated Petites began operations in January 1987 in this neighbourhood in a 1,000 square foot retail space. The store featured a line of executive clothing for the petite female professional.

Sophisticated Petites began with $75,000 equity capital and $10,500 in shareholders' loans. Betty and Edwin had savings of $50,000 and had borrowed $25,000 from Betty's parents. No terms of repayment were negotiated for this loan. In addition, they had borrowed $19,000 from Edwin's parents to be repaid in five years.

While ownership of the business was joint, Betty was responsible for the day-to-day operations. She worked an average of 70 hours per week but did not draw a salary. It was agreed that Edwin would maintain his advertising job and help out with the store only on weekends. Edwin's primary responsibility at Sophisticated Petites was to determine appropriate levels of advertising and promotions.

Betty ordered goods in specified quantities and sizes directly from Canadian manufacturers or from merchandising representatives who operated out of suites in Toronto and Montreal hotels. Purchase commitments were made about nine months in advance of each selling season. Normal industry purchase terms were 2%, 10; net 30[2] and new businesses starting out were often sold on a C.O.D. (cash on delivery) basis. If a supplier wanted the business very badly, terms of 3%, 10; net, 60 were sometimes available. Purchases had to be managed carefully since as much as 65% of sales could occur during the September to December selling season.

Sales were encouraging during 1987 which was the first year of operations. Traffic through the store was high and Betty had begun to notice repeat customers. A survey of customers done in January 1988 indicated general satisfaction with the selection of clothes available, however, a number of customers indicated that the prices were higher than what they would normally be willing to pay. Betty dismissed these responses noting that the quality of merchandise that Sophisticated Petites provided was higher than had been previously offered in this area. In both Edwin and Betty's estimation, the store was a success.

Determined to maintain momentum, the Wongs decided to open a bigger store in the newly built Masonville Mall (a shopping centre located in the north of the city, an area with a high average household income). This opening, which occurred in January 1989, allowed them to expand their line to include casual clothing for the petite professional woman. As with the first store, sales were encouraging.

With the business demanding more managerial time than Betty could provide, Edwin had to quit his job in early 1989 to work full time at Sophisticated Petites. They also hired a total of 12 part-time employees.

During the 1989 fiscal year, Edwin and Betty drew a combined salary of $31,250. They were also able to charge a significant part of their living expenses to the business including their car, a number of meals, and part of their rent since they used one room in their home as an office. They expected to draw a salary of $40,000 in fiscal 1990. Both Edwin and Betty felt that they had a firm grasp of the finances of the business.

---

[2]The invoice is to be paid in full in 30 days and a 2% discount is given if the invoice is paid within 10 days.

The Setback

During fiscal 1989, the Wongs decided to launch a menswear line within the store at Masonville Mall. Like their ladies line of clothing, the men's line was targeted at a niche market—men under 5'6".

In order to help finance the launch of the menswear line, the Wongs had taken out a Small Business Loan of $25,000 from the Confederation Bank. This loan was repayable in monthly payments of $350 plus interest at prime plus 1%. They also took out a Confederation Bank Term Loan of $18,750 repayable in monthly instalments of $300 plus interest at prime plus 2.5%. The loans were being repaid on schedule.

The new business was a complete failure. Men did not feel comfortable shopping in a store called Sophisticated Petites. In addition, they did not perceive the need for a specialized shop since most menswear stores included free alterations with suit purchases—a service which Sophisticated Petites did not offer. The menswear inventory had to be sold off at a deep discount. Furthermore, Sophisticated Petites incurred an extraordinary loss of $20,450 due to the write-off of leasehold improvements in 1989 as shown in the financial statements in Exhibit 1.

Recognizing the need for advice, the Wongs obtained the service of a chartered accountant, Joan Brunelle, who specialized in serving the retail trade. Subsequently, she played an important role in almost all major decisions regarding Sophisticated Petites. Acting on the advice of Joan Brunelle, Edwin and Betty decided to focus only on women's wear.

The Recovery

Under the guidance of Joan Brunelle, business improved. By the end of February 1990, the Wongs felt that the business had turned around. High sales during the fourth quarter of 1989 and favourable feedback from their customers contributed to their optimism. The Wongs estimated a profit of $30,000 during the fourth quarter.

Expansions undertaken to date had been partially trade-financed. Sophisticated Petites had a good relationship with one of its key suppliers and often took advantage of extremely favourable credit terms, sometimes up to 90 days. The Wongs had been told by their suppliers that they would receive such favourable terms until they had completed their startup phase but that they would have to pay under normal terms once they were established. The Wongs realized that they could have to begin paying within at least 60 days if economic conditions began putting pressure on their suppliers. The business rarely had accounts receivable since most customers paid by cheque or credit card, both of which were treated as cash payments. The firm tried to maintain a minimum cash balance of $15,000. An operating line of credit for $10,000 with the Confederation Bank was seldom utilized.

The Current Opportunity

Excited by the recovery and anxious to maintain the momentum, the Wongs planned to open a third store in April in the Galleria, a major mall in downtown London. The timing of the decision was especially important because there were rumours that a competitor was considering the opening of a petites store in the mall and the Wongs felt that if they opened their store first, competitors would withdraw from the market.

Sophisticated Petites had tentatively arranged a seven year lease for a location on the first floor of the mall beginning in March with a monthly rental of $5,000 or 6% of gross sales whichever was larger. They planned to spend $86,000 on such leasehold improvements as a storefront, signage, acoustical ceiling, electrical wiring, mannequins, signage and furnishings. A cash downpayment of $16,000 had been made leaving a balance of $70,000 to be raised. Edwin and Betty wanted to borrow this money through a term loan.

The Wongs were confident that a store in the Galleria had huge potential. The mall had 165 stores located on two stories. The upscale clothing stores such as Harry Rosen, Heritage, Liptons and Susan J were located on the second floor. With popular national stores like The Gap, Eaton's, and The Bay, traffic through the mall was high. In addition, London had excess commercial real estate capacity and property management firms were enticing retailers with generous leasing terms.

The store would be opened for business in April but hiring would begin immediately. The Wongs planned to hire one full time employee as an assistant manager at $30,000 per annum. They also budgeted for an additional eight part-time employees at $8,000 per annum. Benefits would cost an additional 25% of employee salaries.

Projections

The Wongs were optimistic about the success of Sophisticated Petites. The Richmond Row store had shown a consistent profit since its start-up. According to them, this performance would have been repeated by the Masonville store had it not been for the menswear debacle. Betty, Edwin, and Joan Brunelle felt particularly positive about the potential of the proposed Galleria store.

This confidence was reflected in their financial projections. The Wongs predicted that their gross profit margin would stabilize at 40%, the standard in the industry. Management of inventory would be critical and the Wongs expected inventory turnover (using year end inventory rather than average inventory) would be consistent with the local industry standard of three times. The average age of payables was expected to be 75 days. In addition, they expected that the new store would add $20,000 to the fixed General and Administrative Expenses and $5,000 to the Advertising Expense. The Wongs believed that the wages and benefits expenses for the Richmond and Masonville stores would be about the same in 1990 as in 1989. In 1989, of $77,513 General and Administrative Expenses, $45,000 was fixed and the rest was variable with sales.

The Wongs were not overly concerned about the tax implications of their business decisions. The effective small business tax rate was 25%.

Joan Brunelle's projection for the Galleria store for the year ending December 1990 was for sales of $550,000. She anticipated that monthly sales for this store would ultimately be slightly higher than that for either the Richmond Row ($62,500) or Masonville ($58,333) stores because of its excellent location. Sales for all three stores combined were anticipated to reach $2,000,000.

Current Economic Conditions

Anxious to do a comprehensive analysis, Ann Moore reviewed topical economic and business information. The Bank Rate had shown a steady upward trend during the past 2-1/2 years and was currently pegged at 13.25% reflecting the Bank of Canada's war on inflation. Inflation however was persistent and had averaged 5.33% per annum during the first two months of the year. The prime rate was currently set at 14.25%.

The persistent high interest rates had begun to slow consumer spending. Analysts were predicting real Gross Domestic Product to show its first decline in six years during the first quarter of 1990.

The government expected the proposed Goods and Services Tax (GST), scheduled to take effect January 1, 1991, to add another 1.25% to the inflation rate at that time. Lack of confidence in the government's current policies, however, had led economists to forecast even higher inflation rates.

The retail trade was nervous about the impact of the GST. Currently, there was no federal sales tax on clothing. The GST, therefore, would be an entirely new tax on this item. Many retailers expected to see a decline in sales during the first few months of 1991 until customers became accustomed to the new prices. Some analysts had forecast that the economic slowdown combined with the impact of the GST could result in retail sales in some sectors falling as much as 10%.

Competition within the retail sector was intensifying. Consumers were becoming more discriminating and more sensitive to price-value relationships. Combined with slow growth in real personal disposable income and the emergence of new store formats, these factors were forcing stores to focus their marketing and planning to meet special needs.

The elimination of tariffs and other trade barriers under the Free Trade Agreement was expected to provide North American retailers (Canadian and U.S.) with broader North American sourcing opportunities. It could also encourage cross-border investment. This was expected to increase overall economic activity by facilitating the flow of new retail concepts and intensifying competition.

While American retail giants had not rushed into the Canadian market, the successes of the few that had, like The Gap, were notable. There was even talk that Robert Campeau would open a Bloomingdale's in Toronto. The flagship store in New York carried an extensive petite women's line. (The Gap and Bloomingdale's are two upscale department stores in the U.S.)

In the long term, despite slow population growth in Canada, a significant increase in the number of people in the high-spending (35 to 49 year old) age group was expected. This augured well for the retail sector which was expected to outperform the economy in the period to the mid-1990s.

Ann Moore also referred to Dun & Bradstreet Canada's Key Business Ratios—1990 Edition (shown in Exhibit 2) to compare key ratios for Sophisticated Petites with those in the industry. She understood that the ratios presented in this publication were averages based on an analysis of a composite sample of Canadian audited financial statements. The statements of both profitable and unprofitable concerns were included in the Dun & Bradstreet analysis.

The Decision at Hand

It was clear to Ann Moore that the Wongs were extremely dedicated and anxious to succeed. During the interview with the Wongs, Ann had put together a crude personal statement of affairs for the couple (Exhibit 3) and noted that their personal assets were not very large. However, she knew that the Wongs had a number of well-to-do relatives in town.

The Wongs had been longstanding Confederation Bank clients. Until the launch of the menswear line, they had only taken advantage of the Confederation's deposit services. The two outstanding loans were being repaid on schedule. Ann also noted that the current account balance was normally in the $20,000 range, but there had been a few times when the balance had reached a small overdraft situation.

	Exhibit 1

BALANCE SHEET
for the year ending December 31st

	1988	1989
ASSETS		
Current Assets		
Cash	$ 20,778	$ 19,518
Inventory	120,022	268,494
Prepaids	2,750	2,750
Total Current Assets	143,550	290,762
Fixed Assets		
Furniture and Fixtures	2,000	5,000
Leasehold Improvements	59,546	105,540
Fixed Assets	61,546	110,540
Less Accumulated Depreciation	6,155	17,209
Net Fixed Assets	55,391	93,331
TOTAL ASSETS	198,941	384,093
LIABILITIES		
Current Liabilities		
Accounts Payable & Accrued		
Liabilities	79,000	206,176
Current Share of L.T. Liabilities	————	7,800
Total Current Liabilities	79,000	213,976
Long Term Liabilities		
Due to Shareholders	19,000	19,000
Bank Loans (L.T. Portion)		35,950
Total Long Term Liabilities	19,000	54,950
TOTAL LIABILITIES	98,000	268,926
SHAREHOLDERS EQUITY		
Capital Stock		
Authorized: 1,000,000 common shares		
Issued & Fully Paid 7,500		
common shares	75,000	75,000
Surplus	25,941	40,167
Total Shareholders Equity	100,941	115,167
TOTAL LIABILITIES		
& SHAREHOLDERS EQUITY	$198,941	$384,093

	Exhibit 1 (continued)

INCOME STATEMENT
for the year ending December 31st

	1988	1989
Sales	$600,110	$1,300,518
Cost Of Goods Sold		
Beginning Inventory		120,022
Purchases	479,130	965,840
Freight	958	1,958
	480,088	1,087,820
Ending Inventory	120,022	268,494
Cost of Goods	360,066	819,326
GROSS PROFIT	240,044	481,192
Expenses:		
Advertising	10,000	15,000
General & Admin. — Fixed	45,000	45,000
General & Admin — Variable	0	32,513
Bad Debts	600	1,301
Bank Charges	600	600
Credit Card	7,501	16,256
Depreciation	6,155	11,054
Loss Due to Theft	6,001	13,005
Owner's Salary		31,250
Promotion	18,003	39,016
Rent	72,050	141,038
Wages and Benefits	39,543	90,034
Interest	0	5,707
TOTAL EXPENSES	205,453	441,774
Extraordinary Loss		20,450
INCOME BEFORE TAXES	34,591	18,968
Taxes	8,648	4,742
NET INCOME	$25,943	$ 14,226

Exhibit 1 (continued)

NOTES TO THE FINANCIAL STATEMENTS **for the year ending December 31, 1989**

1.   SIGNIFICANT ACCOUNTING POLICY
     Depreciation was calculated by using the straight line method. Assets had an estimated life of 10 years.

2.   LONG TERM LIABILITIES

Bank Loans	December 31/89	Current Portion
Repayable in 72 monthly payments of $350.00 plus interest at prime plus 1%	$20,800	$4,200
Term Loan - Repayable in 60 monthly payments of $300.00 plus interest at prime plus 2.5%	$15,150	$3,600
Shareholders Loans		
No specified repayment schedule	$19,000	
Total	$54,950	$7,800

3.   COMPARATIVE FIGURES

     In January 1989, the company opened a second retail store in Masonville Mall.

4.   BANK INTEREST AND CHARGES
     Bank charges generally averaged $600 per annum. Also included in this item are credit card discounts. Typically, these discounts would equal 2.5% of credit sales. 50% of total sales were made on credit card, 20% with cash, and 30% with cheque.

Exhibit 2

DUN & BRADSTREET CANADA
KEY BUSINESS RATIOS — 1990 EDITION

LINE OF BUSINESS (and number of concerns reporting) DOMAINE D'EXPLOITATION (et nombre d'entreprises étudiées)		Cost of Goods Sold Coût des marchandises vendues Per Cent Pour cent	Gross, Margin Marge bénéficiaire brute Per Cent Pour cent	Current Assets to Current Debt Coefficient du fonds de roulement Times Fois	Profits on Sales Coefficient du profit sur les ventes Per Cent Pour cent	Profits on Equity Coefficient du profit sur l'avoir Per Cent Pour cent	Sales to Equity Coefficient des ventes sur l'avoir Times Fois	Collection Period Période de recouvrement Days Jours	Sales to Inventory Coefficient des ventes sur les stocks Times Fois	Fixed Assets Equity Coefficient des immobilisa-tions sur l'avoir Per Cent Pour cent	Current Debt Equity Coefficient des exigibilités pur l'avoir Per Cent Pour cent	Total Debt Equity Coefficient de la dette totale sur l'avoir Per Cent Pour cent
ALL COMPANIES TOUTES LES COMPAGNIES*	606,562	66.9%	33.1%	1.0	7.1%	11.3%	1.6		7.6	65.0%	124.5%	223.1%
RETAIL TRADE COMMERCE DE DÉTAIL	90,373	74.3%	25.7%	1.4	2.5%	20.9%	8.2		6.4	66.4%	142.5%	217.2%
Auto Acc. & Parts Pièces et accessoires d'automobiles	3,136	70.9%	29.1%	1.5	2.2%	20.6%	9.3		5.4	61.3%	174.8%	257.6%
Book & Stat. Stores Livres et papeterie	1,221	62.6%	37.4%	1.3	2.3%	22.0%	9.4		5.0	90.3%	216.9%	304.7%
Clothing, Men's Vêtements pour hommes	1,914	58.9%	41.1%	1.6	3.5%	12.9%	3.7		4.8	25.7%	79.4%	115.5%
Clothing, Women's Vêtements pour dames	3,706	57.0%	43.0%	1.5	1.9%	12.8%	6.6		5.6	74.4%	139.8%	206.4%
Dept. Stores Magasins à rayons	45	69.0%	31.0%	1.7	1.4%	5.0%	3.6		5.0	29.0%	74.0%	112.5%
Drug Stores Pharmacies	3,788	72.6%	27.4%	1.5	2.2%	20.7%	9.2		5.3	41.3%	161.6%	215.6%
Dry Goods Merceries	2,798	60.6%	39.4%	1.6	1.3%	9.8%	7.3		4.4	77.2%	144.1%	246.1%
Elec. Appliances Repair Appareils électriques, réparation	1,042	57.0%	43.0%	1.7	1.9%	11.9%	6.2		8.3	45.6%	126.7%	179.5%
Florists Fleuristes	1,405	46.4%	53.6%	1.2	2.6%	24.0%	9.2		10.6	115.4%	166.7%	270.9%
Food Stores Magasins d'alimentation	13,460	77.7%	22.3%	1.1	1.0%	10.8%	10.9		15.4	95.9%	113.1%	203.6%
Fuel Dealers Vendeurs d'huile	371	79.3%	20.7%	1.5	3.9%	21.1%	5.4		14.4	72.3%	84.6%	114.8%
Furniture & Appliance Ameublement et appareils ménagers	9,344	69.3%	30.7%	1.5	1.9%	13.0%	6.7		4.7	38.1%	150.8%	200.0%
Gas. Serv. Stns. Stations-service	7,214	81.4%	18.6%	1.2	1.4%	23.1%	16.3		27.3	145.9%	133.9%	277.6%
General Mdse. Marchandises générales	1,195	79.1%	20.9%	1.3	1.7%	13.6%	8.0		7.6	77.5%	117.1%	197.7%
Hardware Quincaillerie	3,371	68.5%	31.5%	1.8	2.6%	14.5%	5.7		4.2	47.1%	110.2%	177.9%
Jewellery store Bijouterie	2,378	54.0%	46.0%	1.8	2.9%	8.3%	2.9		2.2	25.1%	105.0%	168.0%
Motor Veh. Dealers Concessionnaires automobiles	6,405	88.0%	12.0%	1.2	−0.7%	−11.7%	16.9		5.5	125.5%	337.6%	466.9%
Motor Veh. Repairs Réparation des véhicules	9,179	58.8%	41.2%	1.3	2.9%	21.6%	7.4		11.0	109.1%	123.7%	221.1%
Shoe Stores Magasins de chaussures	1,333	57.1%	42.9%	1.5	1.8%	8.1%	4.6		3.5	44.3%	112.8%	139.5%
Tobacconists Tabagies	398	61.0%	39.0%	2.1	−2.0%	−21.4%	10.6		8.3	162.1%	103.8%	1668.6%
Variety Stores Magasins d'articles variés	1,008	71.9%	28.1%	1.6	1.8%	12.1%	6.9		4.9	47.1%	121.8%	158.2%
WHOLESALE TRADE COMMERCE DE GROS	53,026	81.8%	18.2%	1.3	1.9%	14.0%	7.3	39	7.4	39.9%	171.0%	219.0%
App. & Dry Goods Mercerie et habillement	2,608	79.6%	20.4%	1.4	2.0%	15.3%	7.6	49	6.2	23.3%	189.6%	236.4%
Coal & Coke Charbon et coke	19	−103.8%	203.8%	2.2	−0.2%	1.2%	(4.8)	−38	(4.6)	1.2%	80.2%	77.9%
Drug & Toilet Prep. Pharmacie et produits de beauté	770	79.7%	20.3%	1.5	2.0%	15.4%	7.9	45	7.4	30.1%	159.6%	190.2%
Food Alimentation	4,211	87.3%	12.7%	1.3	1.9%	21.4%	11.4	20	16.6	40.4%	137.1%	183.7%
Furn. & Furnishings Meubles et ameublement	1,083	76.5%	23.5%	1.6	1.9%	14.2%	7.5	48	5.8	22.3%	162.0%	205.3%

Exhibit 3					
PERSONAL STATEMENT OF NET WORTH — THE WONGS					

ASSETS		**LIABILITIES AND EQUITY**		
Cash	$5,450	Confederation Car Loan	$4,799	(1)
Value of Company	115,000	Loan from Chen Family	25,000	
Shareholder's Loan	19,000	Loan from Wong Family	19,000	
Nissan '87 Micra	5,500	Student Loans	9,841	(2)
Jewellery &				
Collectibles	6,250	Subtotal	58,640	
Total Assets	$ 151,200			
		Surplus	92,560	
		Total Liabilities & Equity	$151,200	

(1) Monthly payments of $140.98
(2) Monthly payments of $228.23

LONDON SKI CLUB

In early November 1999, Paulette Root looked out the window of her Confederation Bank of Canada office and pondered over the loan request from the London Ski Club (LSC), a local not-for-profit organization. In August, the bank and the LSC had met and agreed on the firm's credit limit for the coming year. However, during the annual pre-season maintenance of the groomer, it was realized that a sizeable investment was needed to get this key piece of equipment ready for the upcoming season. As a result the club had unexpectedly requested an increase in its bank loan of approximately $250,000. Paulette noted that the club had experienced losses during the past two years and wondered whether the extension of the loan could be justified.

LONDON SKI CLUB BACKGROUND

The LSC had been created as a not-for-profit organization with the purpose of providing facilities for various winter and summer activities surrounding the natural splendor of Boler Mountain. The mountain was located in the town of Byron situated 10 kilometres outside the city of London. It had begun as a public initiative to give the local residents a place to ski. This local base had led to the creation of a very close knit community-oriented organization. Many people volunteered to help operate a number of services.

Richard Ivey School of Business
The University of Western Ontario

IVEY

John Siambanopoulos prepared this case under the supervision of Professors Craig Dunbar and James E. Hatch solely to provide material for class discussion. The authors do not intend to illustrate either effective or ineffective handling of a managerial situation. The authors may have disguised certain names and other identifying information to protect confidentiality.

The resort grew to a paying membership of over 1,700 and was a popular place for families to spend a day outdoors.

The ski resort industry had changed over the past decade. Ski resorts were becoming more oriented around families and provided "something for everyone." Recreational skiing had always been the primary winter sport; however, the increase in other new snow-related activities such as tubing and snow-boarding had required many within the industry to commit money and staff to the provision of a wider range of products, while at the same time trying to use existing resources as efficiently as possible. Capital improvements were prevalent throughout the industry in order to accommodate these different interests. For example, the LSC had put in a new tube run for people who wanted the exhilaration of sliding down a hill while sitting in a large inflated rubber inner tube.

Operations at all ski resorts included snow making and grooming. These essential services were provided to maintain optimum ski conditions when nature wasn't accommodating. Changes in snowmaking technology allowed resorts to have a greater degree of control over the length of their operating season and the quality of the snow conditions. The snowmaking equipment could make snow at a temperature of zero degrees but the optimal temperature for snowmaking was less than $-9°$. Typically after a day of skiing, the snow is carved into frozen uneven ridges along the hill. The groomer is a critical piece of equipment for a ski hill. It is a large vehicle, similar to a snowplow, that breaks and evens the snow for optimal skiing. The club purchased the current groomer in 1994.

The Boler Mountain ski hill offered 10 trails with terrain varying from beginner to advanced. A number of activities, including downhill skiing, snowboarding, and tubing, were offered in the winter in addition to mountain biking in the summer. Other services included a ski school, a professional shop, a cafeteria and a lounge. Annual subscriptions and daily passes traditionally made up over 60 per cent of total revenues. Annual subscriptions cost $300 per year and offered the subscriber unlimited use of the facilities at any time. The club held early payment discount drives during September to build up cash for the upcoming season. Subscription revenue had fallen dramatically a couple of years ago, while sales of daily passes picked up much of the decrease. Keeping the subscriptions from declining further would be a challenge in the future, as consumers didn't want to commit to only one form of winter entertainment with a yearly charge.

The target market for the LSC was essentially "anyone who could ski or enjoyed other outdoor winter activities." Marketing efforts revolved primarily around promotion of the club's facilities and services. The LSC had an Internet presence, which listed its major services and its prices, in addition to maps, upcoming events, contact information and other items related to Boler Mountain. The firm had redesigned its brochure and held a "Business After 5" event through the Chamber of Commerce at the club to help raise its profile with London area businesses. Increasing awareness and raising money from membership drives had always been key issues. For the upcoming Canada Games in 2001, the LSC would be hosting the mountain bike races, which would provide positive exposure for the club.

Although there were many ski resorts in the southern Ontario region, most were very similar in their products and services; therefore, most consumers didn't bother travelling long distances to go to another resort when a similar one operated nearby. Unlike the resorts of the Canadian Rockies, most Ontario resorts were smaller and catered to a more regional consumer versus a national or international one. Two resorts, Cobble Hills and Chicopee, operated within one hour of London. The LSC didn't consider these nearby ski resorts to be competitors in the traditional sense; instead they helped each other out by raising general public awareness about skiing. Half a million people lived in the local market.

Other winter activities such as hockey, skating and cross-country skiing were considered direct competitors for the time and money of their participants. Many of these activities required less dependency on the weather than skiing did and therefore could operate for a longer season. Other activities, like hockey, found other revenue sources in the off-season by renting the property to other groups. In terms of financing, arenas were owned and operated by the municipal government which, unlike typical ski resorts, had a large budget for operations and capital needs.

Many resorts had expanded into tennis, golf, hiking and bike trails during the summer months in order to help supplement and smooth yearly revenues and cash flows. However, these expansions involved large capital expenditures.

The board of directors of the London Ski Club and the operational management team at Boler Mountain had a great deal of experience within the recreational ski industry. The firm had a volunteer board of directors, listed in Exhibit 1. Exhibits 2 and 3 provide an organizational chart and a list of key personnel, respectively. The role of the board was to focus on major strategic issues including major capital expenditure decisions, obtaining financing and hiring the operating managers. All of the board members were volunteers who served a three-year term. Although there was no tangible financial incentive to become involved in the operations of the club, people who enjoyed the facilities felt inclined to help as board members or volunteers for other programs. The contribution of unpaid volunteers was very substantial. Two programs that relied heavily on volunteers were the ski patrol that managed the safety of the hills and the group that organized and delivered racing for kids.

In the 1999 fiscal year, certain expectations and goals for the club had not been met, which caused some tension. The general manager, who acted as a liaison between the president and all of the line-managers, had recently been terminated and had not been replaced. This departure had flattened the reporting hierarchy by removing one level of management between the board and the operating managers. Currently, Peter Toms, the operations manager, held a critical position for the LSC and oversaw all activities related to the mountain. The ski school had been purchased a few years ago and the previous owner became an employee of the LSC as manager of the school.

The LSC was set up as a not-for-profit corporation without share capital and was exempt from income taxes other than on investment income greater than $2,000. Financial statements are provided in Exhibit 4.

The LSC had three different methods of financing: cash from operations, loans and fund-raising. Unlike private enterprises, equity financing was not an option since there were no owners and profits could not be distributed outside of the firm. LSC could raise capital through debt financing. At the annual review conducted in early 1999, however, both LSC management and the Confederation Bank had agreed that the club had reached its borrowing limit. Since the LSC was a not-for-profit organization, it could also raise money through fund-raising from individuals and corporations; however, it was not a registered charity so it could not provide charitable donation tax receipts. A consultant had been approached to take on the fund raising task in return for a percentage of revenues received. However she had refused to take on the task without a fixed salary so the initiative had been dropped and total fundraising efforts had provided very little capital to date. Due to the LSC's unique position within the community, government support was also possible; however, due to heavy cutbacks, funding from these sources was doubtful.

The rapport between Paulette Root of Confederation Bank and LSC management had been very good. Confederation Bank had been the sole bank for LSC since the club's inception. Paulette Root had worked with the club for several years. The club had never been delinquent with information or loan payments. Despite the effect that recent weather difficulties had on profits, Paulette felt LSC was a well-run business.

The loan from the bank had been increased a few times in the past in order to meet various capital needs and now totaled $1,091,449. It had been set up as a 10-year mortgage. The loan was secured by all of the club's assets. The property, made up of land and buildings, had been appraised at $6.3 million as of May 17, 1990, and was supported by fire insurance. Various covenants were placed on the loan: the total debt to total net worth ratio could not exceed 1.3; capital expenditures were limited to $250,000; and a minimum tangible net worth of $700,000 was required. These covenants were all monitored annually. Annual audited financial statements were required within 120 days of the March 31st fiscal year-end. The total debt to total net worth covenant was breached during the 1998/99 fiscal year. Confederation Bank waived its right for further action in respect to this breach until the annual review in mid-August, at which time the covenants had been modified at the agreement of both the bank and the LSC. The total debt to total net worth ratio could now not exceed 1.5, capital expenditures were limited to $50,000 without the bank's prior consent and a minimum tangible net worth of $900,000 was required. The two years of losses from 1998 to 1999 had put some strains on the banking relationship, in part because the club didn't have a contingency fund set up for capital projects.

The LSC operated primarily as a cash business. Cash reserves at year-end, therefore, were large. This money was then used to pay down the debt load as operating expenses decreased over the spring and summer. The club had a target year end cash balance of $300,000. In order to ensure smooth cash flows, the LSC had a $100,000 line of credit with the bank, which was used typically during the fall to help bolster the cash from annual dues. Interest on the line of credit was set at prime plus 1.5 per cent. As of August 1999, the prime interest rate was 6.0 per cent.

Accounts receivable tended to be modest and represented the amount still owed from various visiting high schools at the year-end. Accounts payable were owed to suppliers and, although these accounts had increased in 1999, they were expected to return to 1998 levels in 2000 and beyond. The LSC held some inventory in the form of club hats and T-shirts; however, most of the inventory was actually made up of ski uniforms rented by the employees. It was expected that inventory would fall to approximately $20,000 for the upcoming year as more people bought their own uniforms.

Revenues had grown over the last five years, mostly in areas other than skiing such as snowboarding and tubing. However, previous years' weather conditions had not been cold enough during the lucrative Christmas season, which had dampened revenues. According to the Canadian Meteorological Centre, although 1998 had a "below normal" level of snowfall, 1999 was expected to be "above normal" for the LSC's region.

All revenues were expected to increase during the upcoming season. Because of the effort that had been put into improving the mountain biking trails, as well as into a stronger marketing campaign, revenues from mountain biking had already reached $41,000 for the year, a strong increase from the previous summer. Annual dues were aggressively budgeted at around $435,000. By September 30, over $310,000 had already been received from this source.[1] Interest and other income were expected to be $9,000, including the amortization of deferred revenues (see note 2 to the Balance Sheets in Exhibit 4). The club now planned to run various special events, which were to be held in the newly-renovated chalet. This was expected to generate additional revenues of $20,000. Revenues from the new tube run were expected to grow at 40 per cent due to its relative novelty. Revenues from daily passes were expected to grow at a more modest five per cent. All other sources of revenue were expected to grow similarly at five per cent. Mountain biking revenues, annual dues and interest and other income were insensitive to weather conditions. All other revenue projections could be substantially lower if weather conditions were poor. Club management believed that 1998 revenues represented a worst case scenario, given the poor weather during that year.

In the coming year, administration and office, general operating, and property expenses were predicted to be similar to 1999 levels. Due to the expected increased usage of the newly-renovated chalet for special events, chalet expenses were forecasted to be $35,000. All other expenses were considered to be variable and were expected to remain at 1999 levels relative to sales. If weather conditions were favorable, as expected, management believed that operations expenses would be 12 per cent of sales, however.

Future expansion had been planned in three phases. Phase one, which had been completed, included improvement to the chalet, a new tube run and a beginner hill. Phase two, which was ongoing, was oriented around infrastructure improvement such as new pumps, piping, and a garage. Phase three was geared towards a "Hill 2000" concept, which entailed developing and creating a new man-made ski run that would have a much higher elevation than any other part of the current hill. Although the LSC wasn't a large resort, this expansion would greatly improve the quality of the skiing and the overall product that the club offered. The capital requirements for this expansion were massive since the creation of another run called for large infrastructure outlays in addition to the obvious changes to the mountain. The club had no immediate plans to proceed with this phase of expansion.

THE GROOMER PROBLEM

In the fall of 1999, during the pre-season tune-up of the groomer, it was realized that extraordinary repairs of at least $21,000 would be required for the groomer to make it through the season. The groomer currently had a net book value of zero. This increasing upkeep of the groomer and the upcoming season's expected colder weather had called into question the machine's capacity to last another season. Two options had been

---

[1] Of this total, $78,616 was raised in a membership drive in March 1999. These advance payments were recorded as deferred revenue for the year ending March 31, 1999. The club did not plan to begin its membership drive for the 2000/01 ski season until after March 31, 2000.

tabled by management: service the current machine and buy another one within two years, or buy a new groomer this year. The new groomer was quoted at $262,141 including taxes, with an expected useful life of 10 years. Like all other club assets, the groomer would be depreciated on a straight line basis. The club would receive a $35,000 trade-in allowance on its old groomer. The purchase of a new groomer would have a positive effect on snowmaking and grooming expenses. With the new groomer, these expenses were forecast to be $140,000.

Taking on more debt without strong profits and cash flows could hurt the LSC and its future expansion plans. Both the bank and management had agreed that no new debt would be taken on until earnings improved. However, due to the lack of cash that was typical in the fall and the apparent need for a new groomer, management decided to come to the bank for an increase in the club's loan. Besides the groomer, no other major capital expenditures were expected.

The new winter season was quickly approaching and the LSC wanted to begin preparations. Paulette realized she had very little time to decide on the increase.

Exhibit 1
BOARD OF DIRECTORS

Position	Name	Occupation
President	David James	Property Manager
Vice-President	Eric Mitchell	Production Engineer
Secretary	Brian Robertson	Physician (general practitioner)
Treasurer	Ed Stuart	Consultant
	Bob Wright	Salesman
	Fraser Smith	Lawyer
	Wayne Booth	Compression Engineering – Owner
	Larry Noel	Manager of Parks and Recreation, City of London
	Carol Smith	Self-employed
	Nancy Osborne	Nurse
	Mark Chretien	Lawyer
	Randy Harris	Insurance Sales

Note: One third of the positions were re-opened for election each year.

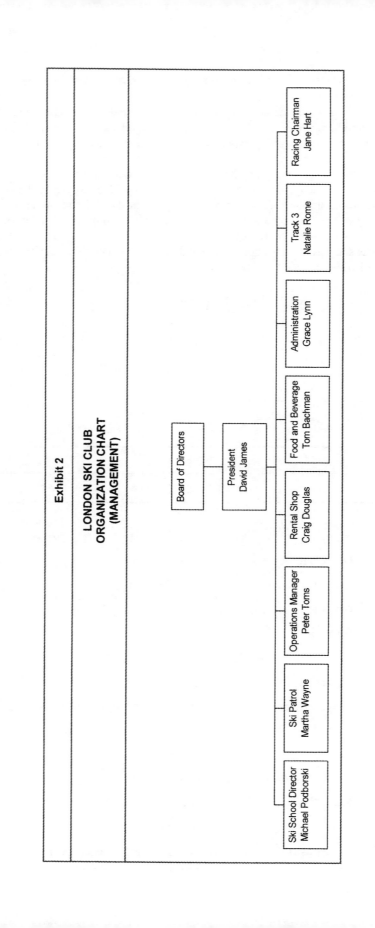

Exhibit 2

**LONDON SKI CLUB
ORGANIZATION CHART
(MANAGEMENT)**

Board of Directors

President
David James

Ski School Director
Michael Podborski

Ski Patrol
Martha Wayne

Operations Manager
Peter Toms

Rental Shop
Craig Douglas

Food and Beverage
Tom Bachman

Administration
Grace Lynn

Track 3
Natalie Rome

Racing Chairman
Jane Hart

Exhibit 3
MANAGEMENT PROFILES

David James, President
- Volunteer and member of the Board of Directors

Peter Toms, Operations Manager
- Nine years experience with the London Ski Club
- Attained diploma in Ski Resorts operation management
- In charge of lifts, property, grooming and snowmaking

Tom Bachman, Food and Beverage Manager
- Four years experience with the London Ski Club
- Six years experience as general manager with another golf and country club

Craig Douglas, Rental Shop Manager
- 10 years experience as a rental shop employee with the last two as manager

Michael Podborski, Ski School Director
- Owned the Ski School since 1988
- When the LSC acquired the School, kept Wayne as director

Grace Lynn, Office Manager
- Holds over 19 years of experience in financial management
- Contributes to business planning, budgeting, oversees the interim statement preparation, payroll and accounting schedules
- With the LSC for the past three years

Exhibit 4

FINANCIAL STATEMENTS

Balance Sheet

Year Ending March 31

	1997	1998	1999
Assets			
Cash and term deposits	346,355	152,222	302,578
Accounts receivable	10,738	9,296	6,421
Loan receivable [1]	30,000	30,000	27,000
Inventory	-	39,066	36,316
Prepaid Expenses	37,323	27,773	26,932
Current Assets	424,416	258,357	399,247
Capital Assets, net	1,278,049	1,901,569	2,209,108
TOTAL ASSETS	$ 1,702,465	$ 2,159,926	$ 2,608,355
Liabilities and Equity			
Accounts payable and accruals	101,261	76,828	147,084
Unearned revenue	-	-	78,616
Current portion of deferred revenue [2]	-	5,600	5,600
Current portion of long-term debt [3]	99,730	123,397	125,156
Current portion of obligation under capital lease [4]	-	-	30,780
Current Liabilities	200,991	205,825	387,236
Deferred revenue [2]	-	128,800	123,200
Obligation under capital lease [4]	-	-	128,139
Long-term debt [3]	342,486	713,760	966,293
Equity			
Retained earnings	1,158,988	1,111,541	1,003,487
Contingent liability [5]	-	-	-
TOTAL LIABILITIES AND EQUITY	$ 1,702,465	$ 2,159,926	$ 2,608,355

---

[1] In lieu of rental payments for the use of building on London Ski Club (LSC) premises, the club established a $30,000 interest free loan to the Ski Patrol, a non-profit organization. The loan is to be repaid by the Ski Patrol beginning in 1999, with 10 annual installments of $3,000.

[2] Deferred revenue is an adjustment to account for the transfer of ownership of a building on LSC premises from Track 3, a non-profit organization, to LSC. LSC's contribution to the construction of the building had previously been expensed. To offset this, the deferred revenue account was established. Deferred revenue is amortized on a straight-line basis over 25 years. The annual amortization ($5,600) is added to the LSC's income statement as non-cash revenue (included in Interest and Other Income).

Exhibit 4 (continued)

---

[3] Long-term debt is a first mortgage repayable in equal monthly payments of interest and principal of $15,750. The interest rate on the mortgage loan is 6.25%. Annual interest and principal payments on the loan are as follows:

Year ending March 31	Total Payments	Interest Payments	Principal Payments
2000	$ 189,000	$ 64,695	$ 124,305
2001	$ 189,000	$ 56,699	$ 132,301
2002	$ 189,000	$ 48,189	$ 140,811
2003	$ 189,000	$ 39,132	$ 149,868
2004	$ 189,000	$ 29,493	$ 159,507
2005	$ 189,000	$ 19,233	$ 169,767
2006	$ 189,000	$ 8,313	$ 180,687
2007	$ 47,250	$ 291	$ 46,959

In addition to the first mortgage, the whole of the indebtedness is subject to a general security agreement covering all of the club's assets.

[4] Annual payments under the capital lease are broken into principal repayments and interest expenses as follows:

Year ending March 31	Total Payments	Interest Payments	Principal Payments
2000	$ 43,235	$ 12,455	$ 30,780
2001	43,235	$ 12,990	$ 30,245
2002	43,235	$ 9,924	$ 33,311
2003	39,629	$ 6,547	$ 33,082
2004	32,311	$ 3,194	$ 29,117
2005	2,626	$ 242	$ 2,384

[5] The club has been notified that it is a defendant in a suit which states a claim for negligence and breach of statutory duty in the amount of $500,000 for general damages and the amount of $100,000 for special damages. The outcome of this claim is not determinable at this time and as such, no liability has been recorded in the accounts.

Exhibit 4 (continued)

Income Statements

Year Ending March 31

	1997	1998	1999
Revenue			
Annual dues	464,562	370,725	370,217
Daily dues	341,681	332,249	426,611
Mountain biking	16,187	25,594	27,405
Rental shop	171,438	202,417	232,701
Snow tubing	-	33,383	71,990
Special events	-	-	-
LSC ski school	203,708	208,763	212,033
Food concessions (cafeteria)	150,416	148,067	162,528
Interest and other income [1]	17,996	11,243	10,574
Racing fees	53,849	48,369	42,480
Lounge	6,619	8,147	10,659
Total Revenue	1,426,456	1,388,957	1,567,198
Cost of Goods Sold (certain areas)			
Rental Shop	675	-	-
Food concessions	51,925	54,624	60,901
Lounge	3,144	2,436	3,693
Total Cost of Goods Sold	55,744	57,060	64,594
Expenses			
Operations	113,814	191,987	212,372
Snowmaking and grooming	175,197	176,032	180,980
Property	84,669	73,901	100,434
Chalet	26,278	26,203	24,642
Lounge	3,515	4,046	3,732
Cafeteria	38,416	32,827	35,597
Rental Shop	75,413	59,867	72,449
Mountain Biking	11,698	26,499	29,209
Ski School	127,695	114,690	104,209
Administration and office	316,941	240,723	278,416
General operating expenses	244,945	161,700	178,712
Racing	50,185	50,114	41,503
Tube run expense	-	33,954	43,716
Capital interest	-	-	5,778
Mortgage interest	40,028	40,142	59,204
Depreciation [2]	-	146,659	239,705
Total expenses	1,308,794	1,379,344	1,610,658
Income taxes [3]	3,105	0	0
Net earnings	58,813	(47,447)	(108,054)

---

[1] Includes amortization of deferred revenue

[2] In 1997 depreciation was included in the expense of each line of business. Depreciation in 1998 and 1999 has been separated.

[3] The London Ski Club is exempt from taxes on income other than investment income greater than $2,000

PEAK ROOFING COMPANY

In January 2000, Gerry Dillabaugh was sitting in his office at the Confederation Bank in downtown Montreal considering the file of a potential new client, Peak Roofing Company (Peak). Pierre Lemieux, president of Peak, had requested a loan to finance an expansion of his roofing supplies business by adding a new site they had found in South Shore Montreal to their three existing sites. Although Peak had used the Cross Canada Bank for all of its previous financing needs, it was not especially satisfied with the service that they had received and was actively considering switching banks. As a result, Dillabaugh saw this as an opportunity to not only make a loan for the expansion, but to take other business away from a competitor.

THE CONFEDERATION BANK

The Confederation Bank was one of Canada's largest banks. It offered a wide range of personal and commercial banking services, as well as investment banking across Canada and in the many other parts of the world. Dillabaugh was under some pressure to maintain and perhaps grow his bank's share of the commercial lending market in the Montreal area. He also knew that the bank was anxious to sell related services such as cash management, personal and private banking and investment banking.

All account managers were expected to abide by the bank's lending guidelines. The bank offered com-

Richard Ivey School of Business
The University of Western Ontario

Professors Stephen Sapp and James E. Hatch prepared this case solely to provide material for class discussion. The authors do not intend to illustrate either effective or ineffective handling of a managerial situation. The authors may have disguised certain names and other identifying information to protect confidentiality.

mercial mortgages to customers that had a five year term and a 10 to 15 year amortization period. The amount of the loan tended to be in the range of 60 to 65 per cent of the appraised value of the properties being pledged. Operating loans were closely tied to the value of pledged accounts receivable and inventory with "normal" margining requirements of 75 per cent and 50 per cent respectively. The bank used the funded debt/EBITDA[1] ratio as a guideline in setting the total loan amount made available to the client.

Term loans were available at either a fixed rate or a floating rate, while all operating loans carried a floating rate. The bank employed loan pricing guidelines for each broad industry class based on ranges of industry ratios. The pricing guidelines which applied to this client were as seen in Exhibit 1. The base rate for five year term loans was called the cost of funds and all loans were priced at some number of basis points above the base rate, depending on the level of perceived risk. Similarly, all operating loans were priced relative to the prime rate. At the present time the base rate was 6.6 per cent and the prime rate was 6.5 per cent.

In addition to the general guidelines employed by the bank, Gerry had recently seen an information circular issued by the economics group and risk management department that appeared to apply to this account. The memorandum had pointed out that construction, real estate and related industries tended to be cyclical in nature. Although the economy was currently growing, there was some concern that the record long growth period could not be sustained for too much longer, so caution was warranted in these industries, especially for weaker accounts.

ABOUT PEAK ROOFING

Founded in 1973 by Marcel Lemieux, Peak had grown to be one of the largest, independent roofing materials suppliers in the greater Montreal region. The company supplied the materials needed by individuals and companies who were installing original roofs or were replacing or repairing roofs on residential and commercial structures. The company prided itself on selling anything and everything related to roofing and having a sales staff capable of providing valuable help on these products. Ninety-five per cent of Peak's revenues came from the distribution of roofing supplies, with the remainder coming from the manufacture of specialty roofing supplies.

At first Marcel Lemieux had worried about the arrival of the "big box" stores in the Montreal market. But Marcel's contacts from his years as a contractor in Montreal and his reputation for being a reliable and knowledgeable supplier of roofing supplies had allowed Peak to remain the largest independent distributor of roofing supplies and tools in Montreal. In fact, his son, Pierre Lemieux, claimed that the arrival of the "big box" stores, such as Reno Depot, did not significantly influence their business because, "we offer our customers the products they need, when they need them and our staff is able to answer any questions they may have." As a result, the Lemieuxs felt that their business had more value added than many of their competitors, with the result that they could achieve higher profit margins. Going forward, the company's strategy was to maintain their loyal customer base and a consistently high profit margin while continuing to grow the business.

Because of its relatively small size, Peak had not tried to compete for the large roofing contracts on new commercial developments. The developers for these projects generally negotiated sizable volume discounts directly from the large national chains or the manufacturers. As a consequence, Peak could not compete with the prices they offered and still maintain an adequate profit margin. Nevertheless, Peak's wide selection of roofing products, reputation for quality service and knowledgeable staff made them very popular with the smaller, independent contractors which tended to be family owned businesses and many of the "do-it-yourselfers." Consequently, a large part of Peak's business was related to re-roofing, roof repairs and renovations (e.g., the roofing on additions to residences). The breakdown of revenues in the most recent year had been 40 per cent commercial re-roofing and repair, 20 per cent commercial construction, 35 per cent residential re-roofing and repair and five per cent new residential construction.

The business had consistently experienced double digit growth over the past 15 years. This growth rate was in contrast with the average annual increase of only three per cent in Canadian Gross Domestic Product. The Lemieuxs attributed their comparatively high rate of growth to the rapid expansion of the Montreal

---

[1]EBITDA is earnings before interest, taxes, depreciation and amortization.

market and the steadiness of the growth to the concentration on re-roofing, which was much less cyclical than the new housing market.

The management of purchases and inventory was a very important part of the business. Marcel Lemieux did not use a formal inventory management system. Instead, he used his many years of experience to determine which products their customers would require and maintained inventory levels consistent with his beliefs. When the demand for roofing products was lower than expected due to such factors as exceptionally mild winters (a mild winter tended to lead to fewer roofing problems and subsequently led to fewer repairs), Marcel Lemieux would simply compensate by ordering less the next year. The exact quantities to be ordered were determined using simple rules of thumb, past experience and an "eyeballing" of the existing stock in the different stores. Generally, this system worked very well and they had few problems. To maintain profit margins at the desired level, Peak frequently ordered large quantities from their suppliers to take advantage of volume discounts. For example, in 1997 prices were expected to increase significantly, so Peak took out a short-term loan to take advantage of the volume discounts and lock in the lower prices. The Lemieuxs felt the lower purchase price of the goods would more than compensate for the costs of carrying the extra inventory.

Marcel Lemieux relied on his old friend Sam Lawson, the owner of a small accounting firm, for his bookkeeping and financial advice. Both Marcel and Sam were financially very conservative. They refused to take on debt unless it was absolutely necessary. This conservatism had been very beneficial to them in the past. In fact, they believed that it was one of the principal reasons for their ability to maintain their target profit margin through the recession in the early 1990s while some of their competitors had financial difficulties.

Even though they were averse to taking on debt, Peak had purchased the property on which they had their original store. They did this because the property had gone up for sale and they preferred to purchase the property rather than risk an increase in rent from a new owner. By taking out a fixed rate term loan to finance the acquisition, they were able to lock in the cost of their property for the next few years. For similar reasons, they had purchased the buildings serving the Laval and West Island regions of the city. These acquisitions had also turned out to be wise investments, with their combined market values now reaching about $8 million—significantly more than their current book value. Coincidentally, all of these mortgage loans were soon to come due and were up for renegotiation at the Cross Canada Bank.

With their most recent property purchase, Peak had acquired some roofing supply manufacturing equipment. Although the manufacturing of roofing supplies only constituted about five per cent of their current sales, Pierre Lemieux saw this as an area of potential growth and was actively planning to increase this line of business over the next couple of years. Moreover, he saw the greatest opportunities for manufacturing in the large American market where Peak currently had a significant price advantage. To take advantage of this opportunity, Peak had recently established relations with a distributor in New York state and was investigating the possible acquisition of a distributor in Chicago.

Despite the rapid growth of the company, its basic structure had changed little since its founding in 1973. Although Marcel Lemieux was 75-years-old and semi-retired, he still exercised substantial control over Peak's major decisions and maintained personal contact with many of its largest and most loyal clients. Since 1995, the day-to-day decisions had been made by Marcel Lemieux's son, Pierre, who was 35-years-old, and his daughter, Marie Bertrand, who was 37-years-old. Both had been working with the company since about 1989. However, it was not until the end of 1994 that Marcel Lemieux had felt they were ready to take over the company. At that time he had loaned them the necessary money to allow each to purchase 50 per cent of the firm's common equity from him.

Pierre Lemieux and Marie Bertrand had divided the day-to-day operations of the business between them. Pierre was the president and, therefore, was in charge of the day-to-day running of the stores. Marie was manager of administration and, among other things, was in charge of managing the sizeable accounts receivable and accounts payable. Because of the seasonal nature of the business (spring and summer were very busy periods), the size of these accounts tended to be highly variable and had been a source of concern to their bank in the past. Marie's active management of these accounts allowed the company to keep 95 per cent of the accounts receivable at less than 90 days and to take maximum advantage of financing opportunities and discounts from its suppliers.

The line of credit received from their existing bank to finance their working capital typically peaked over the May to July period. This was supplemented by a $25,000 personal line of credit on Marcel Lemieux's Visa card. However, the size of the company was now such that the bank believed this personal line of credit should be replaced by a minimum of $8,500 cash balance per store.

ECONOMY AND INDUSTRY SITUATION

Dillabaugh had accumulated information on the Canadian and Quebec economies, as well as the building supplies industry. Real GDP in Canada had grown at a rate of 4.5 per cent in 1999, up from 3.3 per cent in 1998, taking capacity utilization rates up to 84.8 per cent and pushing unemployment rates to record lows of 7.6 per cent. In spite of the rapid rate of economic growth, the consumer price index was up by only 1.7 per cent after a very low growth rate of 0.9 per cent in 1998. The Canadian dollar was trading at US$0.6730 which was an increase from US$0.6550 a year earlier. The Quebec region was experiencing a similar buoyant economy as the rest of Canada, although growth was not as rapid, unemployment was modestly higher and wage pressures were not as great. Growth in housing starts in Quebec in 1999, while up over 1998 levels, was still below the Canadian average.

Based on leading indicators, the outlook for the U.S. economy was excellent and early indications were that Canada would have a substantial current account surplus in the first quarter of 2000. Interest rates in Canada had drifted upward over the past year. Ninety-day Treasury Bills had a yield of 4.85 per cent and 10-year Government of Canada bonds were yielding 6.18 per cent up from an average of 4.89 per cent in 1998. The stock market remained strong as it participated in the longest economic boom in history, but fears were frequently expressed that the Bank of Canada and the United States Federal Reserve would increase interest rates to cool down a potentially overheated economy.

The building supplies industry was characterized by heavy competition between firms selling commodity-like products. Faced with low margins, most industry players attempted to achieve profitability through high volumes. In the building renovations segment of the industry, customers were willing to pay more for better service and margins were correspondingly higher. Although do-it-yourself renovation work made up a substantial portion of the renovations market in terms of numbers of customers, the work undertaken by renovation contractors (including both the labor and materials components) accounted for about two out of every three homeowner renovation dollars. About 60 per cent of all renovation spending was on materials.

The outlook in Canada for new construction and especially renovations was very good for the next couple of years. According to the Clayton Housing Report which had been received in May 1999, it was anticipated that there would be increased spending on residential renovations in both 1999 and 2000 of over three per cent (see Exhibit 2).

Dillabaugh obtained the following economic report on the City of Montreal that had been compiled mid way through 1999 from public sources.

> Following a disappointingly slow recovery from the early 1990s recession, Montreal has finally come into its own over the past couple of years. The revitalization of Montreal's economy is clearly evident in the housing market, as home construction and resale activity have surged so far in 1999 from year-earlier levels. Job creation in Montreal, which was quite weak in the first half of 1999, should rebound strongly over the rest of this year and into 2000. For 1999 as a whole, 24,000 net new jobs are expected to be created, with the tally rising to 27,000 next year. Montreal's unemployment rate, which dropped below 10 per cent last year, is expected to slip to 9.4 per cent on average next year. In this environment, Montreal consumers are expected to remain in a spending mood. The outlook for Montreal's manufacturing sector remains bright over the near term, propelled by continued strong performances in the city's vibrant aerospace, telecommunications equipment, and biotechnology industries. Residential construction activity should remain on an upward track, while non-residential building activity will be boosted by the construction of new entertainment complexes, big-box stores as well as industrial expansions. Although this year and next are shaping up to be good years for the Montreal economy, the city—and the province—need to overcome some obstacles that may limit potential economic growth over the medium term. Two key challenges are to lower provincial personal tax rates, and to reduce the provincial government debt burden, which is higher than that of the other provinces.[2]

---

[2]Source: TD Bank Financial Group, "Current Economic Developments", July, 1999.

As a result of the preceding information, Pierre Lemieux was predicting that Peak's expected growth in revenue from the existing stores for the next couple of years would continue at 10 per cent per year.

FUTURE GROWTH STRATEGY

Since Pierre Lemieux and Marie Bertrand believed that Peak's growth opportunities were reaching their limits in the Central, Laval and West Island markets, they were considering different growth options. There were two principal directions they were considering: increasing their manufacturing revenue by expanding their sales and distribution system for these products in the United States and expanding their roofing supplies sales business into the South Shore Montreal market by either building a new store or purchasing a competitor in this area. Increasing their sales network for specialty roofing supplies in the United States would allow them to take advantage of their lower costs due to the historically weak Canadian dollar relative to the U.S. dollar. Opening a branch in South Shore Montreal would allow them to service the large and growing market in this part of the city that they were currently not servicing.

The requested loan was to finance the purchase of land and a building, the installation of the required leasehold improvements and the acquisition of the necessary inventory to add coverage to South Shore Montreal. They believed the new property was perfect. It was in a central location and located near the highway, providing it with great access from all parts of South Shore Montreal and many of the suburbs. The cost of the new premises was $2 million, of which $500,000 was allocated to the cost of the land and $1.5 million would be associated with the building and leasehold improvements.

PROJECTING NEEDS

As part of his preparation for analysis of the account, Dillabaugh decided to create his own projected income statement and balance sheet for the forthcoming two years. He took as his starting point Peak's historical Income Statements and Balance Sheets (Exhibits 3 and 4).

First he considered existing operations. He knew that the client was expecting sales growth of about 10 per cent per year from the existing stores and that costs for those three stores over the next two years would behave much as they had in the past. Although he knew the tax rate was different for profits below $200,000 and above $200,000, he decided to use an average 23 per cent tax rate in his calculations.

He decided to assume that there would be annual capital expenditures on existing assets at the beginning of each year of about six per cent of the gross book value of the buildings and equipment. Depreciation would be charged on a straight line basis of 10 per cent of the gross book value of the buildings and equipment. Other income from the company's manufacturing operations was expected to grow by six per cent each year and would be unaffected by the new branch. The "extraordinary expenses" in 1999 were nonrecurring. Dillabaugh decided to assume that working capital items would be managed in much the same way as the past.

Turning to the new premises, Dillabaugh noted that the client was expecting the new unit to achieve sales levels similar to those of existing operations after a two year period. In the first year, the average of the sales would only reach two-thirds of the ultimate target, but sales for the second year would be at their target rate— the level achieved by existing operations. While cost of goods sold was expected to vary with sales, general and administrative expenses were expected to be at steady state levels starting in the first year. It was also considered necessary to carry inventory levels in the first year as if the branch was operating at its mature level so as to offer the normal wide range of goods.

THE DECISION

This account presented an interesting opportunity to steal a client from a competitor. But Dillabaugh knew he had to put together a careful analysis of the risks and opportunities and a well thought out deal structure before his boss would approve the deal. He also knew that the deal would have to be competitive in order to attract the client away from its existing bank. To do this, he needed to set up an attractive package for all of Peak's financing needs. This included the loan for this new property, as well as the loans on Peak's existing properties that were currently up for renegotiation and the operating loan. Since the majority of this package was for fixed assets, Dillabaugh was considering maximizing the portion of the loan financing that would be made as a term loan and proposing that the rest be financed using the line of credit. This would better match the maturities of the assets and liabilities while also allowing Peak some flexibility for its seasonal financing needs.

Exhibit 1

LOAN STRUCTURING GUIDELINES OF THE CONFEDERATION BANK
FOR BUILDING PRODUCTS DISTRIBUTORS
Based on Key Financial Ratios

S&P Rating	Investment Grade				BB	B	CCC
	AAA	AA-	A	BBB			
Liquidity							
Current Ratio	2.0	1.8	1.6	1.4	1.2	1.0	.80
Quick Ratio	1.1	1.0	.90	.80	.75	.70	.50
Debt Service Coverage							
EBIT/Interest	12.90	9.20	7.20	4.10	2.50	1.20	(.90)
Leverage							
Funded Debt/EBITDA*	1.60	1.95	2.25	2.85	4.00	5.00	6.25
Funded Debt/Equity*	.21	.29	.33	.41	.55	.68	.75
Total Debt/Equity	.70	1.20	1.90	2.25	2.75	3.80	4.25
Pricing Options							
Term Loan (Cost of Funds+)** Avg. Loan to Value 65%	CoF+25bps***	CoF+50bps	CoF+85bps	CoF+115bps	CoF+200bps	CoF+290bps	CoF+375bps
Operating Line (Prime)**** Margin A/R 75% + Inv. 50%*****	P	P	P+15bps	P+50bps	P+100bps	P+170bps	P+350bps

*   Funded debt is all debt which bears interest.
**   Assume 5 year term loan.
***   A basis point (bps) is 1/100 of 1%.
****   Pricing is flexible but profitability must meet a hurdle rate based on risk adjusted capital.
*****   Excluding Work in Progress. Margin rates can vary based on borrower risk assessment and resale market for finished goods.

Source: Confederation Bank.

Exhibit 2
REALIZED AND PROJECTED GROWTH IN RENOVATION SPENDING

a) Canada Wide Total Renovation Spending[1]

Year	Billions of 1998$	Per cent Change
1994	19.8	
1995	18.7	-5.6%
1996	19.9	6.4%
1997	21.2	6.5%
1998	21.7	2.4%
1999 (projected)	22.4	3.2%
2000 (projected)	23.1	3.1%

b) Total Renovation Spending by Region:[1]

Year	Billions of 1998$							
	Atlantic	Quebec	Ontario	Manitoba	Saskatchewan	Alberta	B.C.	Canada
1998	1.7	5.6	8.2	0.6	0.7	2.2	2.7	21.7
1999	1.8	5.8	8.5	0.6	0.7	2.3	2.7	22.4
2000 (projected)	1.8	5.9	8.9	0.6	0.7	2.4	2.7	23.1

Source: Clayton Research.

---

[1]*Since the report had been prepared in May 1999, the figures for the entire 1999 year were estimates.*

Exhibit 3

BALANCE SHEET
For the years ended December 31
($000)

| | Actual | | | | | | | | Estimated |
	1991	1992	1993	1994	1995	1996	1997	1998	1999
ASSETS:									
Cash	2	2	1	4	1	4	34	22	25
Accounts Receivable - Trade	486	839	926	1,193	1,329	1,977	2,110	2,107	1,850
Inventory	1,986	1,836	1,936	2,438	2,827	2,803	3,403	3,678	5,100
Prepaid Expenses	45	62	47	80	81	104	3	10	10
Total Current	2,519	2,739	2,910	3,715	4,238	4,888	5,550	5,817	6,985
Fixed Assets									
Plant and Equipment	1,882	2,004	2,256	2,482	3,893	4,035	4,503	5,317	5,535
Land	480	480	480	480	1,005	1,005	1,005	1,005	1,005
Gross Fixed Assets	2,362	2,484	2,736	2,962	4,898	5,040	5,508	6,322	6,540
less: Accumulated Depreciation	851	1,058	1,284	1,528	1,880	2,239	2,638	3,074	3,479
Net Fixed assets	1,511	1,426	1,452	1,434	3,018	2,801	2,870	3,248	3,061
TOTAL ASSETS	4,030	4,165	4,362	5,149	7,256	7,689	8,420	9,065	10,046
LIABILITIES									
Notes Payable - Bank	1,177	742	524	820	1,659	1,221	2,498	2,479	2,100
Current Maturities - Long Term Debt	-	-	-	-	95	90	121	91	90
Accounts Payable	342	784	1,066	1,342	905	1,767	1,053	1,171	2,480
Income Taxes Payable	-	1	-	70	49	47	45	44	44
Total Current	1,519	1,527	1,590	2,232	2,708	3,125	3,717	3,785	4,714
Long Term Debt	230	230	230	230	1,759	1,675	1,711	2,245	2,240
Deferred Income Taxes	68	45	41	15	6	7	4	-	-
Total Liabilities	1,817	1,802	1,861	2,477	4,473	4,807	5,432	6,030	6,954
Net Worth	2,213	2,363	2,501	2,672	2,783	2,882	2,988	3,035	3,092
TOTAL LIABILITIES & NET WORTH	4,030	4,165	4,362	5,149	7,256	7,689	8,420	9,065	10,046

Exhibit 4

INCOME STATEMENTS
For the years ended December 31
($000)

					Actual				
	1991	1992	1993	1994	1995	1996	1997	1998	1999
Sales	9,382	10,720	12,316	15,548	17,379	22,520	23,640	22,558	24,200
Cost of Goods Sold	6,902	7,895	9,189	12,008	13,430	17,781	18,787	17,635	19,000
Gross Profit	2,480	2,825	3,127	3,540	3,949	4,739	4,853	4,923	5,200
General & Administrative Expense	1,687	2,166	2,505	2,758	2,902	3,644	3,727	3,737	3,840
Lease & Rental Expense	85	90	90	90	94	94	93	92	91
Depreciation	206	207	226	244	352	359	399	436	405
Total Operating Expenses	1,978	2,463	2,821	3,092	3,348	4,097	4,219	4,265	4,336
Operating Income	502	362	306	448	601	642	634	658	864
Interest Expense	(100)	(101)	(73)	(63)	(300)	(316)	(342)	(422)	(439)
Other Income	145	150	197	231	192	231	256	269	275
Extraordinary Expense	-	-	-	-	-	-	-	-	(190)
Profit Before Tax	547	411	430	616	493	557	548	505	510
Taxes	137	103	95	129	172	28	104	147	117
NET PROFIT	410	308	335	487	321	529	444	358	393

Exhibit 5

KEY BUSINESS RATIOS FOR SIC CODE #5039 WHOLESALERS — CONSTRUCTION MATERIALS
(% of Assets)

	1997	1996	1995
Cash	17.0	11.8	9.2
Accounts Receivable	36.5	31.3	38.2
Inventory	23.1	30.9	24.5
Other Current Assets	17.7	14.8	19.8
Total Current Assets	69.6	66.3	67.8
Fixed Assets	31.6	28.9	30.3
Other Non-Current	5.8	18.5	12.5
Accounts Payable	29.2	32.0	29.0
Bank Loans	14.5	14.0	14.2
Notes Payable	9.1	-	-
Other Payables	21.4	19.9	22.8
Total Current	45.4	51.8	52.4
Other Long Term Debt	25.9	32.2	20.2
Deferred Credit	21.5	21.0	18.1
Net Worth	32.6	21.8	29.7
Net Profit After Tax	10.5	4.5	(2.4)

Source: Dun and Bradstreet.

Exhibit 6

KEY BUSINESS RATIOS SIC CODE 5039 WHOLESALERS — CONSTRUCTION AND MATERIALS
(By Quartiles)*

	1997 UQ	1997 MED	1997 LQ	1996 UQ	1996 MED	1996 LQ	1995 UQ	1995 MED	1995 LQ
Solvency									
Quick Ratio (X)	1.4	0.9	0.6	1.0	0.6	0.4	1.5	0.8	0.4
Current Ratio (X)	2.9	1.5	1.0	2.3	1.2	1.0	2.2	1.4	1.1
Curr Liab./N.Worth (%)	51.6	94.3	214.9	16.8		250.1	70.7	111.7	300.7
Curr Liab/Inv. (%)	145.9	217.1	415.4	83.1	130.8	230.1	160.9	226.7	391.4
Total Liab/N.Worth (%)	40.7	137.9	239.4	53.6	146.1	500.3	99.3	178.6	380.6
Fixed Assets/N.W (%)	30.7	80.1	126.4	13.3	65.3	183.3	6.5	25.8	147.3
Efficiency									
Coll. Period (Days)	26.6	54.0	76.3	22.1	43.6	66.0	17.6	47.5	62.5
Sales/Inventory (X)	31.9	16.9	6.3	10.1	7.5	5.3	17.6	9.2	6.5
Assets/Sales (%)	24.9	37.5	61.8	31.1	48.5	78.6	25.5	41.7	65.7
Sales/Net Worth (X)	14.5	7.9	1.5	13.4	3.5	(4.4)	15.0	5.4	(0.1)
Acc.Pay/Sales (%)	6.3	8.6	15.6	5.1	12.4	18.8	7.5	10.0	13.6
Profitability									
Return On Sales (%)	12.1	6.3	1.7	8.1	1.8	0.3	6.5	3.3	1.3
Return On N.Assets (%)	21.4	12.0	6.0	11.3	5.1	0.4	14.5	9.9	2.1
Return On N.Worth (%)	64.7	44.3	20.5	81.0	22.9	1.1	77.9	27.9	8.0

*   UQ = upper quartile; MED = median; LQ = lower quartile

Source: Dun and Bradstreet.

part two

Accounts Receivable and
Loans Management

SRI OFFICE PRODUCTS INC.

On September 27, 1995, Brian Marshall, credit manager for SRI Office Products Inc. (SRI), emerged from a meeting with Mike Pascal, president, and Deb Neal, vice-president sales, flushed from the heated exchanges among the parties. The meeting was called to discuss the outstanding and seriously overdue account receivable of Macdonald Stationery and Office Supplies Ltd. (Macdonald), SRI's exclusive distributor in the four Canadian Atlantic provinces. The Macdonald account amounted to $2.4 million, was 156 days old, and for the past fourteen months, executives in the company had stonewalled attempts by Marshall to get information. Just a few days ago he had received financial statements from Macdonald after threatening to cut off shipments completely. The statements showed losses for the years ended December 31, 1993 and 1994, and the eight months ended August 31, 1995 (see Exhibits 1 and 2). The accumulated losses had wiped out the retained earnings and the shareholder equity section of the balance sheet was less than two per cent of total assets. When Marshall suggested stopping shipments to Macdonald immediately and considering undertaking bankruptcy proceedings, Neal became very excited and upset.

She argued that SRI did not have a contingency plan in place at this time for another distributor, that she was not advised of this type of action, that competitors would take market share if SRI stopped selling to Macdonald, that SRI had a long and profitable relationship with the Macdonald officers and that SRI owed it to them to give them time to get their financial act together. Pascal stepped into the confrontation between Neal and Marshall to settle them down, but Neal would have none of any mediation and finally managed to get Pascal to assure her that nothing would be done to close down the Macdonald account until she had explored the options fully. She was assured nothing would be done for a week. Meanwhile, Marshall had to put together an immediate action plan, and recommend a longer-term plan for the account.

Richard Ivey School of Business
The University of Western Ontario

Professor David C. Shaw prepared this case solely to provide material for class discussion. The author does not intend to illustrate either effective or ineffective handling of a managerial situation. The author may have disguised certain names and other identifying information to protect confidentiality.

SRI OFFICE PRODUCTS INC.

SRI marketed nationally a broad range of office supplies, including all types of stationery products, diskettes, binders, tape, and office equipment like staplers and calculators. SRI Industries Corp., an affiliated company, manufactured about 65 per cent of what SRI sold; the rest it bought from other manufacturers. SRI Industries Corp. sold products globally through related distribution companies.

In Canada, SRI dealt with several major regional distributors, usually more than one in a region. Distributors originally had an exclusive in a zone; however, as the distributors expanded their business horizons, they competed with each other, and the SRI products were effectively distributed by competing firms in most major centres. SRI's sales for 1995 were budgeted at $195 million. Major competitors included companies producing fine papers, such as MacMillan Bloedel, companies like 3M which sold their own product lines, and many stationery and office suppliers. Competition was intense, and everyone was trying to reduce costs to attract customers with the large box stores, like Office Depot, which had revolutionized the retail business in the large North American urban centres. SRI was the second largest distributor in the business, determined to maintain and grow its market share.

Macdonald had been granted an exclusive distribution franchise by SRI for the four Atlantic provinces (Nova Scotia, Prince Edward Island, New Brunswick and Newfoundland) in Northeast Canada in 1968. Although two other distributors had moved into the region from Quebec and carried SRI lines, their efforts had only marginal effects and 95 per cent of SRI's sales in Atlantic Canada were through Macdonald.

MACDONALD STATIONERY AND OFFICE SUPPLIES LTD.

Macdonald operated as wholesale distributor to retail and small wholesale accounts in a broad range of office supplies, printing supplies, specialty papers, and other related products for as many as 50 national distributors, including SRI. Sales of approximately $22 million in 1994 were handled through the company's main warehouse in Halifax (the capital city of Nova Scotia) and a branch warehouse in St. John's (the capital city of Newfoundland). Macdonald employed 78 persons. Credit sales accounted for virtually all of its sales on terms of net 30 days. The company was originally incorporated in 1922 and its facilities in Halifax were a landmark. The company had built a very loyal customer base over its seventy-odd years of business.

Macdonald was acquired by John Quinn, the president of the company, and four senior officers of the company in January 1993 from descendants of the Macdonald family through a leveraged buy-out. At the time Quinn was a relatively new president, having been appointed fourteen months previously. He had been vice president marketing of a consumer products company in Montreal prior to accepting the presidency of Macdonald. The four other shareholders, all vice presidents, were longtime Macdonald employees, experienced and competent in the business. Quinn owned 33 per cent of the shares and the other four each owned about 17 per cent.

The purchase price of $4.2 million was financed largely by the Confederation Bank through both an increase in the term loan of $1.0 million and an operating line of $3.0 million. The five shareholders invested a total of $0.5 million, much of which they borrowed on their personal accounts. A new company was formed by the buyers which bought the shares of Macdonald. The two companies were then amalgamated into one company under the Macdonald name, but carrying the bank debt incurred to finance the takeover.

Macdonald had distributed SRI products for over 50 years, acting as a distribution centre for over 500 customers by taking title to the products and carrying a full product line at all times. SRI was the largest supplier to the Macdonald firm. Good relations evolved because of the quality of service provided by Macdonald as distributor and credit manager. Prior to the acquisition in 1993, Macdonald maintained its account with SRI on an approximately current basis.

The agreement with Macdonald negotiated in 1968 for the exclusive distribution rights to SRI products in the Atlantic provinces stipulated that Macdonald would receive list price for the volume specified less any discounts allowed on any product line. This was referred to as the best wholesale price. Macdonald was allowed 45 days on most items, but for some items destined for remote island customers, SRI allowed 60 days. Macdonald was encouraged to tender on government contracts and SRI would offer extended terms for special purchases to fill these contracts.

The credit limit granted to Macdonald had risen to $2.4 million by 1992. This credit limit was reviewed and adjusted annually based on information from financial statements requested by SRI's credit manager. The determination of the credit limit was based on a formula tested extensively by major corporations. The formula incorporated the overall financial condition of the firm including working capital and the long-term viability. Credit limits were built up under the formula by adding assigned percentages of the amount of a customer's working capital, net income, and net worth, while reductions were made under the same system of assigned percentages for long-term debt and net losses. A discretionary assignment by the credit manager accounted for past performance and future prospects, trade and bank references, general reputation, or any other factors which may have been unique to the business. This discretionary factor could adjust the credit limit by plus or minus 25 per cent, or possibly suspend credit altogether. A table of company statistics included in the evaluation provided client history and the degree of exposure the creditor faced. The purpose of the formula was to have a structure from which consistent decisions could be made. At SRI, the level of authority required for approval of credit limits depended on the amount requested. The credit manager had authority up to $200 thousand, the treasurer up to $500 thousand, the vice president finance $1 million and the president had unlimited authority. The credit limits established for Macdonald in 1992 and for 1994 and the calculations based on the formula are presented in Exhibit 3.

CRITICAL EVENTS OF THE PAST TWO YEARS

Relations between the two companies had been good prior to the acquisition. In April 1993, Marshall routinely requested audited financial statements for 1992 and some details of the acquisition. The company sent the statements for 1992 as shown in Exhibits 1 and 2. When Marshall requested the 1993 statements and later the 1994 statements, his requests were ignored at first, then denied. On the basis of the 1992 financial results, Macdonald was granted a credit limit of $2.4 million; but now Marshall was worried about a deterioration in the credit bases of the company. In September 1994, a representative of SRI's finance department visited Macdonald and although he neither saw nor obtained copies of the financial statements for the previous year nor the 1994 year to date, he nevertheless came back assured that the company was healthy. The restructuring was explained to him by the shareholders. He indicated that the new board of directors included the five shareholders and their spouses. Current financial statements were promised, but never arrived.

Sales from SRI to Macdonald in 1994 amounted to $5,519 thousand. For the first eight months of 1995, sales amounted to $3,682 thousand. The current receivable balance of $2,412 thousand represented 156 days' sales outstanding. Losses continued at Macdonald, although Quinn assured Pascal and Marshall that July and August were both profitable months. The recent decline in the prime interest rate to 8.00 per cent from 9.25 per cent saved Macdonald almost $50 thousand in interest expenses to date in 1995.

SRI undertook a profit analysis by customer in early 1995. The average trading profit margin to Macdonald was 22.3 per cent. The ratio was stable over time. Shipping costs were relatively high at 1.2 per cent of sales. All accounts were charged selling and administration costs of 9.7 per cent of sales. Based on an average day's sales outstanding at the end of 1994 of 120 days, the return on investment after tax (46 per cent) amounted to 18.7 per cent. This was lower than SRI's target of 20 per cent.

Marshall was concerned about SRI's credit risk because of the significant decline in the economy of the Atlantic provinces in 1993 and after. The decline of the fishing industry, the loss of a major Macdonald client in Halifax due to bankruptcy, a strike among workers at the ports of Halifax and Saint John (a major city in New Brunswick), which significantly affected the region's business level, and weakness in the paper and construction industries hit these provinces very hard. He knew that SRI's sales to Macdonald were down in 1993, and the receivable was up; not a good sign. Interest rates had risen in 1994 and early 1995, with prime hitting a high of 9.75 per cent in March 1995 reducing home construction.

Marshall pushed hard for tough action by Pascal. Initially in 1994, he requested a reduction in the credit limit, but without success. Finally, in September 1995, Pascal threatened to cut off sales and undertake bankruptcy proceedings. Quinn and two of his vice presidents came to Toronto to meet with Marshall and Pascal, and presented financial statements for the years 1993, 1994 and the first eight months of 1995 (Exhibit 2). The losses, negative retained earnings, and slow payment of payables were major topics.

Quinn explained some of the items, the reasons and the actions to date. Dividends on common were paid in 1993 and 1994 to enable the shareholders to make payments on their personal loans to buy the company. They had been curtailed. The non-operating expenses were largely payments of directors' fees; these too were eliminated. Cost controls were introduced in 1994, but a new computer system caused substantial cost increases. Quinn thought these issues were behind the company now and that it could operate profitably. When asked about the high inventory, 61 days' sales, Quinn said that in order to take advantage of volume discounts, the company had to maintain large amounts in inventory. No suggestions were brought forward to improve the inventory situation.

The Macdonald financial results were worse than anyone at SRI had anticipated. The credit limit formula which in 1992 was used to establish the $2.4 million limit, now gave a negative amount as a limit. The equity base at the end of 1994 was only two per cent of total assets. Losses were declining, but retained earnings were negative.

THE OPTIONS AND ACTION PLANS

The first option was to push Macdonald hard to bring the account down to some reasonable level, say 120 days and then to 45 days within six months. Failure would mean suspending shipments and implementing bankruptcy proceedings. Clearly, this would mean searching for a new distribution system, since the chances of Macdonald coming up with the funds to bring the account to 120 days, about $600 thousand, seemed very remote. Quinn indicated that the bank had refused to extend the line of credit beyond $3.0 million, and was actively trying to reduce it to $2.5 million.

There were about ten office supplies distributors in the Atlantic region. Only three covered the entire territory, but there were reasonable prospects if two or three companies replaced Macdonald. Although Neal would not admit it, Marshall knew that she had done some survey work regarding other distribution companies. What worried her the most was the prospect of losing market share, because Macdonald was considered to be the best in the region. If SRI was perceived to be the supplier that shut Macdonald down, then she thought a loss of 15 to 20 per cent of current sales to Macdonald was possible. Replacement distributors would require smaller and more frequent shipments, and posed credit risks not unlike Macdonald's.

A second option was for SRI to start a distribution company in Atlantic Canada. This would require a significant capital investment and would change the pattern of distribution for the company. However, it would stabilize the existing situation. SRI would have to hire salespersons and set up distribution points at various locations.

The third option was to try working with Macdonald to resolve the problem. First, the credit limits had to be reduced and the account balances brought into line. Clear targets would have to be established and plans implemented to accomplish the targets.

One proposal was to ship goods to Macdonald on consignment using a separate bonded warehouse facility. Collections on account from customers would have to be kept separate from other cash by Macdonald, and remitted directly to SRI. Frequent audits of the warehouse and the accounts would be required. The system would be tight. As well, SRI could increase its sales activities in the region and draw goods directly from the separate bonded warehouse.

Suggestions were also made to work with Macdonald to reduce its inventory of SRI products. The senior SRI sales manager indicated that Macdonald had an inventory of SRI products at August 31, 1995 of about $1.075 million. Smaller shipments, more frequent deliveries, shorter times from receipt of order to delivery were recommended. These remedies would probably increase the shipping and administrative costs to SRI by about one per cent of sales. Macdonald's high administrative costs were due in part to a computer system that did not work effectively. SRI had a state of the art system and could help Macdonald get a system that worked well and efficiently.

Pascal wondered out loud about the "do nothing" option. While the Macdonald account was over the credit limit, was very slow and created a problem for the credit department, nevertheless, it was a valuable account, and other creditors were apparently not moving to collect in anything like the aggressive way that Marshall was proposing. Quinn indicated that the other creditors had not asked for financial statements and had not received them.

Pascal knew that a good distribution system was key to achieving and maintaining target market share.

But the Macdonald deteriorated financial position and possible bankruptcy could set SRI back on several levels: lost market share, earnings decrease, and sales declines. Pascal had Marshall on one side encouraging him to take a tough stand on Macdonald and Neal on the other reminding him that to act precipitously was to possibly lose market share big time.

Exhibit 1			
MACDONALD STATIONERY AND OFFICE SUPPLIES LTD. **BALANCE SHEETS** **at December 31, 1992 to 1994** **($000s)**			
	12/31/94	**12/31/93**	**12/31/92**
Current Assets			
Cash	$ 1	$ 1	$ 4
Accounts Receivables	3,754	3,788	1,964
Inventories	5,144	4,172	4,912
Prepaid	162	44	38
	9,061	8,005	6,918
Property, Plant & Equipment	2,480	2,408	2,476
Less: Accumulated Depreciation	1,038	906	774
	1,442	1,502	1,702
Land	368	292	292
TOTAL ASSETS	$10,871	$ 9,799	$ 8,912
Accounts Payable	5,199	4,078	4,090
Income Tax Payables	—	—	58
	5,199	4,078	4,148
Bank Loan			
–Operating	2,856	2,700	—
–Term	2,500	2,600	1,600
Total Bank Loan	5,346	5,300	1,600
TOTAL LIABILITIES	$10,555	$ 9,378	$ 5,748
Shareholders' Equity			
Common Shares	500	500	1,980
Retained Earnings (beginning)	(79)	1,184	763
Less: Amalgamation adjustment	—	(1,036)	—
Add: Earnings	(85)	(127)	471
Less: Dividends	(20)	(100)	(50)
Retained Earnings (end)	(184)	(79)	1,184
TOTAL EQUITY	$ 376	$ 421	$ 3,164
TOTAL LIABILITIES & EQUITY	$10,871	$ 9,799	$ 8,912

Exhibit 2			

MACDONALD STATIONERY AND OFFICE SUPPLIES LTD.
INCOME STATEMENTS

For the Years Ended December 31, 1992 to 1994 and Eight Months
(Unaudited to August 31, 1995)
($000s)

	08/31/95	12/31/94	12/31/93	12/31/92
Net Sales	$14616	$ 22040	$17835	$20447
Cost of Goods Sold	12158	18338	15017	16971
Gross Profits	2458	3702	2818	3476
Operating Expenses				
Selling, Warehouse and Delivery	932	1798	1394	1294
Administration	1292	1634	1240	1164
Operating Expenses	2224	3432	2634	2458
Operating Profit (EBIT)	234	270	184	1018
Interest Expenses	232	408	402	140
Miscellaneous Non-Operating Costs	11	15	28	10
	243	423	430	150
Net Income Before Tax	(9)	(153)	(246)	868
Income Tax	—	(68)	(119)	397
Net Income	$ (9)	(85)	(127)	471
Dividends Paid	—	20	100	50
Ratios to Net Sales:				
Gross Profit	16.9	16.8	15.8	17.0
Operating Profit	1.6	1.2	1.1	5.0
Net Income	(0.01)	(0.04)	(0.07)	2.3

	Exhibit 3		
	CREDIT LINE EVALUATION TECHNIQUE **APPLIED TO MACDONALD STATIONERY AND OFFICE SUPPLIES LTD.** **($000s)**		
	Basis for Establishing a Macdonald Stationery and Office Supplies Ltd.		
	Credit Line	**1992**	**1994**
Working Capital	10%	277	386
Quick Assets	5% (Max 50% of W/C credit)	98	188
Pledged Rec/Inv.	(10%)	—	(890)
Long-Term Debt	(3%)	(48)	(75)
Net Worth	2%	63	6
Net Income	10% or (20%)	47	(17)
Other			
Credit Line		437	(402)
Credit Line Requested		2400	2400
Credit Line Approved		2400	
Working Capital Ratio		1.67	1.74
Quick Asset Ratio		0.47	0.72

ALFRED BROOKS MENSWEAR LIMITED

In early February 1989, Harry Lagerfeld, the treasurer of Alfred Brooks Menswear Limited (known as ABM in the trade), was preparing for an introductory meeting with an account manager from the Confederation Bank. ABM had been dealing for several years with the Metropolitan Bank, but when Lagerfeld told Metropolitan about ABM's plans for a large expansion over the next year, he had been met by a non-committal response. Lagerfeld was surprised at Metropolitan's hesitancy and felt it was an appropriate time to reassess ABM's banking relationship.

Up to now ABM's products had largely been produced and sold in Canada. However, in the past year, Alfred Brooks had personally spearheaded a concerted selling effort to Sutton's, a large national department store in the United States, and this effort had led to a major order. The order would cause fiscal 1989 sales to increase 80 per cent over the sales for fiscal 1988 and Lagerfeld knew that additional working capital would be needed.

At the same time, Lagerfeld and the company buyer were nearing completion of an agreement with a Hong Kong supplier called Leung Manufacturing, for the contract production of the new line of suits. Preliminary manufacturing of "unfinished" suits was to take place in Hong Kong before shipment to Toronto for "finishing." ABM had purchased fabric from abroad in the past, but in order to meet the tight cost targets on this new order, ABM had been forced to follow the strategy of other North American

Richard Ivey School of Business
The University of Western Ontario **Ivey** Steve Cox prepared this case under the supervision of Professor James Hatch solely to provide material for class discussion. The authors do not intend to illustrate either effective or ineffective handling of a managerial situation. The authors may have disguised certain names and other identifying information to protect confidentiality.

garment manufacturers and source more value-added production from the Far East. By importing the clothing in "unfinished" form, ABM would minimize punitive duties and be able to claim Canadian content in the garments subsequently exported to the United States. The rule of origin interpretation for men's suits required that 50 per cent of the cost be Canadian value-added.

THE CLOTHING INDUSTRY

Menswear was a major segment within the clothing manufacturing industry, and suits/sport coats made up 12 per cent of the menswear share of wardrobe dollars. Menswear had enjoyed a reasonably healthy growth in the 1980s as the numbers of men in their 30's and 40's, who were the prime suit purchasing market, increased. At the same time, imports took on an increasing share of the market, as seen in Exhibit 1.

Competition in both Canada and the U.S. within the suit/jacket manufacturers segment was intense. The industry was heavily dependent upon sales of branded and private label menswear to discounters, general merchandise stores (Sears, Ward's, Sutton's), department stores and men's specialty retailers. Additionally, a few manufacturers had set up their own retail outlets.

In 1987, the U.S. and Canada signed a comprehensive Free Trade Agreement (FTA). The clothing manufacturing industry had historically received a high degree of government protection in both countries because of the significant employment the industry generated. Government protection policies included duties/taxes, import quotas and subsidies. As a result of the FTA, the duties on domestically produced clothing traded across the border were to be reduced. However, the duty reduction would not be applied to clothing manufactured abroad and imported into Canada or the U.S. for re-export, unless the finished garments had a significant domestic value-added component (minimum of 50 per cent content). The present U.S. duty on men's suits was 77.2 cents/kilogram plus 20 per cent, and this was to be reduced to zero over a ten-year period in ten equal reductions of 10 per cent.

Lagerfeld was concerned about the impact of the recently passed Free Trade Agreement. Although ABM would benefit under the FTA through lower duties on cross-border shipments of Canadian-made garments into the U.S., Lagerfeld worried that competing U.S. manufacturers who possessed greater resources would soon be making significant inroads into the Canadian market. The larger American competitors were approximately twenty times the size of ABM in terms of sales.

ALFRED BROOKS MENSWEAR

Company Background

Established in 1978 by Alfred Brooks, ABM manufactured men's suits and jackets for wholesale distribution in Canada; a small portion was also wholesaled in the U.S. and Italy. Alfred Brooks, now 55, had started work as a tailor when he was 15 and had spent his life in the industry. Before starting ABM with the proceeds of an inheritance, he had worked for eight years as the general manager of a major Canadian men's clothier.

Alfred Brooks acted as chairman and president of the company. The senior management group included Ben Bulmer, who was the marketing manager, Denham Crawford, who was operations manager, and Harry Lagerfeld, who acted as treasurer. All three senior managers had been with ABM since its inception and had varied backgrounds in the industry prior to joining the company. Alfred Brooks had designed generous compensation packages for each of his senior managers to keep them motivated and loyal to the company.

ABM employed 25 full-time employees: four management (including Brooks), two office support staff, two buyers, two designers, five pattern makers/cutters, three sales people, two shippers and five warehouse workers/inspectors.

Garments were manufactured by casual employees, primarily new immigrants to Canada, who were paid on a piecework basis. Anywhere from 10 to 200 such workers were employed at any particular time and these workers were not unionized.

Manufacturing and Warehousing Facilities

ABM was located in Toronto's Spadina garment district operating out of premises rented under a 15-year lease, and was into the second year of the first five-year term with two renewal options remaining. ABM's administrative, selling, manufacturing and warehousing operations were all located at the leased Spadina facility, although it occasionally rented temporary warehousing space when needed.

Suit Design and Development

Alfred Brooks personally supervised all aspects of suit and jacket design and development. The preliminary design process was spearheaded by two highly experienced designers. Suit patterns were then laid out by pattern-makers who were hired on freelance contracts. Cloth bolts were cut in substantial quantities and the cloth pieces were then sewn together by seamsters working on a piecework basis. ABM occasionally contracted some manufacturing to other Toronto clothiers.

In Alfred Brooks' opinion, ABM had cultivated a quality reputation. ABM was very careful about the materials it chose, picking classic patterns and colors in fabrics with a lasting feel. Brooks instinctively steered away from faddish colors or finishes. ABM also produced sophisticated looking end products, with much handwork involved in the sewing, assembly and pressing of the suit. As a result, ABM's finished product had a sophisticated look to it, resembling European styled suits more than American.

Markets

Over the years Alfred Brooks had developed a good sense of who wore his suits and jackets. In his opinion, ABM's target customer was a white collar male who wanted top-of-the-line quality but at reasonable prices. ABM's suits typically retailed in the $250 to $300 price range, which was below the top-end quality suits at $400 plus (offered by upscale Canadian retailers such as Holt Renfrew and Harry Rosen), but above the mass market suits at the $150 to $200 range (offered by economy retailers such as Tip Top or Moores).

ABM sold most of its suits to a client list of 48 Canadian retailers such as large department stores and menswear chains but roughly 10 per cent of annual sales were to a mix of 11 retailers in the United States. ABM also sold a small number of suits (less than one per cent of sales) to an Italian retailer who had been a customer for several years and Brooks was anxious to expand his sales to other Italian retailers. Lagerfeld provided the Bank with a monthly list of accounts receivable outstanding, which is attached as Exhibit 2, and a listing of inventory on-hand. Both were pledged as security for the company's loans but Lagerfeld was annoyed that the Bank excluded ABM's accounts receivable from American and Italian retailers when calculating the amount of operating funds available to the company. Accounts receivable in the U.S. (and a few in Canada) were protected with insurance from American Credit Indemnity (ACI).

ACI was a commercial credit insurer that established credit limits for an approved list of accounts and insured accounts receivable up to that limit. The insurance fee charged was based on the Dun and Bradstreet ratings for the buyer firms. Although ABM had never had to make a claim under its policy, Lagerfeld had heard that obtaining a claim was difficult in certain circumstances. The insurance did not apply to trade disputes; there was a $100,000 deductible.

All sales were made on an open account basis. Most invoices stated terms of two per cent, 10; net 30 days, although some of ABM's retailers stretched these terms. The larger Canadian clients typically took between 45 and 60 days to pay and some were offered extended terms of up to 90 days. Additional discount terms were selectively offered to ABM's larger customers. Typically, a discount/warehousing allowance ranging between two to six per cent was offered depending on the size of the client and was given in exchange for prompt payment (within 10 days). Discounts were not deducted from the monthly accounts receivable listing, but were allowed only when payment was received. Returns were not allowed, except under special agreement.

Expansion: The Big Order

Late in 1988 Ben Bulmer of ABM had visited the menswear buyer for Sutton's in Dallas to show him the new "swatch books"[1] for the upcoming 1989 fall season. Sutton's was a potentially very important account. The company was a very profitable, large national department store with over 1,000 branches and sales exceeding $9 billion. One of the company's key product lines was clothing.

Sutton's had always received positive customer feedback about the Alfred Brooks line of suits. In particular, their American clientele liked the distinctive European style cuts of the Alfred Brooks suits together with their reasonable prices. Alfred Brooks thought that with a little hard sell they might be able to get Sutton's to double their previous year's purchases of C$800,000.

The ABM team learned that Sutton's planned to feature the ABM suits more widely than ever before. The buyer verbally committed Sutton's to a huge order, saying it would be for at least 70,000 suits. Alfred Brooks was flabbergasted!

On Friday, February 3, 1989, ABM received the purchase order: Sutton's total order would amount to 71,130 suits at US$137.50 each for a total sale price of US$9,780,375. The exchange rate that day was C$1.1858/US$1.00, which worked out to a total order of C$11,597,568. The order was denominated in U.S. dollars.

The purchase order stated that the suits were to be delivered to specified U.S. warehouses in five tranches to be received as follows: on the 15th of July, August, September and October—15,000 suits, and on the 15th of November—11,130 suits. The order specified quantities by fabrics, colors and sizes. The agreed terms of sale were 60 days with an offered discount of six per cent, 10; E.O.M. (end of month). There was no provision for returns, but Sutton's reserved the right to refuse shipments if the quality did not match the samples. No backorders or substitutions were allowed. Freight and duties were to be paid by ABM F.O.B. to the specified warehouse.

The Sutton's order, taken together with the orders already on-hand from other retailers, would mean a huge leap in sales from C$20.9 million in 1988 to C$37.3 million in 1989. Lagerfeld estimated that monthly sales would be as follows:

Monthly Sales
December 1988 - November 1989
($000)

Month		Month	
Dec. 88	$2,993	Jun.	$ 2,742
Jan. 89	1,292	Jul.	3,728
Feb.	2,393	Aug.	5,903
Mar.	1,860	Sep.	5,644
Apr.	308	Oct.	4,547
May	512	Nov.	5,378
		Total	$37,300

Financial Implications

Lagerfeld knew that he would require financial assistance to meet the cash flow demands of the new order. In an attempt to quantify the needs he drew up the annual pro forma financial statements and monthly cash flow forecasts seen in Exhibit 3. Since banks typically require a margining of inventories and accounts receivable, he drew up the schedule seen in Exhibit 4, which indicates the monthly margin position.

---

[1]"Swatch books" were similar to catalogues and indicated different fabric textures, finishes, patterns and colors.

Key Suppliers

ABM's suppliers of fabric (primarily wool knit cloth bolts), buttons, zippers, and thread were Canadian and these raw materials were purchased on an open account basis. Terms varied from two per cent, 10; net 30 to one supplier who extended 180-day terms. Ninety percent of ABM's accounts payable were owed to trade accounts, with the remaining 10 per cent being sundry payables such as deductions from source and vacation pay. ABM maintained very good relations with trade creditors and always kept payments in line with the terms outlined. A schedule of outstanding accounts payable can be found in Exhibit 5.

The fabric and preliminary manufacturing for the Sutton's sale would be sourced from Leung Manufacturing in Hong Kong in order to meet the cost targets for the order. ABM planned a gross margin of C$30 per suit, and had based this on a US$43/suit raw material and labor (cutting and preliminary assembly) component from Hong Kong. The unfinished suits would then be shipped to Canada for finishing: pressing, sewing on zippers, belt loops, buttonholes and buttons, and the final tailoring of pleats and pockets.

The fixed price contract for the Hong Kong production was denominated in US$. It specified delivery to Canada in five tranches of 15,000 suits on the 1st of May, June, July, August and September. ABM had ordered a larger number of unfinished suits than needed for the Sutton's order and planned to sell the excess suits in Canada. Leung Manufacturing was responsible for delivering the unfinished suits to dockside in Hong Kong, and thereafter the costs of freight, insurance and duty were to be paid by ABM.

Leung Manufacturing had been suggested to Alfred Brooks by a close friend who owned a women's outerwear manufacturing company and had used Leung previously. Brooks had made some independent enquiries and found out that Leung had been in business since 1947 and had been managed by two generations of the Leung family. Annual sales were in the US$50 million range and Leung had always been profitable. Mr. Leung had never heard of ABM and wanted some assurance of ABM's ability to pay before he would set the production in motion. Moreover, Leung wanted to be paid within 30 days of delivery and production would not start until the method of payment was confirmed.

Financial Status

The financial statements for the fiscal year ending November 30, 1988 had just been received from the accountants and are shown in Exhibit 6. Lagerfeld was proud of the rebound in profitability from the depressed levels of 1987 when an aggressive effort to expand in the U.S. had been initiated with low introductory prices, which had significantly reduced the overall gross margin that year. Lagerfeld knew that ABM performed well in comparison to the industry and he had put together some of the key industry averages, which are shown in Exhibit 7.

In February 1989, the prime interest rate charged by Canadian financial institutions was set at 12.75 per cent. The prime rate in the United States was 11.0 per cent while the Confederation Bank set a base rate on U.S. dollar loans of 11.5 per cent. Canadian prime rates had increased from the levels of late 1987 when the rate had been set at 9.75 per cent. Further increases in the prime rate were expected, as the Bank of Canada continued its policy of fighting inflation (which was exceeding five per cent) through increases in the Bank of Canada rate. This made-in-Canada interest rate strategy continued to keep the Canadian dollar strong relative to the U.S. dollar in spite of a worsening Canadian balance of payments. The U.S. dollar was currently trading at C$1.1858. The U.S. dollar had weakened steadily since 1987 at which time it was trading at approximately C$1.3200. During the past twelve months the value of the U.S. dollar had been quite erratic relative to the Canadian dollar, fluctuating between C$1.2400 and C$1.1700. The forward rate for Canadian dollars for three months was $1.1883, for six months was $1.1940 and for one year was $1.2032.

Decision at Hand

ABM had been a Metropolitan Bank client since inception. Lagerfeld knew that ABM lacked sufficient working capital and he wanted an expansion in its operating loan to help accommodate increased sales. Lagerfeld estimated that ABM would require an increase in its operating loan ceiling from $8,250,000 to

$12,000,000 in order to finance its expanded production and sales resulting from the Sutton's order. However, the Metropolitan Bank had been hesitant in committing to an increase in the company's operating loans, and Lagerfeld hoped that the Confederation Bank would react more positively. He had also arranged a meeting with a representative from Irving Trust, a large U.S. bank.

Exhibit 1
CANADIAN GARMENT SHIPMENTS 1981 - 1985 **(000's of garments)** [1]

	1981	*1982*	*1983*	*1984*	*1985*
Domestic	372,876	336,112	338,500	339,724	338,706
Less Exports	4,383	4,606	4,426	4,998	5,137
Net Domestic	368,493	331,506	334,074	334,726	333,569
Plus Imports	165,489	166,402	202,453	237,277	247,539
Total Canadian Market	533,982	497,908	536,527	572,003	581,108
Imports/Total	31.0%	33.4%	37.7%	41.5%	42.6%

[1]Government of Canada Report on Apparent Markets for Textiles & Clothing

Exhibit 2
ACCOUNTS RECEIVABLE **as at January 31, 1989** **(in $000s)**

	0-30	*31-60*	*61-90*	*Over 90*	*Total*
		Days Outstanding			
Canada					
Large Diversified Clothing Retailer	$ 144	$ 580	$ 241	$ —	$ 965
Large National Department Store	—	222	395	—	617
Large National Department Store	—	355	—	—	355
Regional Department Store	—	—	292	—	292
Large Men's Clothing Chain	—	145	—	—	145
Other retailers	62	175	220	201	658
					3,032
United States					
Sutton's	—	145	—	—	145
Northeast Department Store	125	—	—	—	125
Midwest Department Store	—	—	60	—	60
Other retailers	—	65	39	43	147
					477
Italy					
Northern Menswear Chain	—	58	—	—	58
TOTAL	$ 331	$1,745	$1,247	$ 244	$3,567

Exhibit 3

PRO FORMA BALANCE SHEET as of November 30, 1989	

Assets

Accounts Receivable	$ 9,925
Directors' Advances	86
Inventory	4,655
Deposits	2
Prepaid Expenses	55
	14,723
Net Fixed Assets	214
TOTAL ASSETS	$14,937

Liabilities

Bank Loans	$6,443
Accounts Payable	2,596
Income Taxes Payable	995
	10,034
Shareholder Loan	1,487
TOTAL LIABILITIES	$11,521

Shareholder's Equity

Capital Stock	339
Retained Earnings	3,077
	3,416
TOTAL LIABILITIES & EQUITY	$14,937

PRO FORMA INCOME STATEMENT
for the year ending November 30, 1989

Sales		$37,300
Cost of Goods Sold:		
Beginning Inventory	$ 4,558	
Purchases & Labour	30,459	
Available for Sale	35,017	
Less Ending Inventory	4,655	
		30,362
Gross Profit		6,938
Expenses		
Selling & Administrative	3,240	
Interest	1,239	
Depreciation	61	
		4,540
Earnings Before Taxes		2,398
Taxes		995
NET INCOME		$ 1,403

Exhibit 3 (continued)

MONTHLY CASH BUDGET
for December 1988 to November 1989

(C$000s)

	Dec	Jan	Feb	Mar	Apr	May	Jun	Jul	Aug	Sep	Oct	Nov	Total
Sales													
Sutton's[1]	$ 0	$ 0	$ 0	$ 0	$ 0	$ 0	$ 0	$ 2,446	$ 2,446	$ 2,446	$ 2,446	$ 1,814	$11,598
Other	2,993	1,292	2,393	1,860	308	512	2,742	1,282	3,457	3,198	2,101	3,564	25,702
Total Sales	2,993	1,292	2,393	1,860	308	512	2,742	3,728	5,903	5,644	4,547	5,378	37,300
Opening loan balance	–3,901	–4,310	–4,709	–4,010	–5,235	–5,507	–7,125	–9,260	–11,769	–12,076	–11,978	–9,347	–3,901
Cash inflows													
Collection[2]													
Sutton's	0	0	0	0	0	0	0	0	0	2,446	2,446	2,446	7,338
Other	2,539	2,634	2,993	1,292	2,393	1,860	308	512	2,742	1,282	3,457	3,198	25,8876
TOTAL AVAILABLE	2,539	2,634	2,993	1,292	2,393	1,860	308	512	2,742	3,728	5,903	5,644	32,548
Cash outflows													
Leung purchase[3]	0	0	0	0	0	0	765	765	765	765	765	0	3,825
Labour	530	530	530	530	530	530	530	530	530	530	530	530	6,360
Material	2,082	2,163	1,371	1,641	1,786	2,580	756	1,306	1,331	1,913	1,585	1,851	20,365
Admin. & Selling	270	270	270	270	270	270	270	270	270	270	270	270	3,240
Interest: Al Brooks[4]	17	17	17	17	17	17	17	17	17	17	17	17	204
Taxes	0	0	0	0	0	0	0	0	0	0	0	0	61
TOTAL OUTFLOWS	2,899	2,980	2,249	2,458	2,603	3,397	2,338	2,888	2,913	3,495	3,167	2,668	34,055
Preliminary balance	–4,261	–4,656	–3,965	–5,176	–5,445	–7,044	–9,155	–11,636	–11,940	–11,843	–9,242	–6,371	
Loan Interest[4]	–49	–53	–45	–49	–62	–81	–105	–133	–136	–135	–105	–72	–1,035
Ending Balance	$–4,310	$–4,709	$–4,010	$–5,235	$–5,507	$–7,125	$–11,769	$–11,769	$–12,076	$–11,978	$–6,443	$–6,443	$–6,443

Assumptions
[1] C$1.1858/US$1.00
[2] 60 days.
[3] 30 days.
[4] Prime rate at 12.75% + 1% = 13.75%

Exhibit 4

LOAN MARGIN CALCULATION
for December 1988 to November 1989

(C$000s)

	Dec	Jan	Feb	Mar	Apr	May	Jun	Jul	Aug	Sep	Oct	Nov	Total
Accounts Receivable	$5,627	$4,285	$3,685	$4,253	$2,168	$ 820	$ 3,254	$ 6,470	$ 9,631	$11,547	$10,191	$9,925	$9,925
Inventory[1]	4,734	6,375	6,328	6,985	9,051	11,744	11,563	11,129	8,950	7,564	6,743	4,746	4,746
Margin	6,587	6,401	5,928	6,682	6,152	6,487	8,222	10,417	11,698	12,442	11,425	9,817	9,817
Operating Loans	−4,310	−4,709	−4,010	−5,235	−5,507	−7,125	−9,260	−11,769	−12,076	−11,978	−9,347	−6,443	−6,443
Surplus/(Deficit)	$2,277	$1,692	$1,918	$1,447	$ 645	$−6,38	$−1,038	$−1,352	$ −378	$ 464	$ 2,078	$3,374	$3,374

Assumptions
[1] Accounts Receivable @ 75%
Inventory @ 50%

Exhibit 5
ACCOUNTS PAYABLE **as at January 31, 1989** **($000s)**

Supplier (month of invoice)

Textile Supplies Inc. (various)	$ 195
Canadian Worsted Knit Products Ltd. (Dec/88)	262
Texfab Manufacturers Ltd. (Nov/88)	542
Toronto Garment Centre Inc. (Oct/88)	606
Sundry payables	217
TOTAL	$1,605

		Exhibit 6		

FINANCIAL STATEMENTS

Auditors' Report

We have examined the balance sheet of Alfred Brooks Menswear (Canada) Ltd. as at November 30, 1988 and the statements of income and retained earnings for the year then ended. Our examination was made in accordance with generally accepted auditing standards, and accordingly included such tests and other procedures as we considered necessary in the circumstances.

Waterhouse Ross
Chartered Accountants

Toronto, Ontario
January 29, 1989

BALANCE SHEET
as at November 30, 1988

	($000s)			
	1988	*1987*	*1986*	*1985*
Assets				
Current Assets				
Accounts Receivable	$ 5,173	$ 7,860	$ 4,079	$ 3,780
Loans Receivable - director	86	55	7	40
Inventory (note 2)	4,558	4,139	3,646	2,762
Deposits	2	2	2	5
Prepaid Expenses	55	39	44	21
Income Taxes Refundable	0	97	0	0
	9,874	12,192	7,778	6,608
Net Fixed Assets (note 3)	275	168	118	110
TOTAL ASSETS	$10,149	$12,360	$ 7,896	$ 6,718
Liabilities & Shareholders' Equity				
Liabilities				
Current Liabilities				
Bank Loan (note 4)	$ 3,901	$ 6,834	$ 2,638	$ 1,518
Accounts Payable	2,687	2,339	1,980	2,395
Income Taxes Payable	61	0	96	61
	6,649	9,173	4,714	3,974
Long-Term Debt (note 5)	1,487	1,487	1,487	1,487
	8,136	10,660	6,201	5,461
Shareholders' Equity				
Capital Stock	339	339	339	339
Retained Earnings	1,674	1,361	1,356	918
	2,013	1,700	1,695	1,257
TOTAL LIABILITIES & SHAREHOLDERS' EQUITY	$10,149	$12,360	$ 7,896	$ 6,718

Exhibit 6 (continued)			
INCOME STATEMENT **for the year ending November 30, 1988**			

	($000s)			
	1988	*1987*	*1986*	*1985*
Sales	$20,965	$21,570	$18,763	$18,144
Cost of Sales				
Inventory, Beginning Year	4,139	3,646	2,762	901
Purchases	13,249	13,985	12,315	12,831
Labour	4,151	4,808	4,195	4,013
Styling & Designing	68	74	35	233
	21,607	22,513	19,307	17,978
Inventory, End of Year	4,558	4,139	3,646	2,762
	17,050	18,374	15,663	15,216
Gross Profit	3,915	3,196	3,100	2,928
Expenses				
Selling (note 6)	1,400	1,314	1,050	1,015
Administrative (note 6)	1,193	965	785	780
Depreciation and Amortization	61	38	31	28
Interest	873	873	687	544
	3,527	3,190	2,553	2,367
Income Before Income Taxes	388	6	547	561
Income Taxes	75	1	109	115
NET INCOME	$ 313	$ 5	$ 438	$ 446

See accompanying notes

Exhibit 6 (continued)

NOTES TO FINANCIAL STATEMENTS
as at November 30, 1988

1. *Accounting Policies*

   Inventory

   Inventory is valued at the lower of cost (first-in, first-out basis) and net realizable value.

   Depreciation and Amortization

   The company depreciates its fixed assets by the declining balance method at the following rates per annum:

Machinery and Equipment	20%
Furniture and Fixtures	20%
Truck	30%
Computer Equipment	30%

   Leasehold improvements are amortized by the straight-line method over the term of the lease for a period of 5 years.

2. *Inventory*

   Inventory consists of the following:

	1988	1987
Raw Materials	$ 628,127	$2,069,144
Work in Process	937,272	491,136
Finished Goods	1,790,542	1,435,504
Goods in Transit	1,201,631	143,462
	$4,557,572	$4,139,246

3. *Fixed Assets*

	Cost	Accum. Depre.	Net 1988	Net 1987
Machinery & Equipment	$140,784	$ 51,066	$ 89,718	$ 64,448
Furniture & Fixtures	91,410	29,564	61,846	25,995
Truck	15,954	4,786	11,168	15,954
Computer	81,202	41,730	39,472	24,037
Leasehold Improvements	120,050	47,383	7 2,667	37,670
	$449,400	$174,529	$274,871	$168,104

Exhibit 6 (continued)

NOTES TO FINANCIAL STATEMENTS
as at November 30, 1988

4. *Bank Loan*

Bank loans are secured by a registered general security agreement covering accounts receivable and inventory to the extent of $8,250,000, and by the issuance of a $5,500,000 debenture which provides for a fixed and floating charge on all assets of the company.

5. *Long-Term Debt*

Long-term debt is payable to the shareholder, bearing interest at bank prime plus 1% per annum with no specific terms of repayment.

6. *Selling & Administrative Expenses*

Selling	1988	1987
Delivery, Freight, Shipping	$ 731,564	$ 633,465
Rent/Warehousing	227,146	157,518
Travel/Entertainment/Promotion	441,059	523,480
	$1,399,769	$1,314,463
Administrative		
Bad Debts	$ 33,190	$ 29,419
Charitable Donations	5,087	34,965
Computer	55,353	46,001
Insurance	68,063	89,550
Management Salaries	208,845	185,644
Professional Fees	113,540	39,831
Rent	45,966	7,956
Repairs & Maintenance	90,852	43,920
Salaries	400,981	353,991
Taxes	67,538	63,535
Telephone	103,391	69,882
	$1,192,806	$ 964,694

	Exhibit 7

KEY INDUSTRY RATIOS
MEN'S & BOY'S CLOTHING ASSET SIZE US$1 - 10 MILLION

	Upper Quartile	*Median*	*Lower Quartile*
Gross Margin		25.8%	
Operating Expenses		19.5%	
Profit Before Taxes		5.2%	
Current Ratio	2.2	1.9	1.5
Quick Ratio	1.6	0.9	0.6
Days Receivable	33.0	51.0	83.0
Days Inventory	39.0	91.0	122.0
Days Payable	13.0	25.0	36.0
Sales/Working Capital	2.9	6.2	10.0
EBIT/Interest	9.3	3.0	1.2
Debt/Equity	0.8	1.5	2.4
Profit Before Taxes/Equity	42.6%	15.3%	2.5%
Sales/Assets	3.1	2.0	1.4

Source: Robert Morris Associates, 1988

part three

Risk Management

ADVANCE TECHNOLOGIES INC.

On October 1, 1992, Eileen Harrison, vice-president finance for Advance Technologies, was contemplating the effects that a weakening Canadian dollar would have upon the company's projected 1993 financial results. The upcoming Canadian Constitutional Referendum (on whether Quebec can secede from the rest of Canada) was having marked effects on the value of the Canadian dollar, which had fallen 3.56 cents in value relative to the U.S. dollar since the first of September. Advance had recently entered into a loan agreement with a major Canadian bank, to finance its expansion into manufactured specialty plastics. To remain in compliance with the covenants of the loan, Advance was required to generate a minimum level of profitability throughout the term of the loan. In light of the recent volatility in currency markets worldwide, Harrison knew it was important to understand the effects that an ever-weakening dollar would have on Advance's income and cash flows, and the tools available to manage them.

THE COMPANY

Advance Technologies was engaged in the manufacture and sale of a wide range of engineered plastic products in the Canadian marketplace. A decision was made in 1990 to pursue a strategy focused on specialty, proprietary products. Management believed this approach to the Canadian marketplace was essential for Advance to build a lasting competitive advantage. After a long search, Advance entered into a

Richard Ivey School of Business
The University of Western Ontario **IVEY** Sandra Galli prepared this case under the supervision of Professor James E. Hatch solely to provide material for class discussion. The authors do not intend to illustrate either effective or ineffective handling of a managerial situation. The authors may have disguised certain names and other identifying information to protect confidentiality.

licensing agreement with Hart Industries, a large plastic resin manufacturer based in New York, on September 30, 1991. The agreement granted Advance exclusive Canadian manufacturing and distribution rights to a revolutionary new plastic called Cryolac. While Cryolac was a premium product it faced competition from Canadian produced plastics. In exchange, Advance was required to pay an upfront sum, a monthly licensing fee of US$250,000, and was required to purchase raw materials necessary to the manufacture of Cryolac from Hart. All such purchases were made in U.S. dollars at prices negotiated annually.

To finance the upfront investment in Cryolac and the purchase of specialty manufacturing equipment, Advance obtained financing from two sources—a Canadian bank and Hart Industries. Contained in the Canadian loan agreement were several covenants regarding profitability. Advance was required to generate, at a minimum, a before tax profit of $9 million. Hart agreed to accept a US$1 million note from Advance as partial payment of the upfront licensing fee. The note was payable in full ten years from the date of the agreement.

THE SITUATION

Advance was exposed to significant foreign exchange risk as a result of the Hart agreement. While all of the company's revenues were denominated in Canadian dollars, a large part of its expenses were paid in U.S. funds. Thus, Advance had to regularly convert its Canadian dollar cash flows to cover expenses in the United States. As the Canadian dollar weakened, Advance's cash flow and profitability were adversely affected.

Harrison was faced with a great deal of uncertainty regarding the relative exchange rate of the Canadian and U.S. dollars over the next twelve months. The historical relationship between these two currencies is illustrated graphically in Exhibit 1. Both domestic and international events were creating unprecedented levels of volatility in currency markets, and the Canadian dollar was dropping rapidly in response. A Globe and Mail article (September 29, 1992) discussing the situation is presented in Exhibit 2.

Harrison's concerns were compounded by the loan covenants regarding profitability. While Advance's projected income before tax of $12.5 million was more than acceptable, Advance's budget was based on a U.S. dollar equal to CDN$1.2195 and the dollar was currently trading at $1.2536. Exhibit 3 outlines the multi-currency budgeted financial statements for the current fiscal year.

Hedging Vehicles

Harrison had investigated various alternatives for hedging Advance's foreign exchange risk. They included: 1) call options, 2) put options, and 3) forward contracts. The purchase of a call option grants the buyer the right, but not the obligation, to purchase foreign currency from the seller at a fixed strike price, on or before a specified date. The amount paid for this privilege is called the option premium.

The purchaser of a put option has the option to sell foreign currency at a set price for a particular time period. The writer of a put option must be prepared to purchase the foreign currency if the holder of the option decides to exercise the right.

Two types of options were available—American and European. American-style options could be exercised any time between the date of purchase and the maturity date, whereas European-style options could only be exercised on the maturity date.

Forward contracts obligate the buyer to purchase a specific amount of foreign currency at a specified date in the future at a locked-in exchange rate. The exercise of a forward contract is not optional.

Alternative Hedging Strategies

Harrison was considering a number of strategies including the purchase of a call option, the simultaneous purchase of a call option and sale of a put option, and the purchase of a forward contract.

Advance could purchase U.S. dollar call options only. This strategy involves the purchase of a number of call options in amounts equal to the anticipated monthly U.S. dollar cash outflow. The result of this strategy would be to set an upper limit to the cost of future purchases of U.S. dollars. The call premiums for options with a strike price equal to the current exchange rate (i.e., 1.2536) are provided in Exhibit 4.

A second strategy that Advance could follow would be to purchase a number of call options as noted above and simultaneously sell a number of put options for equivalent dollar amounts. The impact of this strategy would be to set an upper limit to the cost of future purchases of U.S. dollars and generate some money for the firm from the put premiums. However it would also limit the benefit that would accrue to Advance of any increase in the value of the Canadian dollar. This strategy is called a "collar". Since Advance would be committing to the potential purchase of foreign currency at some future date it would be required to put up "margin" equal to four per cent of the face value of the option. This margin might take the form of a guaranteed line of credit at the bank.

The third strategy considered by Harrison was similar to the second. In this case, the firm would purchase calls and sell an equivalent dollar amount of puts, but the strike price of each contract would be set in such a way that the cost of the call premium would be just offset by revenue from the sale of the put. The advantage of setting up this "zero cost tunnel" is that there is no net cash outlay to create the position. On the other hand, the "protection" afforded by this strategy varies somewhat through time. An overview of the arrangements for a zero cost tunnel is seen in Exhibit 5.

Finally, Advance could purchase forward contracts and lock in the cost of future purchases of foreign currency. Since Advance is committing to the purchase of a fixed amount of foreign currency at some future date, it must put up "margin" equal to eight per cent of the face amount of the purchase. Forward contract rates are seen in Exhibit 6. Advance would be expected to pay the offer price.

Advance's U.S. dollar cash flow requirements are relatively stable throughout the course of the year. Therefore, any hedging strategy would involve the purchase of twelve monthly contracts or options of equal amount, to match Advance's cash requirements.

CONCLUSION

Harrison was unsure which hedging alternative to suggest to Advance management. She wanted to show the other managers the effect on projected income and cash flow of a Canadian dollar at 1.2395, 1.2595, 1.2795, and 1.2995 without the use of a hedging strategy. Then she intended to show the costs and benefits of each of the proposed hedging vehicles. In order to show the worst case scenario she decided to assume that any movement in the exchange rate would occur on the first day of the 1993 fiscal year. Harrison's counterparts would be very interested in the results of her analysis, since if the company did not earn $9 million before taxes, the company would be in violation of the Bank's covenants.

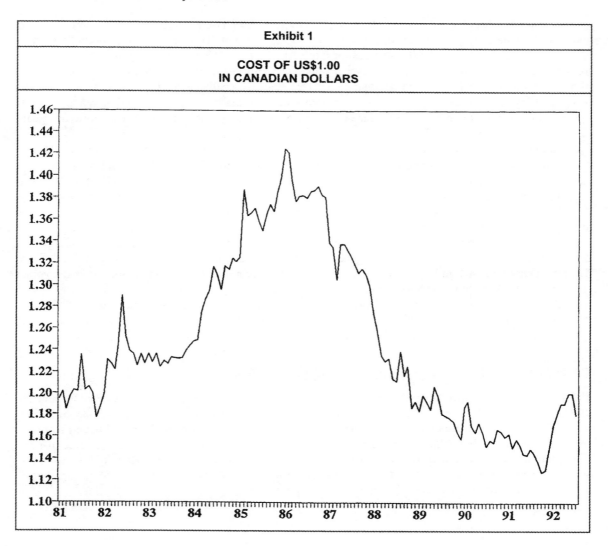

Exhibit 1

**COST OF US$1.00
IN CANADIAN DOLLARS**

Exhibit 2

GLOBE AND MAIL ARTICLE
Tuesday, September 29/92

Fears Torpedo Canadian dollar

By Marian Stinson
The Globe and Mail

The Canadian dollar plunged yesterday to its lowest point in more than four years, amid massive selling sparked by fears that the No side had gained ground in the referendum campaign and by last week's report suggesting there will be economic devastation if the country breaks up.

Despite aggressive intervention by the Bank of Canada, the dollar came perilously close to falling below 80 U.S. cents, a level it has not seen since April of 1988, tumbling 0.51 cents to close at 80.15. It came under heavy selling pressure at noon, and then again about two hours later. Selling began in Tokyo early in the trading day, and continued in North America.

Investors have begun examining their Canadian holdings after recent polls in Quebec and Western Canada showing diminished support for the Charlottetown constitutional accord, along with Friday's Royal Bank report that Canada's standard of living would drop and the jobless rate would soar to 15 percent if the country broke apart.

"The No side has been getting most of the attention, and there has been a lack of progress by the Yes side," said Andrew Pyle, economist with MMS International, a financial market information service. "The situation is looking more dismal."

Although the Royal Bank report appeared to support the Yes camp, in Quebec it was viewed as a scare tactic by an "anglo institution," Mr. Pyle said. With "the Yes side in tatters," he added investors have decided to sell Canadian holdings.

The selling pressure on the currency has been increasing since Labour Day, when turmoil in currency markets over European unity and the French referendum on the Maastricht Treaty sent the British pound, the Italian lira and other weak European currencies reeling. Since the vote a week ago, attention has focused on North America and Canada's Oct. 26 referendum on the constitutional agreement.

U.S. press reports on the weekend speculated about a victory for the No forces. One story dubbed the Canadian dollar the "British pound of North America," referring to the 10 per-cent drop in value of the pound against the German mark in the past two weeks. That conjures up memories of the mid-1980s, when the currency was being labelled the "Hudson Bay peso."

With no end to the market turmoil in sight, the dollar could lose another 1.5 cents in value by the time of the referendum, said Marc Chandler, a New York-based currency analyst with IDEA Inc., a financial market information service. Even after the referendum it is expected to fall further, because the Canadian economy is behind the U.S. recovery by about six months, Mr. Chandler said.

Some of the recent selling of Canadian investments by Japanese institutions relates to adjusting their portfolios halfway through their financial year.

The Canadian dollar has fallen 4.2 per cent in value against its U.S. counterpart since Sept. 1. Since peaking at 89.29 cents last November, it has tumbled 10.2 per cent.

Interest rates on money-market instruments rose dramatically, pointing to a sharp increase in the Bank of Canada rate this week, and a potential jump of half a percentage point in the prime lending rate from its current 19-year low of 6.25 per cent.

Source: Reprinted with permission from *The Globe and Mail.*

Exhibit 3

PRO FORMA INCOME STATEMENTS

Year Ended September 30, 1993
(CAD $000's, USD 1.00 = CAD 1.2195)

	USD Component	CAD Component	Total
Revenue	----	$160,000	$160,000
COGS	$ 45,760	67,935	113,695
Gross Margin	(45,760)	92,065	46,305
License Fee	3,658	—	3,658
Depreciation	----	9,640	9,640
Selling and Admin.	—	19,232	19,232
Interest	91	1,191	1,282
Total	3,749	30,063	33,812
EBT	(49,509)	62,002	12,493
Tax (40%)	—	4,997	4,997
Net Income	$ (49,509)	$ 57,005	$ 7,496

PRO FORMA BALANCE SHEET

As at September 30, 1993
(CAD $000's, USD 1.00 = CAD 1.2195)

	USD Component	CAD Component	Total
Cash	—	$ 678	$ 678
A/R	----	17,280	17,280
Inventory	—	11,555	11,555
Net Fixed Assets	----	30,065	30,065
Total		$59,578	$59,578
A/P	$6,668	$9,492	$16,160
Debt	1,220	13,233	14,453
Equity	—	28,965	28,965
Total	$7,888	$51,690	$59,578

Exhibit 4		
AT-THE-MONEY OPTION **STRIKE PRICE = 1.2536**		
EXPIRY **DATE**	**PUT** **PREMIUM** **(% OF CDN$)**	**CALL** **PREMIUM** **(% OF CDN$)**
Oct. 31, 1992	1.14	1.25
Nov. 30, 1992	1.44	1.52
Dec. 31, 1992	1.65	1.74
Jan. 31, 1993	1.73	1.82
Feb. 28, 1993	1.82	1.90
Mar. 31, 1993	1.90	1.99
Apr. 30, 1993	1.98	2.09
May 31, 1993	2.06	2.20
June 30, 1993	2.14	2.31
July 31, 1993	2.24	2.42
Aug. 31, 1993	2.35	2.53
Sept. 30, 1993	2.45	2.64
Average	1.908	2.034

Exhibit 5		
ZERO COST TUNNEL **STRIKE PRICES**		
EXPIRY DATE	**PUTS**	**CALLS**
Oct. 31, 1992	$1.2491	$1.2690
Nov. 30, 1992	1.2508	1.2749
Dec. 31, 1992	1.2541	1.2799
Jan. 31, 1993	1.2541	1.2821
Feb. 28, 1993	1.2542	1.2842
Mar. 31, 1993	1.2542	1.2863
Apr. 30, 1993	1.2553	1.2880
May 31, 1993	1.2564	1.2897
June 30, 1993	1.2575	1.2915
July 31, 1993	1.2580	1.2927
Aug. 31, 1993	1.2585	1.2938
Sept. 30, 1993	1.2590	1.2950
Average	1.2551	1.2856

Exhibit 6		
FORWARD CONTRACT RATES[1]		
	BID	**OFFER**
1 month	1.2590	$1.2598
2 months	1.2628	1.2639
3 months	1.2669	1.2686
4 months	1.2681	1.2695
5 months	1.2692	1.2706
6 months	1.2703	1.2718
7 months	1.2716	1.2736
8 months	1.2731	1.2750
9 months	1.2745	1.2765
10 months	1.2753	1.2775
11 months	1.2762	1.2784
12 months	1.2770	1.2794
Average	1.2703	1.2719

[1] *Advance expected to pay the offer rate.*

SPENCER HALL

On June 27, 1994, Stu Finlayson, Treasurer of the University of Western Ontario (UWO), was preparing a recommendation to the Spencer Hall Board of Directors that he was scheduled to meet two days later. The recommendation concerned the financing of the $7.7 million expansion to Spencer Hall, a property that UWO used primarily for executive education. The expansion was currently being financed with short-term loans based on either the Prime rate or 30-day Bankers' Acceptances. However, the Board was increasingly concerned with the likelihood that interest rates would increase in Canada and requested that Finlayson reconsider the financing strategy. He realized that if the Board chose to stay with a floating-rate loan, the Board might have to consider a hedging vehicle.

EXECUTIVE EDUCATION AT IVEY

Executive education began at the Ivey Business School in 1948 when the first executives enrolled in the Ivey Executive Program (previously known as the Management Training Course). Forty-six years later, Western attracted participants from across Canada and abroad for its executive education programs, which included an Executive Masters of Business Administration, specific courses designed to help managers in certain functional areas such as marketing or operations, and customized programs aimed at corporations wishing to train employees for specific needs.

Many business schools in North America had well-developed executive education programs and, as a result, competition for enrollment was strong. Many schools had attempted to differentiate their product by offering new programs such as teaching through video-conferencing. Another method of differentiation was achieved by holding programs at sites that were both fully functional and comfortable for the participants. Western achieved this by holding most of its executive education programs at Spencer Hall.

SPENCER HALL

Executive education at Ivey was provided at two sites: The Wettlaufer Centre in Mississauga, Ontario and Spencer Hall in London. While the centre in Mississauga had classroom and dining facilities, Spencer Hall was a fully integrated residential and teaching facility. Located about one kilometer from the main Western campus, the classic Georgian Manor featured thirty acres of parkland, private rooms, dining facilities, break-out rooms, and classrooms designed to facilitate case discussions and group interactions.

Spencer Hall operated as a separate entity from the University, and was owned as a partnership between the University and The Bank of Nova Scotia (Scotiabank). Both groups, as well as other university-based and corporate users, rented the facility for various purposes. Nevertheless, the Business School was the single largest user of the facility.

The executive education programs had limited enrollment due to capacity restrictions on the facilities at Spencer Hall. Consequently, the Business School was interested in securing a facility that would enable their programs to grow and sought an expansion to Spencer Hall. A feasibility study concluded that at 60% occupancy the project could support itself. At the time, it was believed that 60% occupancy was a reasonable estimate based on market research of projected usage by the Business School, Scotiabank, other university users and the corporate community.

The $7.7 million expansion was completed in 1992. Added to the already existing facilities were 65 premium rooms, which were considered more fitting for senior executives than those that were available prior to the expansion, two classrooms, 10 study rooms, and a 150-seat dining room. These additions enabled Spencer Hall to compete for major conference bookings and allowed it to focus on becoming one of Canada's pre-eminent conference centres.

BOARD OF DIRECTORS

Since Spencer Hall was owned as a partnership between the University and Scotiabank, its decision-making body, the Board of Directors, included representatives from each institution. All strategic and operating decisions were made by the Board. Spencer Hall's full-time manager sought approval from the Board for most operating decisions.

Two key decisions that the Board made were the approval of the expansion and its source of financing. The decision, made in November 1990, to approve the expansion was based largely on the strong need exhibited by the Business School and on the business plan's projection that the project would break-even at 60% occupancy and at 12% debt financing. The Board's initial decision to finance the expansion with short-term borrowing was a continuation of the strategy used during construction, which was to borrow on a short-term basis as needed. The difference between short-term and long-term rates had been significant and the use of short-term financing allowed Spencer Hall to achieve savings on its debt charges. For example, a 1% decrease in the rate at which the debt was financed (i.e., from 10% to 9%) translated into annual savings of $77,000.

SHORT-TERM FINANCING

Finlayson helped achieve interest savings for the Spencer Hall expansion by using the short-term money market, as opposed to the charges on a fixed-rate mortgage. He achieved these savings by refinancing the loan every month[1] either by borrowing at the Prime rate from Scotiabank or by issuing 30-day Bankers'

---

[1] Unlike many typical mortgages, the Spencer Hall loan did not have any fixed repayment schedule.

Acceptances (BAs). The Prime rate was the rate reserved for the Bank's best customers. BAs were promissory notes drawn for payment by a corporation and co-guaranteed by a bank, which were usually sold to an investment dealer at a discount from par value. However, by early 1994, Finlayson had two main concerns stemming from the short-term financing. First, in the first quarter of 1994, short-term interest rates were at their lowest level since 1973. As of March 25, the yield curve was very steep (i.e., longer-term bonds had much higher yields than shorter-term bonds) signaling that the market expected interest rates to rise in the future (see Exhibit 1). Therefore, not only was the short-term financing expected to become more expensive in the future, but also, if the Board decided to switch to fixed-rate financing, it was possible that this period represented the best opportunity for quite a while to secure the lowest fixed rate. Second, Finlayson had always been uncomfortable with the fact that the expansion, an asset depreciated over twenty-five years, was being financed with a short-term loan. If interest rates were to increase severely in the future, Spencer Hall would face significant loss. Financial statements are in Exhibits 2 and 3.

The Board developed the view, with the help of information provided by the Scotiabank Economics Department (see Exhibit 4), that interest rates would probably increase sharply in the near future. In particular, they were concerned with the possibility of increasing interest rates in Canada caused by the upcoming Quebec election and the high government debt-levels. The Parti Québécois, a political party whose platform centered on Quebec's secession from Canada, was gaining support among the electorate and it seemed likely that they would win the provincial election scheduled for September 1994. The leader of the Parti Québécois, Jacques Parizeau, had promised that a provincial referendum on the question of secession from Canada would then take place by the end of 1995. This, along with the fact that Canada had one of the highest per capita debt levels among the major industrialized nations, had made foreigners less comfortable with investing in Canada. The result was a Canadian dollar that was experiencing increased volatility relative to other currencies. In order to support the value of the Canadian dollar, the Bank of Canada increased short-term interest rates. Another factor was the U.S. Federal Reserve which was increasing interest rates to fight expected inflation. This also required interest rate increases from the Bank of Canada to support the Canadian dollar.

The Board's interest rate expectations were more pessimistic than the forecast by the Scotiabank Economics Department. The Board believed that interest rates would increase significantly on two occasions over the next two years based on the political situation in Quebec: during the period of the provincial general election and during the referendum. As a result of this view, in March 1994, the Board asked Finlayson to make a recommendation on a strategy that better protected the Spencer Hall expansion from volatility in interest rates. Knowing that a fixed-rate mortgage was still not a favored alternative among the Board members, due to its relatively high interest cost, Finlayson decided to consider hedging vehicles.

HEDGING ALTERNATIVES

With the help of a Scotiabank derivatives marketer, Kathy Chase, Finlayson considered three different hedging vehicles: an interest rate swap, an interest rate cap and an interest rate collar.

Interest Rate Swaps

In the history of financial markets, no product has grown as quickly as swaps. The growth in swaps was due to both the skills of financial engineers who developed the vehicle and the increasing appreciation by financial managers of the importance of risk management in a volatile interest rate environment. Also, investors found the swap market to be a useful one in which to speculate on interest rate beliefs.

Finlayson and Chase considered a "plain vanilla" interest rate swap to be an attractive option (Exhibit 5). In a swap, Spencer Hall would make a fixed-rate payment to Scotiabank and receive a floating-rate payment in return. These payments would be based on the "notional" loan amount of $7.7 million. The swap would be separate from any principal payments; only interest payments would be exchanged.

The swap rate, the rate at which the loan could be fixed through the use of a swap, was set by Scotiabank using the current market yield curves (the available 30-day BA and all-in swap rates[2] on March 25, 1994 are

---

[2]"All-in" rates referred to the effective rates including any fees.

listed in Exhibit 6). The floating payments received from the Bank would be based on the 30-day BAs, reset each month to match the reset period for the loan.

Finlayson felt that there were four good reasons to lock-in the rate using a swap. First, the yield on Government of Canada 91-day Treasury Bills was at its lowest level since 1973. Second, Canada's debt problem and the political uncertainty in Quebec were bound to put upward pressure on interest rates. Third, the swap presented an opportunity to finance the long-term asset with fixed-rate longer-term debt. Fourth, the current 10-year swap rate was 8.24% and was significantly lower than the 12% mortgage rate assumed in the original Spencer Hall business plan.

Interest Rate Cap

Another hedging alternative was a ceiling interest rate agreement, or a cap. The writer, or seller, of a cap paid the cap holder each time the contract's reference rate, the current rate on which the contract was based (such as Prime or BAs), was above the contract's ceiling rate. In return, the writer received an up-front fee. From Spencer Hall's point of view, a cap represented insurance against a sharp rise in floating rates. The up-front fee was set by Scotiabank, the writer, and, like a swap, was based on the current yield curve. Unlike a swap, a cap would allow Spencer Hall to benefit from a decline in floating rates.

Finlayson considered caps for maturities of one to three years and for the full amount of $7.7 million. Cap rates were available as low as 6.50%, and any level above 8.25% was considered to be of little use to Spencer Hall. Exhibit 7 shows pricing for various maturities and rates. For example, a two-year cap with a rate of 8% would cost a fee of 104 basis points (100 basis points equals 1%). For the $7.7 million notional value, this amounted to $80,080 ($7.7 million x 1.04%) as an up-front payment.

Interest Rate Collar

An interest rate collar combined a cap with an interest rate floor. In other words, by simultaneously buying a cap and selling the Bank an interest rate floor, Finlayson could lock-in a range of interest rates that Spencer Hall would pay on its loan. If BAs moved above the cap's level, the Bank would make a payment to Spencer Hall equal to the difference between the cap rate and the market rate. If BAs moved below the floor's level, Spencer Hall would make a payment to the Bank. The advantage of a collar was that the strike levels for the cap and the floor could be chosen so that the fee, or initial cash outlay, was minimized. As the strike level for the cap increased, its price decreased. Likewise, the higher the strike level on the floor, the higher the amount the seller received. The Board did not foresee interest rates falling below 6.5% in the near term. Exhibit 8 shows the fee for different two-year collar combinations. For example, a two-year, 8% cap and a two-year, 4.5% floor would cost a premium of 91 basis points (104 minus 13, from Exhibit 7), or $70,070. In many interest rate environments, a collar could be constructed to result in "zero cost" if a floor was sold at a premium that matched the cap's premium. However, the current yield curve's steep slope made caps relatively more expensive and floors relatively inexpensive.

MARCH 25 DECISION

On March 25, 1994, the Board decided to continue to use floating rate financing until, in their opinion, the financial markets became less volatile. Locking-in a fixed rate at this point seemed to be unwise when interest rates were changing so rapidly. They were also concerned that the level of interest charges required for a fixed-rate loan would create operating losses since Spencer Hall occupancy had not been as high as originally projected in the business plan due to the economic recession of the early 1990s.

JUNE 27 DECISION

All members of the Board were increasingly worried about rising interest rates. Since late March, the U.S. Federal reserve had increased short-term rates twice, and this action had sent long-term rates soaring. Also, the U.S. economy was showing increasing strength which fuelled additional inflation fears. In Canada, these effects, along with the Quebec provincial election, were causing more volatility in the markets than originally expected. The result was that interest rates had recently risen sharply (see Exhibit 9), and the rate at which Spencer Hall could issue BAs had increased from 4.84% on March 25, 1994 to 6.23% on June 27, 1994. The Board's updated interest rate (BAs) view is listed in Exhibit 10. The Board felt that rates would rise steadily until a couple of months after the Quebec provincial election, peaking at 10.5% and then ease off until the summer of 1995. After this, rates would again rise due to the referendum, which was expected to occur by the end of 1995.

However, the Board was still concerned that a fixed-rate mortgage could not be supported by the income from Spencer Hall. The Board felt that they should lock-in for a period of time long enough to ride out the volatility in the markets, which was expected to last about two years, and asked Finlayson to consider a hedging vehicle that would cover them for this period. Rates for swaps, caps and collars (i.e., combinations of caps and floors) as of June 27 are provided in Exhibits 11 and 12. Finlayson had to consider both the costs of financing as well as the risks. One option would be to recommend a continuation of the current policy of unhedged short-term financing.

Exhibit 1

GOVERNMENT OF CANADA YIELD CURVE
As of March 25, 1994

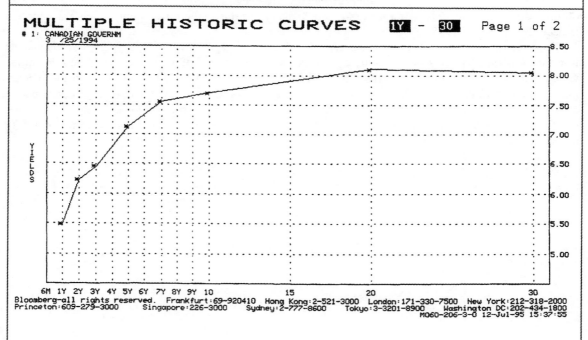

MULTIPLE HISTORIC CURVES 1Y - 30 Page 1 of 2

1: CANADIAN GOVERNM
3 /25/1994

Source: Bloomberg L.P.

Exhibit 2

SPENCER HALL INCOME STATEMENT
For Year Ending April 30, 1994

Revenue	$2,852,570
Direct materials and operating expenses	<u>1,496,705</u>
Operating margin	1,355,865
Overhead Expenses:	
Interest	425,808
Other overhead expenses	487,955
Administrative Expenses:	
Salaries, supplies, marketing and other	<u>535,233</u>
Total Expenses	<u>$1,448,996</u>
Net Income (loss)	<u>($93,131)</u>

Source: Spencer Hall Foundation

Exhibit 3

SPENCER HALL BALANCE SHEET
As at April 30, 1994

ASSETS:

Cash	$50,825
Accounts Receivable	244,015
Inventory	19,120
Prepaid Expenses	42,193
Total Current Assets	356,153
Furniture and Equipment	140,323
Leasehold Improvements	9,222,366
TOTAL ASSETS	$9,718,842

LIABILITIES AND FUND BALANCES:

Accounts payable and accrued liabilities	$85,685
Due to UWO	672,724
Deferred revenue	14,255
Demand note	7,700,000
Other liabilities	200,000
Term bank loans	371,065
Appropriated surplus	470,119
Unappropriated deficit	(822,499)
Equity in fixed assets	1,027,493
TOTAL LIABILITIES AND FUND BALANCES	$9,718,842

Source: Spencer Hall Foundation

Exhibit 4

SCOTIABANK ECONOMIC FORECAST
Spring 1994

Interest Rate Turbulence

The spectre of an impending build-up in U.S. inflation has triggered a broad-based financial market sell-off in North America, Europe and Japan. The U.S. monetary authorities have reacted to these growing financial market pressures by progressively tightening policy in February, March and April.

Despite initial Bank of Canada action to insulate markets from U.S. pressures, spreads off New York have widened sharply after briefly touching decade lows early this year. An accommodative policy bias proved unsustainable with the exchange rate sliding to a seven-year low below 73 cents(US). The best inflation performance in over three decades has not offset investor concerns about Ottawa's deficit-cutting resolve, tolerance for currency weakness and ongoing constitutional uncertainties.

Bank of Canada Governor Thiessen is committed to keeping inflation in a 1-3 per cent range through 1998. When

inflation was 2 per cent or less in the past, money market rates averaged just over 3 per cent and long bond yields were typically around 5 per cent—well below current levels. However, monetary policy cannot prevent sudden interest rate and currency spasms if fiscal deterioration or Quebec election uncertainties give investors the jitters.

Underlying inflation in North America suggests that the run-up in bond yields is overdone. Rates have risen nearly 1 1/2 percentage point since late last year, three times the average erosion at this stage of a cyclical rebound. Unless prices move up sharply, which is not likely, U.S. long-term rates should stay around 7 1/2 per cent into 1995, with Canadian rates fluctuating below 9 per cent.

U.S. private sector borrowings are picking up after a three-year slowdown, underpinned by improving confidence and low financing costs. Willingness to lend also has been enhanced by healthier financial sector balance sheets,

Interest rates stay low ...

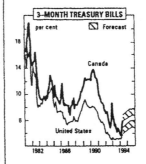

... with the Canadian dollar falling further.

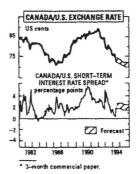

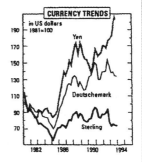

* 3-month commercial paper.

Scotiabank *S*

Source: Scotiabank, Global Economic Outlook, April 1994

Exhibit 4 (continued)

INTEREST RATE OUTLOOK	—(per cent, end of period)—				
	1993	—1941—		—1951—	
	H2	H1	H2	H1	H2
CANADA					
3-month T-bill	3.9	6.4	6.8	7.1	7.1
Mid-term Bond	6.6	8.5	8.7	8.2	7.9
Long Government Bond	7.3	8.7	8.9	8.5	8.2
UNITED STATES					
3-month T-bill (yield)	3.1	4.3	4.8	5.3	5.3
Mid-term Bond	5.8	7.3	7.5	7.0	6.7
Long Government Bond	6.4	7.6	7.7	7.3	7.0
SPREADS					
3-month T-bill	0.8	2.1	2.0	1.8	1.8
Mid-term Bond	0.8	1.2	1.2	1.2	1.2
Long Government Bond	0.9	1.2	1.2	1.2	1.2

EXCHANGE RATE OUTLOOK	—(end of period)—				
	1993	—1941—		—1951—	
	H2	H1	H2	H1	H2
Canadian Dollar (US¢/C$)	76	72-74	71-73	70-72	70-72
Yen (¥/US$)	112	103	100	102	105
Deutschemark (DM/US$)	1.74	1.71	1.78	1.83	1.85
Sterling (US$/£)	1.48	1.47	1.41	1.38	1.37

CREDIT DEMAND	—(end of period, per cent change)—			
	1983–92	1993	1941	1951
CANADA				
Total	9.1	5.9	5.8	5.8
Personal	10.4	5.1	5.5	6.5
Corporate	6.5	2.4	3.5	4.5
Government	10.2	8.7	7.3	8.3
UNITED STATES				
Total	9.6	5.2	6.5	6.9
Personal	9.8	6.3	7.3	7.2
Corporate	7.5	1.0	4.8	4.8
Government	11.8	7.9	7.0	5.5

declining loan delinquencies and reduced regulatory constraints.

Canadian private sector credit demands also are beginning to revive, but will lag U.S. trends through 1995. Public sector borrowings, which have been outpacing private sector credit demands by a factor of three, will remain the dominant source of loan pressures. Huge government borrowings are a pervasive impediment to Canadian longer-term yields approaching U.S. levels despite lower inflation.

Canadian Dollar Tumbles

The Canada/U.S. exchange rate has fallen 6 cents(US) over the past year despite record foreign purchases of Canadian securities. Portfolio capital inflows have been offset by direct investment outflows and by increasing diversification by Canadians in foreign markets. Sudden shifts in these two-way flows have repeatedly buffeted the currency. Look for a similar pattern of erratic Canadian dollar weakness into 1995.

An early turnaround in the currency is unlikely. Domestic activity is lagging U.S. trends. Canadian fiscal and current account shortfalls as a share of GDP are twice as large as south of the border. A revival in the exchange rate requires large deficit cuts, a better economic performance and a big rebound in commodity prices.

The U.S. dollar has been weakened by increased trade frictions with Japan and adverse political developments at home. Despite the Bundesbank's more aggressive interest rate cuts, the dollar has made no headway against the Deutschemark. However, most overseas currencies are likely to soften later this year as higher U.S. rates and lower European yields enhance the attractiveness of U.S. investments.

A tough U.K. budget also will reinforce an accommodative monetary policy and a modest weakening of sterling. Massive Japanese surpluses will probably keep the yen as the strongest currency in the G7.

Exhibit 5
"PLAIN VANILLA" SWAP

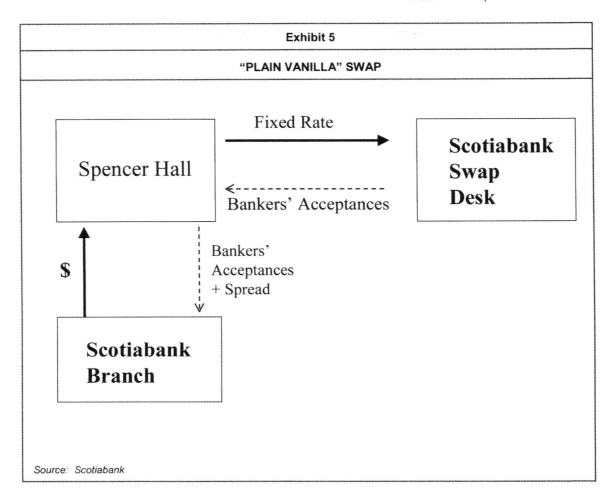

Source: Scotiabank

Exhibit 6
AVAILABLE INTEREST RATES **March 25, 1994**

30-day Banker's Acceptance	4.81%
1 year Swap	5.93%
2 year Swap	6.52%
5 year Swap	7.66%
10 year Swap	8.24%
20 year Mortgage (estimated at 1.5% above 20 year government of Canada bond)	9.50%

Source: Scotiabank

Exhibit 7

INTEREST RATE CAP AND FLOOR PREMIUMS
March 25, 1994 (Basis Points)

CAP	6.50%	6.75%	7.00%	7.25%	7.50%	7.75%	8.00%	8.25%
1 year	37	32	30	24	20	16	14	
2 year	182	165	150	137	125	114	104	95
3 year	420	450	367	343	321	301	283	265

FLOOR	4.00%	4.25%	4.50%	4.75%
1 year	1	2	4	7
2 year	5	8	13	20
3 year	10	16	23	33

Source: Scotiabank

Exhibit 8

TWO-YEAR COLLAR PREMIUMS
March 25, 1994 (Basis Points)

COLLAR	6.50% Cap	6.75% Cap	7.00% Cap	7.25% Cap	7.50% Cap	7.75% Cap	8.00% Cap	8.25% Cap
4.00% Floor	177	160	145	132	120	109	99	90
4.25% Floor	174	157	142	129	117	106	96	87
4.50% Floor	169	152	137	124	112	101	91	82
4.75% Floor	162	145	130	117	105	94	84	75

Source: Scotiabank

Exhibit 9
GOVERNMENT OF CANADA YIELD CURVE **As of March 25 and June 27, 1994**

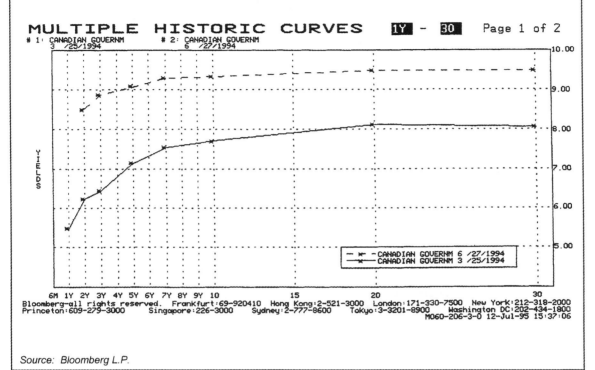

Source: Bloomberg L.P.

Exhibit 10
SUMMARY OF INTEREST RATE VIEW **Spencer Hall Board Of Directors, Late-June, 1994**

Month-end	Projected Interest Rate
September 1994	9.5%
December 1994	10.5%
March 1995	9.5%
June 1995	8.9%
September 1995	9.7%
December 1995	10.5%
March 1996	8.5%
June 1996	7.5%

Exhibit 11

AVAILABLE INTEREST RATES
June 27, 1994

30-day Banker's Acceptance	6.23%
1 year Swap	8.70%
2 year Swap	9.10%
5 year Swap	9.67%
10 year Swap	10.02%
20 year Mortgage	11.00%
(estimated at 1.5% above 20 year	
Government of Canada Bond)	

Source: Scotiabank

Exhibit 12

INTEREST RATE CAP AND FLOOR PREMIUMS
June 27, 1994 (Basis Points)

CAP	6.50%	6.75%	7.00%	7.25%	7.50%	7.75%	8.00%	8.25%	8.50%
1 year	174	158	143	129	117	105	95	85	77
2 year	502	471	440	412	385	360	337	315	295
3 year	824	780	738	698	660	625	591	560	530

FLOOR	4.00%	4.25%	4.50%	4.75%	5.00%	5.25%	5.50%	5.75%
1 year	0	0	0	0	0.5	1	2	3
2 year	0.5	1	2	3	4	6	9	12
3 year	4	6	8	11	15	20	26	33

Source: Scotiabank

part four

Capital Structure Decisions

BORDERS HOTEL CORP.

THE PROBLEM

On November 13, 2001, Karen Daniels, president of Borders Hotel Corp. (BHC), had just returned from a meeting with the directors of BHC. The meeting had discussed three financing proposals to raise $2,275,000 for BHC. Daniels was uncertain of the impact of the three proposals on the financial viability of BHC and on the returns to herself and other investors. The meeting ended with the directors asking her for a recommendation on the preferred financing for a teleconference in two weeks.

HISTORY

After several years as a hotel manager for a national chain, Daniels had established herself in the tourist accommodation business close to the Canada-U.S. border near the Sarnia, Ontario, Canada and Port Huron, Michigan, U.S.A. border crossing. Daniels chose this location because the route was heavily traveled by tourists during the spring and summer months. In 1988, she formed a company known as Huron Motor Courts, Inc., acquired an attractive lot of land and erected an elaborate, modern motel on this site. The buildings provided complete tourist accommodation, shelter for automobiles and spacious dining facilities with entertainment for guests. Daniels considered Huron Motor Courts, Inc. a very successful venture.

Richard Ivey School of Business
The University of Western Ontario

IVEY

Professor David Shaw revised this case (originally prepared by Professor James C. Taylor and later revised by Professor John Humphrey) solely to provide material for class discussion. The author does not intend to illustrate either effective or ineffective handling of a managerial situation. The author may have disguised certain names and other identifying information to protect confidentiality.

With the introduction of the North American Free Trade Agreement (NAFTA), existing and new businesses in the area grew significantly. These businesses were not along the main tourist route on which Huron Motor Courts was situated; consequently, they did not in any way adversely affect the attractiveness of the site as a potential tourist stopover. However, the general expansion in the area attracted many business people who, not infrequently, found it necessary to remain in the area overnight.

THE BHC PROJECT

With these developments in mind, Daniels approached a number of industries in the vicinity in the summer of 2001, with a proposal regarding accommodation for visiting business people. Her suggestion was well received, and several manufacturing concerns expressed an interest in maintaining permanent accommodation for visitors on business. With this encouragement, and in view of the overflow of visitors experienced to date from the tourist business, Daniels conceived the idea of constructing a modern hotel that would attract year-round business by arrangement with the local industries, and could be used to catch the overflow from the Huron Motor Courts during the tourist season.

Daniels then considered the type and size of hotel that would be desirable, and tried to estimate the costs of such a project. A property close to the Huron Motor Courts, which Daniels owned, was 200 feet wide and 350 feet deep, and was appraised at $975,000. After consultation with a local architect, Daniels developed a plan for a hotel building on this site that fulfilled the apparent prerequisites. The plan called for a three-storey structure, containing four suites of two rooms each, 31 twin bedrooms, 30 double bedrooms, a large front store, seven smaller stores and other facilities, which Daniels felt might eventually accommodate a travel agent, hair salon, business center and fitness room.

Daniels then attempted to estimate the profitability of such an establishment. Based on her experience with the motor court business, the income from the four suites and the bedrooms would be $8,100 per day, presuming that all accommodation was occupied. The income from leases of other parts of the building she estimated at $15,000 per month, again with 100 per cent occupancy. Rent would be charged as a per cent of sales and was expected to vary with occupancy. Other income eventually would be derived from gift counters, newspapers, display space and from a large central area, 100 feet by 20 feet in the lower level, for which a purpose had not yet been planned.

Apart from the incorporation expenses, which were expected to be about $50,000, Daniels estimated her yearly operating expenses, again based on 100 per cent occupancy (see Exhibit 1).

Daniels felt that in forecasting the profitability of the hotel, an estimate of 75 per cent average occupancy over a year was realistic, and 50 per cent occupancy the lowest possibility. All store and office spaces were to be leased on a yearly basis. Income taxes were estimated at 40 per cent.

The estimated cost of erecting a brick, concrete and steel hotel, such as the one proposed, was set at $2,300,000. After considerable investigation, Daniels set the estimated cost of furnishing the hotel at $1,100,000. She judged that working capital of $75,000 would be required in order to operate the business. Further, since her estimate of the profitability of the new hotel seemed to warrant a venture into this expanded field of business activity, she was certain that the required capital could be raised.

Accordingly, Daniels met with her associates in the Huron Motor Courts venture, to discuss the establishment of the new business. It was decided, in view of the degree of speculation involved in a new venture of this kind, and also because of the possibility of future expansion in the hotel business, that the business should be established as an independent corporate body with no financial connection whatsoever to Huron Motor Courts, Inc.

Thus, the new company, to be known as the Borders Hotel Corp., was to be incorporated as a company to operate hotels. The head office would be established on the property of Huron Motor Courts, Inc. Daniels would become the president and chairman of the board of directors. The new company would have an authorized share capital as follows:

8% Cumulative preferred shares par value $25	500,000 shares
Common shares without par value	1,000,000 shares

BHC FINANCING PROPOSALS

Considerable progress had been made in planning operations. Daniels felt that attention must be turned now to the matter of providing the permanent capital, which had been previously estimated at $4.5 million: working capital, $75,000; land $975,000; building, $2,300,000; furnishings, $1,100,000 and organization costs, $50,000.

Daniels foresaw the desirability of beginning construction as quickly as possible, so that the interior work could be completed in the winter. It was anticipated that the new structure would be completed in time for the 2002 peak season. Since considerable time would be required to raise the necessary capital, the five outside members of the board and Daniels each invested $25,000 and received 2,500 common shares. This provided the funds to begin construction immediately. The necessary arrangements were completed and construction of the new hotel commenced in September 2001.

As the next step in the financing, BHC would enter into an agreement with Daniels to purchase the land on which the hotel was to be built for $975,000. Under the purchase agreement, BHC contracted to give Daniels 97,500 shares of common stock in consideration for this land.

To finance the furnishings, BHC would negotiate a 10 per cent, five-year term loan of $1,100,000 with the furnishings suppliers. Blended annual payments of $290,160 were due starting at the end of the first fiscal year.

After these three financing arrangements, BHC had raised $2,225,000 with $2,275,000 still required. Daniels arranged preliminary discussions with her associates to decide the most feasible method of raising the capital. She had entertained the thought of a first mortgage on the company's real estate. The mortgage would be for $2,275,000, 20-year term, at eight per cent.[1] The annual principal and interest blended payments would be $231,000, with payments due at the end of BHC's fiscal year. However, Daniels was concerned that the fixed payments might prove too great a risk, with future earnings prospects uncertain.

Daniels' associates made a second proposal: the sale of 24 units at $100,000 per unit with each unit consisting of 10,000 common shares. Legal and other expenses for the issue were expected to be $125,000. Daniels was not enthusiastic about the common stock proposal, as her proportion of the profits would be substantially reduced.

A third proposal, which also involved units, was presented. This time each unit consisted of 3,000 preferred shares and 2,500 common shares. The units would sell for $100,000 with legal and other costs of $125,000. There would be 24 units sold. The preferred shares would have a par value of $25, a preferred dividend rate of eight per cent and dividends would be cumulative. These preferred shares would be redeemable within the first five years of issue at $26 per share. If dividends were passed for two consecutive years, the preferred shares could elect a majority of the board of directors.

After the development of the three proposals, the meeting adjourned. The directors asked Daniels to investigate the three options and report to the board with a recommendation at a meeting scheduled via teleconference on November 27.

---

[1] At this time, long treasury bonds were yielding 5.75 per cent.

Exhibit 1

ANNUAL OPERATING EXPENSES AT 100% OCCUPANCY

	Total Variable Cost	Fixed Costs
Advertising		$ 120,000
Heat, light, water	$ 51,000	54,000
House supplies	52,000	
House wages	227,000	
Repairs and maintenance	41,000	98,000
Insurance		45,000
Salaries		350,000
Laundry	62,000	
Office expenses		51,000
Miscellaneous		12,000
Linen	11,000	
Telephone, fax, etc.		59,000
Automobile and travel	10,000	10,000
Municipal taxes		60,000
Computer systems		224,000
Depreciation		320,000
	$ 454,000	$ 1,403,000

ROCKY MOUNTAIN HIGH SKI RESORT INC. (RMH)

In early November 1993, Christine Hayes, vice-president finance, of Rocky Mountain High Ski Resort Inc. (RMH), was examining the alternatives for financing the proposed Phase 2, $25 million expansion. The well-known Western Canadian all-season resort planned to add several new runs, additional snow-making capacity, another high-speed quad chair lift, a 700 seat restaurant, a new retail ski equipment store, and to upgrade the existing infrastructure. The directors of RMH were scheduled to meet in two weeks to approve both the proposed expansion and financing plans.

RMH was a private company which had relied on debt financing and retained earnings to finance its past growth. Because several of the board members had no previous experience with a public security issue, which was one of Hayes' financing options for board consideration, she knew her presentation required careful and thorough analysis.

THE SKI RESORT INDUSTRY

The ski resort industry had emerged from a period of rapid change, technological advance and consolidation during the 1980s, as a mature industry. Snowmaking technology was refined to allow resort operators to greatly reduce their dependence on natural snowfall. Snow-grooming technology was improved, allowing resort operators to smooth and groom terrain, particularly on beginner and intermediate slopes, eliminating hazardous "moguls," and making skiing a more enjoyable experience for the average skier.

Richard Ivey School of Business
The University of Western Ontario   **IVEY**   Blair Zilkey prepared this case under the supervision of Professor David C. Shaw solely to provide material for class discussion. The authors do not intend to illustrate either effective or ineffective handling of a managerial situation. The authors may have disguised certain names and other identifying information to protect confidentiality.

The most dramatic improvement, however, was the introduction of the high speed four-passenger "quad" chair lifts. This new lift technology virtually eliminated the long lineups at many ski areas, increased the capacity of resorts to handle more skiers, and provided skiers with more actual skiing time for their money.

The capital required for these technologies and the growing "destination skier" segment, which demanded superior facilities, created a fundamental change in the structure of the industry. Small, regional mountains that were undercapitalized or mismanaged, discontinued operations. In 1980, there were 845 ski areas in the U.S. That number had dropped to 529 by 1992.[1] Hayes believed the numbers were similar in Canada. Furthermore, she estimated that by the year 2000, there would only be twenty large-scale, world-class ski resorts in North America.

Murray Derraugh, RMH's president and the major shareholder, knew his resort location was first rate; it had close proximity to an international airport, high quality terrain and snow conditions, a variety of four-season activities that attracted visitors year round and it could support a high quality restaurant, retail, and hotel base. In fact, RMH had been ranked the third best resort in North America by "American Ski Magazine" two years in a row. Derraugh believed the $25 million expansion was key to maintaining its place as the premier ski facility in Canada, and one of the best in North America.

THE SKI RESORT ENVIRONMENT[2]

Skier visits in North America increased by 6.3 per cent to 54 million during the 1992/93 ski season although Canadian statistics showed almost no growth (Exhibit 1). Management had observed a "graying" of the clientele, a trend which seemed to exist throughout North America. In the 1960s, seventy per cent of skiers were under the age of 35. By the 1990s, this number had decreased to 50 per cent. RMH's research showed that older skiers also skied more often (eight to 10 times annually compared to five or six for younger skiers) and demanded a total vacation experience from a resort.

Exhibit 2 describes Canadian winter vacation intentions for the previous five seasons. A continuing weak Canadian dollar (Exhibit 3) made foreign travel more expensive for Canadians and at the same time made Canada a more attractive destination for foreign tourists. About 40 per cent of RMH's visitors were from outside Canada, mainly from Japan and Europe.

The Canadian economy was showing signs of increased activity. Gross Domestic Product (GDP) had grown by 1.6 per cent, third quarter 1993 over 1992, the largest year-over-year increase since the 1989-over-1988 mark of 2.7 per cent. In contrast, the GDP had grown by only .5 per cent, 1992-over-1991, -1.1 per cent 1991-over-1990, and only .9 per cent 1990-over-1989. Management viewed its demonstrated ability to increase cash flow through a recession as a confirmation that its "total resort strategy" was the right one and a reflection of RMH's strength in the market.

RMH: AN HISTORICAL PERSPECTIVE

Winter skiing had taken place on the Evergreen Mountain since the late 1960s. It became a destination resort in 1972 when a 250-room lodge was opened. Ownership changed in 1976 when a local business person purchased the facility and rights to collect lift revenue on the mountain, and presented a plan to expand it into an all-season destination resort. Financial constraints impeded this effort as the 1982 recession squeezed the owner's other holdings. In 1983, Derraugh and a group of five investors purchased RMH.

Derraugh had spent 15 years with a large venture capital firm in Toronto. He had run a number of companies for short periods of time, enjoyed the experience, and always hoped to start or buy his own business when the opportunity presented itself. David Cross, the other major shareholder of RMH and its executive vice-president, had a successful career as a real estate developer in Western Canada. The two men had done business together in the past. Derraugh and Cross looked to RMH as the opportunity to build a successful organization and as a chance to be more involved with a sport they loved.

---

[1]Source: "Corporate Growth Weekly Report," December 6, 1993.

[2]Source: Canadian Ski Council, "Ski Facts and Stats," November, 1993.

In addition to Derraugh and Cross, four other shareholders, not involved with the management of the company, constituted the board of directors. All employees of RMH were on a salary and bonus remuneration plan. Five key employees, including Hayes, owned stock (Exhibit 4). Hayes had joined RMH three years ago after four years in financial management with a chartered bank. She had an MBA from the Ivey Business School.

EVERGREEN MOUNTAIN

RMH was situated at the base of Evergreen Mountain in the Canadian Rockies (Rocky Mountains run across the North American Continent from north to south, almost parallel to the Pacific shore), and was accessible in under two hours by car from several metropolitan areas. Evergreen had an elevation of 7,000 feet and a vertical drop of over 5,000 feet, one of the longest in North America. It had over 100 marked trails covering over 3,800 acres of skiable terrain. The average annual snowfall was approximately 340 inches with the winter ski season averaging 185 days in duration. Glacier skiing was popular in the summer. Heli skiing (where skiers are lifted to the top of the hill by helicopters and ski down the slope) and cross country skiing at RMH were growing in popularity.

RMH owned 500 acres of land at the base of the mountain. Other regional developers were active both at Evergreen and nearby Whitepine Mountain. There were over 2,000 condominium, townhome, or hotel bed units at the mountain's base, of which RMH controlled 50 per cent. Management believed the demand potential justified another 2,000 rooms.

The ski facilities on Evergreen Mountain itself occupied crown land. RMH operated the facilities under various land tenure arrangements which expired in 2025. The provincial government received a royalty of 2.5 per cent of gross lift ticket revenues.

RMH FINANCIAL PERFORMANCE

Income statements for the fiscal years 1988 through 1993 are presented in Exhibit 5. Annual skier visits increased almost 200,000 during this time period and strong growth in revenue per visit reflected the growth in services offered by RMH.

Balance sheets for 1992 and 1993 are presented in Exhibit 6. Buildings and equipment were depreciated over a fifteen-year period. Goodwill arose from the purchase of the Grizzly Bear Lodge, a company with a strong tradition and following among its clientele. Deferred development costs relate to undeveloped land that the company planned to develop within five to seven years.

Sixty per cent of the long-term debt was a fixed rate term loan (at 11 per cent) granted by a large life insurance company, with an annual $2,000,000 sinking fund payment due October 31. The remainder of the debt was a floating rate term loan from the Metropolitan Bank, which carried an interest rate of prime plus one per cent. It had an annual sinking fund payment of $1,000,000, also due on October 31. Both loans were due October 31, 1996.

PHASE ONE EXPANSION

In 1984, RMH purchased the 400-room Grizzly Bear Lodge Corporation, its main resort competitor. Included in the purchase were ski-school and equipment rental and retail operations. A five-year, $40 million capital investment program was implemented beginning in 1987 which would transform RMH from a regional resort to a destination resort attracting skiers from around the world. The development program was two-fold.

Ski facilities were enhanced. Three high-speed quad chair lifts were added; trails were expanded and snowmaking capacity increased to cover over 25 per cent of the skiable terrain. Restaurant and retail capacity was nearly quadrupled. These expenditures doubled daily skier capacity to over ten thousand, reduced travel time from the ski base to the alpine area by 50 to 60 per cent to 15 minutes, and increased the skiable terrain from 1,500 to 3,800 acres.

To diversify its operations, RMH began to develop summer season activities. Glacier skiing was available from June to September. The resort developed two championship 18-hole golf courses. Investments were made to provide tennis and river rafting facilities. Mountain biking, fishing, horseback riding, wind surfing and swimming were also available.

The second part of RMH's strategy involved the development of ski-in, ski-out townhomes and condominiums at the base of the mountain. The company was developing one and two bedroom units in phases of 20 units each. Management cited demographics showing that baby boomers were beginning to enter their vacation home ownership years. The first two phases sold in under seven months. Phase three was scheduled to be completed in time for the 1994/95 winter ski season.

RMH FINANCIAL FORECAST

Hayes forecast revenue growth of 11 per cent for 1994 and 1995 (Exhibit 7). The forecast was based on a $2 increase per year in the winter lift ticket price, and growth in revenue per skier due to RMH's capital improvements. Winter lift revenue accounted for approximately 55 per cent of total winter revenue which included lifts, ski equipment rentals and sales, lessons, food service and lodging. Total winter revenue accounted for 80 per cent of all revenues. Pro forma Balance Sheets are presented in Exhibit 8.

FINANCING OPTIONS

Hayes had carefully explored several financing options in preparing for the board meeting. She knew that once Phase 2 was completed, management did not anticipate capital expenditures to exceed depreciation during the remainder of the nineties. Interest rates were at their lowest in years. Prime had dropped to 5.75 per cent currently, from 13.75 per cent in 1990. Hayes talked to officers in several financial institutions and securities firms and narrowed her options to four.

BANK FINANCING

Metropolitan Bank proposed a financing arrangement which would enable RMH to proceed with the expansion: $25 million term loan at prime plus 2.5 per cent, with the principal repayable over a 12-year period in equal annual amounts, beginning October 31, 1994. The loan would restrict further annual capital expenditures to $2 million and dividends to not more than 50 per cent of annual earnings. The Bank's General Security Agreement on the existing term loan, with amendments, would provide collateral for the new loan. Existing loans, with covenants and securities, would be retained (Exhibit 9).

PENSION FUND PRIVATE PLACEMENT

Hayes made a formal presentation to Michael Smyk, vice president of Pension Associates Inc., a firm which managed a group of large Western Canadian corporate pension funds. The pooled pension, with assets of over $2 billion, was known to invest up to five per cent of the pool in smaller companies operating within the region. Smyk called her back after three days and offered financing as follows:

A $25 million debenture at 9.35 per cent for 15 years secured by a first mortgage on RMH's undeveloped land and a floating charge on the other assets of RMH, subject to the claims held by current lenders on existing loans. This loan, commonly called a bullet loan, had no annual sinking fund payments. It was repayable in full at maturity. The pension fund would also receive 145,000 common shares of RMH for making the loan.

PUBLIC OFFERING OF SECURITIES

Another consideration involved "going public" with an issue of common shares. Hayes discussed this possibility with Melanie Solanson, Vice-President, Underwriting, at Federal Securities, in Toronto. Solanson explained that while initial public offerings in Canada had fallen off dramatically after the October 1987 stock market crash, they had roared back in the past few years. If the current pace continued, the dollar value of preferred and common stock issues would be 60 per cent higher in 1993, compared to 1992.

Hayes knew that, in going public, RMH would have to undergo a rigorous examination of its operations, financial records, and legal situation both by the underwriter and the securities commission. Solanson estimated that the process would take four to six months.

During a second visit, after Solanson had reviewed the company, she pointed out that RMH would have to bear the legal and audit costs of the examination, amounting to about $250,000, as well as pay an underwriting fee of six per cent of gross proceeds. In return, Federal would underwrite the issue, setting the price just prior to the public offering.

Solanson indicated that, based on her assessment of current market conditions, the prospects for the ski industry and RMH, Federal would underwrite the shares at a price of about $13.50 to the public. She suggested that the offer should be for two million shares to assure a reasonable market for the stock and to meet stock exchange listing requirements.

Solanson also discussed a possible placement of straight preferred stock. Solanson and her colleagues believed that a dividend yield of 6.0 per cent would be needed to attract investors. There were also signs that interest rates could be on the rise as a result of the U.S. Federal Reserve Board action to curb what it perceived to be increasing inflation in the United States. Due to this interest rate uncertainty, the investment banker indicated that the RMH issue might have to carry a "retraction" option that would permit investors to cash in on the preferred stock issue within seven years. The company would incur the same investigation and issuing costs with the preferred as with the common offering.

The Metropolitan Bank indicated that it would provide bridge financing for RMH until the proceeds of any public stock offering were received, offering a rate of prime plus 2.5 per cent.

THE ANALYSIS

After speaking with the various parties, Hayes began her analysis of the financing options. She took from her files a recent Statistics Canada publication showing average ratios for the ski resort and real estate industries (Exhibit 10) to use as a basis for comparison. Hayes also prepared a summary of all the financial market information she had accumulated (Exhibit 11).

Exhibit 1
SKIER VISITS IN CANADA

CANADIAN SKI INDUSTRY FACTS AND STATS • NOVEMBER 1993 • 3

ALPINE SKIER VISITS IN 1992/93 SKI SEASON

- Alpine skier visits is the measure of the number of times skiers visited ski areas, and therefore measures skier volume or frequency in a season (as opposed to the number of people who ski).
- Skier visits for 1992/93 were approximately 21, 860,000.
- Although the 1992/93 ski season got off to a slow start in many regions, excellent weather conditions toward the middle and end of the winter enabled many area operators to reach or exceed participation levels of the previous year.
- Moderate gains or losses in regions are a reflection of local weather conditions, particularly in Alberta where difficult weather conditions have contributed to lower skier visits for two consecutive years.

PROVINCE	# SKI AREAS	1990/91 (000)	1991/92 (000)	1992/93 (000)
ONTARIO*	48	7,900	8,000	8,500
QUEBEC	98	7,400	7,400	7,000
B.C./YUKON	61	3,400	3,500	3,900
ALBERTA	36	2,000	1,900	1,600
MAN./SASK.	18	236	280	160
NEW BRUNSWICK*	5	230	212	202
NOVA SCOTIA*	5	219	338	322
NEWFOUNDLAND*	5	140	172	156
P.E.I.*	1	27	27	20
TOTAL SKIER VISITS	277	21,552	21,829	21,860

TABLE 2.1 ALPINE SKIER VISITS

Source: Regional Ski Area Operator's Associations

Where exact statistics were not available, estimates were applied based on volume of business at major ski centres and industry trends.

PARTICIPATION TRENDS

1. MARKET GROWTH OF ALPINE SKIERS:

- Following the recession years in 1981-83, alpine skiing enjoyed a growth in the size of the skier market annually until 1988 reaching a high of 2,163,000 **active alpine skiers** (those who ski six times per year or more).
- From 1988-1990, the skier market shrank 13% to 1,879,000.
- Ski market shrinkage appears to have halted in the winter of 1990/91 with total active skiers back near the 2 million mark (1,982,000).
- The effect of the current recession appears to be less than in the recession years 1981-1983.

YEAR	NUMBER OF ALPINE SKIERS (12 years+)
82/83	1,741,000
83/84	1,642,000
84/85	1,966,000
85/86	2,088,000
86/87	2,093,000
87/88	2,163,000
88/89	1,968,000
89/90	1,879,000
90/91	1,982,000
91/92	2,064,000

TABLE 3.1 ACTIVE ALPINE SKIERS – TEN YEAR PATTERN

Source: Print Measurement Bureau (Active Alpine Skiers ski more than six x/year)*

Exhibit 2

CANADIAN VACATION INTENTIONS AND SKIER CHARACTERISTICS

CANADIAN SKI INDUSTRY FACTS AND STATS • NOVEMBER 1993 • 4

SKIER TRAVEL

1. CHARACTERISTICS OF SKIER TRAVEL

- 2,098,000 "person-trips" over 80 km were made to go skiing during the first quarter (Jan.-Mar.) of 1990.
- 74% of the trips were to go alpine skiing, 26% of the trips were to go cross country skiing.

TABLE 4.1 CHARACTERISTICS OF DOMESTIC TRAVEL (PERSON TRIPS OVER 800KM) 1990

CHARACTERISTICS	% OF X-COUNTRY SKIERS		% OF ALPINE SKIERS	
Male (over 15)		48%		55%
Female (over 15)		21%		25%
Under 15		31%		20%
Most Frequent Age Groups	under 15	31%	under 15	20%
	25-34	26%	25-34	20%
	35-44	21%	45-54	18%
Most Frequent Household Income	$50-$59,000	22%	$80,000+	15%
Most Frequent One-Way Trip Distance	80-150km	52%	80-150km	45%
	160-319km	26%	160-319km	20%
Most Frequent Province of Origin	Ontario	32%	Ontario	34%
	Alberta	27%	Alberta	24%
	Quebec	23%	Quebec	23%
Most Frequent Province of Destination	Quebec	31%	Quebec	29%
	Ontario	24%	Ontario	27%
	Alberta	20%	Alberta	22%
Most Frequent Trip Duration	0 Nights	40%	0 Nights	37%
	2 Nights	29%	2 Nights	32%
Most Frequent Party Size	2 Persons	36%	2 Persons	36%
	3 Persons	28%	1 Person	23%
Most Frequent Accommodation	Private Cottage	41%	Private Cottage	30%
	Friend/Relative	24%	Hotel	26%
Most Frequent Reported Expenditures	Less Than $200	50%	Less Than $200	50%
	$200-$399	11%	$400-599	11%

Source: 1990 Canadian Travel Survey

2. 1992/93 TRAVEL INTENTIONS:

- 52% of the Canadians surveyed for the Consumer Vacation Travel Intentions Survey in September 1993 indicated that they plan to take a winter vacation.
- Of the 52% planning to take a winter vacation, 18% intend to go downhill skiing.
- Canadians expect to be spending the same (36%), or less (35%) as they did on last years vacation travel.

TABLE 4.2
WINTER VACATION INTENTIONS

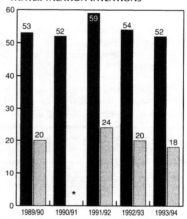

Legend:
- ■ % Intending to take a winter vacation
- ▨ % who plan to take a ski vacation
- * Data not available

Source: Consumer Travel Intentions Survey, Canadian Tourism Research Institute

---

CANADIAN SKI INDUSTRY FACTS AND STATS • NOVEMBER 1993 • 5

TABLE 4.3 TOP 10 1994 WINTER VACATION DESTINATIONS

1. Florida	14%	6. Alberta	6%
2. Quebec	13%	7. Don't Know/NA	4%
3. Ontario	10%	8. Mexico	4%
4. British Columbia	9%	9. Europe	2%
5. Caribbean	8%	10. Arizona	2%

Source: Consumer Travel Intentions Survey, Sept. 1993 Canadian Tourism Research Institute

TABLE 4.4 VACATION SPENDING INTENTIONS
(Do you think you will spend more, the same or less on your vacation in the next six months as compared with the same six months a year ago?)

	Sept. 1989	Sept. 1990	Sept. 1991	Sept. 1992	Sept. 1993
More	52	53	22	27	16
Same	30	26	37	41	36
Less	18	21	41	32	35

Source: Consumer Travel Intentions Survey, Canadian Tourism Research Institute

Exhibit 3

FOREIGN CURRENCY NEEDED TO BUY ONE CANADIAN DOLLAR

YEAR	U.K. STERLING	U.S.$	GERMAN MARK	JAPANESE YEN
1988	.456	.81	1.42	104
1989	.515	.84	1.59	116
1990	.481	.857	1.38	124
1991	.493	.87	1.44	117
1992	.469	.828	1.29	104
Sept. 1993	.501	.757	1.23	80

Source: "Bank of Canada Review", September, 1993.

Exhibit 4		
EXISTING SHAREHOLDERS & PROPOSED FINANCING PLANS		
EXISTING SHARES	**SHARES**	**%**
Murray Derraugh	1,700,000	36.4
David Cross	1,400,000	30.0
Robert Wieler	245,000	5.3
Michael Davis	245,000	5.3
Andy Barstow	145,000	3.1
Janet Christiansen	145,000	3.1
5 Key Employees	785,000	16.8
	4,665,000	100.0
New Shares		
Shares to Pension Fund	145,000	
Shares for Stock Offering	2,000,000	

Exhibit 5						
INCOME STATEMENTS FOR THE YEARS ENDING OCTOBER 31 **'000's (except revenue per visit)**						
	Unaudited **1993**	**1992**	**1991**	**1990**	**1989**	**1988**
Revenue	$41,998	41,789	39,055	32,682	28,476	25,654
Operating Expenses	20,358	19,995	18,769	15,312	12,516	11,288
Earnings from Resort Operations	21,640	21,794	20,286	17,370	15,960	14,366
Administration	3,990	3,800	3,368	2,456	2,232	2,243
Marketing/Promotion	1,439	1,500	1,301	1,298	916	1,144
Miscellaneous	420	500	391	327	252	295
Earnings before Interest, Depreciation, & Amortization (EBITDA)	15,791	15,994	15,226	13,289	12,560	10,684
Depreciation	3,300	3,300	3,300	3,300	3,300	3,300
Amortization of Goodwill	500	500	500	500	500	500
Earnings before Interest & Taxes (EBIT)	11,991	12,194	11,426	9,489	8,760	6,884
Interest	4,528	5,222	6,219	6,918	6,881	6,767
Earnings before Taxes (EBT)	7,463	6,972	5,208	2,571	1,879	118
Tax @ 40%	2,985	2,789	2,083	1,028	752	47
Earnings After Taxes (EAT)	4,478	4,183	3,125	1,543	1,128	71
Dividends	1,343	1,255	937	463	338	21
INCR/(DECR) in Retained Earnings	3,134	2,928	2,187	1,080	789	49
Supplemental Information						
Revenue Growth	0.50%	7.00%	19.50%	14.77%	11.00%	
Skier Visits 000's						
Winter	764	728	746	673	609	570
Summer	22	21	25	24	24	30
Other	66	71	59	61	52	62
Total Visits	852	820	830	758	685	662
Revenue $ Per Visit	$ 49	$ 51	$ 47	$ 43	$ 42	$ 39

Exhibit 6		

BALANCE SHEETS AS AT OCTOBER 31
000's (except ratios)

	1993	1992
Assets:		
Current Assets		
Cash	617	505
Accounts Receivable	3,152	2,900
Inventory-Equipment for Sale	5,722	4,600
Total Current Assets	**9,491**	**8,005**
Property, Buildings, Equipment, Net	49,900	53,200
Goodwill	9,800	10,300
Deferred Development Costs	24,500	21,100
Total Assets	**93,691**	**92,605**
Liabilities:		
Current Liabilities		
Accounts Payable	6,856	6,300
Deferred Revenue	3,188	3,200
Operating Loan	2,993	2,850
Current Portion of Long-term Debt	3,000	3,000
Total Current Liabilities	**16,036**	**15,350**
Long-term Debt	39,455	42,455
Total Liabilities	**55,491**	**57,805**
Deferred Taxes	3,265	3,000
Equity:		
Retained Earnings	16,334	13,200
Paid-In Capital	18,600	18,600
Total Equity	**34,934**	**31,800**
Total Liabilities & Equity	**93,691**	**92,605**
Ratios (1)		
Debt/Equity	1.19	1.39
Debt/Total Capitalization	54.0%	58.0%
Current	0.59	0.52
Interest Coverage	2.65	2.34
Net Profit/Equity and Deferred Taxes	11.7%	12.0%
Gross Margin	51.5%	52.1%

(1)Deferred Taxes Included in Equity

Exhibit 7		

PRO FORMA INCOME STATEMENTS (1) FOR THE YEARS ENDING OCTOBER 31
000's (except revenue per visit)

	1995	**1994**
Revenue	$51,745	$46,618
Operating Expenses	24,837	22,714
Earnings From Resort Operations	26,908	23,904
Administration	4,390	4,190
Marketing/Promotion	2,070	1,450
Miscellaneous	517	466
Earnings Before Interest, Depreciation, & Amortization (EBITDA)	19,931	17,797
Depreciation	4,967	4,133
Amortization of goodwill	500	500
Earnings Before Interest & Taxes (EBIT)	14,465	13,164
Interest	3,993	4,188
Earnings Before Taxes (EBT)	10,471	8,976
Tax @ 40%	4,189	3,591
Earnings After Taxes (EAT)	6,283	5,386
Dividends	1,885	1,616
INCR/(DECR) in Retained Earnings	4,398	3,770

(1)   Financing costs of phase 2 not included. The $25 million capital expansion is assumed to be completed in 1994. All plant and equipment depreciated over 15 years. Half year depreciation taken in 1994.

Supplemental Information

Revenue Growth	11.00%	11.00%
Skier Visits 000's		
Winter	811	783
Summer	23	22
Other	70	67
Total Visits	904	873
Revenue $ Per Visit	$ 57	$ 53

Exhibit 8		

PRO FORMA BALANCE SHEETS (1) AS AT OCTOBER 31 **'000's (except ratios)**		
	1995	**1994**
Assets:		
Current Assets		
Cash	723	583
Accounts Receivable	4,685	3,216
Inventory-Equipment for Sale	9,596	7,293
Total Current Assets	**15,004**	**11,092**
Property, Buildings, Equipment, Net	43,300	46,600
Phase 2 Expansion, Net	22,500	24,167
Goodwill	8,800	9,300
Deferred Development Costs	33,195	29,520
Total Assets	**122,799**	**120,679**
Liabilities:		
Current Liabilities		
Accounts Payable	8,498	7,534
Deferred Revenue	2,927	3,538
Operating Loan	3,300	3,143
Current Portion of Long-term Debt	3,000	3,000
Total Current Liabilities	**17,725**	**17,215**
Long-term Debt	33,455	36,455
Total Liabilities	**51,180**	**53,670**
Deferred Taxes	3,517	3,305
Equity:		
Retained Earnings	24,502	20,104
Paid-In Capital	18,600	18,600
Total Equity	**43,102**	**38,704**
New Financing	25,000	25,000
Total Liabilities & Equity	**122,799**	**120,679**
Ratios (2)		
Phase 2 with Debt		
Debt/Equity	1.39	1.61
Debt/Total Capitalization	58%	62%
Phase 2 with Equity		
Debt/Equity	0.56	0.64
Debt/Total Capitalization	36%	39%
Current	0.85	0.64
Interest Coverage	3.62	3.14
Net Profit/Equity and Deferred Taxes	13.5%	12.8%
Gross Margin	52.0%	51.3%

(1) Financing Costs of Phase 2 not included.
(2) Deferred Taxes included in equity.

Exhibit 9
LONG-TERM DEBT **AS AT OCTOBER 31, 1993**

Instrument	Amount	Charge
TERM LOAN- Life Insurance	$25,680,000	First Fixed & Specific Charge on Developed Property & Projects
TERM LOAN-Bank	$13,775,000	Term Credit Facility General Security Agreement & Real Estate Debenture
	$39,455,000	

Exhibit 10
INDUSTRY RATIOS[4]

	Ski Facilities Average	Hotels/resorts Average
Current Ratio	.4	.6
Debt/Equity	.9	4.2
Interest Coverage (EBIT/Interest)	2.6	1.1
Debt Ratio	.4	.8
Net Profit/Equity	7.1	3.5
Gross Margin	50.7	43.3

[4]Adapted from Statistics Canada, CANSIM DATABASE website http://cansima.statcan.ca/cgi-win/CNSMCGI.EXE

	Exhibit 11			
	MARKET DATA			
	October 1993	**1992**	**1991**	**1990**
Government Of Canada Long-term Bonds[5]	7.35%	8.33%	9.12%	11.15%
Canadian Corporate Long-term Bonds[6]	8.25%	9.57%	10.17%	12.29%
Toronto Stock Exchange '300' Index October 31 High	4255	3336	3515	3081
	1993			
Average P/E Multiples[7] (Real Estate/resorts)	18.8x			

[5]Statistics Canada, CANSIM DATABASE.
[6]Statistics Canada, CANSIM DATABASE.
[7]Bloomberg.

part five

Cost of Capital

TELUS: THE COST OF CAPITAL

OVERVIEW

Barb Williams and Rick Thomas, two managers from service firms, were attending a weeklong executive education course at a well-known business school in November 2001. Both had read an article dealing with the cost of capital as preparation for the next day's classroom session. As they vigorously discussed the concept, it became clear that they had several differences of opinion. Their assignment was to calculate the cost of capital for Telus Corporation (Telus). Telus was a leading telecommunications company providing a variety of data, voice, and wireless services to both businesses and consumers. The data they gathered are presented in Exhibits 1-5.

Rick: What we really want to know is the hurdle rate that Telus should use for its capital investment projects.

Barb: Yes, and we should decide whether the rate ought to be different for different types of projects, such as the purchase of labor-saving equipment or the building of fibre optics underground telecommunications corridors.

Rick: Looking at the balance sheet, I can see that the firm raises funds from quite a few different sources. The best place to start is to look at the cost of the capital raised from each of these sources. The current liabilities except for the "short-term obligations" are mostly trade credit, so their cost is zero.

Richard Ivey School of Business
The University of Western Ontario

Ivey

Professor Stephen R. Foerster revised this case (originally prepared by Professors James E. Hatch and David C. Shaw) solely to provide material for class discussion. The authors do not intend to illustrate either effective or ineffective handling of a managerial situation. The authors may have disguised certain names and other identifying information to protect confidentiality.

Barb: Well, the long-term debt isn't interest free, and some of it is quite expensive. For example, the 2021 Telus bonds were issued with a 10.65 per cent coupon. The newspaper says that long-term government bonds are yielding 5.82 per cent.

Rick: But shouldn't we be using current yields that are much lower than the firm paid in the past? My calculations tell me that based on an average coupon rate of 11.00 per cent on all of the long-term Telus bond issues outstanding, with average maturities of about 15 years and average asking prices of about $118.00 the current average yield is actually 8.81 per cent.[1]

Barb: Notice that Telus borrows money from the banks and through the short-term money market as well. Some of its short-term debt is obtained by issuing commercial paper, but most of it is from bank borrowings.

Rick: Well, the prime rate from banks is 4.50 per cent and I suppose that Telus might qualify for the prime rate wouldn't they? The three-month commercial paper rate is extremely low, currently 2.28 per cent, which is even more attractive to the firm. In case we need more information, I also noted that the current rate on 91-day, government treasury bills is 2.15 per cent.

Barb: Telus was able to issue two major preferred stocks at a cost of only 5.00 per cent in the past. That's a lot cheaper than the debt, even though about $4.00 for every $100 par value share went to the underwriter.

Rick: The two major preferred issues outstanding were issued at par values of $100 per share and $25 per share respectively, and are currently trading to yield about 5.90 per cent each. The company has not issued preferreds for a long time and may not intend to issue them again. Preferreds have a higher after-tax cost than debt according to our instructor, and that makes them less attractive for most issuers.

Barb: Well, if that's true, maybe we can ignore the preferred in our calculations.

Rick: Calculating the cost of common stock is reasonably straightforward. Since the common shareholders are getting regular dividends, we should use the dividend yield.

Barb: No, no! All of the earnings after the dividends to the preferred shareholders belong to the common shareholder, not just the dividends. We should use the earnings-per-share divided by the market price.

Rick: What about issuing costs? Although the current stock price has dropped to around $25.00 per share, Telus would likely have to pay the underwriter and others about $1.75 per share to issue new stock at this price.

Barb: It's not likely that Telus will raise more than one-quarter of its new equity by issuing stock. The rest of the new equity will be retained earnings, which have no cost.

Rick: Retained earnings aren't free capital. They belong to the shareholders. Surely they must expect some type of return!

Barb: I notice from the firm's financial statements that the return on common equity for the company was 7.36 per cent in 2000 and 8.17 per cent in 1999. I realize this is an accounting rate of return computed on the book value of the equity, but I wonder if it can be used to compute the cost of equity capital?

Rick: I would guess that the funds generated by depreciation are free and they are available in large amounts. For example, last year's earnings were over $457 million after deduction of preferred dividends. Depreciation was over $1 billion. Capital expenditures for next year are expected to be about $1.5 billion, so perhaps the bulk of the money can come from depreciation.

---

[1] After allowing for a fee to the underwriter, the cost to the long term debt financing would be 9.31 per cent.

Barb: The assigned reading mentioned the beta of a stock. The beta is calculated by regressing the return for Telus against the return on the market index. I went to the library's Bloomberg system and found the beta, estimated based on three years of monthly data ending November 2001, to be 0.75 with an R-squared of 0.13. The beta seems to be an index of the riskiness of the common stock, but it has to be converted into a required return somehow. What I don't understand is how that return compares with the one we get by simply dividing the earnings-per-share by the stock price.

Rick: What do we do once we have the costs of all sources of financing? Do we just take their average?

Barb: Somehow, the average cost doesn't make sense to me. I think we should just use the cost of the next source of financing. For example, Telus expects to issue $30 million in debt next month. Maybe the interest rate on that issue should be used as the hurdle rate for any new projects that are undertaken with those funds.

Rick: After we get this cost of capital, would you advise Telus to use the net-present value method or the internal-rate of return method to evaluate projects?

Barb: I don't think it matters. The two methods both give the same answer.

Rick: Well, let's get on with this calculation. We have a long night ahead of us. I wish someone would just "Telus" the cost of capital!

Exhibit 1

BALANCE SHEET AS OF DECEMBER 31, 2000[1]   **($ millions)**

ASSETS

Current Assets	$ 1,749.0
Capital Assets (Net)	11,531.0
Deferred Charges	216.0
Future Income Taxes	1,024.0
Leases Receivable	81.0
Investments	18.0
Goodwill	1,795.0
Other	1.0
TOTAL ASSETS	**$ 16,415.0**

LIABILITIES AND EQUITY

Current Liabilities:

Account Payable and Accrued Liabilities	$ 1,326.0
Short-term Obligations [2]	5,033.0
Other Short-term Liabilities	310.0
Total Current Liabilities	6,669.0
Long-Term Debt	3,047.0
Other Long-term Liabilities	281.0
Preferred Shares	70.0
Common Shareholders' Equity	
Common Shares [3]	4,785.0
Retained Earnings	1,563.0
Total Common Shareholders' Equity	6,348.0
TOTAL LIABILITIES AND EQUITY	**$ 16,415.0**

[1]This balance sheet has been simplified somewhat for the ease of discussion.
[2]These were several notes, all of which expired within one year, carrying an average interest rate of 5.86 per cent.
[3]At the end of 2000, there were approximately 287 million common shares outstanding.

Exhibit 2
INCOME STATEMENT FOR YEAR ENDED DECEMBER 31, 2000[1] **($ Millions)**

Revenues	$ 6,433
Operating Expenses	5,156
Net Operating Earnings	1,277
Other Income	30
Interest Expense	317
Earnings Before Taxes, Non-controlling Interest and Goodwill Amortization	990
Income Taxes	496
Earnings Before Non-controlling Interest and Goodwill Amortization	494
Non-controlling Interest	9
Income Before Goodwill Amortization	485
Goodwill Amortization	24
NET INCOME	461
Preferred Share Dividends	4
Common Share Earnings	$ 457

[1]This income statement has been simplified somewhat for the ease of discussion.

Exhibit 3

SELECTED DATA ON TELUS COMMON STOCK, 1969 TO 2000

Year	Common EPS	Common DIV/SH	Closing Stock Price Dec. 31	Total Return[1]
1969	0.51	0.30	14.40	7.20%
1970	0.51	0.30	12.80	-9.03%
1971	0.54	0.32	13.00	4.06%
1972	0.61	0.32	11.30	-10.62%
1973	0.58	0.32	9.80	-10.44%
1974	0.50	0.40	9.40	0.00%
1975	0.69	0.42	11.00	21.49%
1976	0.74	0.46	13.13	23.55%
1977	0.77	0.50	15.25	19.95%
1978	0.78	0.54	17.00	15.02%
1979	0.96	0.58	17.00	3.41%
1980	1.02	0.60	17.00	3.53%
1981	1.11	0.71	15.25	-6.12%
1982	1.05	0.80	17.25	18.36%
1983	1.18	0.80	22.00	32.17%
1984	1.03	0.83	22.00	3.77%
1985	1.10	0.86	26.50	24.36%
1986	1.23	0.86	27.50	7.02%
1987	1.34	0.87	26.25	-1.38%
1988	1.45	0.91	28.13	10.63%
1989	1.58	0.95	18.00	-32.63%
1990	1.72	1.02	19.25	12.61%
1991	1.78	1.10	22.88	24.57%
1992	1.78	1.15	19.63	-9.18%
1993	1.81	1.19	25.38	35.35%
1994	1.88	1.23	24.00	-0.59%
1995	2.00	1.27	25.00	9.46%
1996	1.90	1.31	29.65	23.84%
1997	2.29	1.35	44.50	54.64%
1998	(1.45)	1.40	41.95	-2.58%
1999	1.46	1.40	35.15	-12.87%
2000	1.85	1.40	41.55	22.19%

[1] $r_t = (D_t + P_t - P_{t-1})/P_{t-1}$

Where: r_t =   *Return of year t*
D_t =   *Dividend in year t*
P_t =   *Price of common stock at the end of year t*
P_{t-1} =   *Price at beginning of year 1*

	Exhibit 4		
	MARKET INDEX, SELECTED DATA 1973 TO 2000		
Year	**Index Value Dec. 31**	**Dividend Paid Index Stocks**	**Total Return (1)**
1973	1,207.52	38.28	-0.51%
1974	885.85	49.16	-22.57%
1975	973.78	48.01	15.35%
1976	1,012.10	47.37	8.80%
1977	1,059.59	50.12	9.64%
1978	1,310.00	57.90	29.10%
1979	1,813.20	72.35	43.93%
1980	2,268.70	83.03	29.70%
1981	1,954.20	87.74	-9.99%
1982	1,985.00	80.00	5.67%
1983	2,552.30	82.18	32.72%
1984	2,400.30	88.81	-2.48%
1985	2,900.60	90.79	24.63%
1986	3,066.20	91.68	8.87%
1987	3,160.10	97.33	6.24%
1988	3,390.00	113.90	10.88%
1989	3,969.80	129.02	20.91%
1990	3,256.80	124.74	-14.82%
1991	3,512.40	111.69	11.28%
1992	3,350.40	102.19	-1.70%
1993	4,321.40	97.66	31.90%
1994	4,213.60	100.71	-0.16%
1995	4,713.50	107.00	14.40%
1996	5,927.03	108.46	28.05%
1997	6,699.44	109.87	14.89%
1998	6,485.94	107.67	-1.58%
1999	8,413.75	110.22	31.42%
2000	8,933.68	112.56	7.52%
Arithmetic Average Return, 1973 to 2000			11.86%

[1] $r_t = (D_t + V_t - V_{t-1})/V_{t-1}$
Where: Rt = Rate of return earned by the Index stocks during period
$DIVt$ = Dividend adjusted to Index paid on Index stocks during period t
Vt = Value of Index at the end of period t
$Vt-$ = Value of Index at beginning of period t

Exhibit 5

AVERAGE ANNUAL RETURNS IN NORTH AMERICAN CAPITAL MARKETS OVER THE PERIOD 1926 TO 2000

	U.S.		Canada	
	Arithmetic Average	Geometric Average	Arithmetic Average	Geometric Average
Long-Term Government Bonds	5.7%	5.3%	6.4%	6.0%
Equities (Market)	13.0%	11.0%	11.8%	10.2%

Source: L. Booth, "Equity Market Risk Premiums in the U.S. and Canada." Reprinted by permission from the Fall 2001 edition of <u>Canadian Investment Review</u>. Copyright Rogers Media Inc.

SCOTT'S HOSPITALITY INC.–EVA

Scott's corporate mission is to build shareholder wealth, over time, by operating profitably as an international consumer services company. We continue to seek opportunities for growth through expansion of existing operations and by strategic acquisitions of well managed operations in our core businesses. — *1995 Annual Report*

In May 1995, the management group of Scott's Hospitality Inc. (SHI) was reflecting on the Toronto-based conglomerate's financial performance for the fiscal year just ended on April 30th. Management felt that, through a series of acquisitions and divestitures over the past few years, the organization had been refocused for continued growth and success in three core businesses, all of which had posted strong results in the past year. However, the recent market performance of SHI's shares, which traded on the Toronto and Montreal stock exchanges, had been extremely disappointing. Investors seemed unimpressed by a much improved financial performance in 1995. SHI's share price had only rebounded slightly to $7.88 from a five-year low of $6.75 per share. Bonita Then, senior vice-president and chief financial officer (CFO), knew that the return on capital was too low and that there had been too little ongoing focus on capital employed.

In the fall of 1994, Bonita was intrigued by the concept of Economic Value Added ("EVA"[TM]).[1] Bonita knew that EVA correlated more closely to market price than other traditional measures of share

---

[1]EVA is a registered trademark of Stern Stewart & Co., New York.

Richard Ivey School of Business
The University of Western Ontario

IVEY

John Manning and John McCartney prepared this case under the supervision of Professor James E. Hatch solely to provide material for class discussion. The authors do not intend to illustrate either effective or ineffective handling of a managerial situation. The authors may have disguised certain names and other identifying information to protect confidentiality.

performance. Championed by such U.S. corporate giants as Coca-Cola, Quaker Oats and Briggs & Stratton, EVA was a measure of financial performance that focused on maximizing shareholder value. The concept of EVA had been developed by G. Bennett Stewart III and Joel Stern of the New York-based consulting firm, Stern Stewart & Co. Their book, *The Quest for Value*, and a more recent publication, *Valuation*, by McKinsey & Company, were rapidly gaining popularity in the financial community. Both focused on economic value as the truest measure of corporate performance, particularly where multi-business organizations were concerned. Since Bonita and the rest of the management team were firmly committed to maximizing shareholder value, she wondered whether such an assessment of Scott's on both a divisional and consolidated basis might help the company focus on what really drove shareholder value.

CORPORATE HISTORY—SCOTT'S HOSPITALITY INC.

Established in 1937, Scott's evolved into an international consumer services company with operations in Canada, the United States and Great Britain. The Company's focus was on branded consumer products and services with mass appeal that could be replicated in many locations. Following the 1993 divestiture of Black's Photo Corporation to Fuji Photo Film Canada Inc., the Company's core businesses were organized into three divisions: Food Services, Transportation and Hotels. At year end 1995, the Company employed approximately 18,300 people.

FOOD SERVICES DIVISION

Scott's largest division, Food Services, was one of the premier restaurant and food service operators in North America. The Company was the largest Kentucky Fried Chicken (KFC) franchisee in the world operating over 400 of the 840 KFC restaurants in Canada. These were located primarily in Ontario and Quebec. Scott's had been involved with KFC (owned by PepsiCo) for over 30 years and was currently operating under a recently re-negotiated licensing arrangement which was due to expire in December 2003. After significant cash outlays since 1989 to upgrade its KFC stores, Scott's was on schedule to fulfill the capital expenditure requirements set out in its franchise agreement with PepsiCo. The Company also operated a series of Highway Travel Centre concept restaurants along major 400 series highways in Ontario.

Through the acquisition of a number of oriental fast food businesses in the 1980s, Scott's built the largest North American chain of Chinese fast food restaurants. These restaurants were consolidated under the Manchu Wok brand name. Manchu Wok had reported very poor performance in recent years resulting in a recent management decision to write off $31.4 million of goodwill.

The Company also operated an established chain of home delivery and take-away pizza outlets in Great Britain under the Perfect Pizza banner. Perfect Pizza operated a network of over 200 restaurants predominantly located in the south of England. Perfect Pizza had recently pioneered the 2-for-1 pizza in the UK.

The performance of the Food Services Division was primarily driven by two measures: the traffic volume per store and the average expenditure per customer once in the store. A number of recent promotions, driven by the KFC organization, had been aimed at increasing these measures. An example of this was the MegaMeal, priced at C$19.99, which was aimed at increasing revenue per customer. Exhibit 4 outlines key segmented operating and financial data for the Food Services division. The capital employed in the Food Services Division had increased in recent years due to significant renovations and enhancements in the KFC restaurants and to acquisitions in the Chinese Food and Pizza businesses.

TRANSPORTATION DIVISION

Scott's Transportation Division was the third largest school bus operator in North America (behind Laidlaw Inc. and Ryder System) and was organized as Charterways Transportation Limited in Canada and National School Bus Service Inc. in the United States. These businesses provided bus passenger services to public authorities (eg., school boards and municipalities) on a long-term contract basis. National operated over 3,600 vehicles in Missouri, New York, Illinois, Michigan, Pennsylvania and New Jersey, while Charterways operated primarily in Ontario.

In 1995, Scott's acquired an additional 476 vehicles and associated routes. These acquisitions were primarily in the United States and resulted in a $25.8 million (12.1%) increase in revenue over 1994 for the Transportation Division. The Division actively sought growth through route acquisitions and actively marketed its services to school boards that did not currently use private contractors. The process of public boards switching to privately contracted busing services was known in the industry as conversion.

The outlook for growth in the school bus segment had been mixed. Budget pressures on municipalities and regional governments had squeezed margins for private operators. In addition, the school bus industry was considered mature since North American school age demographics had been flat since the mid-1970s. Although 95 per cent of the school buses in Ontario were operated by private contractors, only about one-third of U.S. school buses were operated by private contractors (with the remainder run by school boards). This presented a significant opportunity for growth via conversion. Segmented operating and financial information on the Transportation Division is available in Exhibit 4.

HOTELS DIVISION

The Hotels Division of Scott's Hospitality comprised 12 full-service hotels and four limited-service hotels throughout England, Scotland and Wales. In 1991, Scott's terminated the management contract for its hotels with Holiday Inn Worldwide in favour of a management arrangement with Marriott Corporation. In 1992, all of the properties were converted and branded to either Marriott or Courtyard hotels. The newly constructed Leeds Marriott Hotel celebrated its official opening in June 1994.

The continued strengthening of the UK hotel market resulted in a strong increase in occupancy, average room rates, and thus revenue and earnings for the Division. Scott's UK Hotels were particularly sensitive to the North American traffic in Britain, targeting the North American Marriott loyal guest, who spent on average 30 per cent more per visit than other guests.

Guidance from Marriott with respect to the design, construction and operation of the hotels was available to Scott's. Marriott published and distributed directories and pamphlets for use in its system and coordinated advertising on an international scale through use of radio, television and other media. Scott's hotels also benefited from being part of Marriott's computerized reservation system, which allowed advance reservations for accommodation at all Marriott locations worldwide.

In exchange for the license to use the Marriott name and system, Scott's paid fees based on a percentage of gross revenues attributable to the rental of guest rooms at the hotel. Each of the 16 hotels operated under a separate Marriott/Courtyard license typically fixed for a term of 20 years. Scott's also owned the exclusive rights to develop three- and four-star Marriott and Courtyard hotels in Great Britain for the next 10 years. Segmented operating and financial information on the Hotels Division is available in Exhibit 4.

CORPORATE PERFORMANCE TO DATE

Based on traditional performance parameters, SHI's financial performance in recent years had been reasonably good. Management felt that a number of positive trends, particularly since 1993, suggested a bright future for the company:

- Positive sales growth over the past three years.

- Impressive increases in operating cash flow each year since 1992.

- 1995 operating cash flow target was exceeded by $9.5 million and was 12 per cent higher than in 1994.

- 1995 cash flow targets for each division were exceeded, capital expenditure came in under budget and financial (interest) expenses were lower than forecast.

- Cash flow from continuing operations had improved steadily in recent years reaching a five-year high of $109.5 million in 1995.

- Long-term debt had been reduced substantially in the past three years resulting in very acceptable debt/equity and interest coverage ratios.

- Net earnings improved by 8.5 per cent in fiscal 1995 vs. 1994 (in face of an objective of 10 per cent growth) while net operating earnings (before non-recurring items, after tax) increased by 21.5 per cent.

- Net earnings per share were $0.53, an 8.5 per cent increase from the $0.49 recorded in fiscal 1994. These results included a $4.2 million increase (roughly 70 percent) in income taxes related to recurring earnings and a $2.2 million non-recurring loss on a disposition.

- Net operating earnings increased by 21.5 per cent from $0.47 to $0.57 per share.

- Return on equity had improved steadily in recent years to a three-year high of 8.5 per cent.

- Exhibit 1 contains more detailed performance data.

SHI MARKET PERFORMANCE

Despite management's belief that SHI had shown improved financial fundamentals and profitability in recent years, the Company's stock performance had been abysmal. From a record high of $19.00 per share in July of 1991, the shares had been in a steady decline closing fiscal 1995 at $7.88 per share. Over the same period, the TSE 300 market index rose from 3,705 to 4,279, an increase of 16 per cent, and the TSE Consumer Products Sub-Index rose from 24,065 to 52,534, an increase of 118 per cent.

In contrast, Scott's share price decline of 59 per cent represented an erosion of equity market capitalization from over $1.1 billion to $470 million. In fiscal 1993 alone, the market value of shareholders' equity dropped by an incredible $450 million. Exhibit 2 shows SHI's market performance since 1990 and Exhibit 3 details the market capitalization values and fluctuations over the same period. Exhibit 6 provides recent research reports written by an investment dealer concerning the attractiveness of an investment in SHI stock.

ECONOMIC VALUE ADDED (EVA)

EVA is defined by Stern Stewart as an estimate of a firm's true economic profit after subtracting the cost of all capital employed. EVA is a period measure of how much value has been created or destroyed through a firm's operations over a specified period. The concept of EVA was based on the desire to develop a performance measure that would properly account for all the ways in which shareholder value could be created or destroyed. EVA was touted as a comprehensive management system that could be used to tie together capital budgeting, financial planning, goal setting, performance measurement, shareholder communication and incentive compensation. According to Stewart, EVA should be adopted by any firm whose focus was to maximize the wealth of its shareholders.

DECISION SUMMARY

Based on the segmented operating and cost of capital information available for the Food Services, Transportation and Hotel divisions, Bonita felt it would be possible to calculate EVA results for SHI. She also felt it would be interesting to do this analysis on both a stand-alone basis for the segmented businesses as well as on a consolidated basis for SHI. Exhibit 5 provides the additional segmented operating data required for this analysis. Management hoped that the analysis would lend useful insight into whether or not each division created or destroyed shareholder value based on the EVA methodology. Perhaps such an evaluation would help management to make strategic capital allocation and restructuring decisions consistent with the corporate mission of "building shareholder wealth."

Exhibit 1

CONSOLIDATED STATEMENT OF EARNINGS For the years ended April 30 ($000)

	1993	1994	1995
Sales			
Food Services	$ 471,090	$ 480,485	$ 462,201
Transportation	213,962	213,019	238,790
Hotels	100,204	116,087	144,658
	$ 785,256	$ 809,591	$ 845,649
Operating Earnings			
Food Services	24,584	17,926	20,371
Transportation	38,316	37,385	40,134
Hotels	($ 3,472)	8,373	16,500
	59,428	63,684	77,005
Net financial expense	($ 27,002)	($ 29,497)	($ 32,591)
Net gain (loss) on disposition and restructuring	0	280	($2,244)
Earnings before income taxes	32,426	34,467	42,170
Income taxes	1,166	5,242	10,454
Net earnings from continuing operations	31,260	29,225	31,716
Discontinued operations	($ 31,253)		
Earnings per share (continuing operations)	$ 0.52	$ 0.49	$ 0.53
Capital Expenditure	139,294	82,302	86,287
Total Assets	977,680	976,701	901,255
Net long-term debt	418,999	341,807	308,792
Shareholders' Equity	370,159	391,065	409,338
Return on Average Shareholders' Equity	8.20%	7.30%	8.50%
Return on Average Assets	3.2%	3.0%	3.4%
Net debt: equity ratio	1.13	0.87	0.75
Interest coverage	2.2	2.2	2.4
Per share Data			
Earnings before non-recurring items	0.52	0.47	0.57
Net earnings	0.00	0.49	0.53
Cash flow from operations	1.58	1.64	1.83
Dividends declared	0.26	0.26	0.26
Book value	6.20	6.55	6.85
Share Price (Year end)	$ 9.25	$ 7.00	$ 7.88
52 Week High/Low	$15.00/$9.25	$11.13/$6.88	$8.88/$6.75
Shares Outstanding (thousands)	59,730	59,725	59,725

Exhibit 1 (continued)			
CONSOLIDATED BALANCE SHEETS **As at April 30 (in thousands)**			

	1993	1994	1995
ASSETS			
Current			
Cash and short-term investments	$ 74,099	$ 124,346	$ 54,665
Accounts receivable	55,635	62,897	56,297
Taxes recoverable	5,195	16,650	15,377
Inventories	21,498	8,069	9,001
Prepaid expenses	15,937	18,023	12,746
	172,364	229,985	148,086
Investments	14,841	16,027	10,287
Land, buildings and equipment	652,681	629,902	638,647
Other assets	137,794	100,787	104,205
	$ 977,680	$ 976,701	$ 901,225
LIABILITIES AND SHAREHOLDERS' EQUITY			
Current			
Accounts payable and accrued charges	$ 89,149	$ 92,534	$ 95,212
Dividends payable	7,777	7,780	7,779
Long-term debt payable within one year	1,389	1,449	1,367
	$ 98,315	$ 101,763	$ 104,358
Long-term debt	491,709	464,704	362,090
Deferred income taxes	17,497	19,169	25,439
Shareholders' equity	370,159	391,065	409,338
	$ 977,680	$ 976,701	$ 901,225

Exhibit 2

SHARE PERFORMANCE AND TRADING VOLUME

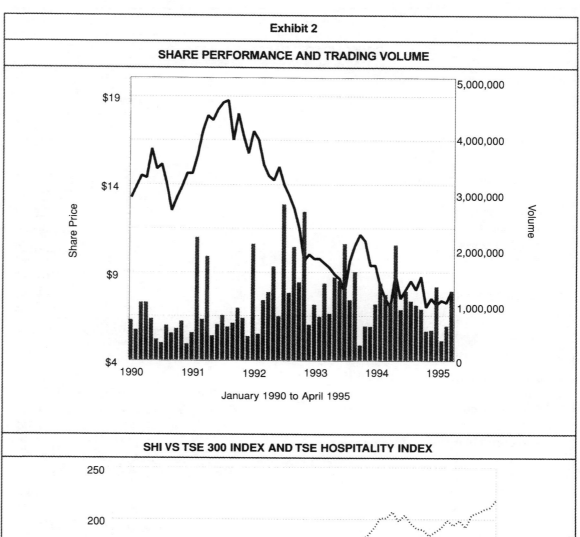

January 1990 to April 1995

SHI VS TSE 300 INDEX AND TSE HOSPITALITY INDEX

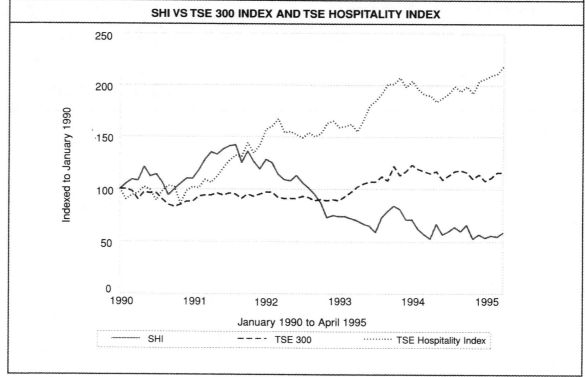

January 1990 to April 1995

———— SHI   – – – TSE 300   ·········· TSE Hospitality Index

Exhibit 3

MARKET VALUATION SUMMARY
(in thousands except per share data)

	at April 30					
	1990	1991	1992	1993	1994	1995
Share Price	$14.38	$17.88	$10.25	$9.25	$7.00	$7.88
52 Week Hi/Lo	$8.88/$6.75	$17.88/$12.00	$19.00/$14.13	$15.00/$9.25	$11.13/$6.88	$8.88/$6.75
Shares outstanding (fully diluted)	59,697	59,717	59,730	59,730	59,725	59,725
Market Capitalization (Year End)	$858,144	$1,067,441	$612,233	$552,503	$418,075	$470,334
Market Capitalization Change (Year-over-Year)	-	$209,297	($455,209)	($59,730)	($134,428)	$52,259

Exhibit 4								
SEGMENTED INFORMATION								

By Business Segment

(in thousands)	Consolidated		Food Services		Transportation		Hotels	
	1994	1995	1994	1995	1994	1995	1994	1995
Sales	$809,591	$845,649	$480,485	$462,201	$213,019	$238,790	$116,087	$144,658
Segmented operating earnings	63,684	77,005	17,926	20,371	37,385	40,134	8,373	16,500
Net financial expense	(29,497)	(32,591)						
Net gain (loss) on dispositions	280	(2,244)						
Income taxes	(5,242)	(10,454)						
Net earnings	29,225	31,716						
Identifiable assets								
Current assets and investments	72,586	72,975	24,798	18,362	35,119	40,563	12,669	14,050
Land, buildings, and equipment	625,276	638,647	190,221	188,862	164,852	171,692	270,203	278,093
Other assets	97,963	102,219	62,033	65,241	30,066	32,847	5,864	4,131
	795,825	813,841	277,052	272,465	230,037	245,102	288,736	296,274
Corporate assets	174,702	87,384						
Discontinued assets	6,174	--						
Total assets	976,701	901,225						
Capital expenditures	82,302	86,287	29,851	30,039	28,694	47,244	23,757	9,004
Depreciation and amortization	$ 68,109	$ 75,264	$ 24,011	$ 26,752	$ 32,246	$ 35,144	$ 11,852	$ 13,368

By Geographic Segment

(in thousands)	Consolidated		Food Services		Transportation		Hotels	
	1994	1995	1994	1995	1994	1995	1994	1995
Sales	$809,591	$845,649	$471,113	$446,000	$192,280	$221,355	$146,198	$178,294
Segmented operating earnings	63,684	77,005	32,751	37,688	23,623	24,746	7,310	14,571
Net financial expense	(29,497)	(32,591)						
Net gain (loss) on dispositions	280	(2,244)						
Income taxes	(5,242)	(10,454)						
Net earnings	29,225	31,716						
Identifiable assets								
Current assets and investments	72,586	72,975	20,898	15,206	34,792	38,586	16,896	19,183
Land, buildings, and equipment	625,276	638,647	237,841	232,550	113,257	123,544	274,178	282,553
Other assets	97,963	102,219	50,913	50,502	27,347	32,364	19,703	19,353
	795,825	813,841	$309,652	$298,258	$175,396	$194,494	$310,777	$321,089
Corporate assets	174,702	87,384						
Discontinued assets	6,174	--						
Total assets	$976,701	$901,225						

Exhibit 5		

ADDITIONAL SEGMENTED FINANCIAL INFORMATION

1. Depreciation and Amortization

Depreciation expenses for Scott's were as follows:

($ 000's)	**1993**	**1994**	**1995**
Food Services Division	18,466	21,203	23,681
Transportation Division	27,439	29,056	31,723
Hotels Division	10,681	10,186	11,635

Amortization expenses by division were as follows:

($ 000's)	**1993**	**1994**	**1995**
Food Services Division	2,530	2,808	3,071
Transportation Division	3,270	3,190	3,421
Hotels Division	1,411	1,666	1,733
SHI Consolidated*	8,835	7,665	8,226

*   Totals do not match due to divestitures of Black's Photography and other businesses.

2. Gains (Losses) on sale of assets

A number of accounting adjustments had been made related to asset sales.

($ 000's) Gains (Losses)	**1993**	**1994**	**1995**
Food Services Division	395	294	(624)
Transportation Division	2,403	1,281	1,157
Hotels Division	—	—	—

Exhibit 5 (continued)

---

3. Lease Commitments

Scott's Hospitality had significant non-cancellable operating leases primarily related to buses in the Transportation Division, properties in the Hotels Division and KFC and Manchu Wok store locations in the Food Services Division. Segmented, non-capitalized annual lease commitments could be broken down as follows:

($ 000's)	1993	1994	1995
Food Services Division	21,225	23,910	22,269
Transportation Division	2,779	3,041	1,637
Hotels Division	4,919	5,258	5,510

For purposes of calculating EVA, Stern Stewart would recommend capitalizing annual lease commitments five years out discounted at the firm's cost of secured indebtedness. This proxy asset value should be included in the firm's invested capital and a financing charge for that capital should be accounted for in the calculation of NOPAT. Scott's employed 9 per cent as a cost of debt.

4. Income Taxes

SHI had significant operations in Canadian, U.S. and U.K. tax jurisdictions. As a result, the company earned significant income in foreign jurisdictions with lower tax rates than would be applicable under Canadian federal and provincial tax legislation. However, for the purposes of valuation and new project investment/divestiture analysis, SHI management decided to use a Canadian statutory tax rate of 40 per cent for the purposes of EVA calculations.

5. Share Capital

	1994	1995
Class C shares	22,960,114	22,938,624
Subordinated voting shares	36,765,266	36,786,756
Total shares outstanding	59,725,380	59,725,380
Options outstanding — Sub-voting	584,546	829,546

Each class C share entitled the owner to one hundred votes while subordinated shares were entitled to one vote per share.

Exhibit 5 (continued)

6.   Inventory Valuation

All inventories in the various businesses were valued based on the FIFO (first-in, first-out) valuation methodology.

7.   Additional Segmented Financial Information

Additional financial information, segmented by division, was as follows:

Food Services

($ 000's)	1993	1994	1995
Accounts Receivable	12,910	7,683	5,209
Prepaids	12,208	12,135	8,132
Inventory	4,566	4,980	5,021
Fixed Assets at NBV	198,355	190,221	188,862
Intangibles at NBV	64,863	62,034	65,240
Accum. Amort.	14,809	17,049	16,753
Accounts Payable	27,162	33,279	31,945
Other Taxes Payable	4,947	5,016	5,062

Transportation Division

($ 000's)	1993	1994	1995
Accounts Receivable	24,841	29,627	34,980
Prepaids	3,135	3,691	3,130
Inventory	1,665	1,800	2,452
Fixed Assets at NBV	162,883	164,852	171,692
Intangibles at NBV	32,380	30,066	32,847
Accum. Amort	11,580	15,470	18,393
Accounts Payable	22,886	26,091	33,511
Other Taxes Payable	635	461	797

Exhibit 5 (continued)

Hotels Division

($ 000's)	1993	1994	1995
Accounts Receivable	7,785	9,935	11,555
Prepaids	1,473	1,467	966
Inventory	1,126	1,267	1,528
Fixed Assets at NBV	255,340	270,203	278,093
Goodwill at NBV	7,315	5,863	4,132
Accum Goodwill Amort	1,851	2,824	4,596
Accounts Payable	13,938	21,073	19,420
Other Taxes Payable	0	0	0

---

8. Statement Consolidation

Due in part to assets and liabilities held within the corporate group as well as discontinued operations in unrelated businesses, the aggregation of the financial results of the Food, Transportation and Hotels Divisions (noted above) does not necessarily reconcile to the consolidated statements of earnings and balance sheet in Exhibit 1.

9. Weighted Average Cost of Capital (WACC) rates

Weighted average cost of capital rates on a division basis were calculated by the treasury group at SHI as follows:

	1993	1994	1995
Food Services	13%	12.5%	11%
Transportation	11%	10.5%	9%
Hotels	16%	14.5%	12%
SHI Consolidated	13.5%	11.5%	10.5%

Exhibit 6

RBC DOMINION SECURITIES

January 18, 1995

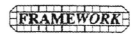

FRAMEWORK

SCOTT'S HOSPITALITY INC.

(SRC - $7.50)

EPS (Trailing 12 M)	$0.52	Trailing P/E	14.4X
ROE (Trailing 12 M)	7.75%	ROE (5 Yr. Avg.)	13.4%
Indicated Dividend	$0.26	Dividend Yield	3.5%
Shares Outstanding(MM)	59.73	Public Float ($MM)	261.95
Average Monthly Volume (000)	903		

Key Shareholders   Fairwater Capital Corp: 8.4% of Sub. Voting;
45.1% of Class C
Langar Co. Ltd.: 4.6% or Sub. Voting; 19.2% of Class C
Caisse de Depot: 10.2% of Sub. voting; 6.5% of Class C

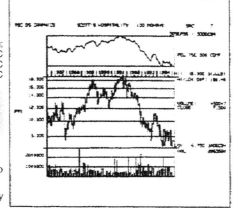

RATINGS			
Fundamental		Price of Growth	8
Company	2	Trend & Cycle TPL	4
Industry	3	Relative Strength	5

RECOMMENDATION

We have upgraded our recommendation on Scott's Shares to a BUY based on strengthening sales and margins in the restaurant division. Also, the U.K. hotel division has already established a pattern of strong improvements. We expect that after a period of three years of essentially flat earnings, the 12% earnings growth forecast for this year end will accelerate to 20% next year and will result in share price appreciation. Based on our outlook for the TSE and our earnings forecast, our projected 12 month trading range is $7.00 to $9.50

HISTORICAL INFORMATION AND ESTIMATES (IN C$)

Fiscal Year End - April 31

	1990	1991	1992	1993	1994	1995*	1996	1997
INCOME								
Revenue Per Share	16.89	12.53	13.15	13.55	14.42	15.14	15.98	17.41
Earnings Per Share (basic)	1.01	0.90	0.52	0.49	0.55	0.68	0.81	1.02
Earnings Per Share (t.d.)	1.01	0.90	0.52	0.49	0.55	0.68	0.81	1.02
CASH FLOW								
Cash Flow Per Share	2.18	1.62	1.58	1.73	1.79	1.96	2.11	2.34
Dividend Per Share	0.26	0.25	0.26	0.26	0.26	0.26	0.26	0.26
Capital Exp. Per Share	3.63	2.21	2.09	1.38	1.26	0.92	0.92	0.92
BALANCE SHEET								
Working Capital Per Share	(0.13)	0.82	0.02	0.09	0.61	0.63	0.64	0.65
Cash Per Share	0.73	0.21	1.24	2.08	1.77	1.64	1.67	1.68
Long Term & Other								
Assets Per Share	13.19	13.45	13.48	12.50	12.56	12.22	11.90	11.20
Total Debt Per Share	7.36	7.31	8.26	7.80	7.78	6.92	6.08	3.98
Other Liab. & Pfd. Per Share	0.62	0.53	0.29	0.32	0.33	0.32	0.32	0.32
Book Value Per Share	5.80	6.64	6.20	6.55	6.84	7.25	7.81	9.23

*F1996

QUARTERLY DATA

Quarterly Earnings Per Share

	Q1	Q2	Q3	Q4	YR.
1993	0.15	0.11	0.10	0.13	0.49
1994	0.16	0.13	0.12	0.14	0.55
1995	0.17	0.15	0.17	0.19	0.68

Quarterly Earnings Per Share

	Q1	Q2	Q3	Q4	YR.
1993	0.07	0.07	0.07	0.07	0.26
1994	0.07	0.07	0.07	0.07	0.26
1995	0.07	0.07	0.07	0.07	0.26

Nancy A. Self, CFA   *Priced as at December 30, 1994*   (604) 257-7037

Exhibit 6 (continued)

SCOTT'S HOSPITALITY INC. (SRC)   *January 18, 1995*

COMPANY PROFILE

Scott's is organized into 3 divisions: Food Service, Transportation and Hotels. Its food service division operates in Canada, the U.S. and the U.K. In Canada its primary operation is the KFC restaurants, while its primary operation in the U.K. is Perfect Pizza, and in the U.S., Manchu Wok. The hotel division owns and operates 12 full service hotels in the U.K. under the Marriott banner and four limited service under the Courtyard by Marriott banner. The transportation division is comprised of Charterway's (the second largest school bus contractor in Canada with 1,960 busses from 26 facilities) and National School Bus (the fourth largest contractor in the U.S.). National has more than 3,500 routes in 10 states which, with its fleet of 3,935 owned and managed busses, gives it an estimated 4% share of the private contract market.

STRENGTHS

Scott's continues to narrow its focus on businesses in which it can have a leading position. This has resulted in the divestiture of smaller restaurant businesses. We would expect this process to continue.

The balance sheet is expected to continue to improve. We estimate that debt (net of cash) to equity will be reduced over the next two years from 0.92:1 at the end F1995 to 0.61:1 at the end of F1997 as a result of the use of net free cash flow to reduce debt. This results in an improved interest coverage ratio (EBITD/interest) from 4.5 times to 6.1 times over the same period.

The hotel division has reported an impressive turnaround over the past year. It has benefitted both from the conversion to the Marriott banner, attracting more American business travelers than the Holiday Inn banner, as well as a general improvement in the U.K. economy. The 104% increase in the operating profit of this division in the second quarter reflected improved occupancy levels as well as higher average total spending per guest per stay.

We estimate that the net realizable value of Scott's separate businesses is $12.71 per share based on forecast F1995 results and cash and debt levels. We judge the 41% discount to this value as larger than required. Our projected 12 month target price of $9.50 assumes a 25% discount to the trailing net asset value.

WEAKNESS

Results have been weak due to the poor performance of the restaurant division. The second quarter was the first quarter the division reported an improvement in its EBIT margin, after reporting nine consecutive quarters of EBIT margin declines. The margin widened by 130 basis points in the second quarter, after reporting a margin decline in first quarter of 43 basis points. This has been an important but still preliminary indication of improvements in this division.

KEY RISKS AND SENSITIVITIES

The KFC concept, the dominant chain within Scott's restaurant division, is mature. Although alternate product formulations, production and distribution techniques are being tested, we do not think that substantial volume growth is likely. Over the past two years, however, Scott's had been engaged in an aggressive capital spending program aimed at generating volume growth. Capital intentions have now been dramatically reduced for this division, which we think more appropriately reflects its mature status.

Exhibit 6 (continued)

SCOTT'S HOSPITALITY INC.

SRC $7.00

EPS	1993	$0.49	P/E		14.3X
	1994E	$0.55			12.7X
	1995E	$0.66			10.6X
Dividend		$0.28	Yield		4.0%
Book Value		$6.84	Price/Book		1.0X
1 Yr. Target		$9.00	Annual Return		32.6%
3 Yr. Target		$12.00	Annual Return		23.7%

IR 3 SR 2. Price of Growth: 7.

Q3 RESULTS STRONG

SRC reported EPS for its third quarter of $0.11 compared with year ago results of $0.10 and our estimate of $0.12.

Despite the fact that Scott's reported a 6.3% decline in restaurant division revenues, the operating profit increased by 349%, reflecting strong KFC results. We understand that the KFC operation doubled its operating profit in Q3 relative to the year ago results.

The operating improvement traced to a higher average cheque in the KFC restaurants, as consumers reacted positively to the "Mega Meal" and delivery promotional activities. The mega meal has served to increase the proportion of the sales mix in the higher margin peripheral products such as salad and fries. Home delivery orders on average are larger than the pick-up business. Operating results were also positively affected by cost savings projects in the quarter.

Of note, these results were achieved despite weaker than expected results in January. Importantly, KFC results

improved in February, auguring well for continued strength in the fourth quarter.

The hotel division continued to report dramatic earnings improvements. The division reported a 30.8% increase in revenues and a 512% increase in operating profit. Its average occupancy rate increased by seven percentage points to 63% for the quarter, relative to the year ago quarter, and was accompanied by a £1.50 increase in the average room rate. On a year-to-date basis, the occupancy rate was 70%. We expect this momentum to slow in the fourth quarter, reflecting the fact that the dramatic increase in results began in Q4 last year.

The transportation division reported a 14% revenue increase and an 8% increase in operating profit. This division also benefitted from the weaker dollar as U.S. results translated into increased Canadian dollar denominated sales and operating profits. We estimate that one-third of the increase traced to the weaker dollar. Of note, both the U.S. and Canadian results were stronger in Q3 relative to Q3 last year, tracing to increased routes.

Interest expense was up marginally in the quarter, however, the increase traced to currency translation issues. In isolation, currency fluctuations resulted in a $634,000 reported increase in interest expense, while lower debt levels reduced interest expense by $150,000 and increased rates increased interest expense by $240,000.

Our preliminary estimate of the asset value net of debt but including cash is approximately $11.75. It is our view that Scott's Hospitality shares should trade at a substantial discount to this value due to the diverse nature of its portfolio of businesses. This is reflected in the 24% discount to this value implied in our $9.00 target price.

 RBC DOMINION SECURITIES

Nancy A. Self, CFA/March 7, 1995

part six

Raising Capital

UNIHOST CORPORATION

Mike McNally, chief financial officer for UniHost Corporation, was sitting at his desk opening his second diet cola of the day and it was only 8:30 a.m. He was concerned about the several piles of papers, each over four inches tall, on his desk representing alternative uses and sources of financing for UniHost Corporation. It was a beautiful May day outside his Toronto office in 1998. Just then, Gord Koros, UniHost's Treasurer, poked his head through the door to announce that the investment bankers had arrived. They were here to finalize UniHost's financing plan and discuss how the financing would fit into UniHost's overall growth strategy.

THE NORTH AMERICAN HOTEL INDUSTRY

The hotel business in North America was divided into multiple segments ranging from six-room roadside motels to four star hotels with several hundred rooms in major urban centers. As a whole, industry performance was positively related to the business cycle and was dependent on a large number of economic factors that affected industry performance. The hotel industry consisted generally of three major types of operation: hotel franchising, hotel management and hotel ownership.

Hotel Franchising operations were considered the least risky of these three activities as they only involved allowing the use of a brand name or "flag" for a hotel in exchange for a small percentage of gross

Richard Ivey School of Business
The University of Western Ontario

IVEY

J.J. McHale prepared this case under the supervision of Professor Craig Dunbar solely to provide material for class discussion. The authors do not intend to illustrate either effective or ineffective handling of a managerial situation. The authors may have disguised certain names and other identifying information to protect confidentiality.

revenues. In addition to the use of the flag, some franchisers also operated hotel reservation systems which franchisees could utilize. Typically, hotels that utilized a flag agreed to maintain a minimum level of standards in terms of quality, customer service and amenities in order to retain the rights to use the flag.

Hotel Management involved the day-to-day operations of the hotel including staffing, billing, food services (if applicable), housekeeping and concierge services. Hotel management agreements tended to be highly variable with either the hotel manager or the hotel owner assuming responsibility for operating costs and the management agreement adjusted accordingly. Management companies generally received compensation based on gross revenues. These fees would amount to three to five per cent of gross revenues after any hotel operating expenses.

Hotel Ownership could be viewed to be a higher risk venture than other real estate activities given the lack of long-term leases and potential changes in consumer preferences inherent to the industry's business. Consequently, the largest portion of any hotel's revenues was provided to the owner of the physical building.

From 1992 to 1997, the U.S. hotel industry had experienced a high level of growth in terms of overall capacity resulting from changes to the U.S. tax legislation. It was generally considered to be "overbuilt", meaning that there was excess capacity of available rooms in the U.S. market which put downward pressure on prices. The excess capacity was more concentrated in the mid-market hotels than at the upscale urban hotels or the low-end roadside motels. The Canadian market was considered to be in better condition, with a four per cent increase in occupancy (from 58 to 62%) combined with an increase in prices of 7.1 per cent (from $69.32 to $74.25 average daily rate) from 1992 to 1996. The Canadian hotel industry was fragmented with two-thirds of hotels independently owned and approximately one-third of these remaining unflagged. Since 1993, UniHost had been a strong performer relative to the Canadian hotel industry as a whole (see Exhibit 1).

UNIHOST HISTORY

In the 1980s, UniHost, then named "Journey's End", was heavily involved in the development, syndication and management of motels and hotels in Canada and the northeastern United States. UniHost developed new properties, built hotels and then sold the majority ownership of the property to a group of individual investors through limited partnerships. Virtually all of the properties developed in this manner were managed by UniHost and operated under one of UniHost's flags.

During the severe real estate and hotel industry downturn of the early 1990s the company sustained heavy losses in its hotel ownership and development activities. UniHost began a period of consolidation and divestiture in which it sold off non-core assets and identified those assets that it viewed as having long-term value. As a result, the company sold all of its U.S.-based properties and exited the U.S. market. The company had formed a joint venture named Choice Canada (with U.S.-based Choice Hotels International) which would allow it to participate in the growth of the network through increasing franchise sales. It reflagged almost all of the Canadian properties that it owned or managed under the Choice Canada brands "Quality" or "Comfort".

LIQUIDITY PROGRAM

Due to heavy pressure from many of the company's limited partners who owned the individual hotels that UniHost managed, the company initiated the Limited Partner Liquidity Program (the "Liquidity Program"). The program was designed to provide the direct owners of the hotels with a means of selling their interest in the various properties and/or obtaining a more liquid form of investment for their ownership interests. The company commenced the implementation of a program to acquire the interests of limited partners who owned 69 hotel and motel properties that were built and managed by UniHost Corporation in June 1997. The limited partners were offered a number of alternatives for liquidating their interests, if desired, including: selling for cash, taking common shares in UniHost and selling for a combination of cash and shares. This program resulted in the company acquiring 100 per cent ownership in 48 properties, 75 to 99 per cent ownership in 15 properties, 50 to 74 per cent ownership in five properties and 36 per cent ownership in the remaining property. Including assumed mortgage debt of $119 million, the gross acquisition cost of the

Liquidity Program was $268.5 million, which the company financed with a $55 million equity issue in December 1997 and a $100 million bridge financing facility from a major Canadian bank. The bridge financing facility required UniHost to maintain an EBITDA to debt service (defined as interest and principal payments on all debt) of at least 1.5 times, a maximum debt to equity ratio of three to one and carry an interest rate of prime + 1.5 per cent.[1]

UNIHOST PORTFOLIO

UniHost owned, managed and operated hotels in a wide variety of market positions. This market positioning was based on brand. In total UniHost held a significant ownership interest in 99 hotels with a total of 9,456 rooms. It also managed an additional 25 hotels with a combined total of 3,576 rooms. Its network of franchised hotels included 227 hotels, 92 of which were owned by UniHost, representing 19,353 rooms (7,966 of which were owned by UniHost). Focused on central Canada, UniHost's portfolio of properties across market positions is summarized as follows:

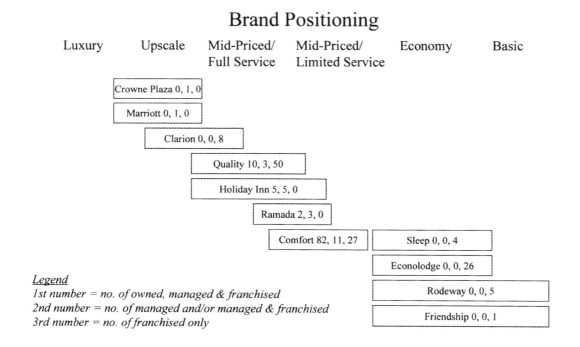

Brand Positioning

CORPORATE STRUCTURE

UniHost's chief executive officer, Tomas Orlando, had set up a unique corporate structure following the last financial restructuring (see Exhibit 2). Virtually all of UniHost's owned hotels were operated as separate companies on either an individual basis or as part of a small group of hotels (usually four or five). These separate companies then arranged individual first mortgage financing. The intended result of this was to insulate the network at large from suffering if one of these separate operating companies became financially distressed. In other words, if a group or "pool" of hotels lost economic viability, they could be cut away from the rest of UniHost's operations to fend for themselves. The creditors of that pool of hotels would only have recourse to the specific properties in the pool and not to UniHost as a corporate entity.

---

[1]Canadian Prime was currently 5.50 per cent.

UniHost Strategy

In a meeting shortly after the conclusion of the Liquidity Program acquisitions, Orlando told McNally: "Now that we dominate the Canadian mid-market, we can pursue our dual strategy for the future growth of this company. I'm really excited about our ventures into the Caribbean." He was referring to UniHost's plans to expand its Canadian operations and enter into the Caribbean market selectively. UniHost wanted to move up the value chain in Canada, increasing its operations in the upscale market segment utilizing the Clarion brand name. The company was also seeking to add some Caribbean assets to its portfolio, and had begun the process of seeking to acquire target properties in the region.

UniHost also planned to acquire a 700-room hotel in downtown Toronto in 1998, and renovate it for the upscale market. This acquisition was considered a critical element in maintaining UniHost's national network status. The cost of this acquisition, including renovations, was expected to be $85 million. The company also had planned capacity additions to various Comfort Inns that would increase the total number of rooms by 400 in 1998 and 800 in 1999 at a cost of $20 million and $40 million, respectively. These capacity additions would come on-stream in the year following the renovation expenditures. Additionally, McNally knew that he had to ensure that the normal capital expenditures in the hotel business were met. These typically came in the form of replacing furniture, fixtures and other operating equipment for all of UniHost's owned properties. These capital expenditure requirements usually amounted to three to four per cent of each hotel's revenues.

By the end of 2000, Orlando wanted the company to expand its operations into the upscale market segment rapidly by acquiring several hotels and renovating some of its existing portfolio. UniHost had already identified hotels representing approximately 2,000 rooms that were well positioned to be a part of the Clarion Strategy. McNally believed that these hotels could be acquired for approximately $90,000 per room. The Clarion strategy also called for adding another 1,000 rooms in the following twelve months for similar prices. In 1998, the company planned to renovate and reflag seven properties to the Clarion market segment at a cost of $15 million. McNally believed that cash flows from acquisitions and renovations would impact UniHost's financial statements in the year following the expenditures.

UniHost had budgeted $5 million in each of the next three years for acquisitions and operational start-up in the Caribbean. Orlando felt that their first hotel should be located in Jamaica. He had visited there in December 1997 on vacation and felt that hotel service had been significantly lacking and that the operation had been extremely disorganized. Orlando envisioned a new network of resort hotels in the Caribbean catering to tourists from North America that could utilize UniHost's existing management techniques and reservation system.

Financing Alternatives

Four investment bankers from Aurora Securities accompanied Koros into McNally's office. Darren Sweeney and Derek Towers were from Aurora's real estate corporate finance group and Carrie Carpenter and Sandra Coveland worked in Aurora's debt capital markets group. Sweeney had been working with UniHost for several years and had always provided McNally with good advice. McNally had only recently met with Carpenter, as UniHost began to consider the possibility of offering public debt securities. Carpenter and her group, of whom Coveland was a member, had exhibited strong success in the fledgling Canadian high yield debt markets. Altogether, Aurora had provided McNally with three separate proposals for raising additional capital. Each of the alternatives had advantages and disadvantages, and the team from Aurora was prepared to assist UniHost in executing any of them. Sweeney and Towers had seen McNally three weeks previously to outline the equity alternatives (common stock or convertible bonds). Carpenter and Coveland had come to UniHost shortly thereafter to discuss the debt alternative. This was new territory for McNally because he knew that his company would not be an investment grade credit, but Carpenter had explained to him that Canada was developing a market for high yield (below investment grade credits) debt. In the past twelve months, she and her team had completed a significant number of high yield transactions and she believed that the appetite in the market for these types of issues was going to grow, not diminish. Based on her presentation, McNally had decided to visit the Canadian bond rating agencies to find out exactly where along the credit spectrum UniHost would fall.

Equity

An equity transaction was the alternative that McNally was most familiar with, having completed such a transaction for $55 million in December 1997. Since December UniHost had become eligible as a Prompt Offering Prospectus ("POP") issuer in the Canadian equity market. This, in effect, allowed UniHost to execute and conclude an equity issue in a matter of days rather than a minimum of six weeks under normal equity registration procedures. In fact, Sweeney had told McNally that Aurora Securities was willing to be the lead underwriter for a bought deal equity issue for any amount up to $40 million. A bought deal transaction was one where the underwriters bought the shares directly from the company, guaranteeing the sale, and assumed the risk for their placement in the marketplace. This was typically done at a larger discount to the current trading price than the more common "marketed transaction" (5% vs. 2.5%) to allow the underwriters some pricing leeway in their sales effort and as compensation to the underwriters for the additional risk they assumed in a bought deal. Sweeney had also indicated that a larger transaction might be possible, but only as a marketed transaction where UniHost would undertake an investor roadshow to tell its story to investors. A marketed transaction could probably be concluded in three to four weeks. Regardless of the method of selling shares, UniHost would need to pay the underwriters four per cent of the total amount raised in commission.

McNally was concerned about the state of the equity markets; since the fall of 1997, the markets had been experiencing what was being called the "Asian flu". The equity markets were highly volatile due to economic uncertainty in Southeast Asia. McNally's largest concern with pursuing a common share offering came from a conversation he had with Eastern Life, one of the company's largest institutional shareholders, following the December equity issue. Eastern had told McNally and Orlando that they would strongly prefer that UniHost not issue any more common stock directly to the market for less than $10.00 per share (see Exhibits 3 and 4 for UniHost's shareholders and stock price performance).

Convertible Debentures

Sweeney and Towers had also presented McNally with a convertible debt alternative for raising capital. Canadian interest rates were at or near historical lows, and thus investors were anxious to purchase higher yielding securities. Aurora had presented UniHost with a term sheet[2] for a two-year issue that would be issued with a yield of 8.5 per cent and would be convertible at a rate of 100 shares per $1,000 bond. This pricing was based on the comparable Canadian convertible bond issues outstanding (see Exhibit 5). The issue would be redeemable at the end of two years in either cash or common stock. However, investors would have the option of converting their bonds into common stock anytime while the bond was outstanding. A convertible bond issue would not require UniHost to submit to any financial or operating covenants. After speaking with the Equity Capital Markets desk at Aurora, Sweeney believed that UniHost could raise between $50 and $75 million through this alternative. The minimum deal size was $50 million in order to provide liquidity for the after market trading. This issue would have to be of the "marketed transaction" variety since the issue would be a new type of security and convertible bond investors were unfamiliar with UniHost's name or operations. Sweeney felt that they could close the deal within two to three weeks and Aurora and the other underwriters would earn a 3.5 per cent commission for a convertible bond issue.

High Yield Debt

McNally was not as familiar with the public debenture alternative as he was with the previous two. Previously, he had negotiated both mortgage financing from institutional investors and the bridge financing facility from the bank. However, the possibility of issuing a public debenture had not been presented to him before Aurora had brought it up. Carpenter and Coveland had laid out a very impressive track record of new issues in the high yield segment of the market over the past twelve months and this had caught McNally's

---

[2] A term sheet outlines all the relevant terms and conditions of a securities issue: price, yield, term outstanding, plan of distribution and detailed language for conversion options or financial covenants.

attention. McNally was aware of the fact that debt financing typically had less negative impact on current shareholders than either an equity or a convertible financing; however, he wasn't sure if that would hold true with a high yield issue. Carpenter explained that the Canadian high yield market was still in its infancy, with approximately 10 to 15 institutional investors who had established high yield funds within their portfolios along with another 10 or so investors who would purchase high yield debt on a case-by-case basis. The core group of high yield investors were mostly new portfolios of existing mutual fund families and they controlled approximately $2 billion in high yield investments in Canadian companies. She also explained the view debt investors take on making an investment: "The best scenario for a debt investor is that they get their money back; they don't see upside, all they do is worry about downside." Carpenter discussed the likely view that debt investors would take on UniHost's growth strategy; she indicated that debt investors would be very uncomfortable with the thought of financing Caribbean operations. Coveland explained that this issue could probably be settled by treating the Caribbean operations as a separate activity for the purposes of the bond issue and that the indenture[3] could be written so that only the Canadian operations would support a potential debt issue.

Carpenter felt that there would be market appetite for a UniHost bond issue in the amount of $60 to $100 million at the current time. The term of the debt could be either five or seven years (see Exhibit 6). Aurora had also provided UniHost with a summary of covenants for other high yield debt issues in the United States, since there were no comparable issues in Canada (see Exhibit 7). Each of the companies in the summary had outstanding debt which would be similar in ranking to a potential UniHost issue. These bonds were all either specifically subordinated[4] or structurally subordinated[5] to first mortgage financing like a UniHost issue would be if it were issued as a general corporate obligation. McNally knew that covenants in the bond issue could restrict the ability of UniHost to use debt as a future financing tool, and also perhaps restrict its operational flexibility as well. He wasn't sure if he wanted to place UniHost in the position where its flexibility would be restricted in making future financing and operating decisions. However, McNally was intrigued enough that he took the next step suggested by Aurora, to obtain an initial rating from the credit rating agencies. Carpenter indicated that Aurora would charge 2.75 per cent of the total amount raised in underwriting commission.

Credit Rating Agencies

Aurora had advised UniHost that should it decide to pursue a Canadian high yield offering, it would be best served by obtaining both a Canadian credit rating and a rating from one of the two major U.S. rating agencies. McNally chose to approach Dominion Bond Rating Service (DBRS) and Standard & Poors (S&P). Typically, the Canadian rating agencies tended to rate companies somewhat higher than the U.S. firms did, usually one or two rating classes, to compensate for a perceived size bias against the usually smaller Canadian firms. McNally and Koros with the assistance of Aurora prepared a presentation of their firm's operations, financial information, strategic goals and operating philosophy and went to visit the two rating agencies. After making a diligent review of the information, DBRS came back with a preliminary rating of BB (Low) and S&P placed an initial rating of B on a potential bond issue by UniHost. With this information, Carpenter and Coveland estimated that UniHost would probably pay a premium over Government of Canada bonds of 325 bps to 375 bps[6] (see Exhibit 8 for current and past government rates).

---

[3]The Trust Indenture is the binding legal contract that governs a bond issue. It sets out all of the terms and conditions of the issue and it empowers a trust company to act on behalf of the bondholders.

[4]For an issue which is specifically subordinated, bondholders have agreed to relinquish first claim on the assets of the company to another debtholder or group of debtholders.

[5]Structural subordination occurs when the assets of a company are held by a subsidiary company with debtholders who hold first claim to the assets of the company. In a bankruptcy scenario, bondholders of the parent company would recoup their investment from the equity payout of the subsidiary company.

[6]Bps = basis points. 1 basis point is equal to .01 per cent.

Financing Strategy

McNally and Orlando had previously discussed what level of financial leverage they wanted for UniHost in order to ensure a reasonable return to shareholders without putting UniHost into an overly leveraged position where they could not effectively operate the company. They also knew that the recent Liquidity Program in spite of the accompanying equity issue had pushed the company's tolerance for financial leverage. They felt that long term they would like to see UniHost with a Total Debt to Total Capitalization Ratio of 60 to 65 per cent on a book basis. Orlando felt that they could re-achieve this level by the end of the year 2000, especially if the Clarion and Caribbean strategies were implemented. McNally knew that the Toronto hotel acquisitions and the hotel acquisitions under the Clarion strategy could raise first mortgage financing for half of the purchase price at approximately a 7.50 per cent interest rate with terms from five to 10 years. But UniHost would have to provide the rest of the cash for purchasing the new hotels from operating cash flow or from issuing public securities.

McNally knew that he had to raise additional funds soon; the bridge financing facility carried a $1 million penalty if it wasn't paid off by June 30, 1998 and there was still $52 million currently outstanding on the facility. The investment bankers had laid out the alternatives for him, but he needed to decide if he could fund all of the things that they wanted to accomplish and how he was going to do it.

Exhibit 1

**NORTH AMERICAN HOTEL INDUSTRY RATES AND UTILIZATION:
1989 TO 2000 (FORECAST)**

Year	UniHost Average Daily Rate	Canadian Industry Average Daily Rate	U.S. Industry Average Daily Rate	UniHost Occupancy	Canadian Industry Occupancy	U.S. Industry Occupancy
1989	NA	$82.00	$67.25	NA	68%	64%
1990	NA	$68.25	$68.25	NA	62%	64%
1991	NA	$68.25	$66.50	NA	57%	62%
1992	NA	$70.50	$72.75	NA	58%	63%
1993	$37.00	$70.50	$79.50	66%	60%	64%
1994	$39.00	$68.25	$86.50	70%	61%	64%
1995	$41.50	$72.75	$92.75	67%	62%	65%
1996	$42.75	$76.25	$98.25	68%	62%	65%
1997 Estimate	$45.50	$80.00	$104.50	69%	63%	64%
1998 Forecast	$48.00	$85.50	$113.25	71%	64%	63%
1999 Forecast	NA	$89.00	$115.00	NA	65%	62%
2000 Forecast	NA	NA	$114.50	NA	NA	62%

Notes:

1. U.S. Data—Smith Travel Research. U.S. data converted to Canadian $ at historical and current rates.
2. Canadian Data—Economic Planning Group & Canadian Hotel Association.

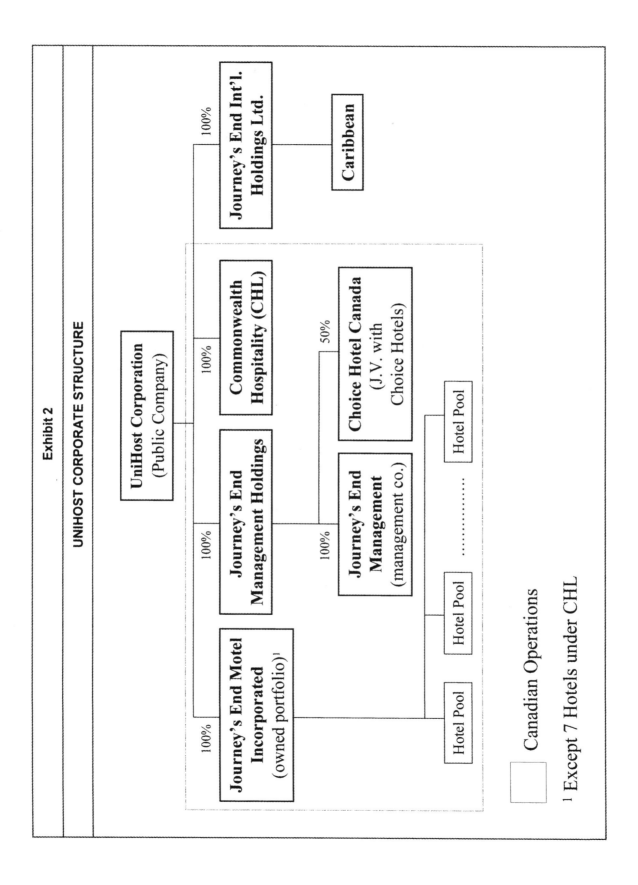

Exhibit 2

UNIHOST CORPORATE STRUCTURE

UniHost Corporation
(Public Company)

Journey's End Management Holdings — 100%

Commonwealth Hospitality (CHL) — 100%

Journey's End Int'l. Holdings Ltd. — 100%

Caribbean

Journey's End Motel Incorporated
(owned portfolio)[1] — 100%

Journey's End Management
(management co.) — 100%

Choice Hotel Canada
(J.V. with Choice Hotels) — 50%

Hotel Pool

Hotel Pool ....

Hotel Pool

Hotel Pool

Canadian Operations

[1] Except 7 Hotels under CHL

Exhibit 3
UNIHOST'S MAJOR SHAREHOLDERS

Shareholder	No. of Shares	% Ownership
Murray Royce [1]	1,488,800	3.9%
P.R. Capital	6,428,772	17.2%
3Qs Investments	4,739,000	12.7%
Eastern Life	3,946,494	10.6%
A1 Management	3,350,000	9.0%
Pegasus Investments	2,478,000	6.6%
Forward Management	1,800,000	4.8%
Arrow Advisors	889,600	2.4%
Soldier Capital	615,900	1.7%
Primal Management	606,700	1.6%
		70.5%

(1) Company Founder and Chairman of the Board of Directors

Exhibit 4

UniHost vs. TSE
Jan. 1, 1997 to May 6, 1998

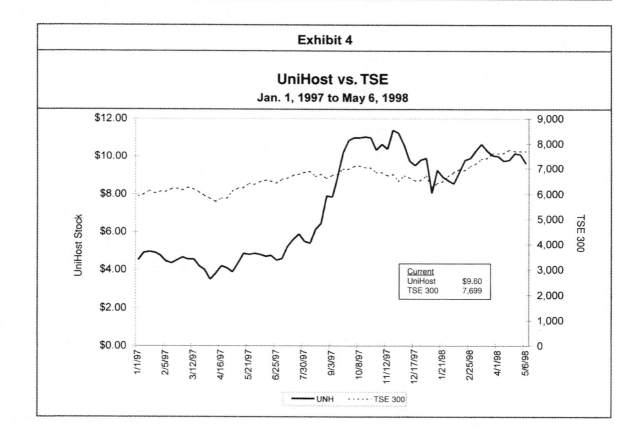

Current
UniHost $9.60
TSE 300   7,699

UNH ····· TSE 300

Exhibit 5

COMPARABLE CONVERTIBLE BOND ISSUE OUTSTANDING

Issuer	Coupon	Issue Date	Maturity Date	Ratings CBRS	Ratings DBRS	Current Yield
Cambridge Shopping Centre	8.00%	Feb. 1988	Feb. 2003	B+ High	BBB Low	8.30%
Revenue Properties	6.00%	Mar. 1994	Mar. 2004	B+ Low	Not Rated	9.55%
Centrefund Realty	7.875%	Jan. 1997	Jan. 2007	Not Rated	Not Rated	8.05%
Brookfield Properties	6.00%	Feb. 1997	Feb. 2007	Not Rated	Not Rated	6.45%
O&Y Properties	5.90%	May 1998	May 2008	Not Rated	Not Rated	9.10%

Exhibit 6

DEBT MATURITY SCHEDULE
(C$ Millions)

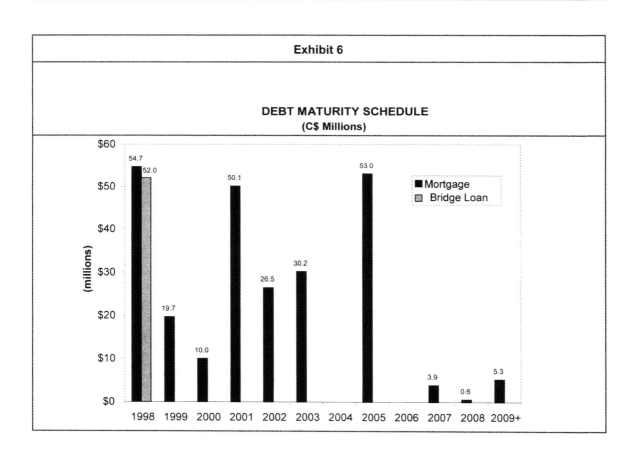

Exhibit 7

COVENANT COMPARISON FOR U.S. HOTEL INDUSTRY DEBT OFFERINGS

Name	Wyndham Hotel Corp.	Motels of America	Prime Hospitality	Embassy Suites (Promus)	Folcor REIT	La Quinta Inns	Sholodge Inc.
Security	Unsecured	Unsecured	Unsecured	Unsecured	Unsecured	Unsecured	Unsecured
Ratings: S&P / Moody's	N/R	CCC+ / B3	B+ / B1	BBB– / Ba2	BB+ / Ba1	BB+ / Ba2	B+ / B1
Ranking:	Senior Subordinated	Senior Subordinated	Senior Subordinated	Senior Subordinated	Senior Notes	Senior Subordinated	Senior Subordinated
Guarantees:	Upstream guarantees from all material subsidiaries.	None	None	Upstream and Downstream guarantees	Upstream guarantees from all material subsidiaries	None	None
Covenants: Maintenance Tests	None	None	None	None	Unencumbered Assets to Unsecured Debt ≥ 150%	None	(i) Minimum Net Worth ≥ $75 million plus 50% of cumulative net income
Incurrence Tests	(i) Fixed Charge Coverage Ratio ≥ 1.75x for the first year; 2.0x thereafter	(i) Fixed Charge Coverage Ratio ≥ 1.50x for the first 2 years, 1.75x for the 3rd year, 2.0x thereafter	(i) Fixed Charge Coverage Ratio ≥ 2.0x	(i) Fixed Charge Coverage Ratio ≥ 2.0x	(i) Total Debt to Adjusted Total Assets ≤ 60% (ii) Secured Debt to Adjusted Total Assets < 40% (iii) Interest Coverage Ratio > 2.0x	(i) Fixed Charge Coverage Ratio ≥ 2.0x	(i) Total Debt to Capitalization ≤ 70%
Limitation on Consolidations and Mergers	(i) Subject to the ability to issue $1 of additional debt (ii) Successor to assume the obligaitons (iii) Net Worth ≥ 100% of Net Worth prior to merger or consolidation	(i) Subject to the ability to issue $1 of additional debt (ii) Successor to assume the obligations	(i) Subject to the ability to issue $1 of additional debt (ii) Successor to assume the obligations (iii) Net Worth ≥ 100% of Net Worth prior to merger or consolidation	(i) Subject to the ability to issue $1 of additional debt (ii) Successor to assume the obligations (iii) Net Worth ≥ 100% of Net Worth prior to merger or consolidation	(i) Subject to the ability to issue $1 of additional debt (ii) Successor to assume the obligations	(i) Subject to the ability to issue $1 of additional debt (ii) Successor to assume the obligations (iii) Net Worth ≥ 90% of Net Worth prior to merger or consolidation	(i) Successor to assume the obligations
Limitation on Restricted Payments	(i) Subject to the ability to issue $1 of additional debt under the incurrence test (ii) Limited to 50% of aggregate Net Income or negative 100% of consolidated negative net income PLUS 100% of any new equity issuance	(i) Subject to the ability to issue $1 of additional debt under the incurrence test (ii) Limited to 50% of aggregate Net Income or negative 100% of consolidated negative net income PLUS 100% of any new equity issuance	(i) Subject to the ability to issue $1 of additional debt under the incurrence test (ii) Limited to 50% of aggregate Net Income or negative 100% of consolidated negative net income PLUS 100% of any new equity issuance	(i) Subject to the ability to issue $1 of additional debt under the incurrence test and subject to a minimum Net Worth amount of $350 million (ii) Limited to 50% of aggregate Net Income or negative 100% of consolidated negative net income PLUS 100% of any new equity issuance	(i) Subject to the ability to issue $1 of additional debt under the incurrence test (ii) Limited to 95% of aggregate Net Income or negative 100% of consolidated negative net income PLUS 100% of any new equity issuance PLUS 100% of Investment Sale proceeds	(i) Subject to the ability to issue $1 of additional debt under the incurrence test (ii) Limited to 50% of aggregate Net Income or negative 100% of consolidated negative net income PLUS 100% of any new equity issuance PLUS $10 million	(i) Limited to 50% of aggregate Net Income or negative 100% of consolidated negative net income PLUS 100% of any new equity issuance PLUS $8.5 million
Limitation on Asset Sales	Asset sales must be for at least 75% cash and any asset sales resulting in $5 MM or more in a 12 month period must be used to repay senior indebtedness or re-invest in hospitality assets	Asset sales must be for at least 75% cash and any asset sales resulting in $5 MM or more in a 6 month period must be used to repay senior indebtedness or re-invest in hospitality assets	Asset sales must be for at least 75% cash and any asset sales resulting in $20 MM or more in a 12 month period must be used to repay senior indebtedness or re-invest in hospitality assets	Asset sales must be for at least 75% cash and any asset sales resulting in 10% of Adjusted Net Tangible Assets or more in a 12 month period must be used to repay senior indebtedness or re-invest in hospitality assets		Asset sales must be for at least 75% cash and any asset sales resulting in $5 MM or more in an 18 month period must be used to repay senior indebtedness or re-invest in hospitality assets	
Change in Control	Company required to offer to repurchase the notes at $101.00 plus accrued interest	Company required to offer to repurchase the notes at $101.00 plus accrued interest	Company required to offer to repurchase the notes at $101.00 plus accrued interest	Company required to offer to repurchase the notes at $101.00 plus accrued interest	Company required to offer to repurchase the notes at $101.00 plus accrued interest	Company required to offer to repurchase the notes at $101.00 plus accrued interest	Company required to offer to repurchase the notes at $101.00 plus accrued interest

Exhibit 7 (continued)

Name	Wyndham Hotel Corp.	Motels of America	Prime Hospitality	Embassy Suites (Promus)	Felcor REIT	La Quinta Inns Inc.
Limitation on Issuance of Capital Stock of Restricted Subsidiaries	(i) No issuance unless issued to the Company or another Subsidiary which is a Guarantor; OR (ii) No issuance unless after such issuance subsidiary is no longer a Restricted Subsidiary	(i) No issuance unless issued to the Company or another Subsidiary which is a Guarantor; OR (ii) No issuance unless after such issuance proceeds are used in accordance with the Limitation on Asset Sales covenant			(i) No issuance unless issued to the Company or another Subsidiary which is a Guarantor; OR (ii) No issuance except up to 20% can be issued to a franchisor affiliate of an acquired or constructed facility	
Limitation on Guarantees by Restricted Subsidiaries	(i) Guarantee must not violate terms of the Indenture (ii) Guarantee applies to the Credit Agreement (iii) Guarantee is pari passu or subordinated to the Guarantee of the Notes (iv) Guarantee existed at the time of the issuance of the Notes		(i) Subject to the incurrence test; OR (ii) guarantee of existing indebtedness		Not permitted unless subordinate to the Notes	
Line of Business Test		Limited to lodging and related businesses	Limited to hospitality related businesses			
Limitation on Transactions with Affiliates			Transactions with Affiliates must be at fair market value and require delivery to the trustee: (i) if less than $5 million – an officers' certificate (ii) if less than $10 million – a fairness opinion from an investment bank or a Qualified Appraiser (iii) if less than $25 million – a fairness opinion from an investment bank	Transactions with Affiliates must be at fair market value and require delivery to the trustee: (i) if greater than $5 million – a Board resolution passed by the majority of the disinterested boardmembers (ii) if greater than $80 million – a fairness opinion from an investment bank	Transactions with Affiliates must be at fair market value and require delivery to the trustee: (i) if less than $5 million – a Board resolution passed by the majority of the disinterested boardmembers (ii) if greater than $5 million from an investment bank	Transactions with Affiliates must be at fair market value and require delivery to the trustee: (i) if less than $10 million – an officers' certificate (ii) if greater than $10 million – a fairness opinion from an investment bank
Limitation on Layering Debt				The Company cannot create any obligation subordinate to the Senior Debt and Senior to the Senior Subordinated Debt		
Fall Away Event					For as long as the Company maintains Investment Grade ratings then the Limitation on Liens, Limitation on Sale and Leaseback Transactions, Limitation on Restricted Payments, Limitation on Restricting Subsidiary Dividends and Other Payments, Limitation on Issuance of Capital Stock of Restricted Subsidiaries, Limitation on Guarantees by Subsidiaries, Limitation on Transactions with Affiliates fall away	

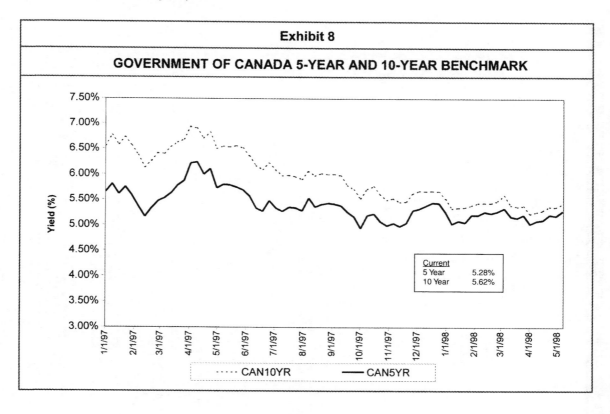

Exhibit 8

GOVERNMENT OF CANADA 5-YEAR AND 10-YEAR BENCHMARK

Current	
5 Year	5.28%
10 Year	5.62%

CAN10YR   CAN5YR

	Exhibit 9	

UNIHOST CORPORATION			
Consolidated Income Statement (Pro Forma the Liquidity Program)			
Years ending December 31			
(Thousands of Dollars)			

	<u>1995</u>	<u>1996</u>	<u>1997</u>
Revenues			
3rd party license & mgmnt agreements	4,383	5,142	5,370
Property ownership interests	162,677	166,392	178,845
Other income	1,790	703	385
Interest income	0	0	1,485
Total Revenues	168,850	172,237	186,085
Expenses			
Mgmnt. & Admin. Expenses	11,994	14,228	11,124
Depreciation & Amortization	1,074	1,490	1,422
Capital Tax	1,140	1,140	1,140
Property Ownership Interests			
- operating expenses	110,590	111,167	118,911
- depreciation & amortization	12,818	12,864	12,863
- mortgage interest expenses	18,310	18,310	18,310
Net recoveries	0	0	(1,977)
Non-controlling interests	574	604	701
Total Expenses	156,500	159,803	162,494
Interest Expense	3,613	3,613	3,613
EBT	8,737	8,821	19,978
Income Taxes			
Current	880	880	880
Deferred	(752)	1,310	6,127
Total Income Taxes	128	2,190	7,007
Net Income	8,609	6,631	12,971
No. of Shares Outstanding			
Current	37,299,945	37,299,945	37,299,945
Fully Diluted	39,082,645	39,082,645	39,082,645

Exhibit 9 (continued)

Consolidated Balance Sheet (Pro Forma the Liquidity Program) Year ending December 31, 1997 (Thousands of Dollars)

	1997
Assets	
Cash & Short-Term Investments	20,705
Accounts Receivables	14,201
Notes and Mortgages Receivable	2,719
Other Assets	20,076
Properties and Investments	494,586
Total Assets	**552,287**
Liabilities	
Accounts Payable & Accrued Liabilities	29,285
Short-Term Debt	0
Deferred Liabilities	2,873
Bank Bridge Indebtedness	58,500
Long-Term Debt	312,890
Total Liabilities	403,548
Non-Controlling Interests	2,610
Shareholders' Equity	
Common Stock	78,000
Retained Earnings	68,129
Total Equity	146,129
Total Liabilities & Equity	**552,287**

THE T. EATON COMPANY LIMITED'S INITIAL PUBLIC OFFERING

Goods satisfactory or money refunded
  —*Timothy Eaton, founder of the T. Eaton Company*

If you don't keep this sweater which fits you perfectly I'll have to write to Monsieur Eaton and explain that you don't want to wear the Toronto sweater. Monsieur Eaton understands French perfectly, but he's English and he's going to be insulted because he likes the Maple Leafs.
  —*Roch Carrier, "The Hockey Sweater and Other Stories,"*
    Stoddart Publishing (reprinted with permission)

Mary Vitug stared blankly at her aquarium screen saver. It was 7:00 a.m. on Friday, May 1, 1998 and she felt no inclination to admire the morning sunshine from her 66th floor office window at Toronto's Scotia Plaza. As she grappled with the decisions concerning The T. Eaton Company Limited's (Eaton's) initial public offering (IPO), she felt a special kinship with those sad and colourful fish doing circle after circle, going nowhere.

The IPO for Eaton's, Canada's largest privately owned department store retailer, was scheduled for early June 1998. A preliminary prospectus had already been filed with the Ontario Securities Commission on April 15.

Vitug was an Associate at Scotia Capital Markets, and was handling the day-to-day work on the

Richard Ivey School of Business
The University of Western Ontario

Ivey

Ahmed Arif prepared this case under the supervision of Professors Craig Dunbar and Steve Foerster solely to provide material for class discussion. The authors do not intend to illustrate either effective or ineffective handling of a managerial situation. The authors may have disguised certain names and other identifying information to protect confidentiality.

Eaton's issue. Next week, she was to meet Sandra Schumacher, a Director at Scotia Capital Markets, and its main contact with Eaton's management, to present analysis on the share offering.

Vitug had to place a value on Eaton's and recommend a share price range prior to meeting with Schumacher. They would then meet representatives from RBC Dominion Securities, who were co-managing the issue with Scotia Capital Markets, to finalize a recommendation for Eaton's board of directors.

The decision on how to value a turnaround company like Eaton's, so recently emerged from bankruptcy protection,[1] was a difficult one. Vitug wondered whether now was even the right time to attempt to raise the $175 million[2] of capital needed. The capital could be raised later once the restructuring had begun to show improved earnings. Alternatively, Eaton's could have a smaller IPO in June, and a second more favorably priced offering once earnings had improved.

Vitug knew that Schumacher would expect clearly reasoned and logical arguments to back up whatever she recommended.

EATON'S BACKGROUND

Timothy Eaton, the founder, started his first store in Toronto in 1869. He was the first retailer in Canada to sell merchandise for cash at fixed prices rather than by the credit and barter system. His marketing strategy rejected the "buyer beware" style of retailing. Instead, he guaranteed "one price for all" and "goods satisfactory or money refunded."

The Eaton's name was one of the most recognised brands in Canadian retailing and the company was considered as Canadian as hockey. As an example of the Eaton's mystique for Canadians, a statue of Timothy Eaton, at the entrance of the Toronto Eaton Centre, had the tip of its left foot shinier than the right because it had become a tradition for people visiting the store to touch the statue's left toe for good luck.

Eaton's policy of trying to be "everything to everyone" had been successful for many decades. By 1996, partly through the success of Eaton's as well as through other family investments in real estate and broadcasting, the Eaton family ranked fourth in Canada on FP Magazine's "most-wealthy" list. By that time, however, the company's run of success had begun to falter.

Eaton's financial performance declined due to internal and external factors. Some of these factors included the unsuccessful "everyday low pricing" strategy implemented from 1991 to 1995, inadequate capital investment in retail operations, several unprofitable stores, weak consumer spending and, most importantly, increased competition. Since 1989, 34 U.S. retailers had begun to compete in Eaton's traditional market. The company faced stiff competition from competitors such as Sears, Wal-Mart, Zellers, Future Shop, Toys "Я" Us, Home Depot, and Gap in every product category.

Consumer research showed that Eaton's was rated ahead of competitors such as The Bay and Sears Canada in the categories of customer service, variety of selection, store lay out and décor, and merchandise quality. However, the 85-store department store chain was unable to convert its superior image into enhanced profitability. Eaton's suffered a $128 million pre-tax operating loss for 1996 and a loss of $80 million for 1995. Sales in 1996 were $1.7 billion, down from $2.3 billion five years earlier.[3]

In November 1996, The Bank of Nova Scotia and Toronto Dominion Bank expressed concern about ongoing losses with respect to Eaton's $200 million operating line of credit secured with them by a pledge

---

[1]Specifically, Eaton's had just emerged from protection under the Companies' Creditors Arrangement Act (CCAA) which is similar to "Chapter 11" bankruptcy protection in the United States. (See Exhibit 1 for more details.)

[2]The Eaton family proposed to purchase $12.45 million of the offering. Other senior corporate officers of the company also proposed to purchase $1.21 million of the offering. Scotia Capital Markets and RBC Dominion Securities had negotiated an underwriting fee of 5% on all other shares sold (total proposed commission of $8.067 million). Other offering expenses (to be paid by Eaton's) would be approximately $1 million. Eaton's also proposed to grant to the underwriters an over-allotment option which would allow Scotia Capital Markets and RBC Dominion Securities to sell an additional $26.25 million in shares if demand was strong (the 5% fee would also apply to these shares). The Eaton family planned to purchase additional shares using aggregate $28.9 million in principal amount of subordinated notes of the Company due February 1, 2000 which the family held. (All amounts are in Canadian dollars.)

[3]"Eaton's and the vultures: A cautionary tale" by Donald N. Thompson, 1997, *Ivey Business Quarterly*.

of shares in Eaton Credit Corp., an Eaton's subsidiary. The banks asked for further collateral, and were offered some on real estate, but not on inventory.

In late January 1997, the two banks reduced Eaton's operating line of credit to $160 million. At the end of February, this line was exceeded when Eaton's paid its $8 million payroll and obtained court-ordered protection under the CCAA.

PRELUDE TO THE RESTRUCTURING PLAN

On February 27, 1997, Eaton's filed an application for and obtained an Order of the Ontario Court granting a stay of proceedings against the creditors of Eaton's, its affiliates and subsidiaries (collectively referred to as the "Applicants"). The creditors of the Applicants were owed approximately $340 million. The stay of proceedings was granted in order to ensure that the Applicants could continue to carry on business and preserve the status quo pending a restructuring which was intended to include divestiture of Eaton's interest in real estate, new financing from GE Capital to provide working capital for the Applicants and a compromise of the amounts owing to unsecured creditors and debenture holders, all of which would be tabled with creditors and filed with the Court for approval.

Early the next month, high-yield funds began to make offers to Eaton's creditors. High-yield funds, sometimes referred to as "vulture funds," buy outstanding bank, bond, or trade debt (frequently distressed) at a discount. They then attempt to sell the debt at a higher price to another institution, or wait until the company is restructured, sold, or liquidated. High-yield funds often get a seat at the restructuring table. At first, high-yield funds were prepared to offer only 50 cents on the dollar for Eaton's trade debt. However, offering quotes rose rapidly when it became apparent that Eaton's might actually survive.

By April, the Bank of Nova Scotia and Toronto Dominion Bank each sold their unsecured and fully extended $80 million lines of Eaton's credit to a syndicate led by Bear Stearns & Co. Inc. for between 91 and 92 cents on the dollar. In addition, by then, high-yield investors had purchased about 60 percent of Eaton's $170 million in trade debt. These new creditors, who owned enough of Eaton's debt to block a proposal for restructuring and, potentially, throw the firm into bankruptcy, insisted that they would settle for nothing less than a 100 percent repayment of their claims.

Eaton's undertook a restructuring with its advisors and court-appointed monitor to pay off its creditors. Certain non-core assets, such as the Eaton Centre in Toronto, other real estate property interests and Eaton's credit operations were sold. The company negotiated a 50/50 division of pension fund surpluses with employee groups. Eaton's share of the surplus in its pension plans was approximately $208.5 million. In addition, in June 1997, Eaton's appointed George J. Kosich as President and Chief Executive Officer to head the turnaround attempt. Before joining Eaton's, Kosich had served 37 years in the retail sector. Since 1990, he was President and Chief Executive Officer of The Hudson's Bay Company.

THE NORTH AMERICAN RETAIL INDUSTRY

Recent Economic Trends

There had been a strong increase in retail spending in North America in recent years. During the second quarter of 1998, consumer confidence was at its highest level in a decade. Interest rates were low—implying lower carrying costs for debt and higher disposable incomes (see Exhibit 2). Major equity indices in New York and Toronto had been enjoying the longest ever bull-runs in their respective markets (see Exhibit 3). Companies operating in the retail industries in Canada and the U.S. had also experienced significant run-ups in their stock prices (see Exhibit 4).

However, the 1997 financial crises in East Asia, recessionary indications in Japan and fears that the U.S. economy might heat up enough for interest rates to rise had some observers concerned about the sustainability of North American equity markets at their current record levels. Most analysts, however, predicted strong economic growth for North America in 1998, though perhaps not at 1997 levels.

Retail Industry in Canada

Canada's indigenous retail industry did not enjoy its fair share of the fruits of the general economic upswing. The industry had become increasingly competitive due to downsizing, consolidations, and, since 1989, an influx of foreign competition.

In particular, gross margins declined for department stores due to the advent of discount stores such as Price Costco, Wal-Mart, and Zellers, and "category killer" stores such as Future Shop, Adventure Electronics, Toys "Я" Us, Home Depot, and Leon's. The discounters had reinforced customer perception that they could have depth of assortments and low prices. A typical buyer looked for exceptional value, purchasing high-end goods on sale at high-end stores, and staples at discounters. This movement of consumers towards "category killers" worked to the detriment of department stores.

Between 1991 and 1996, several Canadian retailers that were positioned poorly, including Simpson's, Woodward's, Woolworth Canada, Pennington's, KMart Canada, Consumers Distributing, and Greenberg and Metropolitan Stores, either shut down, closed outlets, or were acquired by another company.

In 1997 sales of department stores such as Eaton's, The Bay and Sears Canada rose as unemployment fell, and disposable income increased. Market share for such department stores, however, continued to decline. Exhibit 5 summarizes data on Canadian retail industry sales over the past five years and Eaton's share of the market.

Retail Industry in the United States[4]

In 1998, retailing in the United States was experiencing unprecedented growth. At the same time, there were numerous store closures, mergers and consolidations. There was a growing emphasis on business-school-trained management, which focused on markets, competition, competitive advantages, and profitability.

During 1995, the United States had a large number of retailers going out of business, liquidating inventory, closing underperforming stores, or using promotional sales to generate cash flow. For example, Edison Brothers (a multi-concept speciality apparel retailer) closed 500 of its 2,700 stores in 1995; Kmart, a national chain, and Petrie Stores, a New Jersey apparel specialist, each closed about 200 stores; Caldor, a Connecticut-based discount chain, came under bankruptcy reorganization, and Pennsylvania-based Charming Shoppes closed nearly 300 Fashion Bug shops.

America's shopping loyalties had changed over the last decade. Current consumers more often put bargains, nutritional and environmental concerns, and other priorities ahead of brand or store loyalty. Most consumers were brand and store "switchers". A few years ago, the demise of the department store was being predicted. Its prices were too high, its selection too shallow and wide. At a department store, one could buy both lingerie and lawn mowers. Speciality and discount stores were stealing customers from department stores.

However, there was a recent revival in the fortunes of the better-managed department store chains, such as the Federated Department Stores, which had greatly reduced or eliminated furniture, home electronics, automotive, lawn and garden equipment, and hardware. The reason for the revival was the department stores' focus on customers. They focused on particular market targets, differentiated themselves, rid their stores of most hard lines, aggressively developed private-label soft-lines, and cut prices. They were demanding more service from suppliers, and were improving their reputation for customer service. Driving these changes was the recognition that some customer niches preferred the ambience of a department store, and these customers were targeted. As a consequence, analysts were forecasting strong earnings growth of approximately 16 percent per year from 1998 to 2003.[5]

---

[4]This section is based on information from "Retailing trends in the USA: competition, consumers, technology and the economy" by William R. Swinyard, 1997, *International Journal of Retail and Distribution Management*.

[5]Source: Zacks Investment Research (market sector labelled Retail—regional department stores).

EATON'S FUTURE STRATEGY

Eaton's filed a restructuring plan on September 12, 1997 that was to take effect in November. Changes were proposed in the company's operational, financial, and managerial structures.

Operational Restructuring

Eaton's first restructured its existing operations. It closed 18 unprofitable stores and closed or vacated certain warehouse space. The head office was moved from 250 Yonge Street in Toronto primarily due to excess space at the Toronto Eaton Centre store location. Eaton's negotiated rent and other concessions on eight additional store locations resulting in annual savings of $5.2 million compared to contractual rates in effect prior to restructuring. Eaton's then reduced the number of its employees. Over 760 employees accepted a voluntary retirement package that was funded from pension plan surpluses.

Eaton's then began the implementation of its new business plan. The new plan built on the company's key strengths. These included 129 years of goodwill, very strong supplier relationships, and the fact that no competitor could match Eaton's prime store locations. Furthermore, the new strategy attempted to address the company's key weaknesses. Eaton's planned to reposition itself as a fashion department store with an exciting new image. It planned to orient itself towards customers that were fashion- and quality-conscious rather than trying to compete on price.

Eaton's planned to implement "micro-marketing" techniques whereby each store would modify the assortment of goods offered to best reflect the target customer profile in the community it served.

The restructuring plan aimed to rationalise Eaton's merchandise mix by better managing inventory levels and by moving out of the low margin hard-goods business. The company also planned to renovate the appearance of its stores. Already renovated stores were showing a 24 percent increase in sales.

Eaton's planned to implement a variety of merchandising programs, such as an emphasis on "in-shop supplier-stores" offering national and designer brands to improve gross margins. The company would differentiate itself from the other Canadian retailers by positioning itself between The Bay and Holt Renfrew, a high-end Canadian department store, from a target market perspective. Its goal was to be positioned in the under-served "moderate-better" market segment. Furthermore, Eaton's planned to re-engineer operational processes to reduce expenses.

Financial Restructuring

According to the restructuring agreement, Eaton's agreed to repay bank debt to the high yield funds that held it at the rate of 100 cents on the dollar (with a combination of cash and notes). Holders of trade debt also received a combination of cash and notes, whereas landlords received 85 cents on the dollar for their claims.

To pay for the restructuring, Eaton's sold most of its non-core assets, and obtained $208.5 million from pension surplus sharing. The Eaton family invested another $50 million. Having satisfied most of its creditors, the company planned to raise the capital needed for its operational restructuring plan by going through an IPO.

Managerial Restructuring

During the last quarter of 1997, the company instituted certain changes to its governance so that the composition of the board would better reflect the investment of shareholders other than the Eaton family. The size of Eaton's board of directors was increased to 11 and 10 new directors were appointed, including a chairman independent of management.

Nine of the directors on the board were non-management directors and six of the directors were "unrelated" directors in that they had no interest in Eaton's that could materially interfere with their ability to act in the company's best interest. Brent Ballantyne was the new chairman of the board. Ballantyne was the former chairman and chief executive officer (CEO) of Beatrice Foods Inc., prior to which he had been president and CEO of Maple Leaf Foods Inc. Fredrik, Thor and George Eaton remained directors on the board, although George Kosich replaced George Eaton as president of Eaton's. Kosich was hired with a substantial cash salary and a one-time initial cash bonus. He was also granted an option to purchase up to 5 percent of the common share equity of the company outstanding as of October 1997.

Hap Stephen was brought on as director, executive vice-president, and chief financial officer. He was formerly the president of Ernst & Young Inc., and the chairman of Ernst & Young Corporate Finance Inc. While at Ernst & Young, he had acted as the court-appointed monitor of the Eaton's restructuring. His contract at Eaton's provided for a bonus of 50 percent of his base cash salary for meeting targeted performance figures and up to 100 percent of his base salary for exceeding his performance targets. He was also granted certain participation rights based on two percent of the increase in the value of the common shares.

Pierre Daoust was hired as executive vice-president of stores. Prior to joining Eaton's, Daoust had been president of the M Stores division of Steinberg Inc. Among other senior appointments were those of David Murdoch, and Rod Ulmer, both with over 20 years' experience in the retail sector. Murdoch and Ulmer were hired in November 1997, as vice presidents of merchandising. Daoust, Murdoch, and Ulmer were offered competitive salaries with performance-based bonuses and stock options.

Additionally, executive bonus plans were instituted for the payment of annual bonuses. Awards for 1998 were set as a percentage of the individual executive's base salary and were based on meeting or exceeding the forecast EBITDA less interest expense figures for that year, as set in Eaton's prospectus (see Exhibit 6).

A stock option compensation plan was expected to come before the Eaton's board shortly. The maximum number of common shares reserved for issuance under the plan was proposed not to exceed 10 percent of the shares outstanding. Options to purchase approximately 70 percent of this maximum number would be granted immediately, most going to directors and senior executives, such as Kosich, Stephen, Daoust, Murdoch, Ulmer and Ballantyne. The options would have 10-year terms and an exercise price equal to the offering price of Eaton's IPO. This stock option plan was likely to be approved by the board.

THE IPO PROCESS[6]

The IPO process can be initiated by the issuer or, in many cases, by an investment bank. Having decided to do an IPO, the issuer invites presentations from several investment banks. The respective presentations normally include preliminary valuation estimates, and estimates of how much and at what price the investment bank feels it can raise the capital for the issuer. These estimates are based on market conditions, and the issuing company's past performance and future prospects.

The issuer then selects a "lead-underwriter" or "lead-manager". This is the investment bank which puts together a syndicate of underwriters brought together to share, in varying degrees, the risk, marketing effort, and commission related to the IPO. Over the next two to three months, the syndicate works with the issuer to produce the preliminary prospectus for the IPO. This involves an extensive investigation by the underwriters and their experts into the issuer's operations ("due diligence").

Once completed, the prospectus is filed with securities commissions in all provinces where securities are to be sold. The various commissions review the prospectus to ensure that it provides "full, true and plain disclosure" of all material facts relating to the securities being issued. The prospectus must contain, among other things, a description of the issuing company, a description of the securities being sold, a discussion of past operating results, the risk factors associated with the offering, the plan for distributing the shares and the proposed use of proceeds.[7] While not required, the prospectus can contain forward-looking financial information, such as forecasted income statements for up to two years. The preliminary prospectus does not contain information on the offering price (nor information dependent on that price), or the underwriting fees.

Over the next four to six weeks, the various provincial securities commissions review the adequacy of

---

[6]This section is based on a discussion in *Inside Investment Banking*, 2nd Edition, by Ernest Bloch, 1989 *(Dow Jones Irwin)* and information obtained from KPMG Canada and Scotia Capital Markets.

[7]Prospectus content requirements can differ among provinces. The requirements of the Ontario Securities Act are considered to be the most stringent. Therefore, a prospectus prepared in accordance with the Ontario requirements would likely comply with the requirements in other provinces.

disclosure in the prospectus.[8] During this post-filing, or "waiting" period, the underwriting syndicate begins its marketing efforts. It first produces a marketing memorandum or "greensheet" which summarises the investment merits of the offering, provides comparable company information and establishes an initial offering price range. In the two to three weeks prior to anticipated regulatory approval of the offering, the underwriters conduct informational meetings or "roadshows". These are gatherings in major Canadian cities, attended by retail brokers, where the executives from the issuer and the underwriters summarize information in the prospectus and greensheet, and respond to questions. Similar but smaller meetings are held for groups of institutional investors (mutual fund and pension fund managers). Underwriters also make conference calls to investment dealers' retail networks.

During roadshows and conference calls, the underwriters attempt to establish the demand for the offering in a process referred to as "building the book". Investors are asked about their likely demand for shares in the offering at different offering prices.[9] If the initial price range is appropriately set, book building gives the underwriter a good indication of the price required to fully sell the offering. If the price range is too high, there will be insufficient demand. While the underwriters could lower the price range and approach investors again, this is costly and would add to the time required to complete the offering. It could also have the unintended consequence of further depressing demand. If the price range were set too low, demand would be much more than required to fully sell the offering. Again, the underwriters could adjust the price range and repeat the book building process. If the price were not adjusted, it would increase dramatically once secondary market trading commences. The reputation of the investment bank might suffer from the issuer's perspective for leaving too much "money on the table" (i.e., not getting a higher share value for the company).

Once regulators are satisfied with the adequacy of disclosure in the prospectus, the issuer and underwriters can prepare the final prospectus, which includes the final offering price and underwriting fees. After the final prospectus is filed with provincial securities commissions, underwriters confirm the orders gathered during the book building process at the final offering price. The final settlement, or closing, occurs two to three weeks later. At the closing, the underwriters give the net proceeds of the offering to the issuer and the issuer provides the securities to the underwriters.[10]

Eaton's received proposals from several investment dealers in February 1998 and chose RBC Dominion Securities and Scotia Capital Markets as co-leads to jointly manage the underwriting syndicate for its IPO. The underwriting fees would be shared among the members of the underwriting syndicate according to a relatively new system known as "jump-ball economics." In this process, an investing institution can specify the dealer in the syndicate to whom the selling commission generated by its purchases will go.[11] Eaton's also imposed a cap on how much of the allocated selling commissions could be received by the lead managers. In the Eaton's IPO, the co-leads, Scotia Capital Markets and RBC Dominion Securities, were to share the lead underwriters' commission equally.

THE VALUATION PROCESS

Vitug's primary task was to determine the value of Eaton's. For this she first had to choose an appropriate valuation method. Some of the most commonly used methods for valuing a firm were the discounted cash flow (DCF) method, the capitalised earnings (or price-to-earnings) approach based on a comparable companies analysis, and the capitalised EBITDA[12] method based on a comparable companies analysis.

---

[8]The minimum review period is ten days for the primary jurisdiction (e.g., Ontario) plus five more days for other jurisdictions (i.e., other provinces). If there are omissions in the prospectus or "material" adverse changes for the issuer occur after the preliminary is filed, then the issuer must amend the prospectus and re-file with the various commissions. In this case, the review process begins anew. To reduce the chance of significant omissions, commission staff generally agrees to hold "pre-filing" conferences with the issuer. While the focus of the regulatory review is on the adequacy of disclosure, some provincial securities commissions can also review the merits of particular offerings.

[9]While the offering is still under review, these indications of interest are legally non-binding.

[10]Trading on a secondary market, such as the Toronto Stock Exchange, can commence as soon as the final prospectus is filed, even though the issuer has not formally received the proceeds or provided securities. This is referred to as "when-issued" trading.

[11]Traditionally, the commission is shared among the underwriting syndicate according to pre-agreed percentages.

[12]EBITDA (earnings before interest, taxes, depreciation, amortization) is not affected by a firm's capital structure, nor by its abnormal capital expenditures.

In the DCF method, future free cash flows are projected for the firm, often based on "historical" or past earnings and future expectations. "Free" cash flows refer to those cash flows that are available to equity and debt holders once working capital, tax, and capital expenditures have been met. These cash flows are usually projected at least five years into the future and are then discounted to the present at a rate that reflects the risk of the firm. The value of the firm is simply the sum of these discounted cash flows. The discount rate normally used is the firm's weighted average cost of capital, which is the weighted average of the required returns of all of the company's capital providers. The value of the equity portion is obtained by subtracting the value of any debt obligations.

In the capitalized earnings approach, an appropriate forward-looking price-earnings (P/E) multiple is determined and the "intrinsic value" of the equity of the company is estimated to be the product of this P/E multiple and the expected earnings. In the capitalized EBITDA method, the value of the operating assets of the firm, or "enterprise value" (EV), is estimated.[13] The estimated EV intrinsic value is equal to the product of an appropriate forward-looking EV/EBITDA multiple and expected EBITDA. The value of the equity portion is obtained by adding the firm's cash and subtracting the value of debt, preferred shares and minority interests.

The selection of an appropriate multiple (P/E or EV/EBITDA) is crucial to both the capitalized earnings and capitalized EBITDA methods. Rather than using the average multiple of a large group of firms (e.g., all firms in the same industry), analysts typically use the multiple of a small group of "comparable firms" since these firms with similar risks and growth prospects should trade at similar multiples.

To identify comparable firms, analysts examine profitability ratios, such as earnings before interest and taxes (EBIT), EBITDA, and net margins; efficiency ratios like revenues, cash flow, and earnings per average assets employed; financial leverage ratios, and interest coverage ratios. They also look at historic compound annual growth rates for the last two to five years in sales, EBITDA, EBIT, net income, and earnings per share. They will also look for high proportions of sales, cashflow and earnings derived from the same lines of business, and similar figures for market capitalization, share float, and share liquidity measured by the number of shares outstanding and trading volumes. In cases where there are no publicly traded firms in the same line of business, analysts examine companies that operate in a related industry, are in the same stage of development, face similar business risks, have similar growth prospects, or have similar customers. The more similar a company is to the company being valued, the more confidence there can be that the multiples for the two firms should be close.

No matter which method is applied, other factors can affect the value of a company such as management depth, operating expertise, and commitment through stock options and share ownership. A controlling shareholder with a successful track record or a strong strategic partner will increase value. The valuation of the company can also be affected by whether the shares being offered are voting, subordinate or non-voting shares. New investors expect a base of committed institutional shareholders and expect recognised independent members on the board of directors.

To maximize the value potential investors will place on the firm, it is also important to have a proper balance between institutional and retail investors to ensure satisfactory after-market trading. After-market erosion occurs when too high a proportion of the issue has been placed with institutional investors and "thin" trading results. The same problem arises when too many shares are placed with retail investors who may only be interested in "flipping" the issue to take quick profits.[14]

THE DECISION

Vitug pushed away the keyboard, and put her elbows on the table, her forehead in her palms. Her main task focused on estimating a credible post-IPO value of Eaton's equity. After this was determined, a desired IPO issuing price range and post IPO shares outstanding could be determined. Yet, there was much more to it, she realized.

---

[13]In practice, enterprise value is measured as the market value of equity, less cash (and other market securities), plus the market value of debt and preferred shares (for which book values are often a proxy), plus any minority interests.

[14]According to analysts, a 70 percent to 30 percent split between institutional and retail investors, respectively, is generally considered optimal.

She had already compiled a significant amount of data including historic and projected financial statements for Eaton's (see Exhibit 6), and information on firms which she felt were comparable to Eaton's (Exhibit 7). She needed to determine which valuation technique she should use. She wondered how relevant were Eaton's recent troubles and how important was the timing of the issue. Furthermore, the forecasted income statement assumed that only $75 million of the IPO proceeds would be available to generate earnings in fiscal 1998. Since the remainder of the capital raised would be used initially to pay down Eaton's operating line of approximately $194 million[15] (as of April 25, 1998), would it be worthwhile for her to forecast earnings further into the future? Ultimately, she realized she would be asked to recommend an appropriate price range for each share in the IPO.

Mary Vitug raised her head and looked back at the screen. Doing their circles, those sad cyber-fish were still there. And so was she.

---

[15]Eaton's total debt at the time was $245.5 million, excluding the $28.9 million in subordinate notes that the Eaton family planned to swap for common stock as part of the IPO (see footnote 2 for the details of the proposed offering).

Exhibit 1

COMPANIES' CREDITORS ARRANGEMENT ACT (CCAA)[1]

A firm is technically "insolvent" when it is unable to honor its financial obligations as they come due. This may be the case even though the book value of the company's assets exceeds total liabilities. This situation could be temporary and a restructuring of the company's business may be required.

In Canada, an insolvent company can either make a proposal to its creditors under the Bankruptcy and Insolvency Act (BIA) or alternatively, can apply for protection from its creditors by court order pursuant to the provisions of the CCAA. The CCAA grants Canadian Courts jurisdiction to issue a stay of proceedings which stays and suspends all legal proceedings or enforcement processes or any other remedies commenced by any of the creditors, customers, suppliers, lenders, landlords and lessors. Such an order effectively insulates the insolvent company from its contractual obligations and, at the same time, permits the insolvent company to carry on its business pending the implementation of a Plan of Compromise or Arrangement.

Once a stay of proceedings has been issued by the Court under the CCAA, no creditor may take action against the company. However, the Court has the discretionary power to include terms in the Order which provide for the ongoing business of the insolvent company, including the termination of contracts or arrangements of any nature whatsoever, in order to permit the insolvent company to proceed with an orderly restructuring of its business operations.

The insolvent company then negotiates a fair and feasible compromise with creditors. The terms of the restructuring are set out in a Plan or Compromise or Arrangement (the "Plan"). The Plan must be approved by 50 percent by number of the creditors who have at least 75 percent of the dollar value of the creditors in each class voting on the plan. The Plan is ultimately voted on by the creditors. If approved by the creditors, the Plan is then filed with the Court for its approval and is then implemented.

The BIA provides detailed provisions on dealings with creditors but, as a consequence, is very inflexible. The CCAA process allows the Court to use discretionary orders to facilitate and supervise large, complex, corporate restructurings.

---

[1]*This exhibit was prepared by Tom Little under the supervision of Professor Craig Dunbar.*

Exhibit 2
STATISTICAL TRENDS[1]

Canadian Economy

	May 1998	**percent change over last 1 year**
GDP	$706 billion	+ 3.4
Retail Trade	$19.9 billion	+ 4.3
Household credit	$514.8 billion	+ 4.6
Business Credit	$641 billion	+ 9.2
Money Supply (M-3)	$641 billion	+ 21.3
Consumer Price Index	108 (1992=100)	+ 0.9
		1 year ago
Unemployment	8.4 percent	9.5 percent
Prime rate	6.5 percent	4.75 percent
Canada bond yield	5.6 percent	6.99 percent
Corporate bond yield	6.1 percent	7.48 percent

U.S. Economy

GDP Q1	+ 3.6 percent
Consumer Price Index	+ 1.4 percent
Unemployment	- 0.7 percent
Bank prime rate	unchanged at 8.5 percent

---

[1] *Based on annualized and seasonally adjusted figures reported in the <u>Globe and Mail</u>, Report on Business, May 11, 1998.*

Exhibit 3

S&P 500 AND TSE 300 STOCK INDICES BETWEEN 1994 AND 1998[1]

The S&P 500 Index

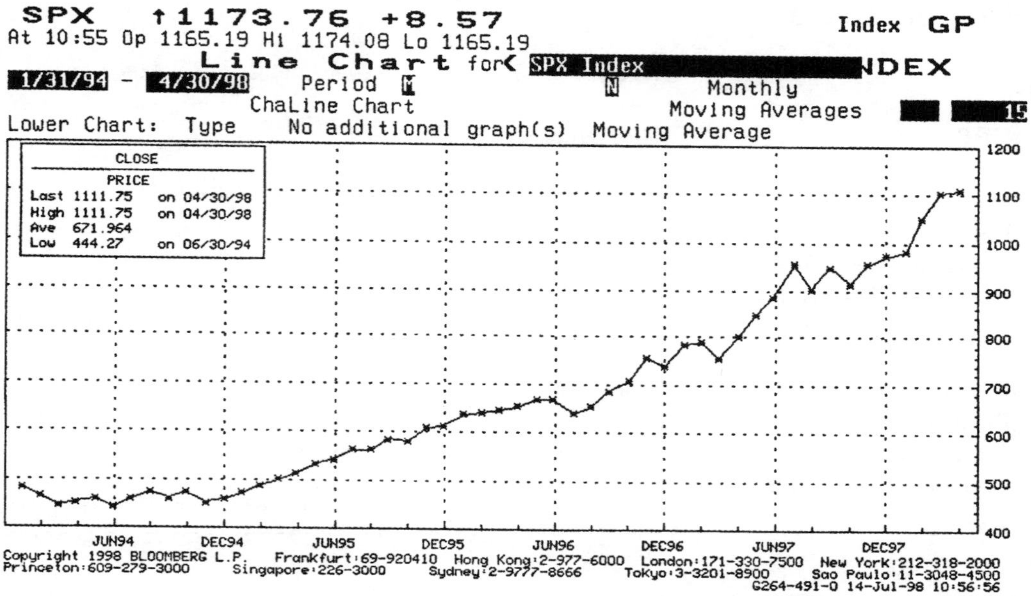

The TSE 300 Index

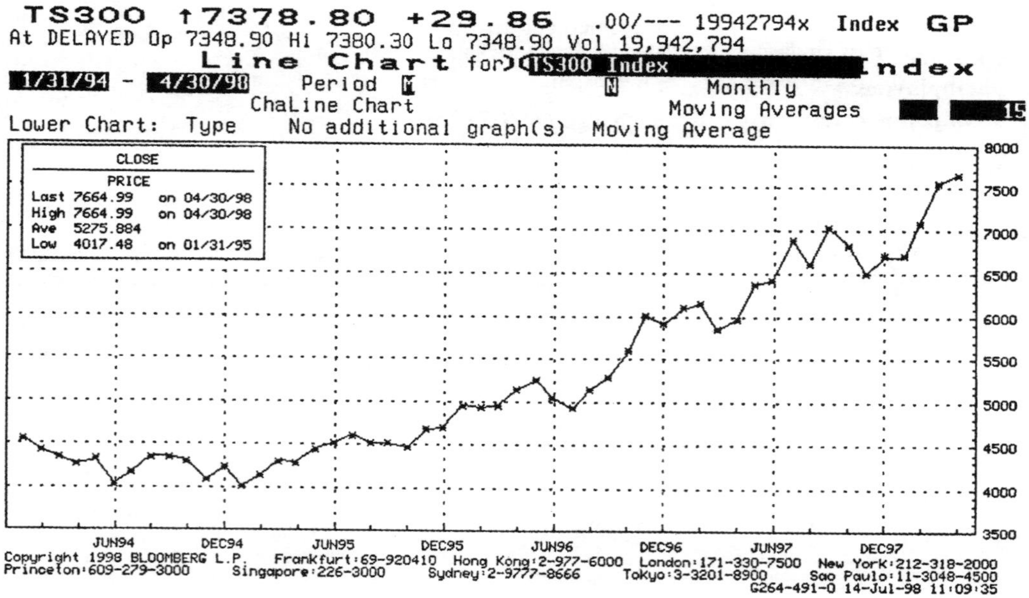

---

[1] *Source: Bloomberg Financial Services*

Exhibit 4

S&P RETAIL INDEX AND THE TSE DEPARTMENT STORE INDEX BETWEEN 1994 AND 1998[1]

The S&P Retail Index

The TSE Department Store Index

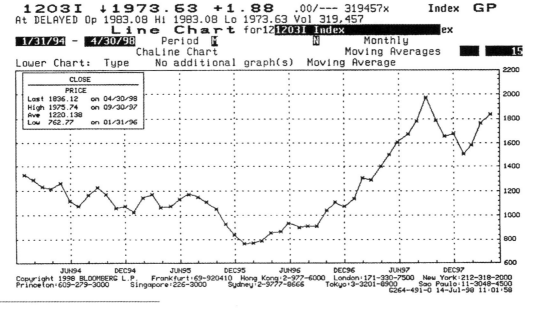

---

[1] *Source: Bloomberg Financial Services*

Exhibit 5

**CANADIAN RETAIL INDUSTRY SALES
(IN MILLION CANADIAN DOLLARS)** [1]

	1993	1994	1995	1996	1997
Major department stores [2]	$ 6,838	$6,764	$6,430	$ 6,402	$6,925 [3]
Eaton's share	28.8%	27.4%	26.5%	26.0%	24.4%
All department stores [4]	$12,794	$13,299	$13,840	$14,447	$15,929
Eaton's share	15.4%	14.0%	12.3%	11.5%	10.6%
Department store type merchandise [5]	$66,316	$69,558	$70,682	$72,484	$77,422
Eaton's share	3.0%	2.7%	2.4%	2.3%	2.2%

(1)   Source: Adapted from the Statistics Canada publication *Retail Trade*, Catalogue 63–005, 1997
(2)   Major department stores include The Bay, Eaton's and Sears Canada.
(3)   Estimate based on 1997 retail sales of Eaton's, The Bay and Sears Canada.
(4)   Includes all major department stores, KMart Canada, Wal-Mart Canada and Zellers.
(5)   Includes all retail sales excluding automobiles, gas, food and restaurant sales.

Exhibit 6
FINANCIAL STATEMENTS AND PROJECTIONS

Balance Sheets (dollars in thousands) – (see note 1)

	Jan. 31, 1998	Jan. 25, 1997
Assets		
Current Assets		
Cash and short-term investments	$7,514	$91,167
Accounts receivable and prepaid expenses (note 9)	56,737	28,063
Merchandise inventories	350,619	272,536
Discontinued operations (note 9)	469,557	-
	884,427	391,766
Fixed assets (note 2)	155,879	238,279
Deferred pension and other assets	5,830	165,761
Discontinued operations (note 9)	38,628	848,470
	$1,084,764	$1,644,276
Liabilities		
Current Liabilities		
Revolving operating line of credit (note 3)	$89,917	$162,894
Notes payable (note 4)	99,109	-
Accounts payable	64,499	129,235
Accrued charges and other current liabilities (note 8)	129,106	105,342
Income and other taxes payable	9,097	26,942
Current portion of other long-term obligations (note 5)	8,646	16,732
Discontinued operations (note 9)	437,406	-
	837,780	441,145
Notes payable (note 5)	33,869	-
Other long-term obligations (note 5)	31,317	129,917
Deferred income	23,684	17,923
Deferred income taxes (note 6)	-	81,485
Discontinued operations (note 9)	27,269	747,101
	953,919	1,417,571
Shareholders' equity (note 7)	130,845	226,705
	$1,084,764	$1,644,276

Exhibit 6 (continued)			

FINANCIAL STATEMENTS AND PROJECTIONS
HISTORIC AND PROJECTED INCOME STATEMENTS
(dollars in thousands)
(see Note 1)

	Fiscal year ending		
	Jan. 31, 1999 - forecasted (note 10)	**Jan. 31, 1998**	**Jan. 31, 1997**
REVENUE	$1,822,000	$1,688,200	$1,666,534
Cost of merchandise sold	1,199,000	1,162,322	1,129,498
Gross Margin	623,000	525,878	537,036
EXPENSES			
Operating, administrative and selling	545,000	602,431	588,861
Depreciation and amortization	31,000	32,090	40,647
	576,000	634,521	629,508
Operating income before interest	47,000	(108,643)	(92,472)
Interest expense (notes 4 and 5)	13,000	17,279	20,693
Operating Income	34,000	(125,922)	(113,165)
Unusual items (note 8)	(16,000)	(124,543)	(80,361)
Income before taxes	18,000	(250,465)	(193,526)
Income taxes (note 6)	(12,000)	(83,170)	(23,364)
Income before discontinued operations	30,000	(167,295)	(170,162)
Earnings from discontinued operations (note 9)	28,000	11,435	44
Net Income	$ 58,000	$(155,860)	$(170,118)
Earnings (loss) per common share (note 7)			
Before discontinued operations	-	(16.92)	(17.21)
Discontinued operations	-	1.16	-
Net earnings (loss) per common share	-	(15.76)	(17.20)

Exhibit 6 (continued)

NOTES TO FINANCIAL STATEMENTS AND PROJECTIONS

1. Significant Accounting Policies

Fixed assets

Fixed assets are recorded at cost. Depreciation for the major asset classes is: Buildings – 5% (diminishing balance); Fixtures and Equipment – 10% (straight-line); Computer hardware and software – 20% to 33% (straight-line); Automotive – 30% (diminishing balance).

Pension plans

The Company's pension plans (available to substantially all full-time and regular part-time employees) encompass both defined benefit and defined contribution arrangements. Pension expenses include the actuarially-computed cost of the Company's contribution to the plans in respect of the current year's service, computed interest on plan assets and pension obligations and straight-line amortization of experience gains or losses, assumption changes and plan changes over the expected average service life of the employee group. As of fiscal 1997 plan assets are recorded at market value.

2. Fixed assets (CDN dollars in thousands)

	January 31, 1998		January 25, 1997	
	Cost	**Book value**	**Cost**	**Book value**
Land	$ 4,300	$ 4,300	$ 5,768	$ 5,768
Buildings	122,617	50,740	130,788	65,532
Fixtures and equipment	262,457	79,051	241,500	74,302
Assets under capital leases	73,486	18,725	139,383	86,805
Computer hardware and software	38,385	1,646	37,500	2,809
Automotive	14,216	1,293	15,503	1,831
Construction in progress	124	124	1,232	1,232
	$ 515,585	$ 155,879	$ 571,674	$ 238,279

3. Revolving operating line of credit

As of January 31, 1998 the Company had a revolving operating credit facility with a maximum borrowing limit of $250 million. The facility has a maturity date of October 30, 2000 but can be terminated earlier by the Company's option or upon the occurence of specified events of default (these include non-satisfaction of financial covenants and cross-default provisions related to other indebtedness of the Company). The facility also imposes limits on indebtedness, dividends, liens and transactions with shareholders and affiliates of the Company. Borrowings can only be made up to amount of the borrowing base (60% of eligible inventory, less certain deductions). Borrowings bear interest at the bankers' acceptance rate plus 2.75% or at the prime rate plus 1%.

Exhibit 6 (continued)

4. Short-term notes payable

On February 27, 1997, the Company filed for protection under CCCA. On October 30, 1997 the company emerged from CCCA protection and settled various liabilities owed to various classes of creditors. Part of the settlement was with short-term notes payable. This included notes payable to parties that were unsecured creditors prior to restructuring and $30 million in partial settlement of the outstanding debt on the Hamilton Eaton Centre.

5. Long-term obligations (CDN dollars in thousands)

	Weighted average interest rate	January 31, 1998	January 25, 1997
Class C Notes, due Feb. 1, 2000	9.5%	$ 28,869	-
Landlord Notes, due Feb. 1, 2000	6.0%	5,000	-
Mortgages various terms due 2005-2015	8.1%	15,799	18,313
Due to shareholders		-	28,910
Obligations under capital lease	10.0%	11,383	93,979
Pension liabilities		12,781	5,447
		73,832	146,649
Current portion due within 1 year		8,646	16,732
		$ 65,186	$ 129,917

The Eaton family held the Class C Notes. They are collateralized by certain real property assets and the proceeds of any sales thereof. The Class C and landlord notes were created under the CCAA reorganization plan. As of January 25, 1997, capital lease obligations included $71.3 million where the lease was either terminated or converted to an operating lease under the CCAA restructuring plan.

6. Income taxes

The average combined statutory income tax rate applicable to the Company is approximately 44%. The Company has accumulated non-capital losses for income tax purposes of $213.1 million as of January 31, 1998 that may be carried forward and applied against future years' taxable income. The Company also has approximately $43 million of additional timing differences for which no deferred tax asset has been recorded. The Company's non-capital loss carryforwards expire as follows: 2001 – $9.0 million; 2001 – $44.8 million; 2002 – $49.6 million; 2003 – $12.1 million; and 2004 – $97.6 million (years refer to fiscal years).

Exhibit 6 (continued)

---

7. Shareholder's equity

Prior to the offering, there were 9,888,733 common shares outstanding. These shares are owned by members of the Eaton family (through corporations, the shares are owned in equal amounts by John Eaton, Fredrik Eaton, Thor Eaton and George Eaton).

8. Unusual items

During fiscal 1997, the Company undertook a major operational restructuring resulting in the closure of 18 stores and a significant restructuring of administrative and support functions. The company also incurred significant CCAA related costs. Restructuring costs for fiscal 1997 include all costs related to store closures announced prior to year-end that will close in the subsequent fiscal year. Restructuring costs for fiscal 1996 include write-downs for the impairment in value of assets based on the restructuring plan adopted in fiscal 1997. Other restructuring costs for the 1996 fiscal year related substantially to severance and voluntary retirement expenses resulting from reorganization of the Company's head office and information systems operations outsourcing.

Unusual items are broken down as follows (CDN dollars in thousands):

	Fiscal years ended	
	Jan. 31, 1998	**Jan. 25, 1997**
Store closure and other restructuring costs	$ (124,526)	$ (18,291)
CCAA costs	(58,815)	-
Write-offs of fixed assets	(4,632)	(63,680)
Total restructuring costs	(185,973)	(81,971)
Gain on settlement of pension surplus	41,907	-
Gain (loss) on sale of assets	18,319	(87)
Other	1,204	1,697
	$ (124,543)	$ (80,361)

9. Discontinued operations

Discontinued operations refer to the Company's Credit and Real Estate Operations. Both operations were terminated after the end of the 1997 fiscal year. On February 16, 1998 Eaton's entered into an agreement with Norwest Financial Capital Canada Inc. ("Norwest") to sell all the shares of its two credit subsidiaries (The T. Eaton Acceptance Co. Limited, or TEAC, and the National Retail Credit Services Limited, or NRCS) for an aggregate proceeds of $126 million. The closing date of the sale was April 28, 1998. Eaton's has agreed that if the Eaton Card fails to achieve certain performance levels of cumulative credit card sales during the five years ending January 31, 2003, Eaton's will pay up to a maximum principal amount of $42.5 million (or a lesser amount if early performance levels are met) to Norwest. As security for such performance warranty obligations, Norwest received a security interest in certain assets of Eaton's up to a maximum principal amount of $42.5 million.

The balance sheet recognition of discontinued operations is summarized as follows. For fiscal year 1997, the current portion of the assets from discontinued operations is solely the credit operations.

Exhibit 6 (continued)

The fixed portion of the assets from discontinued operations is solely the real estate operations. For fiscal year 1996 the assets from the credit and real estate operations are treated as fixed. The credit operations make up approximately 68% of the total fixed assets. For fiscal year 1996, liabilities from credit and real estate operations are treated as long-term. Credit operations make up approximately 72% of the total. In fiscal year 1997, some liabilities are treated as current. Of those current liabilities, approximately 94% are due to the credit operations. Of those long-term liabilities, approximately 47% are due to the credit operations. The income statement recognition of discontinued operations is summarized as follows. For fiscal year 1996, revenue from discontinued operations was $261.7 million and earnings were $0.04 million. For fiscal year 1997, revenue from discontinued operations was $115.6 million and earnings were $11.4 million.

10. Forecasting assumptions

Revenue projections

Revenue is forecast at the merchandise class level for continuing stores based on management's best estimate of the benefits from implementing its Business Plan. Key assumptions include: (a) increased average density per net selling square foot by 35% (to $97), (b) installation of approximately 2,200 supplier shops by the end of the third quarter of fiscal 1998, (c) completion of renovations of 1.3 million square feet of gross leasable area by the third quarter of 1998, and (d) discontinuing sale of hard goods in 21 stores by the end of April 1998 and a reallocation of approximately 400,000 square feet of net selling area to fashion departments.

Cost of goods sold

Cost of merchandise sold as a percentage of sales for continuing stores is assumed to decrease by 2.8% from the prior fiscal year (shift to higher margin goods and reduced use of heavy promotional discounting).

Interest expenses

Borrowing on the Company's operating line is forecast to average approximately $95 million. Interest expense has been calculated based on an assumed prime rate of 6.5%.

Capital expenditures

Fiscal year 1998 planned expenditures amount to $75 million. Approximately 60% will be spent on store renovations and 40% on supplier shop installations. Capital expenditures will be made before the end of the third quarter of fiscal year 1998. In the short run, the proceeds from the initial public offering will be used to pay down the Company's revolving operating credit line. For fiscal year 1999, planned capital expenditures are $100 million. Approximately 60% will be spent on store renovations and 40% on supplier shop installations. No acquisitions of business are planned for the forecast horizon.

Exhibit 6 (continued)

Unusual items

Unusual expenses for fiscal year 1998 include information systems costs related to Year 2000 project ($12 million) and other restructuring costs ($4 million). The forecast also assumes the receipt of cash proceeds of $6 million on the sale-leaseback of the Bramalea City Centre store. The gain on the sale of this store has been deferred and will be amortized over the 20-year lease term.

Earnings from discontinued operations

The sales of Eaton's credit operations to Norwest for $126 million generated a gain on sale of approximately $85 million. Of this gain, $50.5 million has been deferred and will be realized over the next 10 years. The gain of $34.5 million is the most significant component of the revenue from discontinued operations. Applying tax loss carryforwards has offset the income tax on this gain. Earnings from discontinued operations also include $6 million from the sale of the Brandon real estate joint venture. Applying tax loss carryforwards has offset income tax of $2 million on this gain.

Use of proceeds from sale of Eaton's credit operations

The proceeds from the sale of Eaton's credit operations to Norwest were used to pay $99.109 million in short-term notes payable. The remainder was used to reduce the Company's operating line of credit.

Exhibit 7
DESCRIPTION OF COMPARABLE COMPANIES[1]

CANADIAN DEPARTMENT STORES

Hudson's Bay Company

The Hudson's Bay Company is Canada's largest department store chain with 100 The Bay stores and 300 Zellers stores. The Bay targets the mid-range price level while Zellers concentrates on the low/moderate price range.

Sears Canada

Sears Canada operates 110 full-line department stores across Canada and is the 3rd largest major department store chain following The Bay and Eaton's. The company also operates Canada's largest catalogue operation with 1,773 catalogue pick-up outlets, a credit operation, 5 Whole Home Furniture stores, and a home service division.

Canadian Tire Corporation

Canadian Tire supplies merchandise to associate stores located in all the provinces. The stores sell automobile parts and accessories, hardware and household items, leisure-time products, and provide complete automotive service facilities. The company is also involved in real estate, re-manufacturing of auto parts, and consumer credit, as well as operating 197 gasoline stations in Canada.

U.S. DEPARTMENT STORES

Dillard Department Stores

Dillard Department Stores operates approximately 250 department stores located in 24 Southeastern, Southwestern, and Mid-western states of the U.S. The company's stores are primarily located in suburban shopping centres and offer brand name goods in the middle to upper middle price range.

Federated Department Stores

Federated operates full-line department stores and its merchandise includes men's, women's and children's apparel and accessories, cosmetics, home furnishings and other consumer goods. Federated operates more than 400 department stores and 150 speciality stores in 36 states of the U.S. Among the store chains owned by Federated are Bloomingdale's, The Bon Marché, and Macy's.

---

[1] *Based on Scotia Capital Markets analysis.*

Exhibit 7 (continued)

Mercantile Stores Company

Mercantile Stores Company operates 104 fashion apparel stores and 17 home fashion stores in 17 states. The company's retailing strategy is to cater to middle and upper income customers by carrying a wide assortment of national brand items as well as goods sold under Mercantile's private labels. The emphasis is on apparel, accessories, and fashion home products. Its stores compete with other national, regional and local retail establishments, including department stores, mass merchants, specialty stores and discount stores. The company's competitive methodology focuses on value, customer service, fashion, selection, marketing, and store location.

Nordstrom's

Nordstrom's is one of the largest upscale apparel and shoe retailers in the U.S. Nordstrom's has 60 department stores and 20 outlet stores. The company has developed a strong reputation for high quality customer service. Its employees, known as "Nordies," take customer service to new heights, sometimes applauding customers as they walk into new stores and writing personalized thank-you notes after a sale. Members of the Nordstrom family, whose members own about 36% of the company's stock, closely supervise the chain.

Proffitt's Inc.

Proffitt's operates regional department stores and targets middle to upper income customers offering moderate to better brand name fashion apparel, shoes, accessories, cosmetics and decorative home furnishings. Proffitt's stores are primarily anchors in regional or community malls.

Exhibit 7 (continued)

COMPARABLE COMPANY ANALYSIS
Current Balance Sheet and Market Data for Comparable Companies

Canadian Department Stores (CDN$, millions except per share amounts)

Company	Fiscal Year end	LTM period end (1)	LTM Book Value Equity	Share price (April 30, 1998)	Number of shares outstanding	Market Capitalization	Beta (2)	Debt plus preferred (3) (book value)	Cash	Enterprise Value (4)
Hudson's Bay Company	31-Jan	31-Jan-98	$2,010.49	$31.10	73.0	$2,270.30	0.91	$1,307.80	$119.60	$3,458.50
Sears Canada	3-Jan	3-Jan-98	$1,048.37	$26.75	107.1	$2,864.93	1.03	$847.70	$74.00	$3,638.63
Canadian Tire	3-Jan	3-Jan-98	$1,299.75	$35.90	82.2	$2,950.98	0.91	$783.30	$263.40	$3,470.88

U.S. Department Stores (US$, millions except per share amounts)

Company	Fiscal Year end	LTM period end (1)	LTM Book Value Equity	Share price (April 30, 1998)	Number of shares outstanding	Market Capitalization	Beta (2)	Debt plus preferred (3) (book value)	Cash	Enterprise Value (4)
Dillard Department Stores	31-Jan	31-Jan-98	$2,757.99	$36.63	107.6	$3,941.39	0.77	$1,906.40	$42.00	$5,805.79
Federated Department Stores	31-Jan	31-Jan-98	$5,258.65	$49.50	224.8	$11,127.60	0.91	$4,125.00	$628.00	$14,624.60
Mercantile Stores Company	1-Feb	1-Nov-97	$1,573.38	$73.06	36.7	$2,681.30	0.89	$270.90	$52.20	$2,900.00
Nordstrom's	31-Jan	31-Jan-98	$1,476.06	$65.44	74.3	$4,862.19	0.60	$684.60	$24.80	$5,521.99
Proffitt's	1-Feb	1-Nov-97	$1,046.92	$39.75	89.2	$3,545.70	0.63	$640.90	$29.50	$4,157.10

(1) LTM refers to "last 12 months" (ending the date indicated)
(2) Source: Bloomberg Investor Services. For US companies, beta is calculated using the S&P500 index. For Canadian companies, it is calculated using the TSE300 index
(3) Preferred is $0 except for Dillard Department Stores where Preferred is $0.4
(4) Market capitalization of equity plus debt and preferreds minus cash

Exhibit 7 (continued)

HISTORICAL AND FORECASTED FINANCIAL INFORMATION FOR COMPARABLE COMPANIES AND T. EATON CO.

Company	Revenue					Earnings					EBITDA				
	1994	1995	LTM	1998E	1999E	1994	1995	LTM	1998E	1999E	1994	1995	LTM	1998E	1999E
Canadian Department Stores (CDN$, millions)															
Hudson's Bay Company	$5,442.00	$5,829.00	$6,447.00	$7,577.00	$7,947.00	$148.00	$184.00	$51.00	$112.42	$157.68	$451.00	$476.00	$333.00	$510.00	$609.00
Sears Canada	$4,067.00	$3,918.00	$4,584.00	$4,929.00	$5,227.00	$48.00	$33.00	$117.00	$149.94	$176.72	$298.00	$249.00	$379.00	$438.00	$490.00
Canadian Tire	$3,604.00	$3,771.30	$4,057.00	$4,257.00	$4,457.00	$114.80	$121.80	$149.00	$164.40	$189.06	$310.00	$327.00	$353.00	$373.00	$420.00
U.S. Department Stores (US$, millions)															
Dillard Department Stores	$5,545.80	$5,918.00	$6,817.00	$7,146.20	$7,646.50	$251.80	$167.20	$258.00	$277.61	$301.28	$442.10	$529.00	$739.00	$784.60	$837.60
Federated Department Stores	n/a	$15,049.00	$15,668.00	$16,399.00	$17,137.00	n/a	$357.00	$561.00	$674.40	$775.56	n/a	$1,388.00	$1,951.00	$2,125.40	$2,301.60
Mercantile Stores Company	$2,819.80	$2,944.30	$3,118.00	$3,406.80	n/a	$103.40	$123.20	$120.00	$146.80	n/a	$267.30	$291.10	$279.00	n/a	n/a
Nordstrom's	$3,894.50	$4,113.50	$4,852.00	$5,426.00	$6,022.00	$203.00	$165.10	$186.00	$202.84	$247.42	$477.20	$445.60	$501.00	$545.00	$613.00
Proffitt's	$1,063.50	$1,513.40	$3,497.00	$3,750.00	$4,068.00	$25.50	$35.80	$96.00	$160.56	$199.81	n/a	n/a	$193.00	$422.00	$491.80
T. Eaton Co.	$1,698.48	$1,691.02	$1,688.20	$1,821.60	$2,013.90	-$116.52	-$130.41	-$155.90	$58.00	$64.30	n/a	-$61.99	-$76.60	$78.00	n/a

Exhibit 7 (continued)

RATIO ANALYSIS

Company	Fiscal Year end	LTM period end	Market Capitalization	Enterprise Value	Enterprise Value / EBITDA			Price / EPS			Enterprise Value / Revenue		
					LTM	1998E	1999E	LTM	1998E	1999E	LTM	1998E	1999E
Canadian Department Stores													
Hudson's Bay Company	31-Jan	31-Jan-98	$2,270.30	$3,458.50	10.4	6.8	5.7	44.5	20.2	14.4	0.5	0.5	0.4
Sears Canada	03-Jan	03-Jan-98	$2,864.93	$3,638.63	9.6	8.3	7.4	24.5	19.1	16.2	0.8	0.7	0.7
Canadian Tire	03-Jan	03-Jan-98	$2,950.98	$3,470.88	9.8	9.3	8.3	19.8	18.0	15.6	0.9	0.8	0.8
Canadian Average					9.9	8.1	7.1	29.6	19.1	15.4	0.7	0.7	0.6
U.S. Department Stores													
Dillard Department Stores	31-Jan	31-Jan-98	$3,941.39	$5,805.79	7.9	7.4	6.9	15.3	14.2	13.1	0.9	0.8	0.8
Federated Department Stores	31-Jan	31-Jan-98	$11,127.60	$14,624.60	7.5	6.9	6.4	19.8	16.5	14.3	0.9	0.9	0.9
Mercantile Stores Company	01-Feb	01-Nov-97	$2,681.30	$2,900.00	10.4	n/a	n/a	22.3	18.3	n/a	0.9	0.9	n/a
Nordstrom's	31-Jan	31-Jan-98	$4,862.19	$5,521.99	11.0	10.1	9.0	26.1	24.0	19.7	1.1	1.0	0.9
Proffitt's	01-Feb	01-Nov-97	$3,545.70	$4,157.10	21.5	9.9	8.5	36.9	22.1	17.7	1.2	1.1	1.0
U.S. Average					11.7	8.6	7.7	24.1	19.0	16.2	1.0	0.9	0.9
North American Average					11.0	8.4	7.4	26.2	19.0	15.9	0.9	0.8	0.8

HUANENG POWER INTERNATIONAL INC. RAISING CAPITAL IN GLOBAL MARKETS

In early October of 1994, Huaneng Power International Inc. (HPI) was in the process of executing a global equity issue to raise funds for the construction of new power plants. On August 30, 1994, HPI had announced that it would go public and list on the New York Stock Exchange (NYSE) on October 6, 1994. On September 2 it filed the necessary documentation with the Securities and Exchange Commission (SEC), indicating a share price between $22.50 and $27.50. HPI's development plans over the next several years required financing of approximately $4.5 billion, and the equity issue, which was intended to raise between $700 million and $860 million, was a crucial component of that financing.[1] It was important that any issue be seen as a success by both the company and investors, since it would be HPI's first foray into foreign equity markets, and could set the tone for future capital-raising efforts. Recent events, however, indicated that the time might not be right for HPI to try to raise equity capital. A sister company to HPI, Shandong Huaneng Power (Shandong) had raised equity and listed on the NYSE in early August, becoming the first company registered in the People's Republic of China (PRC) to have its primary foreign listing on a U.S. stock exchange. While the entire issue of $333 million had been sold, it was not oversubscribed,[2] and the market value of the issue had fallen substantially since the launch date.

---

[1]Huaneng Power International Inc. *Prospectus,* October 5, 1994.

[2]Peltz, Michael, "Takeovers to the Rescue," *International Investor,* October 1994.

Richard Ivey School of Business
The University of Western Ontario

IVEY

Jerry White prepared this case under the supervision of Professors Steve Foerster and Andrew Karolyi solely to provide material for class discussion. The authors do not intend to illustrate either effective or ineffective handling of a managerial situation. The authors may have disguised certain names and other identifying information to protect confidentially.

Exhibit 1 shows the after-market performance of Shandong and other initial public offerings around the time of Shandong's launch.

Raising equity capital in foreign markets was still a relatively new idea in the PRC. In the past, the PRC had tried to be self-funding where possible and had relied on international debt capital when domestic sources were insufficient. The rapid growth of the past several years had strained internal sources of debt capital, with domestic banks incapable of fulfilling the capital requirements of the larger domestic industries. In addition, economic reforms had encouraged private ownership of previously state-run enterprises. Thus, PRC firms sought to raise equity capital to finance growth. While the country had two stock exchanges, they were in their infancy, with relatively low capitalization and liquidity. As a result, larger PRC firms had begun to look outside of the country to finance their expansion. Several PRC firms had raised equity internationally since July 1993, when Tsingtao Brewery became the first PRC-registered firm to list on an exchange outside of the PRC.[3]

Most PRC firms had raised equity on the Hong Kong exchange, although a few had offered the Hong Kong-listed shares in other countries as well. However, the mixed welcome that these firms had received made predicting the success of a global issue difficult. There was no way to be sure whether foreign investors would be interested in taking an equity stake in HPI, although several foreign stock markets were interested in winning the listings for PRC firms, as evidenced by the September 2, 1994 announcement by NYSE President William Donaldson that he would visit the Shanghai exchange in the PRC. Donaldson cited the importance of the PRC to the U.S. and the expectation that U.S. investors would double their foreign holdings in the next few years as reasons for his visit. As well, the SEC had announced that it would require HPI and other PRC companies to submit only two years audited earnings instead of the usual three years.[4]

Analysts differed as to what was the best foreign market to tap for a PRC company equity issue. Listing on a U.S. stock exchange offered some advantages, such as broader international exposure and access to more institutional investors. This could be important considering the size of the planned HPI offering. HPI had been scheduled to launch the issue on the NYSE in July, but had delayed the issue to the fall due to poor market conditions.[5] The U.S. had experienced an interest rate jump in the spring of 1994 initiated by the Federal Reserve Board in an attempt to control inflation, which was threatening to spiral higher. The sharp increase in interest rates had had an adverse effect on U.S. stock markets, which had been very strong in 1993. Despite the recent lackluster performance of the U.S. markets, domestic initial public offerings (IPOs) had shown few signs, as yet, of slowing down.[6] Also, it was not yet clear whether U.S. inflation had been brought under control. In spite of this uncertainty, the company rescheduled its offering for early October, as it was scheduled to take ownership of a partially completed plant by December and would have to have the funds in place to do so.[7]

PEOPLE'S REPUBLIC OF CHINA

The People's Republic of China was established in 1949 after a Communist revolution. As of 1994, the Communist Party was the only legal political party in the PRC. The government's highest policy and rule-making body was the National People's Congress (NPC), which consisted of nearly 3,000 representatives of provinces, autonomous regions and municipalities. The NPC set economic policy for the PRC, and had recently endorsed the concept of a "socialist market economy."[8] The NPC had the power to appoint the premier of the State Council, the highest administrative authority of the state, as well as several other high-ranking officials. The State Council was responsible for the supervision and co-ordination of all ministries and commissions at the state level, including the power industry. It prepared and supervised the

---

[3]Reuters News Service, July 14, 1993.

[4]"SEC Easy on Chinese," *The Globe and Mail*, June 13, 1994.

[5]Privatization International, no. 71, August, 1994.

[6]The Investment Dealers' Digest, August 8, 1994.

[7]Prospectus.

[8]"China," EIU Country Report, *The Economist Intelligence Unit*, September 9, 1994.

implementation of the state plan and budget. It also had final authority over all administrative orders issued by national and local administrative agencies.[9] The tone for the policy decisions made by the government was set by the leaders of the government. The two most powerful leaders were Deng Xiaoping, who held no official title but was universally recognized as the head of state, and Premier Li Peng.

For several decades, the PRC had a completely state-run and centrally-planned economy, and followed a policy of isolation from the rest of the world. However, beginning in the late 1970s, the PRC began to experiment with limited free-market reforms. The central government relaxed its control over many industries in order to move from a centrally planned economy to more of a market-oriented one. Managers were given more decision-making power and state-owned enterprises (SOEs) were expected to operate at a profit. These reforms had continued throughout the 1980s and 1990s, and contributed greatly to the rapid growth of the PRC economy in recent years. In fact, the economy had expanded at an average annual rate of about nine per cent since 1978, in line with the government's long-term goal target of seven to nine per cent.[10] Exhibit 2 contains selected economic information on the PRC.

However, the rapid growth of the late 1980s, fueled by these reforms, caused problems. The increased demand that resulted from a greater market orientation caused upward pressure on consumer prices. This, combined with the central government's efforts to move away from planned prices, caused high inflation. The high inflation, in turn, caused social unrest as the prices of food and other staples began to skyrocket. The Tiananmen Square protests that followed in 1989 were dealt with swiftly by the PRC government, which then implemented tight controls on capital. These controls reduced demand, moderated gross national product (GNP) growth and brought inflation down to historical lows of 2.1 per cent and 2.9 per cent in 1990 and 1991, respectively. Inflation and GNP started to pick up steam again in 1992, however, with both measures increasing well into the double digits. Despite official government pronouncements that the necessary measures were in place and that inflation had started to moderate, by mid-1994 most economists expressed concerns that the level of inflation experienced in the country at that time, in the mid-20 per cent range, was dangerously high, and that GNP growth of greater than 12 per cent was simply not sustainable.[11] The question was whether the central government had the means to control inflation without the drastic measures that had been used the last time.

A soft correction in inflation was certainly preferable for both domestic and foreign investors, as a sharp correction could destroy the economic growth that attracted foreign investment. Some economists felt that the central government had little power to rein in inflation and growth due to the momentum in the economy and the government's lack of control over monetary growth. Official directives to state banks to tighten credit had little effect due to the unofficial credit that had become widely available. There had been some signs of a slowdown, but the largest slowdowns were among SOEs, many of which were already operating at a loss. These SOEs had been threatened with bankruptcy before if they did not make a profit, but a spate of bankruptcies would cause a worsening of the unemployment problem, further contributing to social unrest. Meanwhile, growth of privately-owned businesses continued at a frantic pace of over 40 per cent per annum. Growth of this nature, because of the inflation it caused, was simply not sustainable without seriously eroding the competitiveness of PRC firms. In light of these competing forces, many observers of the PRC expected little firm action from the central government one way or another.[12]

POLITICAL, ECONOMIC AND LEGAL CLIMATE

The leadership of the PRC had been stable for many years under Deng Xiaoping, but the health of the 88-year-old leader had not been good for some time, and many observers had been discussing the question of eventual succession. Other prominent officials in the government had been jockeying for position for some time in anticipation of Deng's passing. While Premier Li Peng appeared to have the inside track on the

[9]Ibid.

[10]Lehman Brothers Analyst Report, October, 1994, p2.

[11]"China," EIU Country Report, *The Economist Intelligence Unit*, September 9, 1994.

[12]Ibid.

leadership, an orderly transfer of power could not be guaranteed. Nor could there be any guarantee of the continuance of the economic policies and reforms currently in place. Most observers had felt that Deng held back the pace of reform,[13] but it was also well known that there were powerful party figures who felt the reforms had gone too far too fast.

The currency of the PRC, the Renminbi Yuan (Rmb), was currently valued at about 8.6 Rmb to US$1 (USD). The central government had been forced to lower the official exchange rate on the PRC currency by over 40 per cent on January 1, 1994, due to a wide discrepancy between the official rate and the spot rate at which many PRC firms had to purchase foreign exchange. While the government's foreign currency reserves had increased by more than 50 per cent since the beginning of the year, and strong export growth had nearly eliminated the trade deficit in the first half of 1994,[14] there were no guarantees that the currency could maintain its recent stability, especially in light of continued high inflation. Exhibit 3 shows the performance of the renminbi in relation to the U.S. dollar over the previous several years, as well as actual and projected current account balances.

Currently, the PRC tax authority did not withhold tax on dividend or capital gains income earned by foreigners. There was no guarantee that this tax holiday would be continued indefinitely, however, even though observers felt that the central government appreciated the need to maintain an investment climate that was conducive to foreign investment. If the central government was to change its policy in this regard, foreigners earning dividend or capital gains income from shares in PRC companies would be subject to 20 per cent withholding tax unless the investor's home country had a tax treaty with the PRC that reduced the rate of withholding tax.[15] A treaty currently existed between the PRC and the U.S., which pegged the maximum withholding tax at 10 per cent.

The legal history of the PRC suggested that the courts of the PRC would most likely not recognize or enforce against the company, or its directors, judgments obtained in U.S. or other foreign courts. This would affect the ability of any shareholders to successfully bring litigation against the company or its board for breach of fiduciary responsibility should such shareholders feel that management or the board, at any time, did not act in the best interest of the shareholders.[16]

POWER INDUSTRY IN THE PRC

Electricity in the more industrialized parts of the PRC was a scarce commodity due to the rapid growth of the PRC economy. Generally, in rapidly growing economies, the rate of growth in electric supply approximated that of GNP growth, but expansion of the power sector had lagged GNP growth over the past decade,[17] resulting in occasional shortages and rationing of power during peak usage periods. Shortage of electricity was one of the major obstacles to growth in the PRC. Many new plants were needed to meet the expected rapid increase in power requirements in the next few years. The Ministry of Electric Power estimated at the beginning of 1994 that the PRC would need approximately 17,000 megawatts (MW) of new generating capacity per year through the year 2000 to provide the necessary infrastructure to fuel growth.[18] This annual increase was equivalent to the present generating capacity of Hebei and Jiangsu Provinces combined. Together, these provinces represented 11.3 per cent of the population of the PRC. Exhibit 4 shows the growth in electrical generating capacity in the PRC since 1986. This explosive demand, coupled with the need to import much of the generating equipment for the plants from abroad, meant that power companies had to examine ways of raising foreign investment capital, as domestic sources were insufficient to meet the expected demand.

The electricity industry in the PRC was organized under the Ministry of Electrical Power. This ministry had formed an organization, called the China Huaneng Group, to oversee electrical power generation and

---

[13]Ibid.

[14]Ibid.

[15]Prospectus.

[16]Ibid.

[17]Lehman Brothers Analyst Report, October 1994, p2.

[18]Prospectus.

distribution in China in co-operation with local governments. The China Huaneng Group had formed a joint venture with foreign investors called the Huaneng Power International Development Corporation (HPIDC), whose mandate was to develop power plants and distribute power in some of the PRC's fastest growing provinces. HPIDC was the controlling shareholder of HPI. Shandong Huaneng Power was another, unrelated, subsidiary of the China Huaneng Group. Shandong Huaneng operated only in Shandong Province and, thus, did not pose any direct competition to HPI.

HUANENG POWER INTERNATIONAL–MANDATE FOR GROWTH

As the power requirements of the fastest-growing provinces increased, it became clear that the current industry structure would be insufficient to meet the projected demand necessitated by strong economic growth. To facilitate faster growth, HPI was founded on June 30, 1994, with a mandate to develop and operate large coal-fired power plants throughout the PRC using modern technology supplied by leading international manufacturers. Equipment was readily available from international suppliers, and was considered more reliable and efficient than PRC-manufactured equipment. HPI's current plants were about 40 per cent more reliable than the average PRC power plant.[19] The choice of coal as a fuel was due to the fact that the PRC had the largest known reserves of coal in the world.[20] The company was a spin-off of HPIDC, and HPIDC remained the controlling shareholder of the new firm, with 53.64 per cent of the "A", or domestic shares outstanding. The other shareholders were local government investment companies, which had traded in part of the debt owed to them by HPIDC for shares in the new company. The debt had originally been incurred in the construction of the plants transferred to HPI. As part of this arrangement, the local government investment companies agreed to assign all voting rights attached to their shares to HPIDC, so that the parent company could maintain managerial control. This control would continue even after a new share issue, since the new issue would represent only 25 per cent of the company. Thus, HPIDC would continue to control election of all members of the board of directors. A global issue would consist of a foreign class of shares in HPI, for sale only outside of the PRC to non-PRC citizens. Exhibit 5 shows the proposed ownership structure of HPI after a share issue.

The five plants under operation by HPI were all former HPIDC plants completed since 1987. The plants were located in five of China's fastest growing provinces. These provinces represent about 23 per cent of the population, but 31 per cent of the national GDP. In addition to these plants, HPI would acquire the rights to three plants currently under development, with a planned installed capacity of 2,000 MW, by December 31, 1994. HPI was also developing five other plants with an installed capacity of 3,900 MW. The agreement between HPIDC and HPI indicated that HPI would be the exclusive developer of all new greenfield coal-fired plants throughout the PRC that the company was in a position to develop.[21] All planned and projected plants of HPI would be located in provinces in which it currently operated, and would use the same distribution channels. Details concerning the power requirements of these provinces are given in Exhibit 6. The pace of the planned and projected expansions and the use of foreign technology meant that HPI would have to raise capital internationally to finance this expansion, which was the rationale for the formation of the company.

The company estimated that the construction of its planned power plants from 1994 to 1999 would require approximately Rmb 34.3 billion, including start-up costs and interest costs, which would be capitalized during construction.[22] The cost of each plant would then be depreciated over 15 years. Exhibit 7 shows estimated construction costs along with the schedule for completion of the plants. HPI would require additional capital to finance construction of these plants, above what it might raise from an equity issue in 1994. Certainly some of this capital could be raised through internally generated funds and debt issues, but ultimately the source and type of financing of these plants would depend on company performance and the

---

[19]Lehman Brothers Analyst Report, October, 1994, p2.

[20]Prospectus.

[21]Ibid.

[22]Ibid.

market conditions at the time the capital was required. Thus, new equity capital could be required in the future. A schedule of planned capital expenditures appears in Exhibit 8.

OPERATIONAL AND EXPANSION ISSUES

Power plant operation involved many risks which could not always be anticipated or controlled. Equipment might break down or fail to operate to standard, labor disruptions might occur, or natural disasters might strike, all of which could prevent a power plant from meeting the planned output level necessary to achieve profitability. HPI did not carry business interruption insurance to protect it from such occurrences. Nor did the company carry third-party liability insurance coverage for accidents on company property, except during the construction of the plants.[23] Furthermore, while the company was in compliance with all national and local environmental protection laws and regulations, there could be no guarantee that these laws or regulations would not be tightened in the future, which would result in further expenditures to ensure compliance.

Any expansion on the scale of that planned by HPI was not without its obstacles. The plants had a geographical dispersion of 1,600 kilometres among five coastal provinces. With the relatively primitive infrastructure that existed in the PRC, this posed logistical and control problems. Currently, the company received priority allotments of coal and oil to supply its plants from production according to government plans and at preset prices. These allotments had been more than enough to supply company needs; however, there were no guarantees that the company would continue to receive these allotments. The impact of reduced allotments would be that the company would have to purchase coal on the domestic market at going rates. Market rates were very close to planned rates, and with the evolution of the government toward letting prices float, HPI felt this posed little concern for the future. However, the company still had to ensure prompt delivery of coal to its plants. The company purchased the majority of its coal from Shanxi Province and transported it by rail and ship to its power plants, most of which were on the coast. Transportation comprised approximately 50 per cent of the total cost of coal to the plants, with the exception of the Shangan Power Plant, which was very close to the Shanxi Province coalfields. Transportation allotments were held by the company to supply its plants. While the importance of the electrical plants to the PRC economy, and HPI's strong relationship with the central and local governments might enable HPI to secure sufficient transportation, there could be no guarantee of the availability of the transportation, nor of the price the company would pay for it.

More likely, however, the company would face problems in finding and managing sufficient trained personnel to operate the plants. The current management of the company had a great deal of experience at HPIDC in power generation and plant management. Management had built a close working relationship with the central and local governments. In addition, one of the company vice-presidents was the son of PRC Premier Li Peng,[24] who in the early 1980s had served as minister of electrical power. However, if the expected rates of growth in electrical production materialized, the company could face a shortage of skilled operational personnel.

Despite these potential difficulties, some analysts felt that HPI presented an attractive investment opportunity for international investors. This was due in part to its relationship with HPIDC, which was one of the leading power developers in the PRC. It was also due to the successful history of the company while a part of HPIDC. All of the plants currently in operation used foreign equipment and technology successfully. As well, the plants had a profitable operating history, and all were completed on time and within budget. Exhibit 9 shows HPI's income statements for 1993 and the first six months of 1994, and balance sheet as of the date of reorganization.

ALLOWED RATE OF RETURN

It was evident that certain special operating advantages would have to be given to HPI and other power companies seeking to raise capital internationally, due to the higher cost of generating power using foreign tech-

---

[23]Ibid.

[24]"Chinese Capital Feels the Chill," *Euromoney*, December 1994, pp. 25-27.

nology. To facilitate this, the Ministry of Electrical Power persuaded the central government to pass legislation authorizing HPI, Shandong and certain other companies in high electricity usage growth areas to earn a guaranteed rate of return on electrical generating assets as an incentive to attract foreign investors concerned about the risks of investing in the PRC. The return was calculated only on the book value, net of depreciation, of assets involved in the generation of electricity and those assets under construction.[25] This policy allowed HPI to adjust its rates to recover higher input costs such as fuel, fuel transportation and labor. As well, the return was net of interest and taxes. The allowed rate was 15 per cent on equity financed net fixed assets, and on debt financed net fixed assets it was 15 per cent minus the average rate of interest paid on the debt (minimum 7% return). Effectively, this meant that if HPI was entirely equity financed, then the unlevered cost of capital would be 15 per cent, while the maximum cost of debt capital would be eight per cent. Thus, the overall cost of capital would depend on the capital structure of the individual firm.

HPI was the leading independent power company in the PRC and one of the largest independent power producers (IPP) in the world.[26] As an IPP, HPI did not sell its electricity to consumers, but rather to the local distribution grids, which then resold the electricity to the end consumers and subtracted a small percentage fee from HPI. Despite this and the fact that the rates necessitated by the guaranteed return would be higher than other power plants in its operating regions, company management was confident that HPI could sell the amount of power necessary to earn the guaranteed return.[27] This optimism had some merit due to the shortage of power in the provinces in which HPI operated, the support of the central government for the arrangement, and HPI's relationship with the local distribution networks, which were jointly owned by HPIDC and the local governments, which were part owners of HPI through their local investment companies. However, given the history of policy changes in the PRC, and the need for the central government to control inflation, there were no assurances the guaranteed rate of return would exist indefinitely. Further, the local governments sometimes also held operating interests in competing power plants. The central government appeared committed to the development of the country's infrastructure, however, and it appeared to appreciate the importance of the guaranteed return in attracting and retaining the necessary capital.

INTERNATIONAL CAPITAL MARKETS

A PRC firm needing to raise capital had many options to consider, and the choice of the best option could be quite complex. In addition to choosing between debt and equity capital, there was the question of which market to tap and how to enter the market. The Hong Kong investment community was certainly more familiar with PRC companies, and had been a reliable source of capital in the past 14 months, but it was not clear whether the Hong Kong market was getting saturated with PRC companies, or how large an issue the Hong Kong market could absorb. A listing of PRC companies and PRC-related companies that had recently listed on foreign exchanges is shown in Exhibit 10. These firms had received a mixed reception, with some issues heavily subscribed, while others attracted little attention. As well, there had been reports of some haggling over price between the investment bankers and buyers, with the investment banker sometimes lowering the proposed issue price in order to fully sell the issue. This led some market participants to complain that there was a limited choice of good PRC companies.

There was little disputing that 1993 had been an extremely successful year for PRC firms to raise equity. However, it was equally obvious that market conditions and perceptions had changed, and there were no guarantees that new issues would be as warmly received. Still, an indication of the commitment of the Hong Kong market to PRC companies came on August 8, 1994 when the Hong Kong Stock Exchange announced the creation of the Hang Seng China Enterprise Index which was designed to track PRC firms listed on Hong Kong. The index was partially in response to the announcement by the PRC securities commission that 22 more PRC firms had permission to seek international listings in 1994. The first of these firms, Luoyang Float Glass, had been issued at 10.5 times earnings on July 8. Since that time, the share price had fallen

---

[25]Lehman Brothers Analyst Report, October 1994, p2.

[26]Ibid.

[27]Prospectus.

20 per cent, while the Hong Kong market as a whole had risen 11.5 per cent. Hong Kong stocks generally traded at a price/earnings ratio in the nine to ten range. In addition to Shandong and HPI, two other PRC power companies and two power-generating equipment manufacturers had gained permission to seek a global equity issue.

U.S. and international markets offered much potential in terms of their size, higher valuations, and thirst for emerging market investments. Both the NYSE and the National Association of Securities Dealers Automated Quotations (NASDAQ) exchanges had been aggressively promoting themselves in the PRC as the best place for PRC firms to raise international capital. The NYSE had four China country funds among its listings, along with Shandong and four other Chinese firms that operated mainly or entirely in the PRC, but were owned by holding companies in other jurisdictions. NASDAQ had a reputation for being a technology-oriented stock exchange, and its market maker system guaranteed a market for the stock once listed. There was also the possibility of listing on another international exchange, such as the London Stock Exchange. One point that possibly favored U.S. exchanges was the recent deregulation of utilities in the U.S., which had decreased their profitability, and may have made HPI and Shandong's guaranteed return more attractive.[28]

HPI could list a class of shares on the Hong Kong exchange directly if it met the regulatory and reporting requirements. However, if HPI wanted to raise equity capital globally, it would have to use American Depositary Receipts (ADRs). ADRs were a vehicle that facilitated the purchase and sale of the shares of foreign companies. The arrangement involved setting up a depositary agreement between a bank in the country where the shares were registered and a bank in the U.S. The bank in the home country would hold the actual shares in custody while the U.S. depositary bank would issue the receipts, or ADRs, which represented the shares. The holder of the receipts retained the same rights as a normal holder of shares in the company. There were several different levels of depositary receipts. The level a firm chose depended on whether the firm involved wanted to raise capital or simply increase the market for existing shares, or whether the firm wanted to sell shares to the general public or institutional investors only. Exhibit 11 illustrates the characteristics of the various types of ADRs.

To raise equity capital through ADRs, HPI had to apply for either a Level III, a Rule 144A, or a global offering ADR, which was essentially a worldwide distribution using one of the first two methods. The Level III and the Rule 144A had different regulatory and reporting requirements. To make the shares available to a broad range of investors, HPI chose to apply for a Level III, which involved the release of statements in compliance with U.S. Generally Accepted Accounting Principles (GAAP) and full disclosure of all operating results and strategic decisions. This was a level of disclosure to which PRC companies were not accustomed at home. An alternative would have been to list under Rule 144A, which would have allowed HPI to issue shares only to Qualified Institutional Buyers (QIBs), but which also did not have the disclosure and accounting requirements of an exchange listing. At least one PRC electrical utility, Datong Electric, was considering this option. While this alternative was certainly simpler and cheaper, institutional investors were very sophisticated and demanding investors. It was also unclear whether the institutional demand would be sufficient to raise the total amount. Eighty per cent of the Shandong issue had gone to institutional investors,[29] yet some institutional investors had avoided the deal, citing the risks of the economic, regulatory and legal environment.

Now that HPI had decided to issue ADRs, it had to determine a price at which to issue them. The problem was in determining how much 25 per cent of HPI was worth to an international investor. It was possible to estimate future cash flows based on the projected expansion plans and the allowed rate of return, as shown in Exhibit 12, but whether the allowed rate would be enough in light of the perceived risk was unknown (see Exhibit 13 for selected economic and market data). Since all profits would be earned in renminbi, the value of these profits would have to be converted to foreign currency to have any meaning to these investors. Shandong was paying an annual dividend of US$0.50 at current exchange rates, but HPI would not pay any dividends for the foreseeable future in order to help finance expansion.

---

[28]"Investors Prepare for Huaneng, Shandong, and Datong," Going Public: *The IPO Reporter*, September 5, 1994.

[29]Peltz, Michael, "Takeovers to the Rescue," *Institutional Investor*, October 1994.

Nevertheless, HPI wanted a higher valuation than that received by Shandong, which had been priced at 14 times expected 1995 earnings. The rationale for a higher valuation could have been based on many factors. HPI used more efficient foreign technology while Shandong used PRC-manufactured equipment. HPI also had greater diversified operations and greater growth potential due to its mandate to develop power plants country-wide, and its relationships with national and local governments. Exhibit 14 contains a financial comparison of Shandong and HPI, as well as comparable international power generating groups. Lehman Brothers had initially suggested that HPI could issue at a P/E ratio of 30 or greater, but at the beginning of the "book building" process, the price had been narrowed to a range of from 15.5 to 19.0 times expected 1995 earnings, for an issue price of $22.50 to $27.50 per ADR. Each ADR represented 40 international class shares. When the revised prospectus was issued on October 5, 1994, the issue price was set at $20 per ADR, or about 14 times expected 1995 earnings. Flotation costs would be four per cent of the total raised.

Exhibit 1

IPO AFTERMARKET PERFORMANCE (JUNE TO AUGUST 1994)

The IPO 100: A Review of the Initial Public Offering Aftermarket

Company Name	Date Public	IPO Price	Close On 8/24/94	Per Cent Change	Price/Earning Ratio
International Fibercom, Inc.	18-Aug	5.50	4.88	-11.36	neg
Accustaff	16-Aug	10.50	12.00	14.29	75
Marker International	15-Aug	7.00	7.13	1.79	neg
PMT Services	12-Aug	8.00	10.25	28.13	-
Tower Automotive	11-Aug	11.50	12.38	7.61	10.3
Polish Telephone & Microwave	10-Aug	6.75	6.63	-1.85	-
Adtran Inc.	9-Aug	18.00	22.50	25.00	13
Standard Funding Corp.	9-Aug	4.25	4.25	same	neg
Shandong Huaneng Power	**4-Aug**	**14.25**	**13.50**	**-5.26**	**14.0**
Silverado, Inc.	4-Aug	7.00	6.38	-8.93	neg
Systemsoft Corp.	4-Aug	5.50	6.50	18.18	69
Media Arts Group, Inc.	3-Aug	7.25	7.25	same	9.1
Spectrian Corp.	3-Aug	12.50	12.50	same	18.4
Dimac	3-Aug	10.00	10.13	1.25	12.5
Citation Corp.	2-Aug	8.00	9.38	17.19	6.1
Movie Gallery, Inc.	2-Aug	14.00	18.63	33.04	32
Miller Industries	2-Aug	10.50	13.50	28.57	51
NaPro Bio Therapeutics, Inc.	1-Aug	5.00	5.19	3.75	neg
Cascade Communications Corp.	29-Jul	15.00	37.75	151.67	221
Dorsey Trailers, Inc.	28-Jul	13.00	14.25	9.62	-
Heftel Broadcasting Corp.	27-Jul	10.00	12.38	23.75	10.9
Wackenhut Corrections Corp.	26-Jul	9.00	13.88	54.17	64
P.T. Tri Polyta Indonesia	25-Jul	21.00	27.25	29.76	-
Apartment Inv. & Mgmt.	22-Jul	18.50	18.00	-2.70	26
FelCor Suite Hotels, Inc.	21-Jul	21.25	22.88	7.65	-
Matthews International Corp.	20-Jul	14.00	16.13	15.18	9
Bell Cablemedia	15-Jul	17.00	19.00	11.76	-
Grupo Industrial Durangeo	14-Jul	18.00	21.25	18.06	-
WCI Steel	13-Jul	7.50	11.25	50.00	8.5
Xenova Group, PlC	8-Jul	8.00	8.06	0.78	-
1st Nazionale delle Assicurazioni	5-Jul	15.25	14.25	-6.56	-
Doubletree Corp.	1-Jul	13.00	18.00	38.46	14.1
Banpa-s, S.A.	30-Jun	10.00	9.25	-7.50	-
Laboratorio Chile, S.A.	28-Jun	14.50	15.00	3.45	-

IPO Market Performance	**Week Ending**		
	24-Aug	**17-Aug**	**10-Aug**
IPO 100 Index	13.67	9.75	7.58
% Trading Above IPO Price	70	60	58
% Outperforming S&P 500	51	49	56
Number of Issues Added	8	12	6

Source: Going Public: The IPO Reporter, Investment Dealers' Digest, August 28, 1994. A dash indicates no P/E available or reported.

Exhibit 2

ECONOMIC STRUCTURE OF THE PRC

Annual Economic Indicators

Economic Indicators	1989	1990	1991	1992	1993
GNP at current market prices Rmb billion	1,599.3	1,769.5	2,023.6	2,403.6	3,138.0
Real GNP growth %	4.4	4.1	8.2	13.0	13.4
Consumer price inflation %	17.5	1.6	3.0	5.4	13.0
Population, millions	1,126	1,139	1,156	1,173	1,185
Merchandise exports $ billion	52.5	61.3	71.9	85.0	91.8
Merchandise imports $ billion	59.1	52.6	63.8	80.6	104.0
Current account $ billion	-4.3	12.0	13.3	6.4	-11.9
Total debt $ billion	44.8	52.5	60.8	68.3	77.0
Reserves excl gold $ billion	18.0	29.6	43.7	20.6	20.8

Source: EIU Country Report, September 9, 1994.

Economic Highlights January to June 1994

(Rmb billion unless otherwise indicated; current prices unless otherwise indicated)

	Rmb billions	Real % Change
GNP	1,659.9	11.6%
Gross agricultural output	808.4 [a,b]	4.0% [a,b]
Gross industrial output (1992 prices)	1,979.0	18.8%
State-owned enterprises	900.0	5.3%
Collectives	758.3	27.8%
Others (incl. Private & foreign)	320.7	43.7%
Investment in fixed assets	450.5	25.2%
Money supply	1,424.4 [b]	21.6% [b,c]
Domestic credit	3,013.4 [b]	22.0% [b,c]
Bank savings deposits	2,844.0	55.2%
Retail sales	718.8	4.8%
Consumer price index	-	22.0%
Exports ($ billion)	48.4	30.2% [c]
Imports ($ billion)	49.2	21.0% [c]
Foreign exchange reserves ($ billion)	31.8	49.0% [c]

Source: EIU Country Report, Economic Intelligence Unit, September 9,1994 (from other sources).

[a] *EIU estimate.*
[b] *End of December 1993.*
[c] *Nominal growth rates*

Exhibit 3

EXCHANGE RATE AND CURRENT ACCOUNT DATA

Historical Exchange Rates

	Official Exchange/PBOC[a] Rate (expressed in Rmb per USD)				Shanghai Swap Center Rates (expressed in Rmb per USD)			
	Close	Ave.(2)	High	Low	Close	Ave.(2)	High	Low
1989	4.7339	3.7634	4.7339	3.7314	5.7200	6.2300	7.0000	4.7300
1990	5.2352	4.7920	5.2352	4.7329	5.7490	5.6405	5.9300	5.1630
1991	5.4478	5.3343	5.4478	5.2352	5.8980	5.8534	5.9290	5.7490
1992	5.7662	5.5214	5.9007	5.4124	7.7060	6.7497	7.7700	5.8970
1993	5.8145	5.7764	5.8245	5.7076	8.7000	8.6661	10.9230	7.7180
1st Q 1994	8.7080	8.7041	8.7100	8.6900	8.6850	8.6903	8.7564	8.6738
2nd Q 1994[b]	8.6526	8.6656	8.6988	8.6526	8.6280	8.6573	8.7000	8.6280

Source: Prospectus

[a] *People's Bank of China.*
[b] *Determined by averaging the relevant rate on the last day of each month during the relevant period.*

Current Account ($ bn)

	1993[c]	1994[d]	1995[d]
Merchandise exports [c]	75.7	94.6	111.0
Merchandise imports [c]	-86.3	-99.2	-115.0
Trade Balance	-10.6	-4.6	-4.0
Services total	-2.4	-2.7	-2.4
Credit	15.3	19.1	23.9
Debit	-17.7	-21.8	-26.3
Net transfer payments	1.1	1.0	1.0
Current-account balance	-11.9	-6.3	-5.4

Source: EIU Country Report, September 9, 1994.

[c] *EIU estimates*
[d] *EIU forecasts*

Exhibit 4
GENERATING CAPACITY AND GROWTH IN THE PRC

Comparison with Other Countries

	1991 per Capita Installed Capacity (Watts)	1991 per Capita Consumption (kWh)	1991 per Capita GNP (USD)	Real GDP Growth Rate (%)			
				1990	1991	1992	1993
U.S.	3,120	11,333	22,340	1.2	-0.7	2.6	3.0
Japan	1,581	5,965	26,840	4.8	4.0	1.1	0.1
Singapore	1,497	5,527	14,140	8.3	6.7	5.8	9.8
Hong Kong	1,446	4,418	13,580	3.2	4.1	5.3	5.5
South Korea	466	2,736	6,350	9.2	8.4	4.8	5.3
Malaysia	268	1,544	2,520	9.7	8.7	8.0	7.4
Thailand	187	711	1,650	11.6	8.1	7.6	7.8
PRC	130	562	370	3.9	8.0	13.2	13.4
Philippines	104	419	740	2.4	-0.4	0.3	1.8
Indonesia	49	233	610	7.2	6.9	6.3	6.5

Source: Prospectus

Growth

Year	Installed Capacity (MW)[a]	Increase in Installed Capacity (MW)	Electricity Generation (TWh)	Increase in Electricity Generation (%)
1986	93,818.5	6,765.3	449.6	9.5
1987	102,897.0	9,078.5	497.3	10.6
1988	115,497.1	12,600.1	545.1	9.6
1989	126,638.6	11,141.5	584.7	7.3
1990	137,890.0	11,251.4	621.3	6.3
1991	151,473.1	13,583.1	677.5	9.0
1992	166,532.4	15,059.3	754.2	11.3
1993	180,915.4	14,383.0	815.9	8.2

Source: Prospectus

[a] *Includes the installed capacity of all power plants in the PRC, including those not connected to any power grid.*

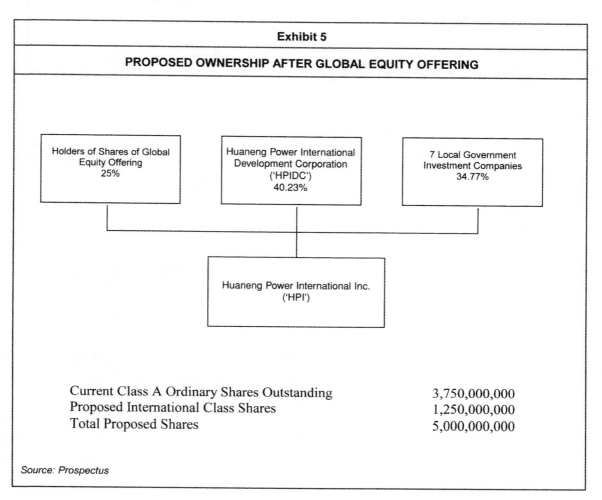

Exhibit 5

PROPOSED OWNERSHIP AFTER GLOBAL EQUITY OFFERING

Holders of Shares of Global Equity Offering 25%

Huaneng Power International Development Corporation ('HPIDC') 40.23%

7 Local Government Investment Companies 34.77%

Huaneng Power International Inc. ('HPI')

Current Class A Ordinary Shares Outstanding	3,750,000,000
Proposed International Class Shares	1,250,000,000
Total Proposed Shares	5,000,000,000

Source: Prospectus

Exhibit 6

PROVINCIAL POWER REQUIREMENTS

Province	1992				2000	
	Installed Capacity (MW)	Total Generation (TWh)	Actual Usage (TWh)	Incr. from Prev. Yr. (%)	Required Capacity (MW)	Expected Usage (TWh)
Liaoning	9,500	48.7	53.6	9.5	14,650	110
Fujian	4,018	16.0	15.0	15.4	12,700	48
Hebei	8,387	45.7	38.0	4.5	16,300	85
Jiangsu	8,280	48.1	43.6	13.2	21,000	115
Guangdong	10,093	43.9	45.2	26.6	27,000	154

Source: Prospectus

Exhibit 7

PLANT DEVELOPMENT SCHEDULE

Plant or Expansion	Province	Actual/ Estimated In-Service Date[a]	Total Cost[b] (Mills. Rmb/ Mills. USD)	Installed (MW)
Current Power Plants				
Shantou Power Plant	Guangdong	Units I&II: Jan. 1987 Unit III: April 1988	215/24.7	2 x 35 1 x 30
Dalian Power Plant	Liaoning	Unit I: Sept. 1988 Unit II: Dec. 1988	1,569/180	2 x 350
Fuzhou Power Plant	Fujian	Unit I: Sept. 1988 Unit II: Dec. 1988	1,713/197	2 x 350
Nantong Power Plant	Jiangsu	Unit I: Sept. 1989 Unit II: March 1990	1,682/193	2 x 350
Shangan Power Plant	Hebei	Unit I: Aug. 1990 Unit II: Dec. 1990	1,959/225	2 x 350
				Subtotal 2,900 MW
Planned Power Plants				
Under Construction Shantou Coal-Fired Plant[c]	Guangdong	Unit I: 2nd half 1996 Unit II: 1st half 1997	3,600/414	2 x 300
Approved by State Planning Commission Shangan Phase II Expansion	Hebei	Unit I: 1st half 1997 Unit II: 2nd half 1997	2,227/256	2 x 300
Dalian Phase II Expansion	Liaoning	Unit I: 2nd half 1997 Unit II: 1st half 1998	4,567/525	2 x 350
Dandong Power Plant[c]	Liaoning	Unit I: 1998 Unit II: 1998	4,750/546	2 x 350
In Approval Process[d] Fuzhou Phase II Expansion	Fujian	Unit I: 1998 Unit II: 1998	4,567/525	2 x 350
Nantong Phase II Expansion	Jiangsu	Unit I: 1998 Unit II: 1999	4,567/525	2 x 350
Jinling Power Plant (51.7% interest)	Jiangsu	Unit I: 1999 Unit II: 2000	10,000/1,149	2 x 600
Shantou Coal-Fired Phase II Expansion[c]	Guangdong	After the year 2000	4,567/525	2 x 350
				Subtotal 5,900 MW
Projected Power Plants				
Dalian Phase III Expansion	Liaoning	-	-	1 x 600
Dandong Phase II Expansion	Liaoning	-	-	2 x 600
Fuzhou Phase III Expansion	Fujian	-	-	2 x 350
Nantong Phase III Expansion	Jiangsu	-	-	2 x 600
Jinling Phase II Expansion	Jiangsu	-	-	2 x 600
Shangan Phase III Expansion	Hebei	-	-	2 x 600
				Subtotal 6,100 MW
				TOTAL 14,900 MW

Source: Prospectus

[a]*Commencement of commercial operations.*
[b]*Including interest expenses during construction (assuming 8% interest) and startup costs. Rmb 8.7 = USD1.0*
[c]*Power Plants to be acquired on or before December 31, 1994*
[d] *The State Planning Commission has not yet approved these plants, but they have been incorporated into the eighth and ninth five-year plans. The company believes that approval will be received in time to meet the above schedule.*

Exhibit 8

SCHEDULE OF PLANNED CAPITAL EXPENDITURES

Power Plant Expansion	1994	1995	1996	1997	1998	1999
			(millions US dollars)			
Dalian Phase II Expansion	-	87	160	173	83	22
Dandong Power Plant	16	79	156	182	89	24
Fuzhou Phase II Expansion	-	87	160	173	83	22
Jinling Power Plant[a]	-	77	89	143	172	95
Nantong Phase II Expansion	-	87	160	173	83	22
Shangan Phase II Expansion	42	72	88	52	2	-
Shantou Coal-Fired Plant	167	139	92	16	-	-
Shantou Phase II Expansion	-	-	-	-	23	159
Totals	225	628	905	912	535	344

Source: Prospectus

[a] *Jinling Power Plant to be 51.7% owned by HPI*

Exhibit 9

SUMMARY FINANCIAL DATA
COMBINED INCOME STATEMENTS—1993 & 1994
(all figures in $ 000s US)

	Six Months Ended June 30, 1994	Year Ended December 31, 1993
Operating Revenues, Net	245,129	470,776
Operating Expenses:		
Fuel	83,967	162,980
Maintenance	6,086	11,413
Depreciation	38,064	76,086
Labor	7,273	14,383
Transmission Fees	28,206	40,837
Service Fees to HPIDC	11,988	21,852
Income Tax	5,807	9,929
Others	8,934	25,902
Total Operating Expenses	190,325	363,382
Refund of Excess VAT Paid	20,868	27,494
Income Before Financial Expenses	75,672	134,888
Interest Charges	24,166	38,719
Exchange Losses (Gains)	(1,227)	-
Total Financial Expenses	22,939	38,719
Net Income	52,733	96,169

Source: Prospectus

Exhibit 9 (continued)

RECONCILED BALANCE SHEET AS OF JUNE 30, 1994
(after reorganization, $000s US)

Assets
Current Assets:

Cash and Cash Equivalents	42,126	
Accounts Receivable	36,686	
Due from HPIDC	32,741	
Materials and Supplies	41,530	
Other Receivables and Assets	56,541	
Total Current Assets		209,624

Long-term Assets

Property, Plant and Equipment, Net[a]	1,146,429	
Other Long-term Assets	5,969	
Total Long-term Assets		1,152,398

Total Assets		1,362,022

Liabilities and Shareholders' Equity
Current Liabilities:

Short-term Bank Loans	21,216	
Current Portion of Long-term Loans	111,179	
Payables and Accrued Liabilities	52,800	
Taxes Payable	27,519	
Staff Welfare and Bonus Fund Payable	10,066	
Total Current Liabilities		222,780

Long-term Loans:

Shareholder Loans[b]	530,094	
Total Long-term Loans		530,094
Total Liabilities		752,874

Shareholders' Equity:

Class A Ordinary Shares		436,361
Additional Paid-in Capital		172,787
Retained Earnings[c]		-
Total Shareholders' Equity		609,148

Total Liabilities and Shareholders' Equity		1,362,022

Source: Prospectus

---

[a] *Market value at reorganization as determined by independent audit.*
[b] *Current foreign and government loans are in name of HPIDC. HPI will make payments to HPIDC for these loans.*
[c] *Reset to zero due to reorganization of plants as a new entity.*

Exhibit 10
A SELECTION OF RECENT PRC-BASED COMPANY INITIAL PUBLIC OFFERINGS

Chinese Companies Listed Overseas

Company Name	Exchange	Issue Date	Offering Size (mills. US$)	P/E Ratio		Times Oversubscribed
Shandong Huaneng Power	NYSE	Aug 4/94	333	14.0		1.03
Luoyang Float Glass	Hong Kong	July 8/94	n/a[a]	10.5		n/a
Quingling Automotive	Hong Kong	July 9/94	n/a	9.0		n/a
Dongfang Electrical[b]	Hong Kong	June 9/94	62	12.0		15
Tianjin Bohai Chemical	Hong Kong	May 18/94	53	11.2	*	1
Yizheng Chemical Fibre	Hong Kong	Mar 29/94	308	13.5		19
Kunming Machine Tool	Hong Kong	Dec/93	17	5.4	*	628
Maanshan Iron & Steel	Hong Kong	Nov/93	128	n/a		69
Beiren Printing	Hong Kong	Aug 4/93	27	15.2	*	n/a
Guangzhou Shipyard Intl.	Hong Kong	Aug 3/93	n/a	10.5	*	n/a
Shanghai Petrochemical	Hong Kong	July 16/93	343	11.3		1.77
Tsingtao Brewery	Hong Kong	July 14/93	115	16.3		110

Sources: Bloomberg, Reuters, AFX News, Privatization International.
* - P/E ratio as of August 23, 1994.

Hong Kong-based Companies with Primary Operations in the PRC

Company Name	Exchange	Date of Issue	Offering Size (Mills. US$)	P/E Ratio	Times Oversubscribed
AES China Generating	NASDAQ	Feb 23/94	160	-[c]	n/a
Consolidated Electric Pwr	Hong Kong	Dec 6/93	150	39	33
Wing Shan International[d]	Hong Kong	April/93	46	24[e]	300

Source: Bloomberg, Reuters, AFX News

---

[a] *n/a - not available*
[b] *Manufactures and sells electrical generating turbines and equipment.*
[c] *New company, therefore no previous revenue or earnings. Price-to-book ratio of 3.2/1. Earnings to August 1994 of $0.02/share.*
[d] *Investment holding company. Principal activity is the generation and sale of electricity in Guangdong Province.*
[e] *P/E ratio as of December 31, 1993.*

Exhibit 11					
AMERICAN DEPOSITARY RECEIPT PROGRAMS BY TYPE					

Different levels of American Depositary Receipt programs are available with various conditions based on trading, SEC registration (Securities Act of 1933) and reporting requirements (Securities and Exchange Act of 1934).

	Level I	**Level II**	**Level III**	**Rule 144A**	**Global**
Description	Unlisted in U.S.	Listed on major U.S. exchanges	Offered and listed on major U.S. exchanges	Private U.S. placement to Qualified Institutional Buyers (QIBs)	Global offer of securities in two or more markets, not in issuer home market
Trading Location	OTC Pink Sheet trading	NYSE, AMEX or NASDAQ	NYSE, AMEX or NASDAQ	U.S. Private Placement Market using PORTAL	U.S. and non-U.S. exchanges
SEC Registration	Registration Statement form F-6	Registration Statement form F-6	Forms F-1 and F-6 for initial public offering	None	Depends: (a) private placement Rule 144A; or (b) new issue, as Level III
U.S. Reporting Required	Exemption under rule 12g3-2(b)	Form 20-F filed annually	Form 20-F filed annually; short forms F-2 and F-3 used only for subsequent offerings	12g3-2(b) exemption or agree to provide information on request	Depends: (a) private placement Rule 144A; or (b) new issue, as Level III
GAAP Requirement	No GAAP reconciliation required	Only partial reconciliation for financials	Full GAAP reconciliation for financials	No GAAP reconciliation required	As above

Source: An Information Guide to Depositary Receipts by Citibank's Security Services Department (1995).

Exhibit 12

PRO FORMA OPERATING DATA

Year (all figures in 000s $US)	1994 (6 mos)	1995	1996	1997	1998	1999
Net generating assets - beg	1,146,428	1,108,214	1,256,785	1,772,223	2,485,395	3,134,899
Equity financed	612,995	812,690	980,645	1,067,107	1,327,489	1,809,042
Debt financed	533,433	295,523	276,141	705,116	1,157,906	1,325,857
LTD/Equity Ratio	0.87	0.36	0.28	0.66	0.87	0.73
Rate structure - equity[a]	n/a	11%	12%	14%	15%	15%
- debt	n/a	7%	7%	7%	7%	7%
Net Income	29,500	110,083	137,007	198,753	280,177	364,166
Interest[b]	21,204	38,212	28,908	20,661	34,457	73,175
Income Tax	2,918	14,305	20,835	29,175	20,120	25,316
Effective Tax Rate[c]	9.0%	11.5%	13.2%	12.8%	6.7%	6.5%
EBIT	53,621	162,599	186,751	248,589	334,753	462,657
EBIAT	48,795	143,900	162,100	216,770	312,325	432,585
Depreciation	38,214	76,429	112,562	191,829	262,495	282,295

Source: Casewriter's estimates based on prospectus.

Note: Working capital does not vary significantly with sales levels.

Exhibit 13

ECONOMIC AND MARKET DATA

PRC Bank Rate - October 1994	10.08%
PRC Official Lending Rate - October 1994	10.98%
S&P 500 Long-term market premium - 1926-1993	4.73%
U.S. Government LT Bond Yield - October 1994	8.09%
Beta of Electrical Power Generating Industry in U.S.	0.52
D/E ratio of Electrical Power Generating Industry in U.S.	1.01
Hong Kong Hang Seng Index Market Premium - 1969-1993	13.05%
Prime Rate in Hong Kong - October 1994	7.75%

Sources: Datastream International, Market Guide, International Financial Statistics, May 1997.

[a] *Allowed rate of return to be phased in by 1998 in accordance with agreements with local governments.*
[b] *Interest on long-term debt assumed at 8%.*
[c] *Effective rate varies due to temporary tax holidays in effect for various plants. Long-term effective rate is 17.37%.*

Exhibit 14
COMPARISON OF SELECTED FINANCIALS

Chinese Power Companies

	Shandong	Huaneng
Net Sales	$146.9M	$470.8M
Assets	$449.0M	$906.0M
Net Income	$47.3M	$96.2M
EPS (expected '95)	$1.02	$1.45
Price-Earnings Ratio (expected '95)	14	14
Book Value/Share	$7.93	$9.67
Price/Book	1.80	1.91
Dividend	$0.50	$0.00
LTD/Capitalization	17%	46%

Sources: Reuters, Prospectus, AFX News, Lehman Brothers analyst report, October 1994.

EPS is based on number of ADRs.

International Power Generating Groups

	Price to Earnings Ratio	Price to Book Ratio	Dividend Yield
Asian Power Producers	15.6x	2.24x	2.8%
South American Utilities	23.0x	2.27x	2.0%
U.S. Independent Power Producers	14.1x	2.47x	n/a
U.S. Utilities	10.2x	1.20x	7.5%
European Utilities	11.4x	1.64x	4.1%

Source: Lehman Brothers Analyst Report, October 1994, p5-6.

Note: n/a - not available.

part seven

Capital Expenditures

PEPSICO CHANGCHUN JOINT VENTURE: CAPITAL EXPENDITURE ANALYSIS[1]

Andre Hawaux, vice-president Finance for PepsiCo East Asia (PepsiCo), finished drinking his can of Pepsi. It was mid-June 1994, and for the past two weeks Mr. Hawaux had been collecting data on the firm's proposed equity joint venture (JV) in the city of Changchun, in the People's Republic of China (PRC). While PepsiCo was already involved in seven joint ventures in the PRC, this proposal would be one of the first two green-field equity joint ventures with PepsiCo control over both the board and day-to-day management. Every investment project at PepsiCo had to go through a systematic evaluation process that involved using capital budgeting tools such as net present value (NPV) and internal rate of return (IRR). The final decision would be made after a presentation to the PepsiCo Asia-Pacific president. Mr. Hawaux wondered if the proposed Changchun JV would be sufficiently profitable based on the information he had collected. He opened another can of Pepsi and got to work.

PEPSI-COLA INTERNATIONAL

PepsiCo Inc. began selling its products internationally in 1934 with its operations in Canada. Currently PepsiCo spanned more than 190 countries and accounts for about one quarter of the world's soft drinks.

---

[1]This case is modified from PepsiCo East Asia Financing Growth in the People's Republic of China, #9A99N043. Certain information and data contained in this case had been modified for classroom discussion.

Richard Ivey School of Business
The University of Western Ontario

IVEY

Peter Yuan and Geoff Crum prepared this case under the supervision of Professors Larry Wynant and Claude Lanfranconi solely to provide material for class discussion. The authors do not intend to illustrate either effective or ineffective handling of a managerial situation. The authors may have disguised certain names and other identifying information to protect confidentiality.

Exhibits 1 and 2 provide the financial statements of PepsiCo Inc. Pepsi-Cola North America included the United States and Canada. Key international markets included Argentina, Brazil, China, India, Mexico, Philippines, Saudi Arabia, Spain, Thailand and the United Kingdom. The company had also established operations in the emerging markets of the Czech Republic, Hungary, Poland, Slovakia and Russia, where PepsiCo Inc. was the first U.S. consumer product to be marketed. The strategy of the international unit was to focus on markets where Pepsi was already strong and on emerging countries not dominated by any beverage company.

THE GLOBAL SOFT DRINK BUSINESS

The carbonated soft drink (CSD) business had, in recent years, become increasingly competitive as Western markets matured and multinational firms began increasing global operations as a means to continue growth. The former USSR, Latin America, and Asia were pinpointed by both Coca-Cola International (CCI) and PepsiCo International (PCI) as prime areas for expansion. Historically, the early mover into a "white" market (an area with no previous distribution of Coke or Pepsi) continued to hold the majority of market share as the market matured. Thus, it was seen as critical to enter new markets as soon as they became politically and economically accessible.

THE SOFT DRINK INDUSTRY IN THE PRC

Politics and Dealmaking

The CSD industry in the PRC was highly fragmented and composed of a multitude of regional players. Owing to geographical issues, namely the lack of an effective wide-area distribution and delivery system, there were no national CSD brands to speak of. However, local CSD players did enjoy relatively high market share within their regional centres. In many areas of the PRC, cases of CSDs would be given as gifts from state-owned enterprises (SOEs) to their employees for Chinese New Year. In fact, some major SOEs, such as coal mines and heavy machinery plants, operated their own CSD bottling lines for staff canteens. However, the growing influx of Western culture into the major cities meant that many Chinese had begun to favor American products, including CSDs. Major CSD companies around the globe considered the Chinese market, with its growing demand for their products, projected high growth rates and standard of living increases, a prime target for expansion.

Prior to 1993, the price of entry into the PRC marketplace was high. The Central Government was determined to limit the growth of foreign companies in order to protect the regional CSD industries, and to ensure that the local firms were given a chance to compete. The only acceptable mode of entry for a foreign CSD company was through a "cooperative joint venture" (CJV) with a local Chinese firm (although the firm was not always involved in the CSD or bottling industry). The structure of a cooperative joint venture was such that the amount of capital injected into the business did not necessarily equal the amount of profit-sharing. For its Guilin CJV, PepsiCo had supplied 80 per cent of the capital, yet received only 17 per cent of the profits.

In 1993, Premier Deng Xiaoping introduced a series of reforms in order to make the Chinese market more attractive to foreign investors. Co-operative joint ventures fell out of favor and a new form of enterprise, the equity joint venture (EJV), was established. Under the new rules, a foreign CSD company could enter into a joint venture with SOEs appointed by the PRC government and hold a maximum of 60 per cent ownership share in the entity—the remaining 40 per cent had to be held by mainland Chinese interests. The profit would be distributed in line with the ratio of capital injected.

The first CSD firm to take advantage of the new regulations was Coca-Cola International. In 1993, CCI signed a Memorandum of Understanding (MOU) for $10 million[2] with the PRC government that gave it the right to build bottling facilities in 10 cities across China. While product could be sold anywhere in China, providing it came from a Chinese JV, once a bottling plant was established in an MOU city, no competitors were permitted to build a plant in the same area for two years. Due to the difficulty of shipping product

---

[2]All figures in US dollars unless otherwise noted.

from neighboring cities, establishing a plant in an MOU city meant that the firm could "own" the surrounding area.

While this practice was designed to facilitate the speed of development (i.e., the faster a firm could build, the faster it could build market share), the Central Government was not keen on creating a monopoly situation. In 1994, a similar agreement was reached with PepsiCo. The $10 million PepsiCo spent was, officially, not only for city rights but also for the overall development of the CSD industry in the PRC. Provisionally, $4 million was to go towards investments in JVs (essentially, to aid the SOEs in financing the equity portion of future JVs with PepsiCo); $4 million for the expansion and development of Chinese local drinks, including investments in technology and equipment; and $2 million for the establishment of "The Chinese Food and Beverage Training and Development Centre." See Exhibit 3 for a map of PepsiCo's and CCI's MOU cities.

THE CURRENT SITUATION

PepsiCo considered the PRC's political and economic outlook to be positive, with a continued commitment to economic reforms. In the past ten years, real per capita GDP growth rates had ranged eight to 12 per cent annually, and the forward momentum in per capita wealth was expected to continue. Total beverage consumption was expected to more than double by the turn of the century from the current consumption of 13 eight-ounce servings per capita. More established demand centres, such as Beijing and Shanghai, had already greatly exceeded this estimate—Beijing's per capita consumption was 84 eight-ounce servings, while Shanghai's was 90.

PepsiCo defined the total Chinese beverage industry as all non-alcoholic beverages, including bottled water (distilled, pure or spring), teas, Asian drinks (including coconut milk, bottled teas and others) and both concentrated and non-concentrated juices. This total basket of drinks was then divided into carbonated soft drinks and non-carbonated soft drinks. Excluded from the definition were most lactose-based pasteurized drinks and tap or non-bottled water. Lactose-based drinks were excluded as the dynamics of that industry were seen as fundamentally different from those of other beverage producers.

Industry-wide, CSDs held a 77 per cent share of the entire beverage industry, representing 680 million eight-ounce cases (one case contained 24 eight-ounce cans). PepsiCo forecast that CSDs would continue growing at 12 per cent annually through the year 2000, and would retain a 67 per cent share of the beverage industry. Within the CSD market, CCI had begun to take the lead. CCI had 13 operational bottling plants and a 15 per cent share of the total CSD market. This 15 per cent share represented 85 million eight-ounce cases of CCI brands and 20 million eight-ounce cases of local brands. PCI, meanwhile, had seven operational bottling plants, and a six per cent market share from 39 million eight-ounce cases of PepsiCo brands and two million eight-ounce cases of local brands.

While these numbers were disturbing to PepsiCo's management, they also realized that it would be premature to suggest that the race had yet been won. With a population of over 1.2 billion—of whom, Mr. Hawaux estimated, only 50 per cent had ever heard of Pepsi or Coke—the PRC still held significant potential for development.

Pepsi's strategic goals were articulated through a platform known within the firm as "Vision 2000." Essentially, Vision 2000 articulated two overarching goals: to close the gap with CCI before the turn of the century and to leverage this into industry leadership beyond the year 2000.

The Changchun Site

The proposed site for the next PCI bottling plant was in Changchun, the capital city of Jilin Province, located in the northeast region of the PRC. Changchun had a population of 15 million within a radius of 150 kilometres, with population growth estimated at 1.2 per cent per annum between 1994 and 2006. Per capita income in 1993 was $1,440, and was forecast to rise to $3,420 by 2006. Nearby cities were Jilin, with a population of 3.8 million, and Siping with 2.3 million inhabitants.

Changchun was considered to be an underdeveloped market with per capita beverage consumption of 21 eight-ounce servings, which was below more established demand centres. PepsiCo forecast total beverage consumption per capita to reach 41 eight-ounce servings in the year 2000. Changchun was seen as a prime target for expansion as there was no international brand in the market. Local CSDs accounted for 95 per cent of the industry, and these brands were not perceived to be satisfying the local demand. Many residents of Changchun had already heard of either Coke or Pepsi and were eager to "experience" a product closely tied to the Western lifestyle. In developed demand centres, it was found that many residents purchased Coke or Pepsi—for a relatively small portion of their disposable income—to buy into and emulate the enticing, fascinating and "sexy" American dream. Both PepsiCo and CCI had found this phenomenon in the former USSR and Eastern European countries as well.

Coke's presence in the Changchun market was relatively insignificant; limited quantities, sourced from CCI's bottling plants in Shenyang, Beijing and Tianjin, were found in certain hotels and restaurants. CCI had no production facilities for its flagship brands and, as per their MOU, couldn't until 1997. However, CCI had recently purchased a plot of land with the intention of producing non-Coke brands prior to 1997. PepsiCo predicted that CCI would begin production of its flagship brands early in 1998. Some PepsiCo products were also found in Changchun, again in extremely limited quantities. It was suspected that they had been smuggled from the eastern coast and from eastern Russia, with which the northwestern provinces of the PRC engaged in a large amount of trade.

In terms of articulated strategy, PepsiCo perceived Changchun as a "build and maintain barriers" site with a "steady phase-in over the first three years." In comparison, areas with a medium to high presence of CCI brands, such as Nanjing, were directed to "break barriers and close the gap" with a "rapid market blitz in the first year."

The Proposed Joint Venture

As per the new PRC regulations on joint ventures, PCI would enter into an equity joint venture, this time with two SOEs which had tentatively been selected by the PRC government as The Second Food Factory Changchun and Beijing Chong Yin Industrial & Trading Company. The Second Food Factory, established in 1932, was the local CSD leader in Changchun with a 30 per cent market share. Beijing Chong Yin, which was based in Beijing, was a subsidiary of the Chinese National Council of Light Industries, with whom PepsiCo had signed the MOU on the 10 joint venture bottling sites.

The proposal was for PepsiCo to control a 57.5 per cent interest in the JV, which would be named Changchun Pepsi-Cola Beverage Company Limited. The Second Food Factory would hold 37.5 per cent and Beijing Chong Yin would hold the remaining five per cent. The agreement would span 50 years, the maximum allowable under Chinese law. Capital infusions from the two Chinese partners would be in cash and/or fixed assets at their fair market value, and would be injected in accordance with the ownership ratio of the JV. PepsiCo's capital would be composed of fixed assets, mainly production lines, and cash in U.S. dollars or the local currency, Renminbi (RMB). In the first year—1994 or year 0 in the financial model—a total capital expenditure of $11.7 million would have to be provided by the joint venture partners and additional amounts would be required in subsequent years. Exhibit 4 provides a schedule of projected capital expenditures, depreciation and amortization. All cash needs would be internally financed as it was against PepsiCo's general policy to use debt financing for these types of projects.

As a green-field setup, the Changchun JV would be considered a mid-sized operation. Please see Exhibit 5 for a comparison with other PepsiCo JVs. Initially, the plant would have one bottling line with the possibility of adding another two lines in the future. Projected future bottling capacity for the three lines was 23.4 million cases of eight-ounce servings. PepsiCo would appoint the general manager while the Chinese partners would be responsible for appointing the deputy general manager. While PepsiCo would initially staff the upper management with expatriates, the firm hoped to develop local management talent over time.

FINANCIAL PROJECTIONS

Common to all large PepsiCo capital requests, a 12-year NPV projection, with sensitivities, was computed by the finance department. The Head Office in the United States determined discount rates for projects in different countries, which included country risk premiums. Currently, PepsiCo used 13 per cent as its weighted average cost of capital. The Chinese partners targeted a 20 per cent return. PepsiCo decided to use a hurdle rate of 16 per cent for the JV.

The current inflation rate in the United States was 3.5 per cent as compared to 12 per cent in China. Based on the concept of interest rate parity,[3] PepsiCo estimated that the Renminbi (RMB) would depreciate annually against the U.S. dollar from the current exchange rate of RMB/US$8.7 at a rate equivalent to the difference in inflation rates between the two countries. The projected future exchange rates used to convert all RMB cash flows into U.S. dollar cash flows are shown in Exhibit 6.

Income Projections

After discussions with colleagues working on the JV, Mr. Hawaux estimated that sales in 1995 (Year 1) would be $4.9 million. They had estimated annual revenue growth rates, gross profit margins and operating expense margins for the next 12 years (see Exhibit 7 for details). Depreciation of fixed assets was included as part of the cost of goods sold (COGS). Operating expenses, which included sales and distribution, marketing, distributors' commissions and general administration expenses, also contained an allowance for the amortization of intangible assets. Besides, PepsiCo estimated that bad debt write-off would amount to three per cent of credit sales, which were projected to be 50 per cent of the total sales.

Realizing that projections that far into the future could often be inaccurate and regional managers could be overly optimistic about their own projects, PepsiCo implemented a net operating profit before tax cap (NOPBT Cap). Based upon its extensive experience around the world, PepsiCo believed that the average NOPBT margin (NOPBT as a percentage of revenue) of bottling plants would be around 11 per cent. This cap set the maximum NOPBT margin allowed in any financial projection of similar projects at this level. Once the estimated NOPBT exceeded this limit, an NOPBT adjustment would be triggered in any capital budgeting analysis to bring the estimation down to the 11 per cent level. The company believed that such a mechanism promoted prudence and conservatism.

Taxation and Statutory Reserves

As part of an incentive program for foreign investment, the JV would enjoy a tax holiday for two years starting from its first profitable year. Tax laws in China allowed loss carry-forwards. After these two years, the JV would enjoy three years of reduced taxes at 7.5 per cent and then the full 15 per cent tax would apply. Additionally, a new local tax was set to take effect in 2001 and was projected to be three per cent. The taxes imposed on the JV were projected to remain at these levels for future years.

PRC laws also stipulated that companies must set aside 15 per cent of their net earnings as a statutory reserve. The reserve was created so that companies were prohibited from distributing all of their earnings. Reserves could be used to offset losses in future periods but could not be distributed to shareholders.

Capital Expenditures and Working Capital Changes

The JV partners would commit considerable capital in the initial years to build up the facility (see Exhibit 4). Bottling lines would be installed in 1994, 1996 and 1999.

The need for working capital would increase as operations expanded. Working capital was defined as accounts receivables (AR) plus inventory less accounts payables (AP). PepsiCo estimated that half of the sales would be cash on delivery (COD) while the other half would have an average credit term of 120 days. On the receiving end, the JV would enjoy an average 45-day payment term, or in other words, AP would be 12.3 per cent of COGS. Inventory would consist of raw materials and finished products. PepsiCo estimated that on average it would have 1.3 months of raw material and 7.5 days (or 0.25 month) of finished products in inventory. Exhibit 8 provides an estimate of net working capital changes over the 12-year projection period.

---

[3] Interest rate parity was an arbitrage process that ensured that the forward discount or premium equalled the interest rate differential between the two currencies. For example, RMB/US$ exchange rate in 1995 would equal: RMB9.4 = RMB8.7 * [(1+12%)/(1+3.5%)].

Bottle and Shell Deposit and Breakage

Bottles and shells were part of the fixed asset investment for the JV. Distributors would provide the bottling plant with a bottle and shell deposit for using these containers. Exhibit 9 provides an estimate of the net bottle and shell deposits Pepsi Changchun expected to receive. PepsiCo calculated an annual amortization charge to cover wear and tear on the bottles and shells in use and these charges are shown in the projected expenses in Exhibit 7.

Concentrate Sales from PepsiCo

In assessing the financial impact of the proposal, Mr. Hawaux understood that there would be two sets of financial projections to analyze: those of the JV, and those of PepsiCo. While the JV would be the bottler and distributor, it would be purchasing the concentrate for the product from PepsiCo at pre-arranged transfer prices. Mr. Hawaux estimated that half of the COGS of the bottling JV would be attributed to the cost of concentrate. In each of the last two fiscal years the net contribution after cost of sales and selling and administrative expenses amounted to 17 per cent of sales for PepsiCo as a whole.

Financial performance for the two entities—the bottler and PepsiCo—would be assessed from different perspectives. From PepsiCo's perspective, it was of critical importance for the JV to gain market share quickly in advance of CCI's entry. Revenues and dividends were essentially a secondary consideration—especially as most dividends would be re-invested and not repatriated by PepsiCo. PepsiCo's returns would be generated by sales of concentrate, as well as the profitability of the bottler.

The Chinese partners would control 43.5 per cent of the JV. While PepsiCo had impressed upon them the long-term nature of the project, the partners would still be eager for dividends in the short term.

Terminal Value

PepsiCo planned to apply for the maximum operation period, 50 years, allowed under the current PRC law governing foreign investments. According to the present stipulations, the JV would be liquidated in 50 years, but many believed that as the economy further liberalized, the JV partners would be allowed to apply for further extensions. Mr. Hawaux felt that a reasonable estimate of the terminal value of the JV beyond the 12-year projection period could be calculated with a commonly used capitalization formula:

Terminal value = [(cash flow) (1 + growth rate)] / [discount rate – growth rate]

He believed that a long-term growth rate (beyond year 12) of five per cent annually was a conservative estimate.

THE CAPITAL BUDGETING EXERCISE

Mr. Hawaux believed that he already had enough information to build an NPV model on the JV project. He also planned to use the base model to conduct a sensitivity analysis based on different projections of sales growth, the profitability ratio and future exchange rates. The proposed Changchun JV represented a key part of PepsiCo's strategic vision for the PRC and the president of PepsiCo Asia-Pacific had asked for the financial analysis to be completed as a top priority. A convincing financial analysis demonstrating a high rate of future profitability would also be useful in convincing all the partners to commit to this new venture.

Exhibit 1		
INCOME STATEMENTS PEPSICO INC. (US$ MILLION)		
	1992	**1993**
Sales	21,970.0	25,020.7
Cost of Sales	9,569.6	10,844.6
Gross Profit	12,400.4	14,176.1
SG&A	8,646.8	9,864.4
Depreciation	1,188.9	1,405.2
EBIT	2,564.7	2,906.5
Interest Expense	586.1	572.7
Nonop Income/Expense	113.7	88.7
Special Items	(193.5)	-
Pretax Income	1,898.8	2,422.5
Total Taxes	597.1	834.6
Net Income	**1,301.7**	**1,587.9**

Source: PepsiCo Inc. Annual Report

Exhibit 2		
BALANCE SHEET PEPSICO INC. (US$ MILLION)		
	31-Dec-92	**31-Dec-93**
Current Assets		
Cash	2,058.4	1,856.2
Receivables	1,588.5	1,883.4
Bad Debt Reserve	6.6	6.4
Inventory	768.8	924.7
Other current assets	420.0	493.4
Total Current Assets	4,842.3	5,164.1
Fixed Assets		
PP&E	7,442.0	8,855.6
Intangibles	6,959.0	7,929.5
Other fixed assets	1,707.9	1,756.6
Total Assets	**20,951.2**	**23,705.8**
Current Liabilities		
Notes Payable	706.8	2,191.2
Accounts Payable	1,164.8	1,390.0
Taxes Payable	387.9	823.7
Other current liabilities	2,064.9	2,170.0
Total Current Liabilities	4,324.4	6,574.9
Long-Term Liabilities		
Total Long-Term Debt	7,964.8	7,442.6
Deferred LT Taxes	1,682.3	2,007.6
Other Long-term Liabilities	1,624.0	1,342.0
Total Liabilities	15,595.5	17,367.1
Equity		
Common Equity	5,355.7	6,338.7
Total Liabilities & Equity	**20,951.2**	**23,705.8**

Source: PepsiCo Inc. Annual Report

Exhibit 3

PEPSICO'S MOU CITIES

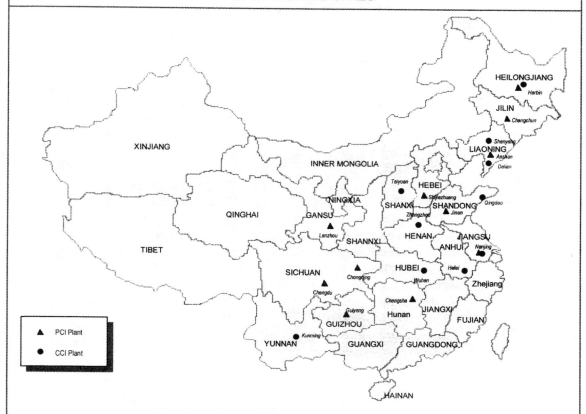

Location	PCI Plant	CCI Plant	Location	PCI Plant	CCI Plant
Harbin	✓	✓	Zhengzhou		✓
Changchun	✓		Lanzhou	✓	
Shenyang		✓	Nanjing	✓	
Anshan	✓		Chengdu		✓
Dalian		✓	Chongqing	✓	
Taiyuan		✓	Wuhan		✓
Shijianzhuang	✓		Hefei		✓
Qingdao		✓	Kunming		✓
Changsha	✓		Guiyang	✓	
Jinan	✓				

Source: PepsiCo company document.

Exhibit 4

SCHEDULE OF PROJECTED CAPITAL EXPENDITURES, DEPRECIATION AND AMORTIZATION FOR THE CHANGCHUN JOINT VENTURE
(US$000)

Calendar Year	1994	1995	1996	1997	1998	1999	2000
Year	0	1	2	3	4	5	6
Capital Expenditures	11,698	5,778	11,086	5,581	1,325	5,375	7,838
Depreciation		896	2,069	2,838	2,843	295	3,362
Amortization		78	551	849	890	3,578	910

Calendar Year	2001	2002	2003	2004	2005	2006
Year	7	8	9	10	11	12
Capital Expenditures	3,426	4,823	5,003	4,445	4,523	5,280
Depreciation	4,018	4,235	4,444	4,506	4,679	4,266
Amortization	729	773	728	735	815	919

Exhibit 5

PEPSICO JOINT VENTURES IN THE PRC

Existing JV	Seasonalized Capacity 8-oz. (mm cases)
Shanghai	46.4
Guangzhou	43.9
Changchun	**23.4**
Wuhan	21.3
Shenzhen	19.8
Chengdu	16.3
Beijing	13.4
Chongqing	12.0
Fuzhou	8.8
Nanchang	7.0
Guilin	5.1

Exhibit 6

PROJECTIONS OF FUTURE EXCHANGE RATES

U.S. Inflation Rate	3.50%
PRC Inflation Rate	12%
Inflation Differential	8.2%

Calendar Year	1994	1995	1996	1997	1998	1999	2000
RMB/US$ Exchange Rate	8.7	9.4	10.2	11.0	11.9	12.9	14.0

Calendar Year		2001	2002	2003	2004	2005	2006
RMB/US$ Exchange Rate		15.1	16.4	17.7	19.2	20.7	22.4

Exhibit 7

PROJECTED REVENUES AND COSTS FOR THE CHANGCHUN JOINT VENTURE

	1995	1996	1997	1998	1999	2000	2001	2002	2003	2004	2005	2006
Revenue	**4,851**	**14,689**	**24,649**	**27,075**	**31,118**	**35,544**	**43,788**	**51,768**	**61,173**	**70,913**	**81,335**	**92,309**
COGS	3,039	7,894	12,923	13,961	15,995	18,272	22,879	27,561	33,334	39,292	45,476	51,731
Other Manufacturing Costs	594	1,579	2,015	2,088	2,207	2,553	2,944	2,962	2,986	3,050	3,077	2,388
Gross Profit	1,218	5,216	9,711	11,026	12,916	14,719	17,965	21,245	24,853	28,571	32,782	38,190
Operating Expenses												
Selling & Distribution	1,020	2,064	3,096	4,098	3,761	4,484	6,533	5,722	6,875	7,346	7,879	8,649
Distributors' Commission	188	585	949	972	1,076	1,304	1,620	1,932	2,315	2,710	3,107	3,506
Advertising & Marketing	480	948	1,517	1,939	2,083	2,255	2,252	2,596	2,851	3,235	3,348	3,708
General & Administration	1,239	1,296	895	854	853	972	1,082	1,191	1,255	1,317	1,387	1,457
Bottle & Shell Breakage & Amort.	193	547	816	802	772	701	466	472	388	366	416	487
Bad Debt Write Off	73	220	370	406	467	533	657	777	918	1,064	1,220	1,385
NOPBT	**(1,975)**	**(444)**	**2,068**	**1,955**	**3,904**	**4,470**	**5,355**	**8,555**	**10,251**	**12,533**	**15,425**	**18,998**
Ratios												
Revenue Growth Rate	N/A	202.8%	67.8%	9.8%	14.9%	14.2%	23.2%	18.2%	18.2%	15.9%	14.7%	13.5%
Gross Profit Margin	25.1%	35.5%	39.4%	40.7%	41.5%	41.4%	41.0%	41.0%	40.6%	40.3%	40.3%	41.4%
NOPBT Margin	-40.7%	-3.0%	8.4%	7.2%	12.5%	12.6%	12.2%	16.5%	16.8%	17.7%	19.0%	20.6%

Exhibit 8

ESTIMATED CHANGES IN WORKING CAPITAL FOR THE CHANGCHUN JOINT VENTURE
(US$000)

	1995	1996	1997	1998	1999	2000	2001	2002	2003	2004	2005	2006
Revenue	4,851	14,689	24,649	27,075	31,118	35,544	43,788	51,768	61,173	70,913	81,335	92,309
COGS	3,039	7,894	12,923	13,961	15,995	18,272	22,879	27,561	33,334	39,292	45,476	51,731
AR	797	2,415	4,052	4,451	5,115	5,843	7,198	8,510	10,056	11,657	13,370	15,174
Days of AR	120	120	120	120	120	120	120	120	120	120	120	120
Inventory												
Raw Material												
(% of COGS)	77%	83%	82%	81%	80%	80%	82%	83%	84%	84%	85%	85%
Raw Material (Monthly)	195	545	878	939	1,072	1,224	1,567	1,904	2,326	2,761	3,208	3,652
Month(s) of Raw Material in Inventory	1.3	1.3	1.3	1.3	1.3	1.3	1.3	1.3	1.3	1.3	1.3	1.3
Closing Balance	253	708	1,142	1,221	1,394	1,591	2,037	2,475	3,024	3,589	4,170	4,748
Finished Products												
(% of COGS)	88%	85%	84%	84%	84%	84%	85%	85%	86%	86%	87%	87%
Finished Products (Monthly)	224	560	908	976	1,116	1,276	1,612	1,952	2,384	2,828	3,280	3,736
Month(s) of Finished Products in Inventory	0.25	0.25	0.25	0.25	0.25	0.25	0.25	0.25	0.25	0.25	0.25	0.25
Closing Balance	56	140	227	244	279	319	403	488	596	707	820	934
Total Inventory Balance	309	848	1,369	1,465	1,673	1,910	2,440	2,963	3,620	4,296	4,990	5,682
AP	375	973	1,593	1,721	1,972	2,253	2,821	3,398	4,110	4,844	5,607	6,378
Days of AP	45	45	45	45	45	45	45	45	45	45	45	45
Total Working Capital	732	2,289	3,828	4,194	4,816	5,500	6,817	8,075	9,566	11,109	12,754	14,478
Changes in Working Capital	(732)	(1,558)	(1,538)	(367)	(622)	(684)	(1,317)	(1,258)	(1,491)	(1,543)	(1,645)	(1,725)

Exhibit 9
ESTIMATED NET BOTTLE AND SHELL DEPOSITS FOR THE CHANGCHUN JOINT VENTURE (US$000)

Year	Amount	Year	Amount
1995	746	2001	455
1996	1,252	2002	568
1997	1,097	2003	515
1998	528	2004	524
1999	644	2005	533
2000	679	2006	600

LAURENTIAN BAKERIES

In late May, 1995, Danielle Knowles, vice-president of operations for Laurentian Bakeries Inc., was preparing a capital project expenditure proposal to expand the company's frozen pizza plant in Winnipeg, Manitoba. If the opportunity to expand into the U.S. frozen pizza market was taken, the company would need extra capacity. A detailed analysis, including a net present value calculation, was required by the company's Capital Allocation Policy for all capital expenditures in order to ensure that projects were both profitable and consistent with corporate strategies.

COMPANY BACKGROUND

Established in 1984, Laurentian Bakeries Inc. (Laurentian) manufactured a variety of frozen baked food products at plants in Winnipeg (pizzas), Toronto (cakes) and Montreal (pies). While each plant operated as a profit center, they shared a common sales force located at the company's head office in Montreal. Although the Toronto plant was responsible for over 40 per cent of corporate revenues in fiscal 1994, and the other two plants accounted for about 30 per cent each, all three divisions contributed equally to profits. The company enjoyed strong competitive positions in all three markets and it was the low cost producer in the pizza market. Income Statements and Balance Sheets for the 1993 to 1995 fiscal years are in Exhibits 1 and 2, respectively.

Richard Ivey School of Business
The University of Western Ontario

IVEY

Rob Barbara prepared this case under the supervision of Professors David Shaw and Steve Foerster solely to provide material for class discussion. The authors do not intend to illustrate either effective or ineffective handling of a managerial situation. The authors may have disguised certain names and other identifying information to protect confidentiality.

Laurentian sold most of its products to large grocery chains, and in fact, supplying several Canadian grocery chains with their private label brand frozen pizzas generated much of the sales growth. Other sales were made to institutional food services.

The company's success was, in part, the product of its management's philosophies. The cornerstone of Laurentian's operations included a commitment to continuous improvement; for example all employees were empowered to think about and make suggestions for ways of reducing waste. As Danielle Knowles saw it: "Continuous improvement is a way of life at Laurentian." Also, the company was known for its above-average consideration for the human resource and environmental impact of its business decisions. These philosophies drove all policy-making, including those policies governing capital allocation.

Danielle Knowles

Danielle Knowles' career, which spanned 13 years in the food industry, had included positions in other functional areas such as marketing and finance. She had received an undergraduate degree in mechanical engineering from Queen's University in Kingston, Ontario, and a masters of business administration from the Ivey Business School.

THE PIZZA INDUSTRY

Major segments in the pizza market were frozen pizza, deli-fresh chilled pizza, restaurant pizza and take-out pizza. Of these four, restaurant and take-out were the largest. While these segments consisted of thousands of small, family-owned establishments, a few very large North American chains, which included Domino's, Pizza Hut and Little Caesar's, dominated.

Although 12 firms manufactured frozen pizzas in Canada, the five largest firms, including Laurentian, accounted for 95 per cent of production. McCain Foods was the market leader with 44 per cent market share, while Laurentian had 21 per cent. Per capita consumption of frozen pizza products in Canada was one-third of the level in the U.S. where retail prices were lower.

ECONOMIC CONDITIONS

The North American economy had enjoyed strong economic growth since 1993, after having suffered a severe recession for the two previous years. Interest rates bottomed-out in mid-1994, after which the U.S. Federal Reserve slowly increased rates until early 1995 in an attempt to fight inflationary pressures. Nevertheless, North American inflation was expected to average three to five per cent annually for the foreseeable future. The Bank of Canada followed the U.S. Federal Reserve's lead and increased interest rates, in part to protect the Canadian dollar's value relative to the value of the U.S. dollar. The result was a North American growth rate of gross domestic product that was showing signs of slowing down.

LAURENTIAN'S PROJECT REVIEW PROCESS

All capital projects at Laurentian were subject to review based on the company's Capital Allocation Policy. The latest policy, which had been developed in 1989 when the company began considering factors other than simply the calculated net present value for project evaluation, was strictly enforced and managers were evaluated each year partially by their division's return on investment. The purpose of the policy was to reinforce the management philosophies by achieving certain objectives: that all projects be consistent with business strategies, support continuous improvement, consider the human resource and environmental impact, and provide a sufficient return on investment.

Prior to the approval of any capital allocation, each operating division was required to develop both a Strategic Plan and an Operating Plan. The Strategic Plan had to identify and quantify either inefficiencies or lost opportunities and establish targets for their elimination, include a three-year plan of capital requirements, link capital spending to business strategies and continuous improvement effort, and achieve the company-wide hurdle rates.

The first year of the Strategic Plan became the Annual Operating Plan. This was supported by a detailed list of proposed capital projects which became the basis for capital allocation. In addition to meeting all Strategic Plan criteria, the Operating Plan had to identify major continuous improvement initiatives and budget for the associated benefits, as well as develop a training plan identifying specific training objectives for the year.

These criteria were used by head office to keep the behaviour of divisional managers consistent with corporate objectives. For example, the requirement to develop a training plan as part of the operational plan forced managers to be efficient with employee training and to keep continuous improvement as the ultimate objective.

All proposed projects were submitted on an Authorization for Expenditure (AFE) form for review and approval (see Exhibit 3). The AFE had to present the project's linkage to the business strategies. In addition, it had to include specific details of economics and engineering, involvement and empowerment, human resource, and the environment. This requirement ensured that projects had been carefully thought through by forcing managers to list the items purchased, the employees involved in the project, the employees adversely affected by the project, and the effect of the project on the environment.

Approval of a capital expenditure proposal was contingent on three requirements which are illustrated in Exhibit 4. The first of these requirements was the operating division's demonstrated commitment to continuous improvement (C.I.), the criteria of which are described in Exhibit 5. The second requirement was that all projects of more than $300,000 be included in the Strategic Plan. The final requirement was that for projects greater than $1 million, the operating division had to achieve its profit target. However, if a project failed to meet any of these requirements, there was a mechanism through which emergency funds might be allocated subject to the corporate executive committee's review and approval. If the project was less than $1 million and it met all three requirements, only divisional review and approval was necessary. Otherwise, approval was needed from the executive committee.

The proposed Winnipeg plant project was considered a Class 2 project as the expenditures were meant to increase capacity for existing products or to establish a facility for new products. Capital projects could fall into one of three other classes: cost reduction (Class 1); equipment or facility replacement (Class 3); or other necessary expenditures for R&D, product improvement, quality control and concurrence with legal, government, health, safety or insurance requirements including pollution control (Class 4). A project spending audit was required for all expenditures; however, a savings audit was also needed if the project was considered either Class 1 or 2. Each class of project had a different hurdle rate reflecting different levels of risk. Class 1 projects were considered the most risky and had a hurdle rate of 20 per cent. Class 2 and Class 3 projects had hurdle rates of 18 per cent and 15 per cent, respectively.

Knowles was responsible for developing the Winnipeg division's Capital Plan and completing all AFE forms.

WINNIPEG PLANT'S EXPANSION OPTIONS

Laurentian had manufactured frozen pizzas at the Toronto plant until 1992. However, after the company became the sole supplier of private-label frozen pizzas for a large grocery chain and was forced to secure additional capacity, it acquired the Winnipeg frozen pizza plant from a competitor. A program of regular maintenance and equipment replacement made the new plant the low cost producer in the industry, with an operating margin that averaged 15 per cent.

The plant, with its proven commitment to continuous improvement, had successfully met its profit objective for the past three years. After the shortage of capacity had been identified as the plant's largest source of lost opportunity, management was eager to rectify this problem as targeted for in the Strategic Plan. Because the facility had also included the proposed plant expansion in its Strategic Plan, it met all three requirements for consideration of approval for a capital project.

Annual sales had matched plant capacity of 10.9 million frozen pizzas when Laurentian concluded that opportunities similar to those in Canada existed in the U.S. An opportunity surfaced whereby Laurentian could have an exclusive arrangement to supply a large U.S.-based grocery chain with its private-label-brand frozen pizzas beginning in April, 1996. As a result of this arrangement, frozen pizza sales would increase rapidly, adding 2.2 million units in fiscal 1996, another 1.8 million units in fiscal 1997, and then 1.3 million additional units to reach a total of 5.3 million additional units by fiscal 1998. However, the terms of the agreement would only provide Laurentian with guaranteed sales of half this amount. Knowles expected that there was a 50 per cent chance that the grocery chain would order only the guaranteed amount. Laurentian sold frozen pizzas to its customers for $1.70 in 1995 and prices were expected to increase just enough to keep pace with inflation. Production costs were expected to increase at a similar rate.

Laurentian had considered, but rejected, three other alternatives to increase its frozen pizza capacity. First, the acquisition of a competitor's facility in Canada had been rejected because the equipment would not satisfy the immediate capacity needs nor achieve the cost reduction possible with expansion of the Winnipeg plant. Second, the acquisition of a competitor in the U.S. had been rejected because the available plant would require a capital infusion double that required in Winnipeg. As well, there were risks that the product quality would be inferior. Last, the expansion of the Toronto cake plant had been rejected as it would require a capital outlay similar to that in the second alternative. The only remaining alternative was the expansion of the Winnipeg plant. By keeping the entire frozen pizza operation in Winnipeg, Laurentian could better exploit economies of scale and assure consistently high product quality.

The Proposal

The expansion proposal, which would require six months to complete, would recommend four main expenditures: expanding the existing building in Winnipeg by 60 per cent would cost $1.3 million; adding a spiral freezer, $1.6 million; installing a new high speed pizza processing line, $1.3 million; and acquiring additional warehouse space, $600,000. Including $400,000 for contingency needs, the total cash outlay for the project would be $5.2 million. The equipment was expected to be useful for 10 years, at which point its salvage value would be zero. On-going capital expenditures, projected to be equal to annual depreciation, would be needed to keep the equipment up-to-date.

The land on which the Winnipeg plant was built was valued at $250,000 and no additional land would be necessary for the project. While the expansion would not require Laurentian to increase the size of the plant's administrative staff, Knowles wondered what portion, if any, of the $223,000 in fixed salaries should be included when evaluating the project. Likewise, she estimated that it cost Laurentian approximately $40,000 in sales staff time and expenses to secure the U.S. contract that had created the need for extra capacity. Last, net working capital needs would increase with additional sales. Working capital was the sum of inventory and accounts receivable less accounts payable, all of which were a function of sales. Knowles estimated, however, that the new high-speed line would allow the company to cut two days from average inventory age.

Added to the benefit derived from increased sales, the project would reduce production costs in two ways. First, the new high-speed line would reduce plant-wide unit cost by $0.019, though only 70 per cent of this increased efficiency would be realized in the first year. There was an equal chance, however, that only 50 per cent of these savings could actually be achieved. Second, "other" savings totaling $138,000 per year would also result from the new line and would increase each year at the rate of inflation.

Each year, a capital cost allowance (CCA), akin to depreciation, would be deducted from operating income as a result of the capital expenditure. This deduction, in turn, would reduce the amount of corporate tax paid by Laurentian. In the event that the company did not have positive earnings in any year, the CCA deduction could be transferred to a subsequent year. However, corporate earnings were projected to be positive for the foreseeable future. Knowles compiled the eligible CCA deduction for 10 years (see Exhibit 6). For the purpose of her analysis, she assumed that all cash flows would occur at the appropriate year-end.

Three areas of environmental concern had to be addressed in the proposal to ensure both conformity with Laurentian policy and compliance with regulatory bodies and local by-laws. First, design and installation of sanitary drain systems, including re-routing of existing drains, would improve sanitation practices of effluent/wastewater discharge. Second, the provision of water-flow recording meters would quantify water volumes consumed in manufacturing and help to reduce its usage. Last, the refrigeration plant would use ammonia as the coolant as opposed to chlorofluorocarbons. These initiatives were considered sufficient to satisfy the criteria of the Capital Allocation Policy.

THE DECISION

Knowles believed that the project was consistent with the company's business strategy since it would ensure that the Winnipeg plant continued to be the low cost producer of frozen pizzas in Canada. However, she knew that her analysis must consider all factors, including the project's net present value. The plant's capital allocation review committee would be following the procedures set out in the company's Capital Allocation Policy as the basis for reviewing her recommendation.

Knowles considered the implications if the project did not provide sufficient benefit to cover the Class 2 hurdle rate of 18 per cent. Entering the U.S. grocery chain market was a tremendous opportunity and she considered what other business could result from Laurentian's increased presence. She also wondered if the hurdle rate for a project that was meant to increase capacity for an existing product should be similar to the company's cost of capital, since the risk of the project should be similar to the overall risk of the firm. She knew that Laurentian's board of directors established a target capital structure that included 40 per cent debt. She also reviewed the current Canadian market bond yields, which are listed in Exhibit 7. The spread between Government of Canada bonds and those of corporations with bond ratings of BBB, such as Laurentian, had recently been about 200 basis points (2%) for most long-term maturities. Finally, she discovered that Laurentian's stock beta was 0.85, and that, historically, the Toronto stock market returns outperformed long-term government bonds by about six per cent annually.

Exhibit 1		
INCOME STATEMENT **For The Year Ending March 31** **($ millions)**		

	1993	**1994**	**1995**
Revenues	$91.2	$95.8	$101.5
Cost of Goods Sold	27.4	28.7	30.5
Gross Income	63.8	67.1	71.0
Operating Expenses	50.1	52.7	55.8
Operating Income	13.7	14.4	15.2
Interest	0.9	1.0	1.6
Income Before Tax	12.8	13.4	13.6
Income Tax	4.2	5.2	5.2
Net Income	$8.6	$8.2	$8.4

Exhibit 2			
BALANCE SHEET **For The Year Ending March 31** **($ millions)**			

	1993	**1994**	**1995**
Assets:			
Cash	$ 6.2	$ 9.4	$13.1
Accounts Receivable	11.3	11.8	12.5
Inventory	6.2	6.6	7.0
Prepaid Expenses	0.3	0.6	2.2
Other Current		0.9	0.9
Total Current	24.0	29.3	35.7
Fixed Assets	35.3	36.1	36.4
TOTAL	$59.3	$65.4	$72.1
Liabilities and Shareholders' Equity:			
Accounts Payable	7.5	7.9	8.3
Other Current	0.7	1.3	2.2
Total Current	8.2	9.2	10.5
Long-Term Debt	16.8	20.4	24.3
Shareholders' Equity	34.3	35.8	37.3
TOTAL	$59.3	$65.4	$72.1

Exhibit 3

AUTHORIZATION FOR EXPENDITURE FORM

Company Name: _____   Business Segment: _____

Project Title: _____

Project Cost (AFE Amount): _____

Project Cost (Gross Investment Amount): _____

Net Present Value at _____%: _____

Internal Rate of Return: _____%   Years Payback: _____

Brief Project Description:

Estimated Completion Date:	Approvals		
_____			
Project Contact Person:	<u>Name</u>	<u>Signature</u>	<u>Date</u>
_____	_____	_____	_____
Phone: _____			
Fax: _____	_____	_____	_____
	_____	_____	_____
Currency Used:	_____	_____	_____
CDN _____ US _____			
Other _____	_____	_____	_____
	_____	_____	_____
Post Audit:			
Company: Yes ___ No ___			
Corporate: Yes ___ No ___			

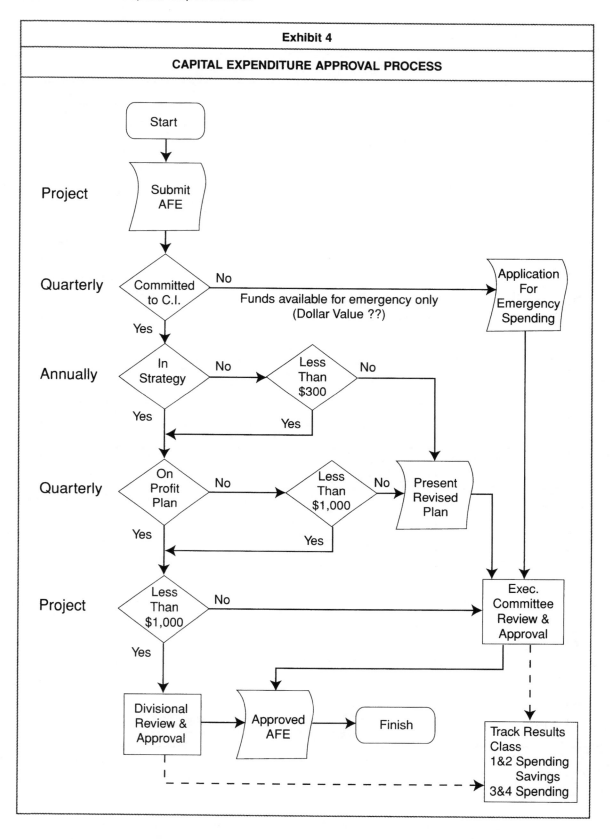

Exhibit 4
CAPITAL EXPENDITURE APPROVAL PROCESS

Exhibit 5

BUSINESS REVIEW CRITERIA
Used To Assess Divisional Commitment To Continuous Improvement

Safety
*   Lost time accidents per 200,000 employee hours worked

Product Quality
*   Number of customer complaints

Financial
*   Return on Investment

Lost Sales
*   Market share % - where data available

Manufacturing Effectiveness
*   People cost (total compensation $ including fringe) as a percentage of new sales
*   Plant scrap (kg) as a percentage of total production (kg)

Managerial Effectiveness/Employee Empowerment
*   Employee Survey
*   Training provided vs. training planned
*   Number of employee grievances

Sanitation
*   Sanitation audit ratings

Other Continuous Improvement Measurements
*   Number of continuous improvement projects directed against identified piles of waste/lost opportunity completed and in-progress

Exhibit 6
ELIGIBLE CCA DEDUCTION

Year	Deduction
1996	$ 434,000
1997	$ 768,000
1998	$ 593,000
1999	$ 461,000
2000	$ 361,000
2001	$ 286,000
2002	$ 229,000
2003	$ 185,000
2004	$ 152,000
2005	$1,731,000

Exhibit 7
MARKET INTEREST RATES **On May 18, 1995**

1-Year Government of Canada Bond 7.37%
5-Year Government of Canada Bond 7.66%
10-Year Government of Canada Bond 8.06%
20-Year Government of Canada Bond 8.30%
30-Year Government of Canada Bond 8.35%

Source: Bloomberg L.P.

part eight

Dividend Policy

CHAMPION ROAD MACHINERY

In late July, 1994, Scott Hall, vice-president of finance and chief financial officer of Champion Road Machinery Limited (Champion), was preparing a presentation on the company's proposed dividend policy for a board of directors' meeting scheduled for the middle of August. It had been only three months since the company completed its initial public offering, at which time the prospectus stated that: "The company does not anticipate paying cash dividends on the common shares in the foreseeable future, but intends to retain future earnings for reinvestment in the business." However, earnings were well ahead of those projected in the prospectus and the company had succeeded in managing cash better than anticipated.

COMPANY BACKGROUND

Champion was founded in Pennsylvania in 1875 as a manufacturer of horse-drawn grading equipment. In 1896, the company moved to Canada and, in 1910, it established its operations at the current location in Goderich, Ontario, a town situated on Lake Huron approximately 100 kilometres northwest of London, Ontario. Champion remained a family-owned business until 1988 when it was sold to a group of investors led by a private investment firm, Sequoia Associates (Sequoia), which held a wide range of investments throughout North America, including a forest products supplier, a manufacturer of home building products and an auto parts manufacturer. Sequoia acquired what it believed were high risk turnaround

Richard Ivey School of Business
The University of Western Ontario

IVEY

Rob Barbara prepared this case under the supervision of Professor Steve Foerster solely to provide material for class discussion. The authors do not intend to illustrate either effective or ineffective handling of a managerial situation. The authors may have disguised certain names and other identifying information to protect confidentiality.

opportunities, including Champion, with the potential for growth in sales, earnings and cash flows, which would translate into stock appreciation.

Immediately after Champion changed hands, the new owners began the first phase of change by moving to secure the financial health of the company. The first move was to replace the company president with Arthur Church, age 41, who had worked at Timberjack Corporation (Timberjack) of Woodstock, Ontario, for Sequoia. Timberjack was a manufacturer of logging and forestry equipment that had been purchased by Sequoia in 1984, taken public with an initial public offering (IPO) in 1988, and then sold a year later to a European equipment manufacturer. Church was a professional engineer with 12 years of engineering, manufacturing and management experience. The board of directors was simultaneously altered to include Mr. Church, three Sequoia representatives and five independent members (see Exhibit 1). The board's chairperson, William Walsh, a founder of Sequoia, was also Champion's largest single shareholder. In addition, management compensation was changed so that a large proportion of total salaries was based on the company's annual profit.

Champion was the world's second-largest manufacturer of graders and other large machinery used in the construction and maintenance of roads, with a 14.4 per cent share of the world market in 1993. Caterpillar, of Peoria, Illinois, was the largest. Champion's products were distributed through independent dealers to customers in 95 countries outside of North America representing 28 per cent of revenues. Canadian and U.S. sales represented 37 per cent and 35 per cent of revenues, respectively.

Champion sold products in five categories. The first category included large load graders. The 700 Series large graders accounted for 65 per cent of revenues. The 700 Series III graders, offered in 16 different models, retailed for around $100,000—an amount that was 20 per cent less than the retail price of Caterpillar's comparable grader. The newer 700 Series IV graders were aimed at the lucrative private contractor market and were built to the specification of a specific purchaser. This market demanded additional benefits, such as a tighter turning radius. Champion sold 39 per cent of its large graders to customers outside of North America.

The second category, soil compactors, was added with the acquisition of the Super-Pac line in January of 1993. Above-average growth was anticipated for this segment also, which represented only four per cent of sales in 1994. The third category Champion entered was the small grader market when it acquired Bud Lee of Charlotte, North Carolina, in 1993. While this segment represented only two per cent of sales in 1994, the company anticipated very strong growth over the next few years. The fourth category, spare parts, represented 12 per cent of sales and this segment was characterized by wide profit margins. The fifth category, the company-owned Ontario dealership, accounted for 17 per cent of the company's sales. All other dealers were independent of the company.

Champion sales were a function of the level of new road construction and maintenance activity, which depended on government budgets and the general state of the economy. The Canadian economy was showing increasing strength as Gross Domestic Product increased by three per cent in the first quarter of 1994 over the same period a year previously. However, since a large amount of the company's sales was driven by maintenance rather than by new road construction, Champion's business was considered moderately cyclical. International sales helped to mitigate the cycle: when sales in one region of the world were flat, it was not uncommon that sales in another region were booming. Much of the growth experienced by Champion in the early 1990s stemmed from developing countries moving quickly to build new road systems. Future growth was expected to come from strong North American markets, improving European markets and continued infrastructure spending in developing countries.

The company was looking to diversify its business further by considering the purchase of a snow removal equipment manufacturer. Champion made profits of $4.7 million in 1993 on sales of $125.4 million in 1993, significantly more than its 1992 earnings of $200,000. Also, the company had been successful at decreasing long-term debt in 1993. Financial statements are provided in Exhibits 2 and 3.

CORPORATE STRATEGY

The new corporate strategy was to be implemented in two phases. The goal of the first phase was to turn-around the company by hiring a new executive, naming a new board, focusing on process improvement, being responsive to customer design recommendations, reducing the work force, and expanding and improving the quality of the product line. This final step would be accomplished by the introduction of the new Series 700 IV large grader, which was planned for the third quarter of 1994. The second phase, which would begin when Champion's financial strength improved, would focus on growth through expanding the company's existing markets, and by acquiring other companies that fit with the core business of manufacturing equipment used for road construction and maintenance.

The management of Champion were patient when looking for acquisitions and, consequently, were able to purchase companies at very reasonable prices. Waiting for the right deal had helped the company reach its target requirement of a 15 per cent return on capital employed for any of its acquisitions. One stock analyst described Champion's capital allocation program as "very successful."

INITIAL PUBLIC OFFERING

Champion common stock was listed on the Toronto Stock Exchange and the Montreal Stock Exchange on April 25, 1994, through an IPO. Management had decided that the company should secure additional financing for several reasons. First, management wanted to repay the $11 million in debt that was outstanding as of April, 1994. Then, if a sufficiently attractive opportunity presented itself, the company would have the flexibility to add debt. Second, because the company wanted to continue to update its production processes, it would require about $3 million to fund capital expenditures planned for 1994. Third, future sales growth would also require additional working capital.

Prior to the IPO, there were 8,750,000 common shares outstanding, owned by 91 shareholders of the company as of February 2, 1994. Almost 40 per cent of the shares were held by the directors and executives. The three largest shareholders were William Walsh, Chairman; Robert Ferris, Secretary; and Arthur Church, President and CEO. An additional 2,420,000 shares were issued at a price of $12 per share, at the time of the IPO, resulting in a total of 11,170,000 common shares outstanding. Gross proceeds from the IPO were $29 million, but the company received $26.6 million after issue costs. As part of the agreement, the 91 shareholders could not sell any stock for one year after the IPO, but were able to sell 1,100,000 shares as part of the IPO. Consequently, a total of 3,520,000 shares were available to the public.

The common stock issue was targeted at investors interested primarily in capital gains. The company had examined the dividend policy issue at the time of the IPO, but had determined that sufficient cash was not available to pay a cash dividend. A cash dividend did not seem to fit with the expectations of the new shareholders. Seventy per cent of the stock had been purchased by institutional investors and 30 per cent by retail investors. The institutional investors included many of the large Canadian-based money managers, such as the Caisse de dépôt et placement du Québec based in Montreal. There were approximately 1,500 retail investors, which included the more than 600 Champion employees. The Champion stock was considered to be eligible for most institutional investments; consequently, investment managers for large pools of investments, such as pension funds, could purchase the stock for their portfolios. Exhibit 4 lists the acts under which Champion was eligible for investment. Historically, eligibility rules required firms to pay dividends each year for a number of years (typically five to seven). More recently, most Canadian federal and provincial legislation relating to financial institutions provided for "prudent investor" standards. Rather than operating under restrictions (such as earnings or dividend history) on individual stocks, the entire portfolio of stocks was judged as a group to determine whether a prudent investor would invest in such a basket of securities. Some exceptions to the prudence test are also listed in Exhibit 4. It was one analyst's opinion that any acts that did not currently comply with the "prudence" standard would have adopted it by the time Champion had built up a dividend history.

Since its initial listing on the Toronto Stock Exchange, the price of Champion's stock had been at its highest point, $12.38, just four trading days after the IPO. This was also the period when trading volume was heaviest, as over 400,000 shares were traded in the stock's first seven trading days. Since then daily volume was generally below 20,000 shares per day. While the price hit a low of $9.25 on June 29, it rebounded quickly to close at just under $12 on July 22 (see Exhibit 5).

DIVIDEND CONSIDERATIONS

Hall re-visited the dividend issue in July, 1994, when he was satisfied that the company had been performing well above expectations and that cash had also been well managed. In the six-month period ending July 2, 1994, Champion had generated $12.3 million in cash, compared with $4.3 million a year earlier. Hall was confident that the company was generating enough cash that it could take advantage of any business opportunity that presented itself. Even if Champion were to purchase the few companies that were likely to meet its criteria, there would still be excess cash. Therefore, if a dividend were paid, it would be paid out of "residual" cash.

Cash flows for future dividends would depend on economic conditions and Champion's debt policies. While the company had a target capital structure that included about one-half debt and one-half equity, Hall preferred to add debt only if an acquisition opportunity warranted. This target capital structure contained a much smaller proportion of debt to total assets than other companies in the industry such as Finning (67 per cent debt) and Caterpillar (82 per cent debt). Shareholders' equity was $45 million as at July 2, 1994.

Only three months earlier, Champion had concluded that a dividend did not fit with the company's goal of growth. Shareholders, who appeared to be more concerned with capital gains, had not bought the company's stock for income. Hall did not think that the profile of shareholders had changed dramatically since April. Nevertheless, he was confident that if investors were convinced that the company was still following a strong and effective capital allocation policy and if, at the same time, there was excess cash, a dividend would be a welcomed source of income.

If a dividend was declared, the company had to be very certain that it could be sustained. Decreasing or eliminating a dividend without a valid reason might result in a fall in the stock price. He thought that the only acceptable reason for the elimination of a dividend would be the opportunity of a large acquisition with a price tag beyond the available cash and debt capacity of the company. The company wanted to issue equity financing only as a last resort, so as to not dilute the existing ownership.

Hall felt that the dividend policies of Champion's competitors would be important to shareholders. The July 1994 annualized dividend yield for the TSE 300 and the Toronto 35 was 2.34 per cent and 2.92 per cent, respectively. Over the last 40 years, the average dividend yield for the TSE 300 had been around 3.5 per cent. Caterpillar's regular cash dividend of $0.15 each quarter translated into a dividend yield of only 0.60 per cent. Two Canadian-based heavy equipment dealers, Finning Tractor and Toromont Industries, had dividend yields of 1.12 per cent and 1.69 per cent, respectively.

A final factor that Hall needed to consider was the tax implications of dividends for shareholders. Dividends and capital gains were taxed differently in the U.S. and Canada. In the United States, dividends were taxed as regular income and were subject to tax at the individual marginal tax rate, which peaked at 39.6 per cent, in 1994 for incomes over $250,000. Unlike capital gains, which were taxable at a maximum rate of 28 per cent, dividends generated an overall higher tax bill for high income investors. In contrast, Canadian tax law provided for a Dividend Tax Credit for dividends of Canadian companies and, therefore, dividend income resulted in a lower tax bill than did an equivalent amount of capital gains. Exhibit 6 shows an example of these differences in tax treatment.

DECISION

If Hall decided to recommend a dividend, he would also need to make a recommendation on the size of a dividend. Armed with a pro forma income statement for the year ended December 31, 1994 (Exhibit 7), he sat down to consider his recommendation.

Exhibit 1
LIST OF DIRECTORS

William D. Walsh, Atherton, California
Chairman, Champion
Partner, Sequoia Associates

Arthur F. Church, Goderich, Ontario
President & CEO, Champion

Robert A. Ferris, Atherton, California
Secretary, Champion
Partner, Sequoia Associates

J. Frank Leach, Atherton, California
Corporate Director and Partner, Sequoia Associates

Raymond F. O'Brien, Los Altos, California
Chairman, Consolidated Freightways Inc.

Ronald A. McKinlay, Toronto, Ontario
Retired Former Chairman of Canada Deposit Insurance Corp.

David J. Sharpless, Toronto, Ontario
Partner, Blake, Cassels & Graydon

Michael D. Smith, Caledon East, Ontario
President, Metaris Inc.

Dennis W. Vollmershausen, Woodstock, Ontario
Chairman, London Machinery Inc.

Source: Champion Road Machinery 1994 Annual Report.

	Exhibit 2		
	INCOME STATEMENTS **For The Years Ending December 31** **($000)**		

	1993	**1992**	**1991**
Net Sales	$125,419	$101,590	$111,392
Cost of Sales	97,427	80,321	87,016
Gross Profit	27,992	21,269	24,376
Selling & Administrative	17,608	18,865	17,838
Profit Sharing Plan	1,301	17	516
Operating Income	9,083	2,387	6,022
Interest Expense	1,519	2,058	3,019
Income Before Taxes	7,564	329	3,003
Income Tax Expense			
Current	3,134	419	942
Deferred	(243)	(297)	50
Net Income	$ 4,673	$ 207	$ 2,011

Source: *Champion Road Machinery Company Prospectus.*

Exhibit 3

BALANCE SHEETS
For The Years Ending December 31
($000)

	1993	1992
Assets:		
Accounts Receivable	$14,851	$9,640
Notes Receivable	1,526	2,132
Inventory	20,275	18,145
Prepaid Expenses	282	256
	36,934	30,173
Property, Plant and Equipment	10,253	9,725
Other Assets	622	128
TOTAL	$47,809	$40,026
Liabilities:		
Bank Indebtedness	$ 4,228	$ 6,032
Account Payable	19,041	12,395
Income Tax Payable	2,301	315
Current Portion of Long Term Debt	2,788	3,409
	28,358	22,151
Long-Term Debt	5,286	6,327
Deferred Income Taxes	655	898
Shareholders' Equity:		
Share Capital	1,578	3,375
Retained Earnings	11,932	7,275
TOTAL	$47,809	$40,026

Source: *Champion Road Machinery Company Prospectus.*

Exhibit 4

ELIGIBILITY FOR INVESTMENT

Eligibility of the Common Shares offered hereby for investment by purchasers to whom any of the following statutes apply is, in certain cases, governed by criteria which such purchasers are required to establish as policies or guidelines pursuant to applicable statute (and, where applicable, the regulations thereunder) and is subject to the prudent investment standards and general investment provisions provided therein:

Insurance Companies Act (Canada)
Trust and Loan Companies Act (Canada)
Pension Benefits Standards Act (Canada)
Loan and Trust Corporations Act (British Columbia)
Insurance Act (Manitoba)
The Trustee Act (Manitoba)
Trustees Act (New Brunswick)
Loan and Trust Corporations Act (Ontario)
Pension Benefits Act (Ontario)
Supplemental Pension Plans Act (Quebec)
An Act Respecting Insurance (Quebec)
An Act Respecting Trust Companies and Savings Companies (Quebec)

In the opinion of Blake, Cassels & Graydon, counsel to the Company and Goodman and Carr, counsel to the Underwriters, the Common Shares offered hereby will, at the date of issue, be eligible investments without resort to the so-called "basket" provisions, but subject to certain investment provisions and restrictions pertaining generally to purchasers, for insurers under the Insurance Act (Ontario), the Insurance Act (Alberta) and the Employment Pensions Plans Act (Alberta). In the opinion of such counsel, the Common Shares if, as, and when listed on a pre-scribed stock exchange, will be qualified investments under the Income Tax Act (Canada) for trust governed by registered retirement savings plans, registered retirement income funds and deferred profit sharing plans.

Source: Champion Road Machinery Company Prospectus.
RBC Dominion Securities

Exhibit 5
STOCK PRICE AND VOLUME

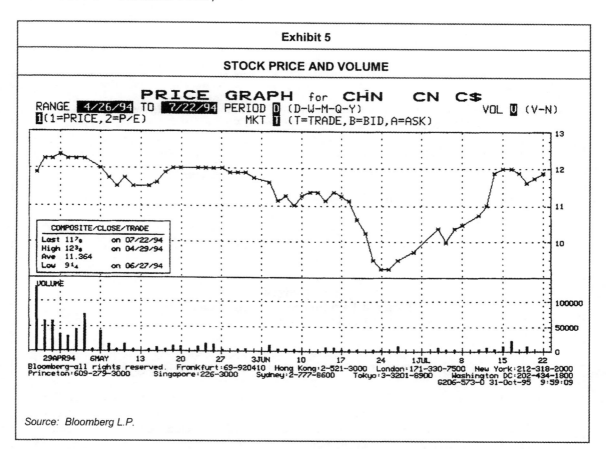

Source: Bloomberg L.P.

Exhibit 6
DIVIDEND AND CAPITAL GAIN INCOME TAX EFFECT

CANADA

$1,000 of Dividend Income:

Gross-Up @ 125% =	$1,250
Federal Tax @ 29% =	$363
Federal Tax Credit @ 13.33% =	$167
Federal Tax Payable =	$196
Provincial Tax Payable	$ 98
(approximately 50% of Federal	
Tax Payable)	

$1,000 of Capital Gain:

Taxable Gain @ 75% =	$750
Federal Tax Payable @ 29% =	$218
Provincial Tax Payable (approximate)	$109

UNITED STATES

$1,000 of Dividend Income:

Taxable @ 39.6% =	$396

$1,000 of Capital Gain:

Taxable @ 28% =	$280

Exhibit 7	

PRO FORMA INCOME STATEMENT
For The Year Ending December 31, 1994
($000s)

Net Sales	$155,000
Cost of Sales	119,500
Gross Profit	35,500
Selling & Administrative Expense	20,500
Profit Sharing Plan	1,400
Operating Income	13,600
Interest Expense	300
Income Before Taxes	13,300
Income Tax	5,200
Net Income	$8,100

Source: Champion Road Machinery Company Prospectus

part nine

Valuation of a Business Interest

RUSHWAY BROTHERS LUMBER AND BUILDING SUPPLIES LTD.

Charlotte Bradley smiled as she reviewed the June 1992 monthly and year to date financial statement she had received that day. "Now," she said, "I'm ready to sell the business. My time in the hot seat is over." As she closed the file, she wondered what the business was worth, how she should go about selling it, and whom she should call first to set the wheels in motion. For the moment she was willing just to savor the good feelings associated with the thought that her term as president, chief executive officer and sole shareholder, as well as order taker, purchasing agent and sometimes shipper, might almost be over and that she had performed well in the various roles.

HISTORY OF THE BUSINESS

Rushway Brothers Lumber and Building Supplies Ltd. (RLBS) was established by George Rushway in 1922 in Ilderton, Ontario as an extension of his lumber mill near Denfield, Ontario. At first the business sold only lumber, but when his two sons, Gordon and Douglas, joined the business in 1945 and 1951 respectively, the variety of products grew rapidly. In addition to serving the retail market for home improvement enthusiasts, the business served the wholesale contractor market for single family dwellings and other buildings. Douglas Rushway started a construction business as part of RLBS, specializing in barns, agricultural warehouses and other such buildings to be constructed within 50 kilometers of

Richard Ivey School of Business
The University of Western Ontario

David C. Shaw prepared this case solely to provide material for class discussion. The author does not intend to illustrate either effective or ineffective handling of a managerial situation. The author may have disguised certain names and other identifying information to protect confidentiality.

Ilderton. The business achieved a reputation for quality products, good service and fine workmanship. The business was reorganized in 1959 after the death of George Rushway with each of the brothers owning 50 per cent of the common stock.

In 1985, after 40 years in the business and upon reaching 60 years of age, Gordon Rushway, Charlotte's father, decided to retire from the business on an active basis and just consult and perform special tasks. He kept his 50 per cent share in the business and participated in the dividends to common shareholders.

Douglas Rushway took over the running of the business in 1985 and ran it single-handedly for three years, delegating the day-to-day work to supervisors. Finally in 1988, he appointed Jack Fairlee as manager of the construction operation and Paul Gaudet as manager of the retail and wholesale products business. Neither person had experience in managing an entire operation, but both had extensive experience with these business segments. However, they had not dealt with financial matters such as budgets, ordering, payroll and employee matters before and the learning process was difficult at times.

In January 1989, Douglas Rushway had a heart attack and was forced to leave the business. The family immediately hired the former manager of the London branch for a national chain of business centres, Charles Conway, to serve as a general manager of RLBS. The hope at that time was that Conway, with Fairlee and Gaudet, would buy the business. The hiring of Conway was thought to be a lucky break for the family, because it was clear that there wasn't any family member who was interested, or available, to take the business over.

Within a year the warning signals were sounding loud and clear that something in the business was wrong. Inventories were way up, correspondingly, so were the bank loan and the interest costs. Salaries and wages were much higher than in previous years. The bank manager called Gordon to say that the company was approaching the upper bound of the bank loan and he was not prepared to extend more on the current terms. Profits to shareholders were down significantly.

Douglas Rushway died in November 1989. Under the terms of a long-standing partnership agreement with his brother, Gordon purchased the shares in the company from the estate using the proceeds of an insurance policy on his brother's life. Almost immediately, Gordon terminated Conway's contract and assumed management responsibilities himself.

At that time Gordon Rushway approached his daughter Charlotte and asked her to take over the operation of RLBS. "I will help you as much as I can," he promised, "and work with you to reduce inventory and get the finances in shape." He pointed out that Jack and Paul were capable managers and with the proper overall supervision and encouragement, they had the potential to bring their divisions back to good health. But someone had to take over the ordering, the credit granting, the general management and control of the business.

Charlotte Bradley lived in Strathroy, a small town west of London, at the time. She was in her early forties, divorced, with two children and a full time job as a secretary. The children were teenagers and relatively independent. While she was not totally familiar with the business, she had been involved with it in some way all her life. As the oldest of three daughters, she was the one who worked after school and on Saturday mornings in the store and on rare occasions in the lumber yard. Although her two sisters and cousin Donald (Douglas's only child who was now a surgeon in Winnipeg) also helped out, it was Charlotte who was the mainstay among the siblings. However, taking over the operation of the business at this stage in her life was not a pleasant prospect to her and she resisted, arguing that her father should sell the business. He maintained that it was no time to sell with the business in such bad shape, and the risk of hiring another manager was too great. When he announced that he had no choice but to continue to manage the business himself, Charlotte realized that she had no choice but to assume the responsibility.

Bradley started full time in January 1990. Gordon came in and worked with her for three months almost on a full time basis. In April he cut back to half time and then in July he and his wife took a vacation which turned out to be a return to his retirement.

Before he left, Gordon transferred all the shares over to Charlotte as her share of his estate. His income from savings, plus his government pension cheques were sufficient to keep him and his wife comfortable. Giving Charlotte the shares now would help to motivate her and to reward her for her efforts in running the business.

THE NATURE OF THE BUSINESS

Ilderton was located about 25 kilometers from London to the west and north of the city of 300,000. Ilderton itself had experienced rapid growth in single family homes and an influx of residents who commuted to jobs in London. The town was situated in the middle of an agricultural stronghold with dairy farming a major segment of the economy of the area. Many of the RLBS customers owned and operated farms, or were brought up on farms and retained a rural lifestyle.

RLBS consisted of two related businesses: merchandising and construction. The merchandising business included a retail store and a lumber yard. The store displayed home building and repair products, including hardware, paint, plumbing supplies and small tools. The order desk in the store issued vouchers to customers which, when presented to the yard personnel, enabled them to pick up lumber, plywood, drywall, roofing shingles and other related products. Most of these products were stored outdoors or in open sided buildings.

Merchandising

The merchandising business had two customer segments. The retail customer was a home owner interested in making repairs, adding on a deck, finishing a basement, or undertaking a project to improve the property. Usually the customer wanted advice and assistance from the staff and so it was very important to have knowledgeable and friendly staff on the floor.

The contractor customer made up the other part of the merchandising business. This group of customers tended to buy large quantities of standard products, lumber, drywall, shingles, etc. and their business was very price sensitive. They demanded service as well, such as delivery on time, but the ability to quote a lower price was critical to this business.

Major competition for both groups of customers came from Beaver Lumber, a large Copps Buildall in the west end of London and the Co-op which sold a broad range of products including building supplies in Ilderton. Other competitors in the towns of Lucan, Strathroy and Parkhill were a lesser threat, but there were competitors on all sides who kept prices tight, especially for contractor customers.

The retail and the contractor customers purchased about equal dollar volumes in 1991.

Construction

The second business involved constructing wood-framed, steel-sided structures for agricultural, commercial, industrial and recreational purposes. Jack Fairlee, the construction manager, was responsible for this division, which employed two or three crews consisting of four persons each.

Construction sales contributed about 50 per cent of total revenues for the year ended 1991. Traditionally, RLBS's construction division operated within a 50-kilometer radius from the Ilderton area, allowing crew members to live at home. Occasionally projects as far to the east as Brantford and to the west as Sarnia, about 100 kilometers, were undertaken.

RLBS employed experienced crew members who knew the business of building wood-framed, steel-clad structures and were efficient, giving RLBS a cost advantage over the competition. RLBS did not have unionized employees.

RLBS acted as a general contractor and maintained a list of subcontractors for such services as excavating, plumbing, electrical, drywall and overhead doors. The main promotion activity for the construction business was a sign announcing "BUILT BY RLBS" at construction sites. Major jobs were awarded through a tender process, but smaller contracts were usually negotiated directly with Jack by the client.

THE OPERATING EXPERIENCE

Bradley began her on-the-job training by learning the merchandising business. Many of the products were totally unfamiliar to her. Trying to remember the various sizes, types, colors, prices and names of suppliers added to the confusion. As well, she had to learn about the customers for the products and the competition.

Prices for lumber and plywood, for example, were volatile, and buying at high prices and being caught with large inventories as prices fell could be very expensive. As she learned the products, she also began to understand the whole process of the merchandising business.

She also took on credit as her responsibility. Many contractors overextended their ability to pay and established large payable balances to suppliers like RLBS. Bradley enforced the practice that a contractor only received discounts off retail, which amounted to as much as 10 per cent, if the bill was paid within 15 days from the end of the month. She also cleaned up old outstanding accounts with a vigorous and tough campaign.

Perhaps her greatest success was with the development of the staff. At the same time that she was learning the business, she was winning with Jack and Paul as a colleague, and hiring new staff members to fit into a team. When the economy softened in 1991 and sales fell, she was able to reduce the payroll because everyone was prepared to contribute more effort to cover for reduced numbers. A friendly and effective staff was critical for good customer relations. Many of the customers were farmers who were used to being recognized and called by name. They preferred informal ways of doing business, and resented any form of bureaucracy.

Bradley was constantly checking prices on lumber, drywall, and other building supplies. She prided herself that RLBS only sold quality Canadian-made commodity products. Some competitors emphasized low prices, but sold inferior lumber and other building supplies. She refused to sell at low prices in order to get the business. "If we can't make our margins, we don't want the business."

In her first year, sales fell by 10 per cent ($2.9 million in 1990 versus $3.2 in 1989) (Exhibit 2) but profits increased from $15.9 to $94.2 thousand. Inventories fell by $185 thousand and the bank loan by $260 thousand (Exhibit 1).

In 1991, the economic recession played havoc with new home construction and the contractor customers of RLBS. Sales fell by more than 15 per cent and prices tightened further. But Bradley and her team reduced costs and inventories and generated a profit of $67.6 thousand, down from 1990, but much better than many competitors who were in serious financial difficulty. The bank loan fell further and now the bank manager was calling trying to get RLBS to borrow its long term funds requirement from the bank and pay off its term loan from another lender.

THE BUSINESS ASSETS

The principal assets of the business were the receivables, the inventory and the land, buildings and equipment. The amounts shown on the books for each of these are presented in the balance sheet at December 31, 1991 and June 30, 1992 (Exhibit 1).

The accounts receivable were current; slow accounts were provided for by an allowance and eventually written off, but still followed carefully by Bradley. RLBS belonged to a purchasing group which paid a rebate at year end based on annual purchases: thus the asset account, Purchase rebate receivable, on the balance sheet. Because the account was not accrued during the year it does not show on the interim statements. The main accounts receivable were from contractors. Retail customers paid either by cash or with a credit card. Construction accounts were usually paid in installments as the work was completed.

The inventory was counted once a year at year end. Interim statements were prepared using an average cost of goods sold percentage of sales and the inventory amount was the difference between cost of goods available for sale (opening inventory plus purchases) and the estimated cost of goods sold. The count itself was carefully undertaken. Old goods were counted, but costed at a price reflecting recovery value. Bradley instituted the idea of a giant yard sale in Ilderton where various community groups could bring goods to the RLBS yard and together with the old stock from RLBS, everyone sold their goods at clearance prices. One service club sold hot dogs and hamburgers and everyone seemed to enjoy the sale. In fact, after the first two such events, RLBS didn't have much more obsolete product to put in the next sale. Bradley was convinced that the inventory dollar amount at year end represented fairly the cost of the goods on hand which were current and the recovery value of the rest.

RLBS owned two pieces of land in Ilderton. The first at 245 Main Street housed the retail business. The retail area took 3,000 square feet and together with storage included an area of about 5,500 square feet.

The property was situated in the center of Ilderton with commercial businesses and residential properties nearby. The business has about 350 feet of frontage on Main St. and about 2.0 acres altogether.

The second piece of land was familiarly known as "the yard." It incorporated about 2.5 acres and was positioned behind the retail site on Queen St. The site included five structures providing 18,000 square feet of storage.

The book value of the properties at December 31, 1991 was about $265,000. In 1988 the properties were assessed by a real estate firm and given values as follows:

Main Street	$495,000
Queen Street	55,000
Total Market value	$550,000

These market values were the basis for a term loan from Commercial Mortgager, but it was questionable whether these values could be realized in the depressed real estate market of 1992.

The other fixed assets included trucks, forklifts and office equipment. Book value was thought to be a reasonable estimate of market.

THE FINANCING

Metropolitan Bank provided all the external financing for the firm. While relations were cordial at this time, only two years before they had been strained indeed. Metropolitan had extended a $440 thousand operating line to RLBS, but in 1989, during the Conway term, the manager demanded a personal guarantee from Gordon to continue the loan. Bradley assumed the guarantee after she took over the business. In late 1991, she requested that the bank remove the personal guarantees. The bank was anxious to develop new business. At the time Bradley offered to borrow $175,000 on a term loan basis from the bank to repay an existing term loan from Commercial Mortgager. The bank agreed to the proposal, but increased the rate on the operating loan from prime plus one-half per cent to prime plus three-quarters per cent. The bank held receivables and inventory as security for the operating line and a mortgage on the property for the term loan. In addition, there were covenants that RLBS had to maintain a working capital amount of $330 thousand and stockholder's equity of $275 thousand.

FINANCIAL PERFORMANCE

The results of Bradley's efforts were slow in coming. Monthly statements throughout 1990 kept showing breakeven and small loss positions in spite of good sales results. The bank loan fell and the cash flow improved. When the year end results were compiled, she was delighted to discover a $94 thousand profit. The problem with the monthly statements was that the estimated trading profit was too low, resulting in reduced profits and inventories. She was elated after all those months of believing that business was barely breaking even. At one stage during the year she was so discouraged by these monthly statements showing losses and worn down by the pressures of the job, that she seriously considered closing the business and selling off the assets.

The recession hit sales in 1991. Business was off by almost 20 per cent. But Bradley was able to cut costs by almost $200 thousand and while profits fell to $68 thousand it was still a success. Perhaps more important than profits, inventories came down from the $543 thousand of late 1989 to about $320 thousand at year end December 31, 1991. The bank loan was reduced to $53 thousand from its high when she took over of $420 thousand. Needless to say, relationships with the bank were easier.

The business turned around in 1992. In the first six months sales were up over 15 per cent and profits more than doubled. All facets of the business were active, but construction especially was very busy. The bank loan stayed low; in fact, the company had positive cash balances for segments of each month.

DECISION TO SELL

Early in 1992 Bradley sat down to look at her options and to make personal plans. For the last two years she had dedicated herself to the company, working on the site 7:30 a.m. to 5:00 p.m. five days a week and Saturdays from 7:30 to noon, plus other time to work out other business issues. She had taken almost no holidays. Now she could have the luxury of thinking through what she wanted to do with the rest of her life. Selling the business was clearly an option to consider. However she was surprised to find that she had grown very attached to the staff and the business generally. It was not an easy decision.

Bradley had compiled personal assets other than the investment in the business which provided security and some income, but she could not live off the investment income. If she sold the business, she would plan to invest the proceeds and probably find a job.

The market for small businesses did not seem very robust. Talking to owners of similar business in her buying group, she discovered that most of them were struggling to reduce costs and lines of business, not adding anything.

The economy was clearly still struggling through the recession. Interest rates were at a significantly lower level than when she took over the business. Financial information is presented in Exhibit 4. While RLBS continued to perform well, many businesses in the area and nationally were failing.

Bradley needed some information. How much was RLBS worth? Where did she go to get advice on how to sell the business? Confidentiality was critical; she did not want her employees to find out from third parties that she was considering selling.

Exhibit 1

BALANCE SHEETS
December 31, 1988 to 1991
With Interim Results at June 30, 1992 and 1991

	6 mos Jan to Jun		1991	1990	1989	1988
	1992	1991				
ASSETS						
Current Assets						
Accounts receivable	$ 617,529	526,503	102,390	274,042	259,027	244,992
Inventories						
Materials for resale	428,134	375,954	318,892	358,499	543,787	464,268
Work in progress	-	-	5,448	7,734	16,777	1,287
Prepaid expenses	20,688	20,730	20,688	21,060	23,185	3,432
Purchase rebate receivable[1]	-	-	54,995	68,417	95,134	84,256
Deposit with supplier	14,630	14,630	14,630	14,630	14,630	14,630
Other current	-	14,178	2,786	12,907	48,486	12,192
Total Current Assets	1,080,981	951,995	519,829	757,289	1,001,026	825,057
Land, Buildings, Equipment						
Land	243,238	243,238	243,238	243,238	243,238	243,238
Buildings	27,420	27,420	27,420	27,420	27,420	27,420
Equipment and furniture	56,449	56,449	56,449	56,059	53,623	53,623
Automotive Equipment	64,922	90,988	93,441	99,574	99,574	95,009
Other	6,410	10,892	6,410	10,892	10,892	10,892
Total Land, Buildings, Equipment	398,438	428,986	426,956	437,183	434,746	430,181
Less accumulated depreciation	115,280	160,585	152,664	163,301	154,334	140,270
Net Land, Buildings, Equipment	283,158	268,401	274,293	273,882	280,412	289,912
Goodwill	101,149	103,509	102,092	104,922	107,532	110,362
TOTAL ASSETS	$ 1,465,288	1,323,903	896,214	1,136,093	1,388,969	1,225,331

[1]Purchase rebate receivable is estimated at year end as a percentage of purchases from Number One Building Centers. The amount is not estimated for interim statements.

Exhibit 1 (continued)

BALANCE SHEETS
December 31, 1988 to 1991
With Interim Results at June 30, 1992 and 1991

	6 mos Jan to Jun		1991	1990	1989	1988
	1992	1991				
LIABILITIES						
Current Liabilities						
Bank loan	$ 378,294	133,964	53,394	157,748	413,382	237,074
Accounts payable and accruals	245,612	215,962	67,074	118,433	229,107	233,867
Taxes payable	11,794	18,689	15,700	9,969	23,953	14,502
Current - long term debt	-	-	22,320	45,116	45,414	44,785
Dividend payable	-	-	55,000	27,500	27,500	27,500
Total Current Liabilities	**635,699**	**368,615**	**213,488**	**359,766**	**742,646**	**557,728**
Long term debt	153,244	358,983	139,678	245,927	196,563	222,734
SHAREHOLDERS' EQUITY						
Common stock	19,754	19,754	19,754	19,754	19,754	19,754
Retained earnings	656,590	576,552	523,294	510,646	430,007	425,115
TOTAL LIABILITIES & EQUITY	**$ 1,465,288**	**1,323,903**	**896,214**	**1,136,093**	**1,388,969**	**1,225,331**

Exhibit 2

INCOME STATEMENTS

| | 6 mos Jan to Jun | | For the years ended December 31, 1987 to 1991 | | | | |
	1992	1991	1991	1990	1989	1988	1987
Sales	$ 1,543,856	1,331,850	2,484,073	2,937,762	3,156,375	2,747,357	2,029,151
Cost of goods sold	1,181,049	1,014,735	1,737,489	1,938,299	2,249,437	1,915,389	1,445,056
Gross margin	362,807	317,115	746,584	999,463	906,938	931,967	584,096
Profit on contracts[1]	20,495	3,639	27,612	2,818	73,026	22,358	10,292
Operating expenses (Exhibit 3)	250,006	254,848	686,342	879,876	959,327	727,148	494,343
Operating earnings	133,296	65,906	87,855	122,406	20,637	127,177	100,044
Income taxes[2]	-	-	20,207	28,153	4,747	29,251	23,010
Net income	133,296	65,906	67,648	94,252	15,891	97,926	77,034
Retained earnings (beginning)	523,294	510,646	510,646	430,007	425,116	382,190	360,155
Dividends	-	-	55,000	13,613	11,000	55,000	55,000
Retained earnings (end)	$ 656,590	576,552	523,294	510,646	430,007	425,116	382,190

[1] Raw materials supplied from RLBS and construction labor are charged to construction contracts at prices above cost and credited to sales revenue. The profit on contracts represents the excess of the contract price over total costs charged to the contract.
[2] Income taxes are not calculated on interim statements. RLBS pays income tax at an average rate of about 25 per cent.

Exhibit 3

ANALYSIS OF OPERATING EXPENSES
For the Years 1987 to 1991
(Dollar amounts are presented in thousands)

	6 mos to June 30		For the Years Ended December 31, 1987 to 1991				
	1992	1991	1991	1990	1989	1988	1987
Salaries, wages and benefits	$ 155.1	152.9	471.9	600.6	663.3	491.7	388.3
Telephone, heat, taxes	14.3	12.1	25.3	25.3	25.3	23.1	24.2
Advertising	4.4	5.5	12.1	9.9	8.8	9.9	4.4
Insurance, legal, accounting	11.0	15.4	29.7	44.0	23.1	39.6	17.6
Repairs, maintenance, tools and supplies	7.7	6.6	14.3	24.2	6.6	3.3	2.2
Office expense and travel	4.4	4.4	12.1	12.1	16.5	14.3	5.5
Truck operations	22.3	26.0	49.4	43.9	46.3	40.7	38.7
Bad debts	1.1	(2.2)	11.0	7.7	1.1	20.9	(2.2)
Depreciation	4.4	4.4	9.9	8.8	12.1	14.3	5.5
Interest	25.3	29.7	50.6	103.4	156.2	69.3	9.9
Total operating expenses	$ 250.0	254.8	686.3	879.9	959.3	727.1	494.3

Exhibit 4			
FINANCIAL DATA			

	July 15 1992	July 15 1991	July 15 1990
Long Term Interest Rates			
Gov't of Canada	8.73	9.90	11.48
Short Term Rates			
Gov't of Canada - Treasury Bills	5.35	8.50	12.76
Prime	6.75 - 7.00	9.75	14.75
TSE 300 Index	3387	3465	3563
P/E Ratios TSE 300 Industry			
Groups Fabricating and Erecting	27.2x		
Consumer Products	20.5x		

OXFORD LEARNING CENTRES INC.: THE CHILDTIME ALTERNATIVE

Dr. Nick Whitehead, president and CEO of the London, Ontario-based Oxford Learning Centres Inc. (OLC), was preparing for his trip to Farmington Hills, Michigan, in late April 1998. He had just received a phone call from Harold Lewis, CEO of Childtime Learning Centers (Childtime). Lewis asked Whitehead to come to Michigan to talk to the directors of Childtime about an offer to purchase a significant stake of OLC. In November 1997, Childtime entered a licensing agreement with OLC where Childtime would operate OLC's supplemental education programs inside two of their U.S. based day-care centres. Dr. Whitehead wondered how he should prepare for the upcoming negotiations.

OXFORD LEARNING CENTRES INC.

OLC was Canada's second largest franchised-based supplemental education provider. As of December 1997, OLC was operating 25 franchises in the southern Ontario region. OLC had developed curricula and programs to provide supplemental education to preschoolers through to secondary students. Although OLC had been operating for over 15 years in London, its growth and establishment as a franchise organization had emerged only within the last four years. OLC had developed from a five-centre operation in 1994 with system sales of Cdn$930,303 to a company in 1997 with system sales of Cdn$4,655,000 (see Exhibits 1 to 3 for OLC historical financial statements).

Richard Ivey School of Business
The University of Western Ontario

Professor Craig Dunbar prepared this case solely to provide material for class discussion. The author does not intend to illustrate either effective or ineffective handling of a managerial situation. The author may have disguised certain names and other identifying information to protect confidentiality.

OLC's initial focus was on the development of teaching programs. Dr. Whitehead and Dr. P.J. Gamlin, an OLC director, spent most of their first 10 years at OLC developing unique cognitive learning programs. Cognitive learning differed from other teaching methods by concentrating on teaching children to "learn how to learn." Developing these skills allowed the child to learn more easily and quickly specific academic skills in areas such as mathematics, reading or writing. OLC also developed a unique assessment method to determine a child's grade level, learning style, and relative cognitive strengths and weaknesses. Whitehead believed that these assessment and learning programs provided OLC a competitive advantage over competitors, whose focus was largely on basic tutoring.

OLC had always planned to grow by franchising since this allowed OLC to minimize its capital requirements. To facilitate franchising, Whitehead realized that his cognitive learning programs would have to be codified. Whitehead and Gamlin developed 10 manuals for franchisees in the areas of start-up, training, education operations, business and administration, marketing, teaching, education directing, philosophy, programming and assessment and site evaluation. To further ensure quality, OLC required all teachers to be certified (holding a B.Ed. degree). As a result, OLC's franchising experience had been very positive. At the end of 1997, all of OLC's franchises were profitable. In addition, OLC had been nominated by its franchisees in 1997 to receive the Canadian Franchise Association's Award of Excellence in Franchise Relations.

While OLC's growth had been smooth, it was beginning to put stresses on OLC's corporate resources. Each OLC franchise had accounting software to track performance. There was no consistency in the timeliness of reports to head office, however. It was becoming evident that additional head office finance staff was required. OLC also required more marketing staff to facilitate future growth.

THE SUPPLEMENTAL EDUCATION MARKET

The total training and education market in the United States was estimated to be US$600 billion in 1996. Of this number, approximately US$70 billion was spent in the workplace training and supplemental education market. The U.S. market for supplemental education consisted of two broad groups. First, there were a large number of small operations (home tutors and school equivalents) that used their location to attract clients. Second, there were large companies that ran professionally managed centres, such as Sylvan Learning Centers with 670 centres and Huntington Learning Centers with over 160 centres in 30 eastern states. Sylvan, which opened its first storefront learning centre in 1979, could dominate the market given its size. Sylvan's strategic focus was shifting from supplemental education to educational testing services such as the Scholastic Aptitude Test national exam (SAT), however. Revenues from educational testing services had tripled in the three years to US$89 million in 1996, compared to supplemental education revenues of only US$30 million. To further illustrate this point, Sylvan, once the dominant supplemental education provider in Ontario, was now second to OLC in this region.

The potential growth in the supplemental education market was huge. There were approximately seven million children in Grades 1 through 8 in the United States that were either in the top five per cent or bottom 15 per cent of their class. Supplemental education companies served a small fraction of these children. Analysts projected annual earnings growth in the market to be over 25 per cent from 1998 to 2002. Data on Sylvan and other publicly traded supplemental education providers are reported in Exhibits 4 and 5.[1]

The Canadian market for supplemental education was extremely fragmented. Although smaller than the U.S. market, no one provider dominated more than one Canadian province. Consequently, opportunities for growth were also high, potentially through consolidation.

THE FIRSTSERVICE AND NOBEL OFFERS

FirstService Franchise Corporation made an unsolicited offer in May 1997 to purchase 60 per cent of OLC. FirstService provided services to more than 260,000 businesses and homes across Canada and the United

---

[1] Huntington is a private company. It attempted to go public in 1997, but cancelled its initial public offering.

States. It owned directly or controlled recognized franchise systems such as College Pro Painters, Nutrilawn International Inc., Certa ProPainters and Action Window Cleaners.

FirstService offered to pay $1.36 million for its stake in OLC. It arrived at this price by first valuing OLC using a multiple of 5 times 1997 EBITDA (earnings before interest, taxes, depreciation and amortization).[2] FirstService arrived at this multiple based on the terms of a recent transaction in the childcare industry. On February 14, 1997, Kolberg Kravis Roberts (KKR) acquired KinderCare Learning Centers, a day-care centre provider in the United States and the United Kingdom, for $500 million, or 5.6 times KinderCare's last 12 months EBITDA.

Dr. Whitehead quickly rejected the FirstService offer for three reasons. First, he did not think that the purchase price was sufficient. Whitehead did not believe that a day-care operation like KinderCare offered similar growth potential to that of OLC. He therefore believed that OLC should be valued at a higher multiple. Second, he did not think that there was a good corporate "fit." Third, and most importantly, FirstService would not support OLC with much needed management resources.

During consideration of the FirstService offer, Dr. Whitehead initiated talks with Nobel Education Dynamics, a U.S.-based private education firm. Nobel operated 120 preschools and elementary schools in the east and mid-west regions of the United States. In the early 1990s, Nobel repositioned itself from a "childcare company" to an "education company." Jack Clegg, Nobel's CEO, thought that education companies both operated with higher margins and traded at higher EBITDA multiples than childcare companies.

Clegg was receptive to talks with OLC because he believed that supplemental education would be a natural extension of Nobel private education services. Nobel had just put a team of educators together to develop a supplemental educational curriculum. Nobel also promised Wall Street analysts that it would be soon entering the supplemental education business. In June 1997, Nobel made a formal offer to purchase 60 per cent of OLC. The initial terms of this offer are given in Exhibit 6.

Dr. Whitehead was intrigued by this offer for three reasons. First, Nobel was likely to be a good strategic partner. Nobel had over 120 schools in the east and mid-west United States. OLC's supplemental education program would likely have immediate demand from existing students. Second, Nobel had an established management team and would participate in the development of the OLC concept in the Nobel Schools. Third, Dr. Whitehead had developed a good relationship with Nobel's CEO, Jack Clegg, and anticipated a good future partnership.

Dr. Whitehead's primary concern was the purchase price. Like FirstService, Nobel had offered to purchase OLC for 5 times EBITDA, again citing the terms of the KKR acquisition of KinderCare Learning Centers as justification for this valuation. In a June 25, 1997, letter to Clegg, Whitehead indicated, "We are looking for a higher multiple (closer to 10)." Whitehead was also concerned about tying a value to 1997's EBITDA since he expected further growth. After extensive negotiations, Nobel presented a revised offer on September 15, 1997, which is summarized in Exhibit 6.

While Dr. Whitehead found the new offer more acceptable, the purchase price was still not high enough. Whitehead also uncovered some information during the negotiations that made Nobel a less attractive partner. While Nobel had over 120 "schools" in operation, most (about 100) would more accurately be described as day-care centres. Whitehead did not think this would provide as good a fit. Nobel also became frustrated with the pace of the negotiations and had approached other companies, including Sylvan. Whitehead learned that Sylvan rejected the alliance without investigation. Ultimately Whitehead decided in late September 1997 to reject the Nobel offer.

CHILDTIME LEARNING CENTERS

Although talks with FirstService and Nobel had not lead to a positive conclusion, Dr. Whitehead believed that a strategic partnership with some U.S. company was the best alternative to facilitate growth in the North American market. In October 1997, he approached Harold Lewis, CEO of Childtime Learning Centers.

---

[2]Using a multiple of 5 times EBITDA, FirstService determined that OLC was worth $2.27 million (see Exhibit 2 for 1997 EBITDA). Its 60-per-cent stake in OLC would, therefore, be worth $1.36 million.

Childtime, a 1990 spin-off from Gerber, operated over 230 childcare centres in 15 states and the District of Columbia with over 25,000 enrolled students (Gerber incorporated this childcare subsidiary in 1967). Their services were provided throughout the year for children between six and 12 years old. Most of Childtime's centres were located in suburban areas, but many were based at work sites for companies like Prudential Insurance and Schering-Plough. Analysts believed that there was a significant demand for firms that could combine childcare and education. They were also impressed with Childtime's experienced management team. Childtime and OLC, therefore, appeared to be a natural combination.

Rather than acquiring OLC, Childtime initially was interested in pursuing a joint venture whereby Childtime would operate the OLC concept inside their U.S. centres. Through this joint venture, a U.S. subsidiary corporation would be created. Childtime and OLC would jointly own this corporation. Childtime would provide 80 per cent of the capital required for expansion with OLC providing the remaining 20 per cent.[3] Either party could terminate the joint venture at one of three test stages.[4] Childtime would pay OLC a 10 per cent royalty on revenues for the right to use its educational methods. Whitehead and his management team would manage the new corporation in the first year. Once the company was up and running, a new management team, independent of OLC and Childtime, would be retained.

While he was intrigued by it, Whitehead quickly decided against the joint venture. The termination clause led him to question Childtime's commitment, as they could easily back away from the venture virtually at any time. More importantly, the deal would require OLC to come up with 20 per cent of the capital for the venture. Whitehead preferred to minimize his capital commitment.

Whitehead proposed that Childtime simply license the OLC methods for use in its centres. Under the licensing agreement, Childtime would deliver programs itself after being trained by Whitehead's team. Childtime would pay OLC a 10 per cent royalty on revenues in return for the right to use OLC's programs. In effect, the licensing agreement allowed Childtime to become an OLC franchisee. Harold Lewis agreed to the arrangement in November 1997 and began operations at two Michigan Childtime sites in January 1998.

In early 1998, Lewis became increasingly excited about the supplemental education business. The early reports on the two Michigan centres were positive. Lewis was also convinced, like Nobel's Jack Clegg, that changing focus from childcare to education would enhance Childcare's margins and valuation. In early April 1998, Dr. Whitehead received a call from Lewis asking him to come to Farmington Hills, Michigan for a meeting with Childtime's board to talk about purchasing a significant stake in OLC.

As he prepared for his trip, Whitehead reflected back on the Nobel negotiations. The purchase price would likely remain a potential stumbling block. Nobel quickly became anchored in its valuation based on Kolberg Kravis Roberts' purchase of KinderCare. Several acquisitions have occurred in the industry since, based on different multiples. On April 14, 1998, Sylvan Learning Systems acquired Aspect, a provider of English-as-a-second-language programs for college-aged students, for US$65 million, or 12 times Aspect's last 12 months EBITDA. Even in the childcare industry, which Whitehead believed to have lower growth potential, analysts were beginning to base valuations on forward-looking EBITDA multiples in the 7 to 8 range.

In the upcoming negotiations, Whitehead thought it would be useful to present valuations based on several methods. He computed implied OLC valuations using various multiples determined using the trading prices of comparable public firms (see Exhibit 7). He also prepared forecasts of OLC income statements for the next five years as the first step in a discounted cash flow valuation (see Exhibit 8). In order to determine OLC's cost of capital for the discounted cash flow valuation, Whitehead collected recent financial market data (see Exhibit 9).

Whitehead also wondered if this was a good time to sell. OLC's growth has been strong and it could have sufficient revenues in a year or two to make it an attractive initial public offering. In the fall of 1997, CorporateFamily Solutions and Bright Horizons had successful initial public offerings in the United States, suggesting the market was receptive to offerings by supplemental education firms. Childtime itself had a suc-

---

[3]By investing more than 50 per cent, Childtime would be able to consolidate this subsidiary on its balance sheet.

[4]The first phase would involve installation of the OLC concept in five Childtime centres over three to four months. The second phase would involve installation of the OLC concept in an additional 25 centres over the next six months to one year. Phase three would involve installation of the OLC concept in the remaining Childtime centres.

cessful initial public offering in February 1996. At the time, it had revenues of only US$12 million. Whitehead also believed that he could possibly achieve a higher valuation if he waited to sell OLC for a year or two, given trends in both OLC cash flows and comparable firm multiples. Armed with considerable amounts of data, Whitehead sat down to map out his strategy.

Exhibit 1				
HISTORICAL FRANCHISE SYSTEM DATA 1994-1997 **(Data are for the fiscal year beginning April 1 of the year noted)**				
	1994	**1995**	**1996**	**1997**
Average Number of Centres	5	14	19	25
Annual Growth in Number of Centres	67%	80%	36%	32%
Average Revenue per Centre	$186,061	$ 84,537	$ 97,567	$ 186,200
Total Franchise System Revenue	$930,303	$1,183,513	$1,853,764	$4,655,000
Growth in Franchise System Revenue	-	27.22%	56.63%	151.11%

Exhibit 2

CORPORATE INCOME STATEMENTS 1994-1997
(Data are for the fiscal year beginning April 1 of the year noted)

	1994	1995	1996	1997
Franchise Related Revenues				
Franchise System Royalties	$ 48,306	$ 71,345	$ 171,693	$ 418,904
Advertising Fund	10,735	15,855	32,221	89,670
Curriculum Fees	31,641	84,994	54,749	113,010
New Franchise Fees	5,000	25,000	171,693	225,624
Total Franchise Revenue	95,682	197,194	430,356	847,208
Franchise Related Expenses	63,516	175,000	330,085	545,921
Franchise Related EBITDA	32,166	22,194	100,271	301,287
Corporate Centres Revenue	393,567	390,786	348,882	467,454
Corporate Centres Expenses	231,029	273,791	233,783	314,273
Corporate Centres EBITDA	162,538	116,995	115,099	153,181
Total EBITDA	194,704	139,189	215,370	454,468
Tax (44%)	85,670	61,243	94,763	199,966
Net Income	$ 109,034	$ 77,946	$ 120,607	$ 254,502

Exhibit 3

CORPORATE BALANCE SHEETS 1994-1997
(Data are for the fiscal year beginning April 1 of the year noted)

	1994	1995	1996	1997
Assets				
Cash and Equivalents	$ 55,633	$ 32,696	$ 824	$ 73,200
Accounts Receivable	24,907	74,974	122,993	79,694
Other Current Assets	-	-	7,779	9,136
Total Current Assets	80,540	107,670	131,596	162,030
Fixed Assets (net)	1,614	6,984	13,828	16,435
Other long-term assets	818	818	818	818
Total	82,972	115,472	146,242	179,283
Liabilities and Equity				
Short-term borrowings	-	7,979	-	-
Accounts payable	750	3,925	16,530	78,521
Long-term debt, current portion	-	-	-	-
Other current liabilities	8,408	3,390	30,237	10,808
Total Current Liabilities	9,158	15,294	46,767	89,329
Long-term debt	-	-	-	-
Common equity	10	10	10	10
Retained earnings	73,804	100,168	99,465	89,944
Total	$ 82,972	$ 115,472	$ 146,242	$ 179,283

Exhibit 4

COMPARABLE FIRM DATA (AS OF DECEMBER 1997)
(Dollar amounts in millions except per share amounts)

	Number of shares (million)	Market value of equity [1]	Long-term debt [2]	Total Enterprise Value (TEV) [2], [3]	Beta [4]	Number of centres [2]	1997 Revenue [2]	1997 EBITDA [2]	1997 EPS [2]	Next 5 year EPS growth [5]	Revenue growth 1994-97 [6]
Children's Discovery Centers	6.801	$ 66.30	$ 17.10	$ 69.20	0.56	248	$ 93.00	$ 10.53	$ 0.37	N/A	19%
Childtime Learning Centers	5.228	71.90	3.20	74.50	0.42	237	91.90	9.01	0.78	18.5%	18%
Nobel Education Dynamics	6.015	30.50	31.50	59.30	0.82	129	81.00	5.03	(0.07)	21.7%	33%
Sylvan Learning Systems	28.964	1,129.60	0.90	1,108.20	0.93	670	246.20	33.34	1.02	33.4%	73%
CorporateFamily Solutions	4.491	96.60	-	84.50	N/A	95	77.70	2.87	0.24	29.3%	N/A
Bright Horizons Inc.	5.531	103.70	0.70	104.40	N/A	155	85.00	N/A	0.27	N/A	N/A

[1] Number of shares outstanding multiplied by the closing price per share on December 31, 1997 (Source: Bloomberg Investor Services)

[2] Source: Edgar filings (10k and 10Q)

[3] Total Enterprise Value (TEV) is defined as the market value of equity plus total debt (short- and long-term) minus cash and marketable securities

[4] Source: Bloomberg Investor Services

[5] Mean forecast annual growth rate in EPS for the next five fiscal years (Source: Zacks Investment Research)

[6] Defined as $[(Revenue_{1997} / Revenue_{1994})^{1/3} - 1]$ (Source: Edga filings)

Exhibit 5
COMPARABLE FIRM DESCRIPTIONS

Children's Discovery Centers

Children's Discovery Centers operates 248 schools in 22 states plus the District of Columbia. Enrolment currently exceeds 25,000 students. Founded in 1983, Children's Discovery Centers serves children from infants to Grade 8. The company also provides employer-sponsored programs through affiliations with over 50 governmental agencies, hospitals, and private companies such as Amoco and GE Capital Services Corporation.

Childtime Learning Centers

Childtime provides care for children from six weeks to 12 years of age. Services include nine-to-five childcare (including educational readiness programs) on weekdays, before- and after-school care, and summer programs for school-aged children. Most of Childtime's 240 centres are in suburban areas, but some are based at work sites and some on the premises of companies like Prudential Insurance. A 1990 spin-off from Gerber, more than 25,000 children are enrolled and in facilities covering 17 states.

Nobel Education Dynamics

Nobel provides high-quality child care, preschool and private school education and development to children that is affordable to middle income working families. The company's private schools are primarily located in California, but expanded to the Eastern United States in 1995.

Sylvan Learning Systems

Sylvan provides educational services to families, schools and businesses. The company operates through three segments: computer-based testing for academic admissions, information technology and certification programs, and instructional services.

CorporateFamily Solutions

CorporateFamily Solutions is a leading national provider of a broad range of management and consulting services for employers seeking to create a "family friendly" work environment by providing their employees with workplace childcare, education and other family support programs. The company manages 94 employer-sponsored Family Centers for 68 corporate clients in 27 states. Founders include the original "Captain Kangaroo" Bob Keeshan and former secretary of education Lamar Alexander.

Bright Horizons Inc.

Bright Horizons provides corporate-sponsored work-site childcare. The firm operates more than 150 centres in 30 states and offers emergency backup care, before- and after-school care, summer camps, special-event childcare, and elementary school (kindergarten through Grade 2) education. Company sponsorship (such as Motorola, Glaxo Wellcome, Mattel and Time Warner) absorbs some of Bright Horizons' start-up costs. The company meets the National Association for the Education of Young Children accreditation standards.

	Exhibit 6

	TERMS OF THE ORIGINAL AND REVISED NOBEL PURCHASE OFFERS

	The May 1997 offer	**The September 1997 offer**
Initial purchase of 60% of OLC's equity	• price based on 5 times OLC's 1997 EBITDA • 50% paid in cash with remainder using a five-year promissory note (7.5%/yr)	• Initial price based on 5 times OLC's 1997 EBITDA • additional payment ("earn-out") in 1998 based on 5 times the difference between OLC's 1998 and 1997 EBITDA • up to 50% paid in cash with remainder using a five-year promissory note (7.5%/yr)
Royalty	• none	• Royalties based on total OLC revenues (Canada and United States) • Royalty of 6.5% in 1998, 6% in 1999, 5.5% in 2000 and 5% thereafter.
Exit strategy (purchase of remaining 50% of OLC's equity)	• after five years, either party could trigger purchase at 5 times OLC's most recent year's EBITDA	• Nobel can initiate purchase in year five on. In year five, price would be 7 times OLC's most recent year's EBITDA, in year six, the price would be 6 times OLC's most recent year's EBITDA and in year seven on, the price would be 5 times OLC's most recent year's EBITDA • OLC can initiate sale in year five on. The price would be 5 times OLC's most recent year's EBITDA
Management	• Whitehead would manage OLC in Canada and the United States and would report directly to Nobel's CEO	• Whitehead would manage OLC in Canada and the United States and would report directly to Nobel's CEO
Funding of OLC growth	• Nobel provides at its borrowing cost plus 1%	• Nobel provides at its borrowing cost plus 1%

Exhibit 7

COMPARABLE FIRM-BASED VALUATION OF OXFORD LEARNING CENTERS INC.

	Valuation Ratios [1]				Implied OLC value (in millions of dollars) based on			
	TEV/1997 EBITDA	TEV/1997 Revenue	Price/1997 EPS	Price/1998 EPS [2]	TEV/1997 EBITDA [3]	TEV/1997 Revenue [4]	Price/1997 EPS [5]	Price/1998 EPS [6]
Children's Discovery Centers	6.57	0.74	26.35	N/A	2.99	0.98	6.71	N/A
Childtime Learning Centers	8.27	0.81	17.63	14.50	3.76	1.07	4.49	4.22
Nobel Education Dynamics	11.79	0.73	(72.44)	21.10	5.36	0.96	-	6.15
Sylvan Learning Systems	33.24	4.50	38.24	45.30	15.11	5.92	9.73	13.19
CorporateFamily Solutions	29.44	1.09	89.62	46.70	13.38	1.43	22.81	13.60
Bright Horizons Inc.	N/A	1.23	69.44	N/A	N/A	1.61	17.67	N/A

[1] TEV (Total Enterprise Value), 1997 EBITDA, Revenue and EPS are from Exhibit 4

[2] Stock price as of December 31, 1997 (*Source*: Bloomberg Investor Services) divided by the mean EPS forecast for the 19989 fiscal year (*Source*: Zacks Investment Research).

[3] TEV / 1997 EBITDA ratio for comparable firm multiplied by 1997 EBITDA for Oxford Learning Centres Inc. (from Exhibit 2)

[4] TEV / 1997 Revenue ratio for comparable firm multiplied by 1997 Revenue for Oxford Learning Centres Inc. (from Exhibit 2)

[5] Price / 1997 EPS ratio for comparable firm multiplied by 1997 Net Income for Oxford Learning Centres Inc. (from Exhibit 2)

[6] Price / 1998 EPS ratio for comparable firm multiplied by 1998 Net Income for Oxford Learning Centres Inc. (from Exhibit 8)

Exhibit 8

FORECASTS FOR CANADIAN OPERATIONS, 1998 TO 2002
(Data are for the fiscal year beginning April 1 of the year noted)

	1998	1999	2000	2001	2002
Franchise Information					
Number of Start-Up Centres	9	13	14	12	12
Number of Second year Centres	-	9	13	14	12
Number of Mature Centres	24	24	33	46	60
Start-Up Centre Revenues	$ 688,500	$ 994,500	$1,071,000	$ 918,000	$ 918,000
Second-Year Centre Revenues	-	1,350,000	1,950,000	2,100,000	1,800,000
Mature Centre Revenues	5,760,000	5,760,000	7,920,000	11,040,000	14,400,000
Total Franchise System Revenue	6,448,500	8,104,500	10,941,000	14,058,000	17,118,000
Projected Income statement					
Franchise Related Revenues					
Franchise System Royalties	$ 709,335	$ 891,495	$ 1,203,510	$ 1,546,380	$ 1,882,980
Advertising Fund	-	-	-	-	-
Curriculum Fees	75,000	135,000	225,000	310,000	400,000
New Franchise Fees	270,000	390,000	420,000	360,000	360,000
Total Franchise Revenue	1,054,335	1,416,495	1,848,510	2,216,380	2,642,980
Franchise Related Expenses	474,451	637,423	831,830	997,371	1,189,341
Franchise Related EBITDA	579,884	779,072	1,016,681	1,219,009	1,453,639
Corporate Centres Revenue	650,000	748,000	860,000	891,000	926,000
Corporate Centres Expenses	455,000	524,000	602,000	624,000	648,000
Corporate Centres EBITDA	195,000	224,000	258,000	267,000	278,000
Total EBITDA	774,884	1,003,072	1,274,681	1,486,009	1,731,639
Tax (44%)	340,949	441,352	560,859	653,844	761,921
Net Income	$ 433,935	$ 561,720	$ 713,821	$ 832,165	$ 969,718

Exhibit 9

FINANCIAL MARKETS DATA
(As of April 22, 1998)

Interest rates

1-month Government of Canada Treasury Bill	4.57%
10-year Government of Canada Treasury Bond	5.36%
30-year Government of Canada Treasury Bond	5.67%

Historical average annual returns (1950 to 1996)

Toronto Stock Exchange 300 index	12.14%
Long-term Government of Canada Bonds	7.24%
Short-term (1-month) Government of Canada Bills	6.40%

Source: Passport Financial Services Inc., Risk and Return Measurement System, 1997 Edition.

part ten

Financing Rapidly Growing Businesses

TREMBLAY LTEE.

In June 1987, Susan Spencer, a Montreal based Royal Bank of Canada account manager for the Tremblay Ltee. (Tremblay) account, was assessing her client's financial position and needs. The company had $18 million in term loans outstanding with the Royal Bank and required additional financing to buyout a minority equity interest in Tremblay held by Le Groupe Marechal (Marechal). Term debt was clearly an option; however, Spencer had some concern about the impact of additional term debt on Tremblay's leverage position. Spencer had suggested to Tremblay's president and majority owner, Andrew LeBlanc, that additional equity be considered, and she now wondered if a referral to Royal Bank Capital Corporation (RBCC) was appropriate.

Spencer knew that LeBlanc had received overtures from Societe d'Investissement Independent Ltee. (SDIL), a major Quebec based securities firm, about taking Tremblay public by way of an initial public offering. LeBlanc had obtained a $2.5 million loan from SDIL in February 1986 to assist in his purchase of the controlling interest in Tremblay, and SDIL was eager to play a larger role in the company's financing activities. In addition, the Confederation Bank, which had been the company's banker before the Royal, had recently made several calls on Tremblay.

COMPANY BACKGROUND

Tremblay, headquartered in Montreal, was the holding company for two operating subsidiaries as shown in Exhibit 1. The original subsidiary, Transport Tremblay Ltee., had been incorporated in Quebec by Marc

Richard Ivey School of Business
The University of Western Ontario

IVEY

Steve Cox prepared this case under the supervision of Professor Larry Wynant solely to provide material for class discussion. The authors do not intend to illustrate either effective or ineffective handling of a managerial situation. The authors may have disguised certain names and other identifying information to protect confidentiality.

Beaubien and a partner in 1966. Beaubien had bought out his partner in 1971 and watched the company grow to become one of Canada's major trucking firms.

Andrew LeBlanc, who worked as a vice-president with SDIL up until 1978, was a longtime friend of Marc Beaubien. In 1978, LeBlanc left SDIL to pursue several real estate investments and, within a year, LeBlanc made $400,000 in two land development transactions. He parlayed this gain into an investment in a Montreal packaging company with several partners. LeBlanc managed this company for one and a half years and then sold it to a major competitor at 10 times the original investment value, leaving LeBlanc with a gain of over $4 million. In 1980, LeBlanc joined Transport Tremblay Ltee. as the company's chief financial officer (CFO).

In 1986, the elderly Beaubien decided to sell off a controlling share of his ownership in Transport Tremblay Ltee. He had been highly impressed with the performance of LeBlanc as CFO, and approached him with an offer for an 80 per cent interest in Transport Tremblay Ltee., which LeBlanc accepted and paid for with the personal capital he had accumulated from his earlier ventures and the $2.5 million loan from SDIL. LeBlanc was a very private individual and he had not disclosed to Spencer the terms of the loan with SDIL. However, Spencer speculated that SDIL wanted to take the company public and would likely have structured repayment of the loan to a public stock issue.

Subsequent to this transaction, LeBlanc became chief executive officer and Beaubien retired, agreeing to serve as a consultant for the next three years and to retain his seat on the board. Beaubien's salary and bonuses had previously amounted to roughly $1 million per annum; however, LeBlanc set his own compensation at $300,000 per year.

As seen in the financial highlights presented in Exhibit 2, Beaubien and LeBlanc managed the company profitably through the recession of the early 1980s and revenues increased on average 12 per cent yearly during this period. In fiscal 1985, Transport Tremblay Ltee. acquired several routes from a competitor, which caused revenues to increase by 42 per cent. LeBlanc felt that the scheduled deregulation of the transport industry would result in increased competition and only the large players would be able to survive. As a consequence, he began to actively pursue acquisition opportunities. LeBlanc learned that Marechal was interested in divesting Transport Larochelle Ltee. from their group. Negotiations followed and Beaubien and LeBlanc reviewed the Transport Larochelle Ltee. operation in detail. They developed specific plans to combine Larochelle into Transport Tremblay Ltee. and to improve operating efficiency by eliminating Larochelle's excessive middle management, demarketing marginal accounts, closing down several unprofitable terminals, and introducing Tremblay's state-of-the-art computer costing and logistics system.

On Aug. 23, 1985, an agreement was reached and the deal was set to close on March 12, 1986. Transport Tremblay Ltee. acquired Transport Larochelle Ltee. from Marechal for $21,204,000, paid for with $10,704,000 in cash (drawn from cash on hand and Royal Bank loans) and $10,500,000 in convertible preferred shares. The preferred shares carried an eight per cent annual dividend, a term of five years, and were convertible at any time at Marechal's option into an equivalent number of common shares of Tremblay Ltee., which was incorporated as the holding company.

As part of the agreement, Marechal retained two seats on Tremblay's board until the preferred shares were redeemed. Assuming conversion of Marechal's preferred shares, shareholdings in Tremblay (as shown in Exhibit 1) would consist of 64 per cent held by LeBlanc, 16 per cent by Beaubien, and 20 per cent by Marechal.

Transport Larochelle Ltee.'s longtime banker had been the Royal Bank, and when the acquisition occurred, the Royal made a concerted effort to gain as much of the connection's business as possible. Tremblay split its banking connection, with Transport Tremblay Ltee. maintaining its outstanding loans with the Confederation. The acquisition needs and Transport Larochelle Ltee.'s facilities were financed by the Royal. In October 1986, Spencer successfully persuaded LeBlanc to move all banking to the Royal Bank.

INDUSTRY OVERVIEW

Freight could be transported overland by truck or by rail. Poolcar and piggyback operators were trucking firms that combined these two modes of transportation by using rail trucks to transport freight to or from rail terminals and using rail to transport freight between terminals. Poolcar operators sorted freight at terminals and loaded it on empty cars, while piggyback operators drove loaded trailers onto rail flatcars. Tremblay was engaged in all of these operators.

There were two main types of carriers in the trucking industry. The first group consisted of public carriers, like Tremblay, whose main activity was for-hire-carriage and accounted for 45 per cent of truck freight movements. The second group entailed private carriers (captive carriers of companies such as Sears or Canada Post) that owned their own fleets and generated the other 55 per cent of industry shipments. The division of revenues between public and private had remained stable for much of the past decade. Most public carriers utilized a mixture of employee-operated and owner-operated equipment to move freight over a long distance. A single trailer could often be hauled by several different tractors over the course of its movements.

There were two basic services offered by the industry: full truckloads (TLs) and less than truckloads (LTLs). The larger trucking firms, which had sufficient infrastructure to pick up, group and deliver loads according to their destination, were able to service both the LTL and TL clients. The smaller trucking firms competed exclusively in the TL market which experienced significantly more price competition and lower profit margins than the LTL market.

Large trucking companies enjoyed economies of scale. A large volume of traffic enabled firms to achieve a more efficient pickup and delivery network and have fewer empty trips. However, heavy traffic required complex and sophisticated logistical systems. The larger trucking companies tended to be unionized and any independent truckers were contracted on union terms. Smaller carriers were generally not unionized which gave them the advantage of lower labor costs and increased operational flexibility.

Deregulation

All trucking operations in the U.S. were deregulated as a result of legislation introduced in June 1980, and this had facilitated entry into the U.S. market for Canadian firms. In Canada, deregulation of trucking operations was to be introduced in January 1988 and was expected to follow the U.S. model. Under current regulation, operators were required to hold licences in order to transport on the roads and across provincial borders, and these licences were awarded once the transporter could demonstrate to the regulatory authority that the public required the service. Licence applicants had to demonstrate sufficient market demand and a lack of adequate service by companies presently servicing the market. With deregulation, licences were to be awarded provided the operator could meet certain financial and safety criteria.

The impact of deregulation was not expected to be as severe[1] on the Canadian industry as the American deregulation had been for U.S. transporters. Deregulation in the U.S. had coincided with the deep economic recession of the early '80s and caused numerous bankruptcies to occur. Economists expected most new entrants into the industry would compete in the TL segment of the market which did not require terminal facilities to sort and pool partial freight loads into full truckloads. In the long run, deregulation was expected to translate into efficiency gains for the industry as the larger, LTL/TL carriers acquired smaller and less efficient TL carriers. However, many were opposed with feelings summed up by the owner of Reimer Transport who was critical of deregulation:

> I'm a firm believer in the maxim: If it ain't broke, don't fix it. We have a system with good rates and a great deal of competition. Why ruin it? The new legislation will spawn over-competition and in the long run, higher prices, poorer service, and more concentration of ownership. There is more competition today than I've seen in 35 years in the business, and a lot of companies are in financial trouble. If shippers are expecting lower rates when the bill takes effect, they're going to be surprised. Rates are as low as they're going to go.

---

[1]The initial impact of deregulation in the U.S. was an upsurge in new entrants into the industry, with a 39 per cent increase in certificates issued in 1982, a recession year. Despite the increase in the number of firms, the business failure rate was below that of American industry and was more influenced by the recession than by deregulation. From 1978 to 1983, the rate of failure rose from 0.10 per cent to 0.50 per cent, while the comparative failure rate for American industry rose from 0.24 per cent to 0.61 per cent during the same period.

Economic Outlook

Exhibit 3 presents Canadian trucking industry data over the 1981 and 1984 period. Revenues were estimated to have exceeded $8.5 billion in 1986. The Canadian trucking industry had benefitted in recent years from strong economic growth. Over the 1983 to 1986 period, the annual average growth in operating revenues had been roughly 10 per cent and reflected an increased volume of traffic as well as the industry's success in enlarging its share of total freight traffic, primarily to the detriment of the railways. Trucking carriers had steadily increased their share of the total freight market, handling 25 per cent of tonnage shipped in 1986 compared to 19.1 per cent in 1983 and 13.7 per cent in 1965. The top 10 trucking competitors accounted for only 25 per cent of the total industry revenues and a financial profile of these companies can be found in Exhibit 4. Detailed stock market information on publicly traded companies is provided in Exhibit 5.

A 1987 sectoral analysis from the Royal Bank's economics department predicted that growth would moderate and price increases would be minimal due to heightened competition resulting from deregulation. The department forecasted volume growth to average four per cent over the 1987 to 1990 period and to increase slightly to six per cent thereafter.

Included in the forecast was a marginal increase in revenue growth as a result of an anticipated "free trade" deal that would emerge from discussions between the Canadian and U.S. governments. However, some industry analysts worried that free trade might eventually mean the end of Canadian east-west transport as trade became more regionally oriented in the North American market.

COMPANY OVERVIEW

Tremblay Ltee. was one of Canada's major trucking haulage firms and was able to offer its customers a broad range of services: LTL or TL freight, poolcar, rail piggyback, local pickup/delivery, freight brokerage across borders, and cargo express. The majority of Tremblay's revenues were from the LTL products which accounted for roughly 65 per cent of its revenues, and the company's 16,000 active client accounts were spread across all major industry sectors. No client accounted for more than two per cent of revenues. Client freight movements were tracked by way of a sophisticated computer system, and this had led to almost perfect delivery reliability (98 per cent on-time) and claim-free (99 per cent without claims) performance. Tremblay's operations were nationally balanced with Transport Tremblay Ltee. specializing in Canada east-west freight while Transport Larochelle Ltee. was concentrated in the east, serving Quebec, Ontario and the northeastern U.S. In June 1987, Tremblay owned 275 tractors, 1,000 trailers, 75 trucks, and two cranes. The company followed a conventional replacement policy and its fleet was considered to be reasonably well-maintained.

Management

LeBlanc, at 41, was a large, heavyset man, and a tough, open-door manager. While experienced in dealing with senior level managers, he could be at ease talking to truckers down in the terminals. He knew he had not been in the industry very long, but made up for this by soaking up information on the industry at every opportunity. He was also a pragmatist, often telling Spencer: "I'm not married to this business (trucking). If the right offer came along tomorrow, I'd grab it." LeBlanc personally dabbled in the stock market, always investing in very safe, blue-chip stocks. His lifestyle was modest and unassuming.

Tremblay's senior management team had experience in the freight forwarding/trucking business dating back to the 1960s. After acquiring his controlling interest in the company, LeBlanc became the driving force behind the company, while Beaubien adopted a more laidback management stance. Operationally, the company was managed by Raymond Brousseau, 38, the vice-president of operations and Martin Coutlee, 50, personnel manager. Jean Tardiff, 48, was promoted to replace LeBlanc as chief financial officer, and Rene Rousseau, 42, remained as vice-president of sales. All of the key officers had been with the company for a number of years and LeBlanc was confident that his management team would continue to be successful in the highly competitive trucking industry.

Employee Relations

Tremblay employed 2,000[2] people in the various facets of its operations. This total included 350 tractor owner-operators working under contract to the company. Approximately one-half of the company was unionized, and these workers were represented by nine separate collective bargaining units. Contracts with various provincially based unions were for varying terms and expired on an ongoing basis. Employee relations were stable, and Tremblay, like many of its competitors in the industry, had been able to obtain favorable contracts in recent negotiations with various unions due to an oversupply of truckers. Transport Tremblay Ltee. and Transport Larochelle Ltee. had not suffered a strike or other significant labor disruption since the early 1970s. Tremblay negotiated separately with its owner-operators usually under exclusive one year contracts that set prices on a negotiable basis and complied with union safety and benefit stipulations.

If Tremblay decided to go public at some future date, LeBlanc was considering establishing an employee share option plan which would enable certain employees to subscribe in the aggregate for up to five percent of the common shares of the company.

Buyout of Marechal's Minority Interest

Marechal's preference shares carried an annual dividend of eight per cent and were to be fully redeemed by Tremblay five years after the date of the Transport Larochelle acquisition. LeBlanc realized that a refinancing of the preferred shares with interest-bearing, tax deductible long-term debt could generate substantial savings. In addition, he was dissatisfied with the presence of the two Marechal members on the Tremblay board who were continually questioning and trying to obstruct the company's plans to streamline operations by closing down inefficient terminals and laying off redundant employees. In LeBlanc's opinion, Marechal contributed little to the management of Tremblay. Marechal was opposed to LeBlanc's expansionary plans and had made clear that it did not want to increase its investment in Tremblay and would retire its preferred shares at maturity. LeBlanc stated "that even if he had to pay the full $10.5 million now, it would be worth it just to get rid of Marechal's influence."

LeBlanc knew that Marechal had alternative uses for the money it had invested in Tremblay so he approached Marechal's president with an offer to retire the preferred shares prior to the March 1991 maturity date. The negotiations were tough and protracted, but finally Marechal agreed to an $8 million payment. Marechal's willingness to accept the $2.5 million discount reflected their cash needs for other investments and their concern about the future of the trucking industry.

Financial History

Tremblay's consolidated financial statements for the year ending March 31, 1987, can be found in Exhibit 6. Revenues and expenses had increased as a result of the Larochelle acquisition.

As of March 31, 1987, the company had long-term debt outstanding of $18 million as part of a total Royal Bank facility of $26 million in revolving[3] term loans. The revolving term loan had initially been set at $21 million to assist in financing the Transport Larochelle Ltee. buyout, but had been increased by $5 million in October 1986 to payout the Confederation Bank loans and to allow the Royal Bank to become exclusive banker to the connection. At this time, the debt was moved to the holding company level. The loan rate on the first $16 million was set at the Royal Bank Prime (RBP) or the Royal Bank Prime Acceptance Fee (RBPAF) for bankers' acceptances; and the remaining $10 million was set at RBP[4] plus ¼ per cent or RBPAF

---

[2]By occupation: drivers 772; clerical 500; dockhands 348; marketing/sales 141; management and supervisory 172; and maintenance 67.

[3]The revolving term loan was for general operating purposes and for realignment of acquisition financing for Transport Larochelle Ltee. It was revolving until April 1, 1988, with the balance outstanding after that date to be split as follows:
  (a) demand, operating loans to a maximum of 75 per cent of good accounts receivable;
  (b) amount in excess of (a) to be termed out over a period not exceeding 5 years, repayable in 20 equal quarterly installments.

[4]RBP was 9.5 per cent in June 1987.

plus 1.4 per cent. The credit facility was secured by accounts receivable and inventory as well as a fixed and floating charge over all of the company's assets.

The revolving term facility was seen by both Spencer and LeBlanc as a bridge financing arrangement until a more permanent capital structure evolved. LeBlanc had discussed the possibility of arranging mortgage financing to pay down some of the term facility. He felt that a fixed rate might help in stabilizing financing costs and place Tremblay in a stronger financial position to deal with industry restructuring and future expansion.

Company-Prepared Forecasts

Income and expense forecasts can be found in Exhibit 7. These forecasts assumed a 15 per cent drop in volume in fiscal 1988 caused by three factors: an anticipated economic recession, the pruning of unprofitable Larochelle accounts and price reductions expected to result from deregulation.

Despite the anticipated sales drop, LeBlanc was optimistic about the upcoming year. The bottom line would be improved by several actions: a saving in financing costs due to the replacement of the preferred shares with debt; a reduction in CEO salaries; and an annual $1.1 million year pre-tax saving from closing down unprofitable terminals and reducing layers of redundant middle management, although these moves would necessitate a one-time expense of $1.6 million in separation and restructuring costs.

LeBlanc envisaged making further acquisitions over the next five years. He believed that deregulation and free trade would create numerous opportunities to pick off weaker competitors and this would give Tremblay growth well above the industry averages. LeBlanc saw the three main goals of Tremblay as: (1) expansion through acquisition, (2) an eventual public issue to strengthen the company's capital base, and (3) an emphasis on providing reliable on-time delivery to maintain its competitive edge and preserve its market share.

FINANCING ALTERNATIVES

Spencer knew that LeBlanc was considering financing the Marechal buyout with $8 million in term debt, the unused portion of the revolving term loan facility. Spencer had come to understand LeBlanc quite well. She observed a classic dealmaker, with a highly analytical mind that was challenged by complexity. LeBlanc enjoyed taking "well calculated risks." He knew the trucking industry well, and at their annual meetings he would often relate interesting developments that were ongoing at competitors.

LeBlanc estimated Tremblay's real estate assets (land and buildings) had a market value between $16 and $18 million, and he thought that mortgage financing on these properties might result in lower and more stable interest costs over the long term. He had had preliminary discussions with several trust and insurance companies about fixed rate mortgage financing.

Royal Bank Capital Corporation (RBCC)

During their meeting, Spencer told LeBlanc that she would gather some background information on RBCC (see Exhibit 8). Spencer called Daniel Mathews, a vice-president at RBCC and discussed some of the guidelines that RBCC sought in new investment decisions. Mathews told her that RBCC invested by way of a convertible subordinated loan or a common stock purchase. RBCC had a target return on investment of 20 per cent. However, Mathews pointed out that since a portion of RBCC's portfolio earned little, if any, returns, the successful investments would have to generate a return in excess of 20 per cent of RBCC to achieve its overall target.

SDIL's Financing Proposal

Spencer knew that SDIL wanted very badly to underwrite an initial public offering (IPO) of Tremblay stock. That motive was evident when it extended to LeBlanc a $2.5 million personal loan to assist in consolidating his ownership. SDIL was attracted to Tremblay because of its strong track record and solid industry reputation and believed Tremblay was an exciting story it could successfully market in selling shares. SDIL was in the process of determining an offering price. LeBlanc told Spencer that SDIL was attempting to price the issue at a price/earnings (P/E) ratio comparable to other trucking companies in the market, but that he thought it would propose an offering of 750,000 common shares at a price of about seven dollars per common share.

Underwriting fees and the legal and audit costs associated with the examination and prospectus would amount to roughly 10 per cent of the gross proceeds from a stock issue. SDIL had just about completed its due diligence examination of Tremblay. If an underwriting agreement was reached, SDIL planned to market the issue in September 1987, and would likely qualify Tremblay's shares under the Quebec Stock Savings Plan.

Exhibit 1		
CORPORATE STRUCTURE **June 1987**		

Shareholdings by:

	LeBlanc	Beaubien	Marechal
Common Shares	80%	20%	0%
After Conversion of Preferred Stock	64%	16%	20%

HOLDING COMPANY

100%	100%
Transport Tremblay Ltee.	Transport Larochelle Ltee.
- Canada-wide service - LTL, TL & poolcar	- Ontario, Quebec, Atlantic, U.S. - LTL, TL & piggyback freight
REVENUES: 35%	65%
EMPLOYEES: 625	1,375

Exhibit 2						
SELECTED CONSOLIDATED FINANCIAL INFORMATION **FOR THE YEARS ENDED MARCH 31** **($000s)**						
	1987	**1986****	**1985***	**1984***	**1983***	**1982***
Revenues	$ 156,289	$ 92,831	$ 40,258	$ 28,250	$ 24,641	$ 21,960
Operating profit before interest and tax	8,580	4,505	2,692	2,369	1,402	2,084
Net income	3,967	1,674	563	8	79	132
BALANCE SHEET DATA						
Total assets	$ 55,111	$ 57,023	$ 10,995	$ 8,958	n/a	n/a
Long-term debt	18,365	16,649	418	687	n/a	n/a
Equity	16,620	13,493	3,169	2,733	n/a	n/a

*   Transport Tremblay Ltee. figures only.
** 1986 results include Larochelle from August 1985, the effective date of acquisition.

Exhibit 3				
CANADIAN TRUCKING INDUSTRY DATA[1]				
	1981	**1982**	**1983**	**1984**
($000,000s)				
Total revenues	$ 6,047	$ 5,929	$ 6,088	$ 7,115
Net income	130	70	156	231
Cash flow	465	411	473	594
BALANCE SHEET DATA				
Working Capital	(94)	(215)	(117)	(78)
Total Liabilities	2,473	2,384	2,502	2,727
Long-term liabilities	1,096	1,024	1,079	1,252
Shareholders' equity	974	941	1,010	1,052
FINANCIAL RATIOS				
Current ratio	0.93:1	0.84:1	0.92:1	0.95:1
Liabilities/ equity	2.54:1	2.53:1	2.48:1	2.59:1
Long-term liab./equity	1.12:1	1.09:1	1.07:1	1.19:1
Interest coverage	2.04x	1.60x	2.45x	2.82x
OTHER DATA				
Employees	90,782	83,989	80,546	83,689
Total equipment	135,002	133,523	133,178	138,819

[1] Adapted from Statistics Canada, _Canada Year Book_, Catalogue No. 11-402, 1985.

			Exhibit 4					

	THE TOP 10 CANADIAN TRUCKING COMPANIES (RANKED BY REVENUES) ($ millions)							

	Name/Fiscal Yr	Where	Revenue	Income	Assets	Fixed Assets	Total Liab./ Equity	ROE
1	CP Trucks 1986	Canada/ U.S.	$ 410	subs.*				
2	TNT Canada 1986	Canada/ U.S.	410	subs.*				
3	Kingsway 1986	Canada/ U.S.	300	pvt.**				
4	Trimac 1986							
	Trucking Division	Canada/ U.S.	202					
	Total Company		294	3.5	357.5	245.4	1.59	1.3%
5	Canadian Motorways 1986	Canada/ U.S.	175	pvt.**				
6	Reimer 1986	Canada	171	0.7	94.1	43.6	6.41	5.5%
7	GTL 1986	Ont/Que	169	4.7	128.4	90.8	5.90	25.2%
8	Tremblay 1987	Canada/U.S.	156	4.0	55.1	24.1	2.22	23.9%
9	Cabano 1987	Que/Marit	93	1.3	64.8	33.3	2.72	7.5%
10	Laidlaw 1986							
	Trucking Division	Ont/Que/U.S.	77					
	Total Company		717	66.2	901.7	454.7	0.38	18.3%

* Subsidiary does not report results separately.
** Privately held company — no public data available.

Exhibit 5

STOCK MARKET INFORMATION
ON SELECTED CANADIAN TRUCKING FIRMS

| | LAIDLAW TRANSPORTATION | | TRIMAC | | TRANSPORT DORVAL | |
	Aug 31 '85	Aug 31 '86	Dec 31 '85	Dec 31 '86	Dec 31 '85	Dec 31 '86
EPS	$0.31	$0.42	$0.06	$0.04	$0.74	$0.65
EPS % growth	34.00	34.00	(122.00)	(33.00)	12.00	(12.00)
Revenue % growth	23.00	31.00	3.00	(18.00)	5.00	(16.00)
Dividends/share	$0.06	$0.07	$0.09	$0.09	-	-
Average P/E ratio	21.40	34.10	54.10	69.40	not listed	10.80
Average market/book value of stock	4.20	5.30	1.10	0.90	not listed	1.80
Book value per share	$1.61	$2.69	$3.06	$3.05	-	$3.90
Return on common equity (%)	21.80	18.30	1.90	1.30	13.20	13.00
Debt/equity ratio	0.47	0.38	1.69	1.59	1.35	1.41

Source: Royal Bank Information Resources.

		Exhibit 5 (continued)	

HISTORICAL P/E RATIO

		TSE 300	TSE Transportation Sector*
1980		8.8	5.9
1981		7.9	5.2
1982		19.3	10.6
1983		22.4	26.1
1984		15.2	13.0
1985		14.5	14.9
1986		17.4	28.9
1987	January	18.9	28.6
	February	19.3	33.1
	March	21.4	30.2
	April	20.9	28.1
	May	20.3	31.5

* Includes Algoma Central, Greyhound Lines, Laidlaw Transportation, Pacific Airlines and Trimac.

Exhibit 6

CONSOLIDATED STATEMENT OF INCOME
($000s)

	March 31		
	1987		**1986**
	(note1)		
Revenue	$ 156,289		$ 92,831
Operating expenses	144,214		86,136
Depreciation and amortization	3,495		2,190
Earnings before interest and taxes	8,580		4,505
Interest expense	1,424		1,017
Income from operations before income taxes	7,156		3,488
Provision for income taxes	3,549		1,814
Income before extraordinary items	3,607		1,674
Extraordinary items (note 5)	360		-
Net income for the period	3,967		1,674
Preferred dividends	840		28
Net income available for common shareholders	3,127		1,646
Income per common share:			
Income before extraordinary items	0.69		0.41
Net income	$ 0.78		$ 0.41

CONSOLIDATED STATEMENTS OF RETAINED EARNINGS
($000s)

Retained earnings, beginning of period	$ 2,677		$ 1,031
Add net income for the period	3,967		1,674
Less preferred dividends	840		28
Retained earnings, end of period	$ 5,804		$ 2,677

(See accompanying notes)

Exhibit 6 (continued)

CONSOLIDATED BALANCE SHEET
($000s)

| | March 31 | |
	1987	1986
ASSETS		
Current assets:		
Cash	$ 1,714	$ -
Accounts receivable	22,554	22,092
Inventories	553	649
Prepaid expenses	1,845	2,210
	26,666	24,951
Other assets (net of depreciation):		
Fixed assets (note 2)	24,075	27,640
Licences	833	833
Goodwill	3,537	3,599
TOTAL ASSETS	$ 55,111	$ 57,023
LIABILITIES AND SHAREHOLDERS' EQUITY		
Current:		
Bank indebtedness	$ -	$ 4,084
Accounts payable	16,468	19,605
and accrued liabilities		
Income taxes payable	2,025	1,155
Current portion of long-term debt	105	809
(note 3)	18,598	25,653
Long-term debt (note 3)	18,260	15,840
Deferred income taxes	1,633	2,037
Shareholders' equity:		
Capital stock (note 4)		
Preferred shares	10,500	10,500
Common shares	316	316
Retained Earnings	5,804	2,677
	16,620	13,493
TOTAL LIABILITIES AND		
SHAREHOLDERS' EQUITY	$ 55,111	$ 57,023

(See accompanying notes)

	Exhibit 6 (continued)	

CONSOLIDATED STATEMENT OF CHANGES IN FINANCIAL POSITION **($000s)**		
	1987	**1986**
Cash provided by (used in):		
Operating activities -		
Income before extraordinary items	$3,607	$ 1,673
Items not involving cash:		
Depreciation and amortization	3,495	2,190
Deferred income taxes	(404)	995
Gains on disposals of fixed assets	(400)	(329)
Net change in non-cash working capital	(2,699)	(1,607)
Cash provided by (used in) operating		
activities	3,599	2,922
Financing activities -		
Increase in long-term debt	1,716	14,312
Issues of preferred shares	-	10,500
Preferred dividends	(840)	(28)
Cash provided by financing activities	876	24,784
Investing activities-		
Purchase of Transport Larochelle Ltee. (note 1)	-	(21,204)
Addition to fixed assets	(861)	(6,050)
Proceeds from disposals of fixed assets	517	665
Proceeds from sale of extraordinary items		
(net of tax)	1,667	-
Cash provided by (used in) investing activities	1,323	(26,589)
Net change in cash during the period	5,798	1,117
Bank indebtedness acquired on acquisitions	-	(3,393)
Bank indebtedness, beginning of period	(4,084)	(1,836)
Bank cash balance (indebtedness),	$1,714	$ (4,112)
end of period		

(See accompanying notes)

Exhibit 6 (continued)

EXCERPTS FROM NOTES TO CONSOLIDATED FINANCIAL STATEMENTS **($000s)**

MARCH 31, 1987

1. Purchase of Transport Larochelle Ltee.

Effective August 23, 1985, the company acquired 100 per cent of the issued shares of Transport Larochelle Ltee. from Le Groupe Marachel. Transport Larochelle Ltee.'s business consists of over-the-road freight transportation. The acquisition was accounted for using the purchase method and the results of operations are included in the consolidated financial statements from the effective date of acquisition. Details of the net assets acquired at assigned values and the consideration paid on the acquisition are as follows:

Working capital (including bank indebtedness of $3,393)	$ 648
Fixed Assets	20,418
Licences	762
Goodwill	1,016
	22,844
Long-term debt	608
Deferred income taxes	1,032
	1,640
Purchase price of net assets acquired	21,204
Consideration:	
Cash, including cash on acquisition	10,704
Preferred shares (note 5)	10,500
	$21,204

The closing date for this acquisition was March 12, 1986.

2. Fixed Assets

		March 31, 1987		March 31, 1986
	Cost	Accu. Dep.	Net B.V.	Net Book Value
Land	$ 5,459	$ -	$ 5,459	$ 5,666
Buildings	8,776	3,514	5,262	5,540
Trucks, tractors and trailers	36,291	24,504	11,787	13,992
Other equipment	5,234	3,790	1,444	2,296
Leasehold improvements	161	38	123	146
	$ 55,921	$ 31,846	$ 24,075	$ 27,640

Exhibit 6 (continued)

NOTES TO CONSOLIDATED FINANCIAL STATEMENTS

3. Long-term debt

	March 31 1987	March 31 1986
Revolving loans	$18,000	$15,028
Lease obligations	365	512
Term loans, at varying interest	0	1,109
rates from prime plus ½ per cent	18,365	16,649
to prime plus 1 per cent		
Less current position	105	809
	$18,260	$15,840

The terms of the revolving loans extend to April 1, 1988 at which time the company has the option to convert the amount not designated as an operating loan to term loans which are repayable in equal quarterly installments over five years. Interest during the revolving period is at prime when loans outstanding are under $16 million and prime plus ¼ per cent when loans exceed $16 million. Interest on the term loans will be at the fixed money market rate (as defined) plus ¾ per cent.

Under the loan agreement, the company is required to maintain the following financial ratios: a minimum equity of $13 million; a working capital ratio greater than one to one; a debt/equity ratio not exceeding 3.5 to one until April 1, 1988 and reducing to two to one thereafter. As at March 31, 1987, the company complied with all restrictive covenants and financial tests.

4. Capital Stock

Issued

As at March 31, 1987 and March 31, 1986, issued share capital consisted of:

	Number	Amount
Preferred	1,000,000	$10,500
Class A common	4,000,000	316

5. Extraordinary items

During the year, the business, goodwill, and all tangible assets of certain Transport Larochelle Ltee. properties and terminals were sold. Total proceeds of $1,841 were received resulting in a gain of $360 (net of taxes of $174).

Exhibit 6 (continued)		

NOTES ON THE CONSOLIDATED FINANCIAL STATEMENTS

6. Segmented information

Geographic segmented information is as follows:

	U.S.A.	Canada	Total
1987			
Revenue	23,786	132,503	156,289
Net income for the period	749	3,218	3,967
Identifiable assets	548	36,832	37,380
1986			
Revenue	12,841	79,990	92,831
Net income for the period	233	1,441	1,674
Identifiable assets	609	32,384	32,993

	Exhibit 7

**INCOME FORECASTS
FOR THE FIVE YEARS ENDING MARCH 31, 1988 TO 1992**

	1988	**1989**	**1990**	**1991**	**1992**
Revenues	$ 138,835	$ 130,505	$ 168,352	$ 191,921	$ 211,113
Operating Expenses	129,117	121,370	153,200	174,648	192,113
Depreciation and amort.	3,691	3,810	3,871	4,104	4,413
	132,808	125,180	157,071	178,752	196,526
Operating income (EBIT)	6,027	5,325	11,281	13,169	14,587
Interest on existing revolving term debt *	2,160	2,160	2,160	2,160	2,160
Net income before taxes dividends or any other incremental financing costs	3,867	3,165	9,121	11,009	12,427
Taxes @ 50 per cent	1,933	1,582	4,560	5,504	6,213
Net income after taxes	$ 1,934	$ 1,583	$ 4,561	$ 5,505	$ 6,214

* Assumed to be 12 per cent

	Exhibit 7 (continued)				

PROFORMA BALANCE SHEETS
FOR THE FIVE YEARS ENDING MARCH 31, 1988 TO 1992

ASSETS	1988	1989	1990	1991	1992
Current Assets					
Accounts receivable	$ 22,822	$ 21,594	$ 27,674	$ 31,549	$ 34,704
Inventory	554	577	599	623	648
Prepaids	1,845	1,845	1,845	1,845	1,845
	25,221	24,016	30,118	34,017	37,197
Fixed Assets	24,810	25,221	26,770	28,832	31,192
Licences	833	833	833	833	833
Goodwill	2,811	2,722	2,634	2,545	2,457
	28,454	28,776	30,237	32,210	34,482
TOTAL ASSETS	$ 53,675	$ 52,792	$ 60,355	$ 66,227	$ 71,679
LIABILITIES AND EQUITY					
Current Liabilities					
Accounts payable	17,687	16,626	20,986	23,924	26,317
Income taxes payable	1,258	1,258	1,258	1,258	1,258
	18,945	17,884	22,244	25,182	27,575
Revolving term loan	18,000	18,000	18,000	18,000	18,000
Deferred taxes	2,874	2,874	2,874	2,874	2,874
TOTAL LIABILITIES	39,819	38,758	43,118	46,056	48,449
Common	316	316	316	316	316
Contributed surplus	2,500	2,500	2,500	2,500	2,500
Core retained earnings *	5,804	5,804	5,804	5,804	5,804
New retained earnings	1,934	3,517	8,078	13,583	19,797
TOTAL EQUITY	10,554	12,137	16,698	22,203	28,417
TOTAL LIAB. & EQUITY	50,373	50,895	59,816	68,259	76,866
FINANCING NEED*	3,302	1,897	539	(2,032)	(5,187)
TOTAL LIAB. & EQUITY	$ 53,675	$ 52,792	$ 60,355	$ 66,227	$ 71,679

Assumptions:
Contributed surplus represents the difference between the $10.5 million face value of the preferred shares and the $8 million redemption value. Retained earnings were $5,804 at March 31, 1987. Year over year additions to retained earnings do not reflect any new financing.
*These numbers exclude the costs of any new financing.

Exhibit 8

ROYAL BANK CAPITAL CORPORATION (RBCC) PROFILE

Background

Royal Bank Capital Corporation (RBCC) provides capital to well managed and established companies, through equity and subordinated debt. RBCC's experience, expertise, financial resources, and track record of innovative deal structures are fully committed to help businesses succeed.

RBCC is a wholly owned subsidiary of the Royal Bank of Canada. Chartered in 1869, the Royal Bank is Canada's largest bank with assets in excess of one hundred billion dollars, a network of 1,500 branches and 5,300 correspondent banking relationships in nearly every country in the world. With its 75 per cent ownership of RBC Dominion Securities, the Bank has consolidated its position as Canada's leading financial institution.

Originally established as a financial services company in 1974, RBCC today represents one of Canada's most active merchant banking/private investment pools, with corporate offices located in Montreal, Toronto, and Western Canada.

Financial Flexibility

RBCC invests its own funds and can therefore be highly flexible in structuring financial packages that best suit individual needs. The scope of operations encompasses a wide range of minority and mezzanine capital investments beyond the limitations of conventional bank debt.

RBCC's investment professionals are skilled in analyzing, structuring, financing, and monitoring a diverse investment portfolio.

Investment Opportunities

RBCC will provide risk capital to dynamic, privately owned and emerging public companies with potential for significant capital appreciation and cash flow generation. Preferred areas of investment are Canadian manufacturing or service oriented firms beyond the startup stage. RBCC will also assist in the structuring of management and leveraged buyouts and advise clients concerning the optimum use of senior and secured debt.

TOM.COM: VALUATION OF AN ASIAN INTERNET COMPANY[1]

Tom.com seemed to embody everything the Internet frenzy is about. The start-up aims to be a multi-lingual mega-portal focusing on delivering China-related content worldwide…as the Internet wave peaked [sic] the interest of local Chinese investors and international investors. A number of competitors already have jumped into the Chinese markets hoping to tap the potential of one billion consumers, most of whom have never used a computer. Tom.com is distinguished from its competition much in part due to its connection with Hong Kong's most high-profile tycoon Li Kai-Shing.[2]

On Feb. 19, 2000, the day after Tom.com Limited (Tom), a Hong Kong based Internet portal, released its prospectus for the planned $640 million[3] initial public offering (IPO), Andy Lau, a portfolio manager for EuroGlobal Funds, was immersed in digesting the 200-page information package. EuroGlobal was one of Europe's leading families of mutual funds. Its Asia Growth Fund had more than US$800 million of funds under management and had been in the top quartile of Asian based funds ranked by total return performance for all five of the years the fund had been in existence.

---

[1]This case has been written on the basis of published sources only. Consequently, the interpretation and perspectives presented in this case are not necessarily those of Tom.com or any of its employees.

[2]Gabriella Faerber, "Tom.com: Just an Illusion?", *Worldlyinvestor.com*, April 2000

[3]Unless otherwise stated, all currencies in the case refer to Hong Kong dollar. US$1 = HK$7.75

Richard Ivey School of Business
The University of Western Ontario

IVEY

Peter Yuan prepared this case under the supervision of Professors Larry Wynant and Steve Foerster solely to provide material for class discussion. The authors do not intend to illustrate either effective or ineffective handling of a managerial situation. The authors may have disguised certain names and other identifying information to protect confidentiality.

Tom had been a focus of attention by the financial community since the announcement of its IPO. Headline after headline had been reporting the grand scale of the mega-portal for China-related content, its affiliation with the Li family and, most of all, its potential market price. Emerging out of the two-year-long Asian financial crisis, the "get rich fast" Hong Kong spirit would not likely see such an event pass without plenty of buzz. However, Lau knew his job was to make professional opinions on the value of such an investment and its appropriateness for different investors. Valuation of "dot-com" companies had been one of the most controversial subjects in the investment realm ever since the technology stock-dominated NASDAQ index shot up almost 84 per cent in 1999,[4] powered mostly by Internet related companies (and biotechnology companies). Various new valuation techniques had been suggested to replace the more traditional Discounted Cash Flow (DCF) and Price Earnings Multiples (P/E) approaches. With only four days left until the closing of applications, Lau decided to use a variety of valuation methods he knew and "try to unveil" the true value of Tom.

TOM.COM LIMITED[5]

Creation of Tom

In 1996, Metro, an information, entertainment and radio programming business owned 50 per cent by the Cheung Kong Group and 50 per cent by the Hutchison Whampoa Group,[6] launched its first Web site, *metroradio.com.hk*, to provide on-line details of Metro Radio's programming. In 1998, a second Web site, *104fmselect.com*, was launched to provide information and live streaming of radio programming. In July 1999, a third Web site called *sochannel.com* was launched to provide up-to-date information on local and international music and the entertainment scene.

As penetration of the Internet accelerated in Hong Kong, Hutchison Whampoa and Cheung Kong realized that the target market should be expanded beyond the limited potential of the existing Metro Web sites. They saw that there was the potential of a portal which offered a total China experience, particularly to mainland and overseas Chinese communities. In order to provide a new and refreshing brand for the range of content being developed, "Tom" was created as the single brand under which to launch and promote the broader portal concept. Subsequently, through reorganization, all of the Web sites and event production expertise of Metro were acquired by Tom for a cash consideration of $310 million. On Oct. 5, 1999, Tom.com Limited was registered in the Cayman Islands.[7]

The Business Plan

Tom intended to leverage its core strengths in technology, media foundation, content acquisition and presentation, as well as shareholder support to achieve its goal of becoming the leading multi-lingual China-related mega-portal.[8] The mega-portal would provide "Lifestyle for Chinese" content and e-commerce to the worldwide Chinese population both in the Greater China region and overseas Chinese speaking communities and broad "China Experience" content and e-commerce to the rest of the world.

Believing that Hong Kong had always acted as a natural bridge between China and the rest of the world for popular culture and entertainment exchange, Tom would focus on three core markets:

---

[4]NASDAQ closed at 2208.05 on Jan. 4, 1999 and 4069.31 on Dec. 31, 1999.

[5]Much of the information in this section is drawn from the prospectus of Tom.com Limited.

[6]Both the Cheung Kong Group and the Hutchison Whampoa Group were listed companies on the Hong Kong Stock Exchange. The Cheung Kong Group was the majority shareholder of Hutchison Whampoa Group. Mr. Li Ka-Shing and his immediate family members had effective control over Cheung Kong Group through their shareholdings.

[7]Many public companies in Hong Kong were registered in Cayman Islands for tax and political reasons. The bulk of their operation was still centered in Asia.

[8]Portals, such as Yahoo!, were Web sites that attract visitors by offering free information or free services on a daily basis. The portal site would be used as a basis to explore the Web. A portal was an entry point and gateway for surfing the Internet that provided useful Web-related services and links.

1. The non-Chinese-speaking audience, which would be interested in "China Experience" style content;

2. The PRC audience, which would be more interested in "Lifestyle for Chinese" content; and

3. Overseas Chinese-speaking audiences, which would be interested in both.

The "China Experience" content would provide a comprehensive guide to China covering classical and contemporary topics including news and business, travel information and services, classical arts and literature, modern arts and literature, wisdom and popular culture. On the other hand, the "Lifestyle for Chinese" content would cover day-to-day interests for Chinese people, such as food and wine, sports and leisure, entertainment and music, fashion and beauty, popular technology and fun and self improvement.

To propel Tom into a leading China-related portal, Tom built and launched a new and unique Chinese language information and entertainment content platform branded Tomcast. It provided a personalized real-time information channel and Internet navigation tool. Subscribers to *tom.com* were asked to sign up and download a small piece of software onto their hard drives.

Some analysts had expressed concern over a potential user's acceptance of such hurdles to accessing the Web site. They had also questioned whether there was a lack of focus by targeting such a broad range of audiences with a relatively wide range of contents. Besides, marketing to the worldwide Chinese audience would be extremely expensive.[9]

Revenue Model

Exhibit 1 provides the audited financial statements of Tom for the two years ending Dec. 31, 1999.

Directors of Tom stated that the company would target four revenue streams over time. Advertising revenue had been the major source of income for Internet portals. Like traditional media companies, Tom would sell advertising space on its Web sites to advertisers. Advertising revenue was linked to the number of page views that Tom expected to generate. The quality of content was a key factor in increasing page views. As Tom increased its online e-commerce capability, it would also receive revenue from transactions and subscriptions from products and services offered through *tom.com*. Commission revenue was generated through commission agreements with companies who had banner advertisements or hyperlinks placed on the *tom.com* Web sites. With an extensive content provision network in place, Tom also expected to sell syndicated content to both cyber and other media.

Current Businesses

By January 2000, Tom had 143 staff and had established five operating units: Super Channel, Super Web, itravel, ECLink Shenzhen and OneAsia (see Exhibit 2).

Super Channel

Super Channel was a wholly owned subsidiary created to operate the Web sites and manage strategic investments. Tom used cutting edge software and hardware components, both developed in-house and procured from third party vendors, to build a common backend infrastructure that provided a reliable and scalable platform. The company also planned to deliver its products via local or mirror servers located in the vicinity of the target markets. The overall architectural design of Tom's infrastructure would follow the principles of distributed Web architecture to enable maximum information availability and provision efficiency to end-users.

Super Channel also supervised the web content management team. To date, Tom had entered into 10 content provision and license contracts with external content providers regarding travel, culture, science, learning, arts, fashion, games, news, sports and "infotainment." The content would be repackaged and edited, while at the same time, Tom would also develop its own content. These content providers included PRC

---

[9]Gabriella Faerber, "Tom.com: Just an Illusion?", *Worldlyinvestor.com*, April 2000.

organizations, Metro and OneAsia. Due to the short history of Tom, most of the license agreements were still subject to finalization. (Several content provision agreements and joint venture agreements with PRC companies were subject to PRC government approval.)

Super Web

Super Web was established in November 1999 to hold the Web sites acquired from Metro for a total cash consideration of $310 million in December 1999. According to the company's internal data, the Metro Web sites comprising *metroradio.com.hk*, *metro997.com*, *metro104.com* and *sochannel.com*, had reached 100,000 daily pageviews and 7,000 registered members within two months from the re-launch in July 1999. These Web sites focused on updated on-line local and international news in Hong Kong.

itravel

A joint venture between Tom and CTN Holdings, itravel would sub-brand its Web sites with tom.com to offer travel related products and services both in B2C (business to consumer) and B2B (business to business) markets. Tom had invested $16.7 million for 55 per cent of itravel, while CTN Holdings owned by China International Travel Service Head Office (CITSHO), the largest PRC state-run travel agency, would bring expertise in servicing inbound tourists. itravel planned to launch its Web site in the first quarter of 2000, and would enter into a commercial agreement with Tom to share transaction revenue generated by users entering itravel through Tom's portal.

ECLink Shenzhen

ECLink Shenzhen, a wholly owned subsidiary of Tom, had been involved in the development of Electronic Data Interchange ("EDI") customs declaration software to provide a secure electronic transaction platform. It would bring Tom capability in software development, electronic network systems and other computer network systems in PRC.

OneAsia

OneAsia.com was a Web site that sold Chinese produced music and video products to Chinese communities in the Greater China region and Chinese communities living overseas. At the time, it was one of the few companies that had payment handling and fulfillment capabilities. Tom indirectly held 15 per cent of OneAsia and had the option to increase its shareholding to 50 per cent. OneAsia would sub-brand with *tom.com*. The two companies were also in discussion to amalgamate their customer databases.

Tom had also entered into a number of content provision and license contracts with providers for cultural events, sports, culinary arts and games.

Future Businesses Plans

Tom would initially focus on the "China Experience" themed content, targeting a worldwide audience, as the company believed that the more advanced distribution infrastructure and established e-commerce models outside of China provided a more ready market. Tom would establish mirror sites in major cities in the world with local editorial teams to develop local content.

SIGNIFICANT SHAREHOLDERS

After the reorganization, Tom had six major shareholders: Easterhouse, Romefield, Cheung Kong, Schumann, Handel and Pacific Century CyberWorks Limited (PCCW).

The Li Family

Through their subsidiaries, Mr. Li Ka-Shing and his family members held 62 per cent of Tom immediately before the IPO through three related entities. Easterhouse, a wholly owned subsidiary of Hutchison, held 38 per cent of Tom. Romefield, a wholly owned subsidiary of Cheung Kong, held 19 per cent and PCCW held five per cent.

Cheung Kong, the flagship investment holding group controlled by the Li Family, owned 49.9 per cent of Hutchison. Both companies were listed on the Hong Kong Stock Exchange with a broad business scope ranging from property development and investment, ports operation, telecommunications, retailing and manufacturing. Including its majority shareholdings in two other listed companies, Cheung Kong Infrastructure (Holdings) Group and Hong Kong Electric Group, Cheung Kong had $59 billion of consolidated profits attributable to its shareholders in 1999.

Richard Li, one of the sons of Mr. Li Ka-Shing, served as chairman and chief executive officer of PCCW, a joint venture that Intel had a 13 per cent stake in. A leading technology company, PCCW was developing an innovative satellite to cable distribution system to deliver broadband Internet service in Asia. It was also actively involved in the investment and development of the Cyberport, an information infrastructure project initiated by the Hong Kong government to create a strategic cluster of information technology and Internet service companies and a critical mass of professional talent in Hong Kong.

Being one of the first companies to invest in Mainland China, Cheung Kong was also the most successful. Its PRC portfolio included properties, infrastructure, ports and retail projects. Through their philanthropic activities and extensive business dealings, the Li family was generally recognized to enjoy good *"Guanxi"* (the Chinese term for personal network) with different levels of the PRC government.

Hutchison and Cheung Kong recently announced the establishment of two other internet-related projects focused on the development of the groups' overall e-commerce ability. One was an alliance between Hutchison and *priceline.com*. The other one was *iBusinessCorporation.com*, a joint venture between Cheung Kong, Hutchison, Hong Kong and Shanghai Banking Corporation (HSBC) and Hang Seng Bank.[10]

Schumann and Handel

Schumann and Handel were engaged in the provision of management consulting services and owned and managed by a group of consultants with extensive experience in the planning and development of projects in China, such as the Beijing Oriental Plaza, a US$2 billion investment by Cheung Kong. The consultants helped Tom to secure the content provision and license agreements with various PRC partners. Schumann held 23.75 per cent of Tom while Handel had a 14.25 per cent stake.

THE SHARE OFFERING

The planned share offering would float 15 per cent of Tom, a total of 428 million shares excluding the over-allotment option[11] on the recently established Growth Enterprise Market (GEM)[12] of the Hong Kong Stock Exchange (see Exhibit 3). The offer price of the common shares would be between $1.48 and $1.78 for total net proceeds of about $640 million (see Exhibit 3). The final offer price would be set by the underwriters at the end of the application period and would depend on the strength of the interest shown for the Tom issue. The proceeds would be used for capital expenditures, promotion and marketing activities, development of the e-commerce business, strategic investments and general working capital (see Exhibit 4).

---

[10]Total assets of HSBC in 1999 were US$559.2 billion. Hang Seng Bank is a member of the HSBC Group with total assets of HK$442 billion.

[11]Over-allotment up to an aggregate of 64,200,000 additional shares could be exercised at the discretion of the underwriters.

[12]GEM was established by the Stock Exchange of Hong Kong in 1999 to accommodate companies with high investment risks and were targeted at professional and informed investors. Companies listed on GEM were not required to have a track record of profitability or forecast of future profitability. By the end of 1999, seven companies were listed on GEM which raised an aggregate of $1.6 billion. In January 2000, daily trading volume averaged $83 million. Total market capitalization of the GEM stocks reached $11 billion by the end of January.

Placing

Ninety per cent of the 428 million offered shares, or 385.2 million shares, would be placed with professional institutional investors, qualifying subscribers and certain employees and executive directors of Tom at the offer price. Professional investors included brokers, dealers, fund managers in Hong Kong, Europe and other jurisdictions outside the United States. Allocation would be based on several factors, including the level of demand and whether or not investors would likely buy further shares, or hold or sell their shares after the listing.

Ten thousand seven hundred Hong Kong residents, registered as subscribers of Tom's Internet services and selected by Tom, would be qualifying subscribers, each entitled to subscribe to 2,000 shares at the offer price. Qualifying subscribers were generally individuals who had visited Tom's Web site and joined on-line as a Tom member.

Up to one per cent of the offer shares would be offered by Tom to certain employees and executive directors of Tom at the offer price.

Public Offering

Forty two million eight hundred thousand shares representing 10 per cent of the shares being offered would be for public subscription. Applicants would be required to pay, on application, the maximum offer price of $1.78 per share, in addition to a brokerage and stock exchange transaction levy. Allocation of public offer shares would be based on the level of application. Shares would be allocated on a pro-rata basis and could involve balloting if the shares were heavily over-subscribed, a norm in Hong Kong for such high-profile IPOs. Already, there was speculation that Tom could break the 1,200 times over-subscription record held by Beijing Enterprise Holdings that had its IPO on the Hong Kong Stock Exchange in 1997 (see Exhibit 5). Funds accompanying an application would be held for about a week until the application was deemed successful. If an application was not successful, payment for the shares would be refunded without interest to the unsuccessful applicant. In addition, if the issue was priced at less than the specified maximum, the difference between the final offer price and maximum offer price would also be refunded to successful applicants.

Waivers

The GEM Listing Rules required the initial management shareholders of a new issuer not to dispose of their interests for a period of two years from the listing date, which was referred to as the moratorium period. A moratorium period was implemented to ensure commitment by the initial management and significant shareholders to the growth of the company. However, as a result of an application made on behalf of Tom, the Hong Kong Stock Exchange had granted an adjustment in the moratorium period applicable to Easterhouse and Romefield, which together held 48.4 per cent of the issued share capital of Tom after the IPO, to be reduced to six months.

Tom had also applied for and was granted a waiver regarding the number of shares that it could issue to its employees in a Stock Option Scheme. Tom was allowed to increase the Stock Option Scheme limit from the regular 10 per cent up to 50 per cent of authorized shares.

THE INTERNET IN GREATER CHINA

Emerging economies in Asia had always been among the most aggressive in investing in new technologies. According to International Data Corporation (IDC), a global leader in information technology analysis, the number of Internet users worldwide would grow from approximately 155.6 million at the end of 1998 to 526 million by the end of 2003, while the user base in Asia (including Japan) would increase from 24 million to 155 million over the same period, a compound annual growth rate of 45.4 per cent. The Internet explosion was supported by a progressive penetration of computers and peripherals. The PC penetration rate in Asia was 1.3 per cent in 1998 and expected to reach 5.3 per cent in 2003.

Tom believed that the substantial growth in the number of Internet users and Web sites was fuelling the expansion of two key Internet business areas: on-line advertising and e-commerce. IDC estimated that worldwide e-commerce revenues would grow from US$48.4 billion as of the end of 1998 to US$1.3 trillion by 2003, representing 93.3 per cent cumulative annual growth rate (CAGR). Over the same period, Asian on-line spending would grow at 104 per cent CAGR, reaching US$118.4 billion in 2003.

A lot of attention had been focused on the adoption of the Internet in the PRC, but little verified industry data was available. China Internet Network International Center, an institution under the PRC Ministry of Information, estimated that at the end of 1999, Internet penetration in the PRC was about 0.74 per cent.[13] Some of the most popular PRC portals, *Sina.com*, *163.com* and *Sohu.com*, reported page views[14] per month ranging from 210 million to 399 million. According to IDC, e-commerce spending would grow from US$43 million in 1999 to US$6.5 billion by 2003. However, according to The New York Times, China's on-line advertising industry only generated US$12 million in 1999, while according to AC Nielsen, a leading market research firm, advertising expenditures on traditional media was US$4.1 billion.

Besides the infancy of the Internet in PRC, it was also not clear what policies the PRC government would adopt to develop the Internet. It had from time to time halted the distribution of information over the Internet that it believed to be socially destabilizing by blocking Web sites maintained outside of China. Currently, the Internet sector was off-limits to foreign investment, even though it was expected to gradually open up. Foreign investors,[15] such as Tom, had been trying to participate through content provision agreements. In addition, within the PRC, access to the international gateway was controlled by the government's backbone. Tom also relied on this backbone and China Telecom, the state-owned monopoly in the PRC, to provide data communications capacity and depended upon the PRC government to establish and maintain a reliable Internet infrastructure.

THE VALUATION CHALLENGE

Valuing these high-growth, high-uncertainty, high-currently-unprofitable Internet firms had been a challenge, to say the least. Some practitioners had even described it as a hopeless one.[16] To be more precise, the real challenge had been to justify the incredibly high values that the market had awarded these dot-coms when many of them were simply producing interesting concepts instead of earnings. For example, in 1999, Amazon had a loss of US$720 million with revenues exceeding US$1.6 billion.

Calculating the Implied Average Revenue Growth Rates

After identifying and studying 133 publicly traded Internet companies with market capitalization over US$100 million, Anthony Perkins and Michael Perkins summarized their findings in a book called "The Internet Bubble." Based on their assumptions of how the Internet industry would turn out to be in the future, they found that the current share prices implied extremely aggressive revenue growth rates in the next five years for most Internet companies.

Assumptions[17]

The Perkinses' approach assumed the Internet companies would experience a period of hyper-growth for a limited time period, such as the next five years, during which time revenue growth could be phenomenal.

---

[13]Based upon a population of 1.2 billion.

[14]Page views were a commonly used statistic for measuring Web site activity. One page view was recorded each time a single page on a Web site is viewed. Another statistic used was called a "hit". One hit was counted each time a user accesses a different file on a Web site. Each page viewed on a Web site might contain many such files, so a single page view could account for multiple hits.

[15]The PRC government classified and treated investment from Hong Kong, Taiwan and Macau as foreign investments.

[16]Driek Desmet et al, "Valuing dot-coms," *McKinsey Quarterly*, Number 1, 2000.

[17]Source: www.redherring.com/internetbubble/

After that time, growth would diminish to more normal levels, profits would be achieved and the stock would be valued in more traditional ways. The Perkinses assumed that by the end of the hyper-growth period, the average P/E ratio would be in the range of 20 to 40 times and the net profit margin would be in the normal range experienced by traditional businesses, between five and 15 per cent (see Exhibit 10).

The Perkinses further assumed that investors in Internet companies would expect a return on capital of 15 to 25 per cent. This assumption was based on examining the betas of more traditional technology companies. By applying the forward-looking discount rate, the future market capitalization of Internet companies in five years could be derived. For example, the market capitalization of Amazon in the second quarter of 1999 was US$17.1 billion. If a 20 per cent required rate of return was assumed, Amazon would need to grow to a market capitalization of US$42.6 billion in June 2004 in order to generate the return required by investors.

Because most Internet companies used stock options in employee remuneration, the Perkinses further assumed a dilution in the equity base of five per cent. In the case of Amazon, the market capitalization would need to grow to US$44.7 billion.

Using a P/E ratio of 40 times and a net profit margin of five per cent, earnings and revenue of Amazon would need to reach US$1.1 billion and US$22.3 billion respectively in five years. By comparing the future revenue to Amazon's past 12-month revenue of US$816.3 million, revenue growth in the next five years would have to achieve a cumulative annual growth of 94 per cent.

The Perkinses categorized 133 Internet companies into commerce, content, enabling services, enabling software and enabling telecom services. Based on stock data and revenue data as of second quarter 1999, they calculated the average Internet company in the set would need to generate revenue growth of approximately 80 per cent every year for the next five years (see Exhibit 6 for selected companies from the Perkins analysis).

Other Valuation Approaches

Lau realized that investment professionals used a variety of other valuation approaches for Internet companies. The most popular valuation method, the discounted cash flow analysis, required an estimation of future earnings, growth in those earnings, the capital and working capital expenditures required to fuel growth and the company's cost of capital. Analysts often estimated earnings over the next five years and then applied a constant growth rate beyond that period. However, Tom would more than likely experience negative free cash flows in the foreseeable future because of high marketing expenses and high development spending. To deal with these issues, elaborate projections over an extended period of time would have to be made.

A related approach was based on scenario analysis. While it was particularly difficult to determine the one "best guess" of projected cash flows for these types of firms, a variety of free cash flows were projected based on "most likely", "pessimistic," "optimistic" and other possible scenarios. After discounted cash flows were estimated for each of the scenarios, a probability was attached to each in order to estimate a weighted-average current value. Scenario analysis allowed for incorporating a small probability of a large potential value with more realistic (and more probable) possibilities.

Relative valuation was widely used on Internet companies, as most investors who invest in these firms did not do so because of their judgements on intrinsic value, but more on their judgement of relative value, the value of a firm relative to how similar firms were valued by the market at the moment. Multiples such as price-earnings, price-book value, price-sales were some of the most popular. However, because most Internet companies had negative earnings, and their book values did not reflect their earnings power, price to sales (P/S) was most widely used with Internet companies. Exhibit 7 provides information of several U.S. based Internet companies.

Besides the P/S ratio, various new multiples for valuing Internet companies were being introduced. Among them, Price to Monthly Page Views[18] and Price to Unique Users[19] were often used for portals. Monthly Page Views measured the number of pages of a particular Web site accessed by the market, and

---

[18]NetRatings Inc., a subsidiary of AC Nielsen, provided page view information of major Web sites.

[19]Media Metrix Inc. provided unique user information of major Web sites.

Unique Users measured the number of users that the Web site possessed. As portals derived most of their income from advertising, and advertisers pay for the size, quality and frequency of the audience their message reached, the value of portal companies was driven principally, it was argued, by the number of viewers they attracted, much like the traditional media companies.

THE DECISION

Andy decided to start with the cumulative average growth rate approach to examine the revenue growth implied in Tom's current IPO price. Exhibits 8 and 9 provide information on risk free rates and equity risk premiums in Hong Kong and the United States. He agreed that one advantage of this approach was that it was based upon past revenue data, which was readily available. Besides, it avoided the almost impossible task of forecasting future cash flows since Tom, like most Internet companies, had a very short history and immature business models. This approach produced one yardstick, cumulative average revenue growth in the next five years, to assess what an Internet company had to achieve during the hyper-growth stage.

Lau realized that even with the revenue growth data, he still didn't have enough information to decide whether such growth would be attainable. However, by comparing the revenue growth data of Tom with those of other Internet companies, Lau believed that he at least had some indication whether Tom was a relatively good Internet stock to buy at this moment.

The EuroGlobal Fund family had always looked to long term value in choosing its investments. Therefore, Lau knew his decision would be based on Tom's value and its prospects of becoming an industry leader in the budding Internet sector in Asia. However, the temptation to view any IPO as a quick-in and quick-out opportunity was particularly high for Tom. Even if Tom's long term prospects could not justify its offering price, Lau wondered whether the Asian Growth Fund should buy into Tom and benefit from a short term boost in prices while the frenzy for Internet based stocks continued.

Exhibit 1		
INCOME STATEMENT **(For years ending December 31)**		
HK$'000	**1998**	**1999**
Turnover	39,717	51,695
Cost of Sales	(31,051)	(43,492)
Gross Profit	8,666	8,203
Other Revenue	1,160	410
Website/Portal Development Costs	(906)	(29,945)
Software Development Costs	(1,090)	(1,113)
Advertising and Promotion Costs	-	(7,364)
Distribution Costs	(2,837)	(2,861)
Administration Expenses	(22,017)	(31,726)
Amortization of Goodwill	(16,022)	(16,022)
Operating Loss	(33,046)	(80,418)
Finance Costs	(61)	(711)
Loss for the Year	(33,107)	(81,129)
Minority Interests	279	-
Loss Attributable to Shareholders	**(32,828)**	**(81,129)**

Source: Prospectus of Tom.com Limited

Exhibit 1 (continued)
BALANCE SHEET

	As at December 31, 1999 HK$'000
Intangible Assets	288,404
Fixed Assets	25,129
Current Assets	
Receivables and Prepayment	8,843
Cash and bank balance	22,369
	31,212
Current Liabilities	
Amounts due to related companies	8,039
Other payables and accrued charges	29,588
	37,627
Net Current Liabilities	(6,415)
Net Assets	307,118
Deduct:	
Loans From Shareholders	362,877
Net Liabilities	**(55,759)**

Source: Prospectus of Tom.com Limited

Exhibit 2
HEADCOUNT OF TOM.COM LIMITED

	Headcount	
	December 1999	February 2000
Management	11	19
Information technology/Web development	16	47
Finance & Administration	11	16
Sales & Marketing	1	7
Business Development	2	3
Operations/other support staff	8	51
	49	**143**

Source: Prospectus of Tom.com Limited

Exhibit 3

SHARE OFFERING PLAN

	Number of Shares	Percentage
Shares to be issued under the Share Offer	428,000,000	15.0%
Placing Shares	385,200,000	13.5%
Public Offer Shares	42,800,000	1.5%
Shares in issue	2,421,000,000	85.0%
Easterhouse	920,000,000	32.3%
Romefield	460,000,000	16.1%
Schumann	575,000,000	20.2%
Handel	345,000,000	12.1%
PCCW	121,000,000	4.2%
Total Outstanding Shares	**2,849,000,000**	**100.0%**
Mid Point of the offering price per share ($)	1.63	
Market Capitalization ($)	4,643,870,000	
Total Offering Proceeds ($)	697,640,000	
Total Issuing Cost ($)	58,000,000	
Net Offering Proceeds ($)	**639,640,000**	
Over-allotment	104,646,000	

Source: Prospectus of Tom.com Limited

Exhibit 4

USE OF PROCEEDS (US$ millions)

Capital expenditure in relation to technology development and content development for the year ending Dec. 31, 2000	$ 240
Promotion and marketing activities for the year ending Dec. 31, 2000	150
Development of e-commerce business for the year ending Dec. 31, 2000	10
Strategic investments and additional general working capital	240
Total	$ 640

Source: Prospectus of Tom.com Limited

Exhibit 5

OVERSUBSCRIPTION RATIO OF SELECTED COMPANIES LISTED ON THE GEM MARKET OF HONG KONG STOCK EXCHANGE

Listing Date	Company	Subscription Ratio (times)
1999/11/25	China Agrotech Holdings Ltd.	58.7
1999/11/26	Pine Technology Holdings Ltd.	66.0
1999/12/02	SIIC Medical Science and Technology (Group) Ltd.	495.2
1999/12/02	T S Telecom Technologies Ltd.	200.3
1999/12/16	Asian Information Resources (Holdings) Ltd.	394.0
1999/12/17	Qianlong Technology International Holdings Ltd.	312.0
Average		254.4

Source: The official Web site of the Hong Kong Stock Exchange, http://www.sehk.com.hk/

Exhibit 6

IMPLIED REVENUE GROWTH RATE OF SELECTED INTERNET COMPANIES **BASED ON THE PERKINS METHODOLOGY** [1] **(Data as of second quarter 1999)**

($ millions) **Name**	**Market cap**	**Revenue**	**Future revenue**	**Implied CAGR**
Commerce				
Amazon.com	17,100.0	816.3	22,338.9	94%
eBay	20,800.0	75.4	10,869.0	170%
Priceline.com	13,600.0	84.6	7,106.6	143%
Content				
America Online	107,700.0	4,190.0	70,348.0	76%
Lycos	3,660.0	109.4	3,187.5	96%
Yahoo	27,600.0	258.7	24,037.2	148%
Enabling Software				
Broadvision	1,500.0	59.3	653.2	62%
Inktomi	4,460.0	39.9	1,942.1	118%
Enabling Telecom Service				
Earthlink	1,400.0	214.4	914.5	34%
Global Crossing	22,100.0	602.1	14,435.4	89%
MindSpring	1,980.0	154.9	1,293.3	53%

[1]*www.redherring.com/internetbubble/*

	Exhibit 7			
SELECTED INFORMATION FOR U.S. BASED INTERNET COMPANIES **(As of Dec. 31, 1999)**				
	Yahoo!	**Ebay**	**Amazon.com**	**AOL**
Revenue 1999 (US$ Million)	588.6	224.7	1639.8	4777
Revenue 1998 (US$ Million)	245.1	86.1	609.8	3091
	343.5	138.6	1030	1686
Cumulative Revenue Growth in the Past 4 Years	355.9%	745.4%	652.7%	110.5%
Current Assets 1999 (US$ Million)	945.9	459.8	1012.2	1979
Current Debt 1999 (US$ Million)	192.3	88.8	738.9	1725
	753.6	371	273.3	254
Current Assets 1998 (US$ Million)	617.7	97.6	424.3	1263
Current Debt 1998 (US$ Million)	95.9	24.7	161.6	1155
	521.8	72.9	262.7	108
	231.8	298.1	10.6	146
Beta	2.64	2.39	1.63	1.54
Price to Book	33.9	19.1	450.8	19.2
Price to Sales	74.7	60.8	5.8	19.1

Source: Bloomberg. Cumulative revenue growth rate of Ebay is for the past three years.

	Exhibit 8	
	YIELDS **(AS OF FEB. 19, 2000)**	
	Government Debt Yield (%)	
	Hong Kong	**U.S.**
3 month	5.86	5.75
6 month	5.98	6.03
1 Year	6.33	6.23
2 Year	6.70	6.63
3 Year	6.91	n.a.
5 Year	7.19	6.70
7 Year	7.37	n.a.
10 Year	7.65	6.49
30 Year	n.a.	6.19

Source: Bloomberg.

Exhibit 9

RETURN AND P/E OF S&P 500 INDEX, NASDAQ INDEX AND HANG SENG INDEX **(1995-1999)**

	S&P 500	**NASDAQ**	**Hang Seng Index**
Total Return (%)			
1999	20.9	86.0	72.7
1998	28.3	40.0	(3.0)
1997	33.1	22.1	(17.0)
1996	22.7	23.0	36.9
1995	37.1	40.8	26.8
P/E (1995-1999)			
Hi	34.7	n.a.	28.5
Low	16.0	n.a.	8.1
Average	23.5	n.a.	15.7

Source: Bloomberg.

Exhibit 10

NET INCOME OF SELECTED U.S. COMPANIES FOR FY1999 **(US$ million)**

Company	Revenue	Net Income	Net Profit Margin
Computer-Services			
Microsoft Corp.	19,747.0	7,785.0	39.4%
Oracle Corp.	8,827.3	1,289.8	14.6%
Adobe Systems Inc.	1,015.4	237.8	23.4%
Novell, Inc.	1,272.8	190.8	15.0%
Citrix Systems, Inc.	403.3	116.9	29.0%
Publishing			
Time Warner, Inc.	14,582.0	168.0	1.2%
McGraw-Hill Cos., Inc.	3,729.1	341.9	9.2%
Dow Jones & Co., Inc.	2,158.1	8.8	0.4%
Washington Post Co,	2,110.4	417.3	19.8%
Retail			
Wal-Mart Stores, Inc.	139,208.0	4,430.0	3.2%
K Mart Corp.	33,674.0	518.0	1.5%
Venator Group Inc.	4,555.0	3.0	0.1%
Advertising			
Interpublic Group of Cos. Inc	3,968.7	309.9	7.8%
Omnicom Group, Inc.	4,092.0	285.1	7.0%
Grey Advertising, Inc.	935.2	25.9	2.8%

Source: Mergent Industry Review, Vol. 19, No. 3, Jan. 21, 2000

part eleven

Corporate Acquisitions

CANADIAN OCCIDENTAL PETROLEUM LTD. THE WASCANA ENERGY INC. DECISION

Roger Thomas, vice-president of planning and investor relations, walked into the Calgary, Alberta, boardroom of Canadian Occidental Petroleum Ltd. (CanadianOxy) in preparation for a meeting of the company's acquisitions team. It was March 15, 1997, and the team had been meeting at least daily for weeks to review the proposed takeover bid for Wascana Energy Inc. (Wascana), a Regina, Saskatchewan-based oil and gas producer. On February 12, 1997, rival Canadian oil and gas producer Talisman Energy Inc. (Talisman) had announced an unsolicited $1.8 billion bid[1] for all the outstanding shares of Wascana. The Wascana board had recently rejected the Talisman bid of $18.50 per share of Wascana as inadequate. Further, the board had been soliciting offers for Wascana from other interested parties in the hope of attracting a higher bid. CanadianOxy management had been in talks with Wascana management for several weeks now, and along with several other parties, had gained access to confidential Wascana data by signing a confidentiality agreement. In doing so, the CanadianOxy acquisitions team had gathered the necessary information to value Wascana so that it could determine whether a higher bid than Talisman's was warranted. That analysis was now substantially complete and the officers gathering in the boardroom had to discuss the analysis and decide whether to make an offer for Wascana, and if so, at what price.

---

[1] All figures are in Canadian dollars unless otherwise stated. At the time of the case $1 Cdn = $ 0.7247 US.

Richard Ivey School of Business
The University of Western Ontario **IVEY**   Steve Foerster, Andrew Karolyi and Jerry White prepared this case solely to provide material for class discussion. The authors do not intend to illustrate either effective or ineffective handling of a managerial situation. The authors may have disguised certain names and other identifying information to protect confidentiality.

Thomas noted that all team members were now present, and knowing that the discussions would be long and arduous, he called the meeting to order.

CANADIAN OCCIDENTAL PETROLEUM LTD.

CanadianOxy was a global energy and chemical producer with core producing operations in Canada, the United States and Yemen. The company was divided into three divisions: International Oil & Gas (the largest division), North American Oil & Gas, and Chemicals. The company had a market capitalization of $3.2 billion, ranking it among the top 10 oil and gas exploration and production companies in Canada, and comprised about 4.9 per cent of the Toronto Oil and Gas Producers (TOGP) Index. In operation since 1971, CanadianOxy had net sales of $1.4 billion and net cash flow of $766 million in 1996, versus sales of $1.2 billion and cash flow of $630 million in 1995. Exhibit 1 shows CanadianOxy's recent financial performance. Average production in 1996 was 137,600 barrels (bbl) of oil per day (bbl/d), most outside of Canada, and 244 million (mm) cubic feet (cf) of natural gas per day (mmcf/d). The company had proven and probable reserves on December 31, 1996, of 581 mmbbl (360 mmbbl proven) and 824 billion (b) cf (617 bcf proven).[2] In addition, CanadianOxy held rights to 8.6 million acres of undeveloped land which could be used for exploration. The value of undeveloped land depended upon many factors including time to lease expiry, prices of recent land auctions, and potential for oil and gas deposits. An industry rule of thumb was that undeveloped land was in the $50 to $75 per acre range.

Approximately two-thirds of CanadianOxy's production assets were outside of Canada, specifically in Yemen and the United States. One of the company's strengths was the quality of its assets. However, with the majority of its production located outside of Canada, especially in its Yemen project, it was also seen as a higher risk firm. It was not certain whether production from the Yemen project could be maintained at high levels. Because of this, CanadianOxy stock had been trading at a lower price-to-cash flow multiple than that of comparable Canadian oil and gas producers. In 1996, the total return on CanadianOxy stock was −1.4 per cent, while the TOGP Index jumped 37.2 percentage points and the Toronto Stock Exchange (TSE) 300 Composite Index rose 25.7 percentage points. While these factors, combined with CanadianOxy's healthy cash flow and moderate debt levels, were often ingredients for a firm to be a takeover target, Los Angeles-based Occidental Petroleum Corporation's 30 per cent stake in CanadianOxy made this unlikely.

WASCANA ENERGY INC.

Background and Regulatory Environment

Wascana was also one of Canada's 10 largest oil and gas exploration, production and marketing companies. With a market capitalization of about $1.3 billion in early February, 1997, Wascana represented about 3.4 per cent of the TOGP Index. In contrast to CanadianOxy, Wascana's development and operational activities were mainly in Saskatchewan, although it did have some international exploration sites in Venezuela, Algeria, and the northern United States. The firm's oil assets consisted mainly of heavy oil, which required more processing than lighter oil and thus commanded a lower price.

Wascana began as the Saskatchewan Oil and Gas Corporation (Saskoil) in 1973. The Saskatchewan government created this Crown corporation, or government-owned firm, during a worldwide energy crisis in an effort to capture some of the benefits of oil and gas development for the province's citizens. Saskoil grew quickly, mostly through asset acquisition rather than exploration, but was not very profitable. In 1981, it lost $6 million on sales of $60 million. By 1984, however, it had cash flow of $63 million and profit of $44 million on sales of $161 million,[3] and the province saw an opportunity to partially privatize the Crown corporation. In 1985, 42 per cent of Saskoil was sold to the public, netting proceeds of $110 million, most of

---

[2]In the oil and gas industry, for the purposes of reporting, imperial units are used. Note that "m" refers to thousands, "mm" refers to millions, and "b" refers to billions when followed by either "bbl" (barrels) or "cf" (cubic feet).

[3]The Globe and Mail, February 14, 1997, p.B7

which went to the Saskatchewan government. The legislation which facilitated the privatization restricted individual ownership in the company to 4 per cent of outstanding shares, and permitted foreigners to own only non-voting shares. Through this and subsequent share offerings, the company raised funds to further its growth through acquisition.

By 1990, Saskoil had spent $500 million on acquisitions and accumulated $330 million in debt. The stock price had peaked at $16. Subsequently, gas prices fell and Saskoil's financial performance and stock price fell with them. Between 1991 and 1994, the company lost a total of $100 million, although cash flow growth was healthy. In 1992, with the stock price at $5, the government relaxed the ownership restrictions to 10 per cent per individual and 35 per cent total foreign ownership—eliminating non-voting stock—in an effort to create a wider market for the firm's shares. In 1993, the company changed its name to Wascana, the Cree name for the river that runs through Regina.[4]

In the spring of 1996, the Saskatchewan government announced that, at the request of the Wascana board of directors, it would lift all ownership restrictions on Wascana, effective December 31, 1996. The Wascana Energy Act made it possible for an individual or firm to take over the company, although the act still contained some regulatory restrictions. These covenants required that any purchaser maintain Wascana's head office and staff levels in Regina; that 50 per cent of the directors of Wascana be residents of Saskatchewan; and that Wascana not sell, lease or exchange all or substantially all of its assets, thereby leaving a shell company. The Saskatchewan government still held 5,842,910 shares, or 7.2 per cent of the 80,790,440 shares outstanding at this time.

In anticipation of a possible takeover attempt, the Wascana board had approved a shareholder rights plan (SRP) in November, 1996. Shareholder approval was to be sought at a shareholders' meeting on May 1, 1997. In the event of a "hostile," or unauthorized, takeover attempt, the SRP gave each shareholder not associated with the hostile bid the right to buy additional shares of the company at half the going market value, thereby blocking a hostile bid. Only the board could waive the application of the SRP, although some plans had been successfully challenged in court. The SRP was designed primarily to allow more time for alternative or competing takeover bids.

Finances and Operations

Wascana's financial and operational performance had begun to improve markedly over the previous two years. In 1996, the firm earned $35 million on revenue of $539 million, although $18 million of this was from extraordinary items. In 1995 it had reported earnings of $13.1 million, but this was later re-stated to $0.6 million to reflect an accounting change in the way the company assessed asset impairment. Cash flow was $215 million in 1996 versus $191 million in 1995. For the period 1992 to 1996, cash flow growth per share averaged 11.8 per cent. Detailed financial results are presented in Exhibit 2. Although 1996 represented an impressive turnaround for Wascana, its financial results would have been even better had it not engaged in a hedging program during the year. By using future contracts to lock in the prices at which it would sell future oil and gas production, Wascana lost out on much of the increase in oil and gas prices during 1996. The foregone profit was as much as $50 million by one estimate.[5] Wascana president and CEO Frank Proto defended the hedging program by stating that it was crucial to ensure the company had the internal cash flow necessary to finance the company's aggressive exploration and development program. In the first quarter of 1997, hedging had a substantial positive impact on profits.

Smaller oil and gas companies often hedged commodity prices to reduce the uncertainty of cash flows. Companies that were stable enough to weather cash flow volatility, such as CanadianOxy and Talisman, usually did not engage in hedging activities. For 1997, Wascana had hedged prices on over two-thirds of the company's projected crude oil cash flow. The company had also hedged nine per cent and had fixed sales contracts on an additional 18 per cent of its expected natural gas volumes. Wascana expected this hedging to cost it about $29 million in 1997 if commodity prices followed their projections. The company expected oil

---

[4]Calgary Herald, January 28, 1997, p.F4

[5]"Husky to Look at Wascana", The Financial Post, March 1, 1997, p. 9.

prices to fall only five to 15 per cent over the year, but the hedging would protect against a sharp drop in oil and gas prices that could threaten the company's exploration and development plans. Wascana had hedged minimal volumes of its anticipated 1998 production, which it expected would cost about $2 million in lost revenue if commodity prices met expectations. Wascana also hedged exchange and interest rates, since the company's revenues and expenses fluctuated with changes in these rates. Because a substantial amount of the company's revenue was in U.S. dollars, Wascana borrowed U.S.-dollar-denominated debt and used currency derivatives to hedge a portion of future U.S. dollar revenues. Many oil and gas producers hedged against currency fluctuations.

Wascana had a very successful exploration and development year in 1996, the most active in the company's history. Drilling activity increased 49 per cent over 1995 to $284 million in capital expenditures, and Wascana's reserve replacement rate was 220 per cent of production, reversing a trend which had seen Wascana's reserves decrease an average of 12.1 per cent between 1992 and 1996. The firm added proven plus probable reserves of 71 million barrels of oil equivalent (boe).[6] Production averaged 51,400 bbl/d for the year, and 55,200 bbl/d in the fourth quarter. Natural gas production averaged 200 mmcf/d for the year. About 60 per cent of its total production was in Saskatchewan. As well, the company retained 2.5 million acres of undeveloped land.

THE CANADIAN ECONOMY

The Canadian economy had been experiencing healthy growth in 1995 and 1996, with real GDP growth of 1.4 per cent in 1996 as compared with 2.3 per cent in 1995. Forecasts for 1997 were predicting growth to increase to 3.4 per cent.[7] As well, both the federal and provincial governments had taken significant steps to reduce budget deficits and work towards a balanced budget. In fact, the Province of Alberta had reported a budget surplus in 1996 thanks to a growth rate above three per cent and an unexpected increase in oil and gas royalties. These factors had combined to raise confidence in the Canadian dollar among international investors, and the dollar had been gaining ground against major world currencies, despite the historical low interest rates that were prevailing in the country at the time. The Bank of Canada rate for short-term loans to major institutions was at a 35-year low of 3.25 per cent and 10-year government bonds were yielding 6.5 per cent. These low rates were due largely to stubbornly high unemployment, which was at 9.7 per cent, low inflation, and growth below that of the United States, Canada's largest trading partner and neighbor to the south. Exhibit 3 contains selected Canadian economic data.

The rapidly expanding U.S. economy had raised concerns that inflation, which was already higher in that country than in Canada, might start to gain momentum. This fear had caused the U.S. Federal Reserve to indicate that it might raise interest rates to cool the American economy. Most economists predicted this rise would be at least 0.5 per cent if and when it came. The jitters that this announcement sent through U.S. financial markets was also felt in Canada, since so much of the Canadian economy was linked to exports to its larger neighbor, and because an increase in interest rates in the United States has historically been closely followed by a matching rise in Canada. Bank of Canada Governor Gordon Thiessen had suggested, however, that the relative strength of the Canadian dollar against the U.S. dollar might allow Canada to avoid matching a U.S. rate increase. This could lead to some downward pressure on the Canadian dollar, which had already fallen from $1.347 Cdn/US at the end of January, 1997, to about $1.380 by mid-March. Many economists suggested that this weakness would be short lived, however, with some predicting a $1.32 Cdn/US exchange rate by year end.

TAKEOVER ACTIVITY IN CANADIAN OIL AND GAS INDUSTRY

The Canadian oil and gas sector had experienced a flurry of takeovers in the preceding 18 months. In 1996, industry mergers and acquisitions had totaled $10.1 billion, up from $7.3 billion in 1995. The rapid

---

[6]Natural gas reserves and production are translated into barrels of oil equivalent (boe) as follows: 10,000 cubic feet (cf) of gas is equivalent to one barrel (1 bbl) of oil. For example, 200 mmcf/d is equivalent to 20,000 bbl/d boe.

[7]"Canada", EIU Country Report, The Economist Intelligence Unit, February 4, 1997, p.9.

transaction pace, combined with the simultaneous increase in oil and natural gas prices, drove the market value of company shares up sharply, and the cold winter of 1997 in Canada had pushed share prices even higher. Consequently, the price paid for acquisitions was also increasing rapidly. In 1995, the median price paid per barrel of reserves in an acquisition was $5.05, but in 1996 this increased to $6.17. This price was based on a company's proven reserves and half of its probable reserves. Industry observers wondered how long such a boom cycle could continue, but 1997 was off to a very quick start.[8] Exhibit 4 compares recent mergers and acquisitions in the industry.

There were many factors which combined to create the environment for all this acquisition activity. As mentioned, oil and gas prices had steadily increased, with oil rising $8 bbl Canadian and natural gas prices doubling during 1996.[9] The industry benchmark West Texas Intermediate (WTI) oil averaged $22.01 in 1996, the second highest average since 1985, while gas prices were setting record highs. High prices for both fuels had rarely been seen at the same time.[10] Actual and projected commodity prices are presented in Exhibit 5. As well, the extended low interest rate environment had kept the Canadian dollar low relative to the U.S. dollar, meaning profits on international oil business, which were denominated in U.S. dollars, were even more profitable for Canadian firms when converted back into Canadian dollars. Profitability and cash flow were both at record highs in 1996, and records were set for most wells drilled, most money raised and most equity raised.

These factors meant that the industry was flush with cash looking for a place to invest, which had created a speculative atmosphere. However, a downturn in commodity prices would have a negative impact on the success of any deal. Some observers thought that a more defensive strategy was in order due to some predictions of commodity price weakness; however, stock market investors were not looking for defensive performance; they were looking for high growth. In 1994 and 1995, the share prices of companies that acquired others were generally penalized, but most acquirers were now being rewarded with higher share prices.[11] Shareholder expectations were high due to the overall bull market, and company executives were under pressure to deliver higher cash flow and earnings every quarter. This accomplishment would be difficult unless commodity prices continued to increase, yet failure to keep pace with industry peers would mean a rapid decrease in the value of the company's stock, as impatient investors took their funds elsewhere in search of above-average growth. An undervalued stock price relative to the rest of the sector would leave a firm vulnerable to a takeover attempt.

Acquisition was a faster and possibly less costly way of increasing production and cash flow than bidding for and developing exploration lands. As well, since the smaller, less efficient companies in the industry did not always command as high a price-to-cash flow multiple as the larger players, in some cases large firms could pay a premium for the smaller firm and still deliver value to their own shareholders. Many large firms used stock swaps to finance takeovers of smaller firms in order to take advantage of the difference in cash flow multiples. Acquisitions had become a matter of growing in order to be competitive. Companies were being pressured to become bigger and more efficient as it became evident that only the fittest would survive, while the weak ones would be taken over.[12]

VALUATION OF OIL AND GAS PRODUCTION COMPANIES

The oil and gas sector was segmented into two groups: the upstream segment, which involved oil and gas production and processing (like CanadianOxy, Talisman, and Wascana), and the downstream segment, which involved transportation and refining. The upstream segment relied upon exploration. Oil and gas contained in underground reservoirs was known as resources. Exploration, which involved geologists and geophysicists, focused on finding resources that could be economically produced (reserves). Technological

---

[8]"Canadian Mergers and Acquisitions: Great Expectations", Oil and Gas Investor, April 1997, pp 73-75.

[9]"Takeover Fever Likely to Continue for Integrateds", The Financial Post, Jan.4, 1997, p.15.

[10]"Canadian Mergers and Acquisitions: Great Expectations", Oil and Gas Investor, April 1997, pp 73-75.

[11]Ibid.

[12]Ibid.

advancements were key in the industry. However, before exploration could occur, firms needed to obtain rights from the owner of the property (for example, provincial governments). Firms then leased the property from the owners in return for royalty payments from production, which typically amounted to around 15 to 20 per cent of a firm's revenues. Once drilling occurred, the reservoirs were connected to the surface and these resources were referred to as reserves. The fraction of reserves that was actually recoverable was quite variable depending on reservoir characteristics such as porosity and permeability, the characteristics of the hydrocarbon (light versus heavy oil, sour versus sweet gas), and often depended heavily on technology as well.

Independent reservoir engineers were hired, usually annually, to provide estimates of volumes of economically recoverable reserves and various classifications of oil and gas. Proven reserves were reserves from producing fields, where development activities and historic production levels provided the firm a high degree of confidence in estimating the reserves expected to be produced from the field over its anticipated life. While there were stringent industry definitions for proven reserves, determining reserves levels was not an exact science. Accuracy depended on the experience of the assessing engineers with the geological formations in the field area and with the field itself. Thus, reserves estimates became more accurate as a producing field became older. Probable reserves were based on extensive exploration, but little, if any, production experience, and thus left a lot of room for discretion. Some companies were very aggressive in stating probable reserve levels, while others were more conservative, possibly feeling that overstating reserves did little for the company other than to make it a more attractive takeover target. Because of the discretion involved with probable reserves and the lack of firm evidence to back up claims, production forecasts generally discounted probable reserves by half.

Valuation of oil and gas production companies usually depended upon either comparable analysis or discounted cash flow analysis (or both). Comparable analysis often relied heavily on net cash flow (rather than earnings). This was because some analysts thought that income could be manipulated in many ways (for example, by choosing full cost versus successful efforts accounting) to present favorable-looking results, while net cash flow allowed all companies to be judged on an equal cash footing. For reporting purposes, net cash flow in the oil and gas industry was defined as: net income after-tax plus non-cash expenses (such as depletion, depreciation and amortization), and less any increases in working capital. For comparable analysis purposes, capital expenditures were not deducted from cash flows, since exploration and development projects were not expected, on average, to recover more than the company's cost of capital. Adjustments could be made on an individual basis if a company had a particularly strong or poor exploration and development record or if a company's exploration prospects were especially good. Comparisons among companies were done on a price-to-cash flow basis in much the same way that most firms are compared on a price-to-earnings basis. Companies with short reserve lives generally traded at lower price-to-cash flow multiples.

The discounted cash flow approach involved projecting "free cash flows" after-tax based on the company's current proven and probable reserves, discounted at an appropriate rate. Reservoir engineers who examined a firm's properties estimated reserves, expected production, required capital expenditures, pre-tax cash flows and derived present values based on a variety of discount rates. Analysts also needed to account for undeveloped oil and gas properties which offered the prospect of future production and revenues.

THE TALISMAN OFFER

Talisman Energy Inc. was a senior Canadian oil and gas explorer and producer averaging 171,000 boe/d of production in 1996. The company's major areas of operations were in Western Canada, the North Sea and Indonesia. Proven and probable reserves were at 430 mmbbls of oil and 3,446 bcf of natural gas. Talisman also had 5.9 million acres of undeveloped land. Net cash flow had been $734.4 million in 1996 and $493.4 million in 1995, with cash flow growth per share averaging 40.5 per cent between 1992 and 1996. The company had grown aggressively through acquisition in the previous few years, most notably through the purchase of Bow Valley Energy for $1.8 billion in 1994, and had a market capitalization of $4.6 billion as of February 28, 1997. Talisman represented a 10.8 per cent weighting in the TOGP Index. Company financial statements are presented in Exhibit 6.

Talisman's bid on February 12, 1997, was for all outstanding shares of Wascana and consisted of cash of $18.50 per share, to a maximum of $615 million (representing a maximum 33.2 million shares), or 0.41

shares of Talisman. Given the 80,790,440 shares and 3,247,275 options for common shares outstanding, this placed the equity value of the deal at about $1.55 billion. Talisman would also assume $220 million in Wascana debt. The offer was set to expire March 24, 1997. The offer was conditional on, among other factors, 90 per cent of the outstanding shares being tendered to the deal, and the Wascana board's waiving Wascana's shareholder rights plan. The offer price was a 12.8 per cent premium to Wascana's prior day close of $16.40 per share. While Talisman shares had initially gone up from $44.90 to $45.15 the day the bid was made public on February 12, 1997, they had since fallen to $43.95. It was unclear whether this decrease was connected to the Wascana offer or related to the decrease in oil and gas prices in early March.

Talisman had acquired 1,048,100 shares of Wascana, at an average cost of $15.08, prior to announcing the offer, and had since entered into a lock-up agreement with Altamira Management Ltd. for their 7.5 million shares, for a total of 10.58 per cent of the total company shares outstanding. The lock-up agreement meant that Altamira had agreed to sell the shares owned by its funds only to Talisman at the offer price of $18.50, unless Talisman increased its offer to other shareholders. Talisman had also held lengthy discussions with the Saskatchewan government regarding their shares, and had pledged to abide by the terms of the Wascana Energy Act and maintain current staff levels for at least five years, despite the view of some industry analysts who thought there might be a legal way around the legislation. Talisman also agreed to fund a chair in heavy oil research at a Saskatchewan university for seven years if the deal was consummated. Analysts greeted the Talisman offer with enthusiasm. They saw Talisman as a good fit with Wascana, although Talisman had very little experience with heavy oil production. It would also help Talisman achieve its goal of increased focus on oil, as the purchase would increase Talisman's oil production by 51 per cent and its gas production by 30 per cent.

Wascana's Response

Wascana's response to the offer was less than enthusiastic. Proto indicated that the Wascana board of directors would review the deal, but that they thought Wascana was worth more. Wascana retained petroleum engineering consultants Ryder Scott Company to review the company's assets, and investment bankers RBC Dominion Securities and Goldman Sachs to provide fairness opinions on the offer. On February 26, 1997, the Wascana board approved an employment termination compensation agreement which would pay severance to any employee whose job was eliminated in the 12 months following a takeover. The amount of the compensation would be based on the employee's salary and years of service. On February 28, the board approved the granting of 308,000 share options to senior officers of Wascana at an exercise price of $18.50.

On March 6, 1997, Ryder Scott submitted its report to Wascana. The estimates it contained included a 29 per cent increase in proven and probable reserves, to 219 mmbbl of oil (172 mmbbl proven) and 846 bcf of gas (635 bcf proven). The Ryder Scott report was based on an audit of 80 per cent of Wascana's operating assets, with numbers supplied by Wascana forming the basis for the evaluation of the remaining 20 per cent. Ryder Scott stated that a portion of the assets not reviewed by it had been audited the previous year and that the numbers submitted by Wascana should be within normal engineering and geologic accuracy. Subsequently, on March 10, 1997, both RBC Dominion and Goldman Sachs expressed their opinions that the Talisman offer was financially inadequate to the shareholders of Wascana. The Wascana board then announced it was rejecting the takeover bid and recommending that shareholders not tender their shares to Talisman. The Wascana board did not trigger the SRP, although it retained the right to do so.

Talisman reacted aggressively to this news by questioning the results of the Ryder Scott report and Wascana's 1997 financial and operating projections, which Talisman thought were overly optimistic. Talisman's opinion was that the announcements had been conveniently timed to get more money for Wascana shares. Despite this negative reaction, arbitrageurs[13] had pushed the price of Wascana stock to $19.40 on March 14 in anticipation of a higher offer than Talisman's. Exhibit 7 contains a comparison of Wascana's, Talisman's and CanadianOxy's share prices, as well as the TOGP and TSE 300 indexes. Wascana had begun

---

[13]Arbitrageurs are speculative investors who trade shares of takeover targets on a short-term basis, hoping to profit from small gains in a stock's price.

seeking other parties interested in making an offer for the company almost as soon as the bid was announced. Several large Canadian oil companies had held preliminary talks with Wascana management, including CanadianOxy, Crestar Energy, PanCanadian Petroleum, and Husky Oil.[14] Some of these firms had signed confidentiality agreements to gain access to the Wascana data room, where they could gather important financial and operational data to assess the value of Wascana to their firm. Talisman requested access to these data when it learned that Wascana was seeking other suitors, but had thus far been denied access.

CANADIANOXY NEGOTIATIONS

Prior to the 1990s CanadianOxy was regarded as an intermediate Canadian oil and gas producer. In 1991, the company declared commerciality for a major project in Yemen. In 1993, oil and gas production in Yemen came on-line and the Yemen project became so successful that it dominated the business of the firm. The view internally was that international projects were "the place to be." Stock market participants gave CanadianOxy credit for its move into Yemen and the stock price rose accordingly. The Yemen project generated a large cash flow and profits, which the company needed to determine how best to utilize.

However, some concerns arose that tempered the market's enthusiasm for CanadianOxy. CanadianOxy's focus was not viewed as "international" per se, but rather narrowly focused on Yemen. Furthermore, the 1994 civil war in Yemen caused market participants to be skittish. Consequently, any benefits that CanadianOxy was able to derive from the Yemen project were already priced by the market, yet risk remained a major concern. CanadianOxy's price-to-cash flow multiple was less than four times, considerably below the industry average.

CanadianOxy management were frequently concerned with strategic issues that impacted the firm. In particular, management recognized that the turn-around cycle between development and production was much longer internationally than domestically. Although CanadianOxy had begun revitalizing its Canadian oil and gas business in 1994, it was recognized that the company needed to do something different and significant in order to rebalance its portfolio. Consequently, CanadianOxy recognized it needed to make an acquisition.

CanadianOxy had been eyeing Wascana as a potential takeover target for several months, but did not want to be the first one to make a bid, as they were not prepared to be hostile bidders and had concluded that there were inherent disadvantages to doing so. Instead, in December, 1996, after CanadianOxy's board of directors had approved, in principle, an acquisition bid, CanadianOxy retained investment bankers ScotiaMcLeod Inc. to advise it on any potential transaction, and started accumulating Wascana stock. CanadianOxy now held 3,349,500 shares, or 4.15 per cent of the total outstanding, at an average cost of $16.25. CanadianOxy was first contacted by Wascana on February 19, 1997, regarding making a friendly takeover offer, and readily expressed interest. Between March 4 and March 9, CanadianOxy and ScotiaMcLeod representatives made several visits to the data room Wascana had set up at its Calgary office. There they gathered the information necessary to confirm their valuation of Wascana and gathered forecasts of Wascana's financial performance. This information, which is presented in Exhibit 8, also shows how Wascana's projected results would vary with changes in various economic factors. In addition to reviewing the information gathered, however, Thomas and his team had been impressed by the Wascana team that they had dealt with, and had determined that the cultures of the two firms would mesh well.

There were many factors to consider in deciding whether and how much to offer for Wascana. Any offer would have to be perceived as superior to the Talisman bid in order to entice investors to sell their shares to CanadianOxy instead. It would also have to be high enough to discourage a higher bid from a competitor, as several others had access to the same data, and Talisman might persuade Wascana to allow access to the data room if Wascana thought a better offer would be forthcoming. Yet any deal made must also produce a benefit for CanadianOxy shareholders. Some market comparables used in the evaluations are presented in Exhibit 9.

To complicate matters, even the decision to make a bid was an important one, since if CanadianOxy did bid, the company would incur legal, financial and advisory fees whether the bid was successful or not. As

---

[14]The Financial Post, March 1, 7, 15 and April 24, 1997.

well, the bid process would consume senior executives' resources and time that they could expend on other projects. The company's chief financial officer Victor Zaleschuk was confident that CanadianOxy could arrange the financing necessary for a takeover through either bank debt or a bond issue. CanadianOxy had an A+ rating from the Canadian Bond rating service which would allow it to issue debt at approximately 50 basis points above comparable government of Canada debt.[15] However once the company engaged for a bid, this financing arrangement would require payment of a facility fee, or fee to set up a financing arrangement, whether the arrangement was used or not. While the company had already incurred some expenses in examining and analyzing Wascana's financial and operational data, the company had also purchased Wascana shares at a price several dollars below the Talisman bid price and stood to gain on the price appreciation regardless of the outcome. CEO David Hentschel wanted to make sure that the decision to continue in the bid process was in the best interest of CanadianOxy shareholders and Thomas's team would also have to be prepared to discuss this point with Hentschel and Zaleschuk.

The bid process was not entirely number oriented, however. There were significant political ramifications concerning the Saskatchewan government's holdings. Talisman appeared to have won initial support from the Saskatchewan government in part from the promises contained in its bid and, thus, CanadianOxy would also have to gain this approval if it wanted to ensure that its bid would be successful. Thomas and other executives at CanadianOxy were also concerned that Wascana be a good strategic fit. Including Wascana's production, CanadianOxy production would be 264 mboe/d of oil, with 115 mboe/d in Canada, making the company one of the top three producers in Canada. The steadier cash flow that could result from such a union could help ensure sufficient funds for future development projects in Canada and abroad, a goal CanadianOxy had been looking to achieve. Another potential source of synergy was that many of CanadianOxy's exploration and production lands in Saskatchewan bordered on Wascana lands, which might provide some efficiencies in exploration, development and production. CanadianOxy also had expertise in heavy oil production. Nevertheless, Zaleschuk also knew that acquiring a company the size of Wascana could hurt short-term earnings. He had estimated this cost could reduce 1997 earnings by up to $0.50 per share.[16]

Another concern was a cultural one: CanadianOxy was a fairly conservative firm with a tradition of growing slowly and was not viewed as being as aggressive in terms of acquisitions as other firms such as Talisman. As well, a major concern was whether the potential acquisition would be recognized by market participants as a fix to some of CanadianOxy's strategic concerns and result in a higher price-to-cash flow multiple.

In addition to determining what price to offer for Wascana, management also had to determine how to structure the deal. CanadianOxy could offer all cash, a stock swap, or a combination of the two as Talisman had offered. There were implications for different investors for each of the alternatives. It was difficult to know which option the majority of Wascana shareholders would prefer, and which options were possible considering the size of the deal and the need to maintain the financial integrity of CanadianOxy. While there were many complicated factors to consider, Thomas knew that a decision must be made within the next few days, as Wascana was actively soliciting bids from other suitors.

---

[15]It was estimated that Talisman (A rated) and Wascana (B++ rated) faced spreads of 100 and 150 basis points, respectively. A basis point was 1/100 of a per cent.

[16]"Wascana", The Globe and Mail, Mar 19, 1997, p. B1.

Exhibit 1

CANADIAN OCCIDENTAL FINANCIAL STATEMENTS
(millions of dollars, except per share data)

Consolidated Statement of Operations
(year ended December 31)

	1996	1995	1994
Revenues			
Net Sales	$ 1,362	$ 1,180	$ 1,015
Profit from Disposition of Assets	18	23	28
Interest and Other Income	18	25	14
	1,398	1,228	1,057
Expenses			
Cost of Sales	395	376	365
Selling, Administrative and Other Operating	74	75	66
Depreciation	91	84	71
Depletion and Amortization	345	342	279
Exploration	119	49	42
Interest, Net	55	62	73
	1,079	988	896
Income Before Income Taxes	319	240	161
Provision for Income Taxes	129	99	65
Net Income	$ 190	$ 141	$ 96
Net Income per Share	$ 1.40	$ 1.05	$ 0.72
Dividends per Share	$ 0.30	$ 0.22	$ 0.19

Source: Canadian Occidental Annual Report, 1996.

Exhibit 1 (continued)		

Consolidated Balance Sheet
(as of December 31)

Assets	1996	1995
Current Assets		
Cash and Short-term Investments	$ 109	$ 45
Accounts Receivable	242	205
Income Taxes Receivable	4	16
Inventories and Supplies	62	53
Pre-paid Expenses	11	13
Total Current Assets	428	332
Property, Plant and Equipment	1955	1882
Deferred Charges and Other Assets	21	37
Total Assets	$ 2,404	$ 2,251
Liabilities and Shareholders' Equity		
Current Liabilities		
Accounts Payable and Accrued Liabilities	$ 270	$ 237
Income Taxes Payable	7	-
Accrued Interest Payable	11	10
Dividends Payable	10	8
Total Current Liabilities	298	255
Long-term Debt	572	674
Deferred Income Taxes	197	183
Dismantlement and Site Restoration Allowance	117	113
Other Deferred Credits and Liabilities	53	56
Minority Interest	44	40
Shareholders' Equity		
Common Shares	314	294
Contributed Surplus	14	14
Retained Earnings	715	566
Cumulative Foreign Currency Translation Adjustment	80	56
Total Shareholders' Equity	1123	930
Total Liabilities and Shareholders' Equity	$ 2,404	$ 2,251

Source: Canadian Occidental Annual Report, 1996

Exhibit 2	

WASCANA ENERGY FINANCIAL STATEMENTS
(millions of dollars, except for per share amounts)

Consolidated Statement of Operations
(year ending December 31)

	1996	1995 (restated)
Revenue	$ 539.3	$ 485.7
Royalty expense	117.0	90.8
Operating and administrative expense	166.1	162.4
Restructuring expense	5.4	11.6
Interest expense	17.4	16.4
Depletion, depreciation, and amortization	141.1	141.5
Exploration expense	43.7	47.2
Gain (loss) on property dispositions	4.5	(1.4)
Earnings before taxes	53.1	14.4
Capital and large corporation taxes	18.5	13.8
Earnings	$ 34.6	$ 0.6
Earnings per share - basic	$ 0.43	$ 0.01
- fully diluted	$ 0.41	$ 0.01

Consolidated Balance Sheets
(as of December 31)

	1996	1995 (restated)
Assets		
Current assets		
Accounts receivable	$ 188.5	$ 182.1
Inventories and prepaid expenses	27.6	26.5
	216.1	208.6
Plant, property and equipment	831.2	713.5
Total Assets	$ 1,047.3	$ 922.1
Liabilities		
Current liabilities		
Accounts payable	$ 220.2	$ 192.2
Current portion of long-term debt	-	2.5
Long-term debt	244.8	185.2
Other liabilities	27.6	26.5
Total Liabilities	$ 492.6	$ 406.4
Shareholders' Equity - Share capital	$ 573.4	$ 569.0
- Retained Earnings	(18.7)	(53.3)
	$ 554.7	$ 515.7
Total Liabilities and Shareholders' Equity	$ 1,047.3	$ 922.1

Source: Wascana Annual Report, 1996

Exhibit 3
SELECTED CANADIAN ECONOMIC DATA

	1995	**1996**	
Real GDP Growth %	2.3	1.4	a
Exports US$ billion	189.9	213.3	a
Imports US$ billion	167.5	178.8	a
Current Account US$ billion	-8.7	3.4	a
Consumer Price Inflation %	2.1	1.6	
Exchange Rate avg. ($CAD/$1USD)	1.37	1.36	
Bank of Canada Rate % avg.	7.24	4.67	
Government of Canada 30-year bond rate % avg.	8.17	7.23	
Population (million)	29.6	30.1	

Sources: EIU Country Report, February 4, 1997; Datastream International.

Notes: (a) EIU estimate.

Average Annual Returns in Canadian Capital Markets: (1924 - 1994)

	Geometric Average	**Arithmetic Average**
Treasury Bills	5.01	5.11
Long-term Government of Canada Bonds	5.51	5.84
Inflation Rate	3.19	3.29
Common Shares	10.11	11.79

Source: Laurence Booth, "On Shaky Ground", Canadian Investment Review, Spring, 1995.

Exhibit 4

RECENT OIL AND GAS MERGER AND ACQUISITION TRANSACTIONS

Asset Value (C$ millions)	Buyer	Acquisition	Reserve Value (1) per Proven BOE ($)	Reserve Value per Proven + Probable BOE ($)	Price to Trailing Cash Flow	Premium (2) (%)
$ 104	HCO Energy	Chancellor Energy Resources	6.24	4.26	2.9x	-6.9
25	Stampeder Exploration	Independent Energy	7.07	4.06	7.4x	37.9
123	Tarragon Oil and Gas	Strike Energy	8.21	5.85	5.8x	0.1
787	Petro-Canada	Amerada Hess Canada	7.91	5.77	6.9x	Private
250	Gulf Canada Resources	Pennzoil Canada	5.84	N/A	N/A	Private
80	Barrington Petroleum	Sherritt Energy	N/A	4.05	N/A	Private
90	Crestar Energy	Petrostar Petroleums	10.97	7.75	11.8x	-3.6
168	Morgan Hydrocarbons	International Colin	4.99	4.43	4.0x	4.6
132	Stampeder Exploration	Ballistic Energy	6.54	5.26	4.4x	17.6
712	Canadian Natural	Sceptre Resources	6.43	4.51	4.9x	27.1
105	Northrock Resources	Inland Oil & Gas	10.74	6.20	N/A	Private
240	Poco Petroleums	Gardiner Oil and Gas	8.44	6.58	7.7x	24.3
539	Stampeder Exploration	Morgan Hydrocarbons	6.21	4.74	4.98x	3.1
56	Sunalta Energy	Paloma Petroleum	5.26	4.12	3.9x	6.7
135	Pembina Resources	Serenpet Inc.	7.72	4.94	5.6x	18.9
53	Chauvco Resources	Tidal Resources	6.99	3.88	8.3x	20.6
83	Jordan Petroleum	Transwest Energy	4.07	3.43	3.0x	-8.4
45	Encal Energy	Morrison Petroleums (Property)	5.54	4.27	N/A	Private
705	Canadian 88 Energy	Morrison Petroleums Ltd.	10.62	9.02	8.1x	18.8
$4,434		AVERAGE	$7.21	$5.17	6.0x	11.5

Source: *Scotia Capital Markets*

Notes: (1) - Reserve value is market capitalization plus long-term debt, working capital deficiency and other net liabilities.
(2) - Premium of the acquisition price over the closing market price the day prior to the initial bid.

Exhibit 5
ACTUAL AND PROJECTED COMMODITY PRICES

	Actual	Projected	
	1996	1997	1998
Oil - WTI (US$/bbl)	$22.01	$20.40	$20.51
Oil - Wascana Average Price* (Cdn$/bbl)	20.31	19.46	19.97
Gas - NYMEX (US$/mmbtu)+	$2.55	$2.03	$2.10
Gas - AECO (Cdn$/mmbtu)	1.32	1.63	1.88
Gas - Wascana Average Price* (Cdn$/mcf)	1.50	1.65	1.82

Notes: (+) - mmbtu = million British thermal units of natural gas
(*) - The Wascana average price is the price resulting from hedging. The forecast predicts hedging losses of $29 million in 1997 and $2 million in 1998.

Source: Wascana Directors' Circular, March 10, 1997.

Exhibit 6

TALISMAN ENERGY FINANCIAL STATEMENTS

Consolidated Statement of Income (millions of dollars, except per share figures)	Year ended December 31, 1996	Year ended December 31, 1995
Revenue (net of royalties)	$ 1,212.8	$ 899.2
Expenses		
Operating	299.5	245.0
General and administrative	56.3	56.6
Depreciation, depletion and amortization	420.6	369.1
Dry hole and exploration expense	128.9	76.3
Interest on long-term debt	68.7	86.4
Other (net)	(26.2)	(30.3)
	947.8	803.1
Income before Taxes	265.0	96.1
Taxes		
Income taxes - current	51.3	10.8
Income taxes - deferred	84.3	50.5
Petroleum revenue tax	34.5	-
	170.1	61.3
Net Income (from continuous operations)	$ 94.9	$ 34.8
Net Income per Common Share	$ 0.91	$ 0.36
Cash Flow per Common Share	$ 7.07	$ 5.11

Consolidated Balance Sheet (millions of dollars)	December 31, 1996	December 31, 1995
Assets		
Current assets	$ 361.7	$ 255.8
Pension and other assets	56.9	51.0
Property, plant and equipment	3,332.6	2,733.5
Total Assets	$ 3,751.2	$ 3,040.3
Liabilities and Shareholders' Equity		
Liabilities		
Current liabilities	$ 337.7	$ 224.9
Other liabilities	107.4	78.9
Long-term debt	898.7	906.0
Deferred taxes	313.4	204.2
	1,657.2	1,414.0
Shareholders' Equity		
Share capital and contributed surplus	1,863.6	1,490.8
Retained earnings	230.4	135.5
Total shareholders' equity	2,094.0	1,626.3
Total Liabilities and Shareholders' Equity	$ 3,751.2	$ 3,040.3

Source: Talisman Energy Inc. Annual Report, 1996.

	Exhibit 7				
	STOCK PRICE COMPARISON				
Date	Wascana Energy	Talisman Energy	Canadian Occidental	TSE 300 Index[1]	TOGP Index[2]
1/1/96	$12.88	$27.63	$22.37	4713.50	4794.10
1/1/97	15.80	45.60	22.05	5927.03	6577.16
2/3/97	16.65	47.40	25.35	6140.93	6973.51
2/4/97	17.00	47.20	25.15	6145.41	6895.28
2/5/97	17.00	46.25	24.95	6112.41	6805.12
2/6/97	17.25	44.80	24.20	6071.89	6607.20
2/7/97	16.75	44.40	23.25	6101.74	6523.84
2/10/97	16.10	43.20	23.15	6081.27	6331.16
2/11/97	16.40	44.90	23.40	6126.92	6425.59
2/12/97	16.95	45.15	23.40	6165.38	6440.56
2/13/97	19.00	46.25	24.10	6225.78	6568.83
2/14/97	19.10	46.30	24.10	6214.24	6590.21
2/17/97	19.10	46.30	24.55	6217.60	6608.40
2/18/97	19.00	46.45	24.40	6238.22	6599.34
2/19/97	18.90	45.80	24.15	6248.86	6506.90
2/20/97	18.60	44.15	23.65	6205.07	6389.06
2/21/97	18.75	45.65	23.80	6226.95	6443.09
2/24/97	18.85	46.00	24.10	6242.52	6448.74
2/25/97	18.55	45.05	23.65	6247.78	6376.68
2/26/97	18.50	45.40	23.40	6201.43	6369.86
2/27/97	18.60	44.75	23.40	6187.46	6351.14
2/28/97	18.45	44.45	23.10	6157.84	6233.96
3/3/97	18.40	44.30	22.85	6145.98	6214.07
3/4/97	18.55	44.95	22.85	6155.05	6282.36
3/5/97	18.90	44.50	22.75	6203.12	6319.11
3/6/97	18.70	44.15	22.70	6214.73	6304.29
3/7/97	18.75	44.45	22.50	6268.39	6397.69
3/10/97	18.95	44.25	22.70	6332.87	6432.57
3/11/97	19.10	43.90	22.95	6305.46	6443.49
3/12/97	19.15	44.20	22.90	6257.21	6414.83
3/13/97	19.40	44.00	22.80	6165.86	6323.13
3/14/97	19.40	43.95	23.45	6197.71	6375.23

Notes: (1) - Toronto Stock Exchange Composite Index   (2) - Toronto Oil and Gas Producers Index

Source: Datastream International.

	Exhibit 8

WASCANA FINANCIAL FORECASTS

Consolidated Statements of Operations Forecasts
(millions of dollars except for per share amounts)

	1997	1998
Revenue		
Operating	$653	$866
less Royalties	(131)	(156)
	522	710
Expenses		
Operating	152	184
General and Administrative	36	38
Depletion, Depreciation, and Amortization	161	210
Exploration	61	57
Interest	21	22
	431	511
Earnings Before Taxes	91	199
Capital and Large Corporation Tax	19	23
Current Income Taxes	-	33
Deferred Income Taxes	23	24
Earnings	$49	$119
Earnings per Share - basic	$0.61	$1.46
Earnings per Share - fully diluted	$0.60	$1.43
Change in Working Capital Balances	(7)	(9)

Note: Cash flow sensitivity - (millions of Canadian dollars)

	1997	1998
Oil price change - US $1.00 per bbl of WTI	$8.8	$16.5
$1.00 per bbl change in heavy oil differential	5.9	6.5
Gas price change - $0.10 per mmcf	5.2	5.4
Royalties - change of 1%	5.4	5.1
$0.01 change in US/Cdn exchange rate	2.5	3.1
Interest rate - change of 1%	0.5	1.1

Source: Wascana Directors' Circular, March 10, 1997.

Exhibit 9

ANALYSIS OF OIL AND GAS MARKET COMPARABLES

	Share Price[1] ($)	Price/1996 E[2] CFPS (times)	Price/1997E CFPS (times)	Total BV of Debt/1997E Cash Flow (times)	Asset Book Value per BOE/D of Production ($)	Asset Book Value per BOE of Reserves ($)	Beta
Wascana Comparables							
Crestar	29.75	5.5	5.3	1.3	26,114	8.48	0.95
ELAN	11.80	5.1	4.9	0.7	24,304	6.16	0.85
Poco	13.95	7.4	6.2	1.2	35,646	10.43	1.19
Ranger	13.50	8.0	7.4	0.5	33,000	9.99	1.11
Rigel	14.90	6.2	5.8	1.3	28,554	7.38	0.56
Stampeder	8.00	6.9	5.6	1.2	25,709	7.00	1.00
Tarragon	15.15	7.0	5.8	1.3	37,612	7.85	0.87
AVERAGE		6.6	5.9	1.1	30,134	8.18	0.93
Wascana	15.80	6.2	5.3	0.9	20,105	6.19	1.15
CanadianOxy Comparables							
Alberta Energy	32.25	8.7	6.7	1.6	49,375	8.44	0.95
Anderson	17.90	7.1	6.3	1.4	32,369	5.95	1.17
Canadian Natural	38.40	9.4	7.8	1.2	53,865	13.58	N/A
Gulf Canada	11.85	7.0	6.3	3.7	39,823	10.02	1.16
Norcen Energy	31.70	5.7	5.5	1.6	26,547	7.07	0.97
PanCanadian	52.80	7.5	6.9	0.9	31,801	9.68	0.71
Renaissance	49.15	9.6	8.9	0.6	56,005	12.42	1.11
Talisman	48.00	7.3	6.8	1.2	37,783	9.65	1.01
AVERAGE		7.8	6.9	1.5	40,946	9.60	1.01
CanadianOxy	24.30	4.4	4.4	0.8	23,971	7.81	1.14

Source: Scotia Capital Markets (except betas from Bloomberg)

Notes: (1) Closing share price as of January 15, 1997.
(2) - Price to 1996 expected cash flow per share.

UNITED GRAIN GROWERS LIMITED

On February 20, 1997, Alberta Wheat Pools and Manitoba Wheat Pools, two farmer-owned agricultural co-operatives, announced their intention to jointly make a cash offer to purchase all of the shares of United Grain Growers (UGG) for $13.75 per share. Scotia Capital Markets, the long-time financial advisor to UGG, had been called upon to mount a defense to this hostile takeover. On February 14, 1997, in anticipation of a bid, UGG implemented a shareholder rights plan. On February 26, 1997, UGG instructed Scotia Capital markets to create "data rooms," containing non-public operating and financial information for UGG, and contact third parties regarding their interest in UGG.

As part of their response to the takeover bid, UGG also asked Scotia Capital Markets to prepare a "fairness opinion." This would involve a formal review of UGG's business and the terms of the offer. Most importantly, Scotia Capital Markets would have to assess the adequacy, from a financial point of view, of the offer to UGG shareholders.

Scot Martin, head of investment banking and UGG relationship manager for Scotia Capital Markets, met with his team on the evening of March 3, 1997, to finalize their fairness opinion. As he entered the meeting, Martin thought about some important questions. What was UGG worth? Would an acquisition by Alberta Wheat Pools and Manitoba Wheat Pools be in the best long-term interests of UGG shareholders? Would the shareholder rights plan buy UGG enough time to identify other viable alternatives?

Richard Ivey School of Business
The University of Western Ontario

IVEY

Professor Craig Dunbar and Gabriel Vinizki prepared this case solely to provide material for class discussion. The authors do not intend to illustrate either effective or ineffective handling of a managerial situation. The authors may have disguised certain names and other identifying information to protect confidentiality.

UNITED GRAIN GROWERS LIMITED (UGG)

UGG was founded in 1906 and later incorporated in 1911 under a special act of the Canadian Parliament (the "UGG Act"). UGG provided a wide range of goods and services to farmers across Western Canada. In addition, it marketed agricultural commodities domestically and internationally. In 1997, the company competed by offering western Canadian grain and livestock farmers value-added products and services in four distinct but interrelated businesses: grain handling and marketing, crop production inputs, livestock production inputs, and farm business communication and information services (see Exhibit 1).

UGG's principal business was grain handling and marketing, where it acted both as an agent for the Canadian Wheat Board and for its own account. In 1997, UGG received approximately 5.5 million tonnes of grains, such as wheat and barley, and oilseeds, such as canola. It typically received these and other crops at one of its 160 Western Canada elevator facilities, and earned tariffs and other revenues for the handling of the commodities prior to their shipment to domestic and international markets. In 1997, UGG controlled approximately 19 per cent of the elevator storage capacity in Alberta, 12 per cent of the capacity in Saskatchewan, and 20 per cent of the capacity in Manitoba. UGG owned two terminal elevators in Thunder Bay, Ontario, and one in Vancouver, British Columbia, and owned a 16.3 per cent interest in a terminal elevator in Prince Rupert, British Columbia.

THE 1990S: A TIME OF CHANGE

The Canadian Grain Market

From the mid-1950s to the early 1990s, the number of firms engaged in grain handling in Canada dropped from 43 to 17. Also, the number of grain facilities dropped from approximately 2,000 in 1958 to just less than 1,000 in 1992. In 1992, six major private companies dominated the grain-handling industry in Western Canada: Alberta Wheat Pool, Saskatchewan Wheat Pool, Manitoba Pool Elevators (collectively called "the Pools"), Pioneer Grain Company, Cargill Limited and UGG.

The pools were organized on a provincial basis and, for the most part, were confined to performing their core operations within their home province. The pools were farmer-owned co-operatives, formed, on average, 65 years ago. While the Pools achieved market share dominance in each of their respective provinces, their shares had begun to decline. From 1987 to 1992, Alberta Wheat Pool's market share in Alberta dropped from 63 per cent to 62 per cent, Manitoba Pool Elevators' market share in Manitoba dropped from 54 per cent to 52 per cent, and Saskatchewan Wheat Pool's market share in Saskatchewan dropped from 63 per cent to 61 per cent. Besides the Pools, UGG with 16 per cent of Canadian grain deliveries had the largest market share. Pioneer and Cargill had 10 per cent and seven per cent market share, respectively.

Forces of Change

Grain handling and marketing and crop production always had high fixed costs, making scale desirable. In the early 1990s, deregulation and changes to trade barriers would increase the importance of scale. Within Canada, constrained resources of both the federal and provincial governments were expected to lead to changes in policies toward the agricultural sector. A 1989 Government of Canada policy paper, entitled "Growing Together—A Vision for Canada's Agri-Food Industry," argued that the industry needed to become more market oriented, and that government should design its programs so as to encourage more self-reliance. One expected future change, the elimination of rail transportation subsidies, would likely make freight rates more dependent on volume. Only those grain companies with elevator facilities capable of multiple-car loading would be able to take advantage of any volume discounts on freight.

Internationally, the Uruguay Round of General Agreement on Tariffs and Trade (GATT) negotiations, which began in 1986, had yet to conclude. This round of the GATT attempted to introduce its most sweeping trade liberalizing policies to date. Agriculture had historically been exempted from many of the rules covering commodities. The Uruguay Round now addressed agriculture, attempting to find some solutions to the distorting effects that export subsidies and other restrictive programs were having on global trade. A GATT agreement mandating a decrease in the level of export subsidies would likely lead to higher grain export prices. While Canadian firms would appear to have an advantage in a competitive world grain market, given Western Canada's abundance of quality farmland, increased scale would be needed.

As a backdrop to these market changes, new international environmental standards were forcing agribusiness firms to build new warehouses, or to upgrade old ones. The cost would be substantial (approximately $75,000 for each new 1,800 square foot of warehouse space), and many smaller firms were thought to be unwilling or unable to make these kinds of financial commitments.

Combined, these forces were leading to accelerating consolidation in the US$550 billion agricultural chemicals industry worldwide. Surviving firms would need to make substantial capital expenditures to upgrade facilities and expand.

Some firms, including UGG, were also increasing expenditures on research and development (R&D) in an attempt to enhance market share and profitability. UGG, through an intensive R&D program involving alliances with several leading domestic and international breeding organizations, had developed the largest varietal seed program in Western Canada. Future sales were looking very promising. In addition to advances made possible through biotechnology, there had been considerable resources devoted to certified seed development. This was in anticipation of new legislation designed to encourage seed research through the recognition and protection of the breeding company's proprietary interest in new seed varieties. The development of new seed products sold under the Proven® Seed label had provided UGG's crop production services division with a distinct product. From 1990 to 1992, UGG's market share had more than doubled, making it the largest single seed distributor in Western Canada. UGG's continued commitment to R&D as a differentiation strategy would require a substantial amount of capital in the coming years.

UGG's Financial Strategy

The problem facing UGG, as well as its competitors, in the early 1990s was how to finance the heavy capital expenditures that would be needed to better position them for the new competitive environment. The first part of UGG's solution was to hire Scotia Capital Markets (then called ScotiaMcLeod) as an advisor. In 1991, UGG amended its bylaws to allow for the appointment of a non-farmer chief executive officer. What followed were a number of other key additions to senior management positions within the company. The company redefined its mission statement and goals. UGG divested two of its businesses: printing and oilseed processing. Realizing that in order to compete effectively in the anticipated period of deregulation and change, it would need to achieve a stronger and more flexible capital structure, UGG began to transform itself into a public company. During the company's 1992 annual meeting, a plan was ratified to reorganize UGG's capital structure (see Exhibit 2).

On July 15, 1993, UGG issued two million limited voting common shares at $8 per share as part of an initial public offering (IPO) and a secondary offering. Scotia Capital Markets was the lead underwriter for the offering. At the time of the IPO, UGG's board structure was also amended. Farm members would elect 12 directors to the board who had to be members and shareholders of UGG, and shareholders would elect the remaining three directors, who could not be members of UGG. For any fundamental changes to pass a board vote, 75 per cent of the votes had to move in favor of the particular motion.

UGG was able to raise additional public funds on a number of occasions following its IPO, as summarized below. In all transactions, Scotia Capital Markets was the lead underwriter.

Date	Issue	Amount (millions)
April, 1994	Additional new common stock issue	$ 18.0
July, 1995	Securitization program	$300.0
June, 1996	Increased long term debt facility	$ 35.0
November, 1996	Additional new common stock issue	$ 22.0

Of UGG's domestic competitors, only the Saskatchewan Wheat Pool followed UGG's lead and completed an IPO on April 2, 1996. Around the same time, Alberta Wheat Pool members voted against a motion at their annual meeting which proposed that the pool consider going public. Manitoba Wheat Pool has never considered such a motion.

Exhibits 3 and 4 show the recent financial performance of UGG. Exhibit 5 shows UGG's stock perform-ance from its IPO through March 1997. Exhibit 5 also shows the performance of the TSE 300 over the same period and the performance of the Saskatchewan Wheat Pool after its IPO. While UGG's stock lagged behind the TSE 300 up to April 1996, it has since outperformed both the TSE 300 and Saskatchewan Wheat Pool.

ALBERTA WHEAT POOL AND MANITOBA POOL ELEVATORS' BID FOR UGG

Alberta Wheat Pool was a farmer-owned co-operative formed under the Alberta Wheat Pool Act. For the year ending July 31, 1996, Alberta Wheat Pool had sales of $2.1 billion, income from operations of $46.9 million, net income of $28.2 million, total assets of $625.8 million, and 1,366 employees. Alberta Wheat Pool also had 57,000 members, 187 elevator points, and 67 agro-outlets to handle and market grain, seed and oilseeds both domestically and internationally. Manitoba Pool Elevators was a farmer-owned co-operative formed under The Cooperatives Act of Manitoba. For the year ending July 31, 1996, Manitoba Pool Elevators had sales of $1.2 billion, income from operations of $18.7 million, net income of $5.5 million, total assets of $383.2 million, and 692 employees. Manitoba Pool Elevators also had 16,000 members, 124 elevator points, and 75 agro-outlets to handle and market grain, seed and oilseeds both domestically and internationally.

On February 5, 1997, Alberta Wheat Pool and Manitoba Pool Elevators announced that they had acquired 999,700 of the limited voting common shares of UGG through 3339351 Canada Ltd., a company jointly owned by the two Pools (hereafter referred to as Alta-Man). The press release also stated that Alta-Man now owned 1,616,700 shares of UGG, representing 13 per cent of the 12,497,963 issued and outstanding shares. No reference, however, was made to any intention to make an offer to acquire UGG.

On February 13, UGG received a request from Alta-Man for UGG's shareholder lists, pursuant to the pro-visions of the Canada Business Corporations Act. Obtaining a shareholder list was a necessary legal step in any acquisition, as a formal offer to take over a firm, by law, must be mailed to all shareholders. On February 14, Alta-Man announced by press release that it had acquired on February 12 and 13 an additional 255,000 shares of UGG through its advisor, Griffiths McBurney and Partners, increasing its ownership to 14.98 per cent.

On February 20, 1997, Alta-Man publicly announced its intention to make a cash offer to purchase any and all of the issued and outstanding limited voting common shares and associated rights of UGG for $13.75 per share. The offer was set to expire on March 27, 1997. Exhibit 6 shows UGG's stock trading price between January and March 1997.

In its offer to purchase UGG, Alta-Man identified several benefits from the transaction. The purchase of UGG would: (1) improve economic efficiencies; (2) meet the desire of many western Canadian farmers for a modern, efficient co-operative market alternative; (3) retain Canadian ownership in the western Canadian grain industry; (4) produce a co-operative venture capable of competing globally; (5) expand the geographic supply base for specialized grain, special crops, seed and oilseeds, thereby ensuring customer satisfaction during periods of climatic variability; and (6) maximize utilization of existing terminal facilities in Vancouver, British Columbia and Thunder Bay, Ontario.

Alta-Man indicated that it intended to integrate UGG with the operations of the two pools. Effectively, UGG would be taken private, with its shares ultimately being delisted from the Toronto and Winnipeg Stock Exchanges. This would repatriate UGG to its co-operative roots, reversing the decision to be a public com-pany (made five years earlier with 97 per cent approval of UGG shareholders).

UGG's Response to the Alta-Man Offer

The Shareholders Rights Plan

On the evening of February 13, 1997, the day Alta-Man made a request to receive UGG's shareholder lists, the board of directors of UGG adopted a shareholders rights plan. The board was concerned that Alta-Man was mounting a "creeping" take-over bid. The plan was designed, according to UGG, to encourage the fair treatment of shareholders if there were to be an unsolicited takeover bid. Effective 7:00 a.m. (Winnipeg time) on February 14, 1997, one right would be attached to each outstanding common share of UGG. Although the rights plan was effective immediately, the exercise of rights was subject to receipt of applicable regulatory approvals, including approval of the Toronto Stock Exchange. Shareholders would be asked to confirm the rights plan at the next scheduled shareholders meeting.

Should a person acquire beneficial ownership[1] of 15 per cent or more of UGG's outstanding limited voting common shares without complying with the "permitted bid" provisions of the plan,[2] or without approval of the board of directors, a "flip in" event would be deemed to occur. At that time, each right, other than rights held by the acquiring person and related persons, would entitle its holder to purchase 8.5 common shares of the company at a 50 per cent discount to the market price at the time.[3]

The trigger point in most shareholder rights plans is 20 per cent. UGG chose a lower trigger of 15 per cent, in part due to its unique voting structure. As noted previously, 75 per cent shareholder approval was required for fundamental changes to pass a board vote. A shareholder would, therefore, need to own 75 per cent of UGG shares to gain outright control of the firm. A flip side of this structure, however, was that only 25 per cent ownership was required for any party to exert "negative control" (i.e., prevent anyone else from gaining outright control). In practice, an individual shareholder could effectively gain negative control with a lower ownership stake, given the difficulties in obtaining large blocks of shares. The 15 per cent trigger was, therefore, chosen to make it practically impossible for some party to gain outright control of UGG.

UGG was concerned about two issues in the event a flip-in event occurred. First, small investors may not have the resources to exercise their rights. While the rights could be sold on the Toronto Stock Exchange, investors would face transaction costs. To account for this, UGG created a "small shareholder selling and purchasing arrangement" which would allow small shareholders (owners of less than 100 shares) to sell rights at market prices with UGG paying the commission. UGG was also concerned that the market would react negatively to the large cash infusion that would result from the exercise of the rights. It therefore committed to repurchase shares, using a Dutch auction mechanism with the proceeds from the rights exercise.

Other Responses to the Alta-Man Offer

Part of UGG's response to the Alta-Man bid involved legal actions. UGG petitioned the Canadian Competition Bureau to intervene, arguing that the takeover would be anti-competitive and detrimental to farmers. By early March, farmers seemed to be leaning in UGG's favor. On March 3rd, for example, the Western Canadian Wheat Growers Association announced by press release that it would file an objection to the transaction with the Competition Bureau.

On February 26, 1997, UGG's board of directors met with its financial and legal advisors to consider possible courses of action. Scotia Capital Markets was instructed to broadly identify and pursue strategy alternatives to enhance shareholder value. On February 27th, UGG approved the creation of data rooms containing non-public operating and financial information for UGG to which certain third parties, who had entered into confidentiality and standstill arrangements,[4] would be permitted access. At the request of UGG, on March 3, 1997, Scotia Capital Markets began contacting third parties in search of a "white knight" or "white squire" for UGG.[5] The "potential purchaser" list included other Canadian grain elevator companies, U.S. and international agribusiness concerns, fertilizer producers, and any other kinds of companies that might be interested in UGG (commodity trading companies, financial buyers, etc.). Initial firms contacted included Saskatchewan Wheat Pool, Pioneer, ConAgra, Cargill, Archer Daniels Midland, Continental Grain, Bunge, and Pattison Enterprises.

---

[1] Beneficial ownership was defined broadly in the plan. This includes: (1) securities purchased by a person or that person's affiliates or associates; and (2) options to purchase shares by a person or that person's affiliates or associates.

[2] Takeover bids which are: (1) made to all shareholders; (2) remain open for 60 days; (3) provides that no shares will be taken up or paid for unless 50 per cent of the outstanding shares held by shareholders other than the offeror have been tendered to the bid; and (4) the offeror must announce publicly when 50 per cent of shares have been tendered, providing at least another 10 days for other shareholders to tender their shares.

[3] Technically, the UGG plan defined market price as the weighted average trading price of UGG's stock over the 20-day period prior to the flip-in event date.

[4] A standstill arrangement prohibits the party accessing the data room from making further investments in the company for a specified period of time.

[5] A "white knight" is a more acceptable merger partner sought out by the target of a hostile bidder. A "white squire" is a third party, friendly to management, who helps a company avoid an unwanted takeover without taking over the company on its own.

While co-ordinating this white knight or white squire process, Scotia Capital Markets also were asked to provide a "fairness opinion" on the Alta-Man offer. This involved a formal review of UGG's business and the terms of the Alta-Man offer. Most importantly, Scotia Capital Markets would have to assess the adequacy, from a financial point of view, of the offer to UGG shareholders. This would involve a stand-alone valuation of UGG as well as a valuation of synergies.

Martin and his team first determined the stand-alone value of UGG based on a discounted cash flow analysis using five years of financial forecasts provided by management (see Exhibit 7). For valuation purposes, they used a target capital structure of 65 per cent equity-to-capital, a tax rate of 46 per cent, a beta of 1.0, and a market risk premium of 6.5 per cent. In late February 1997, the yield on 10-year Canadian government bonds was 6.20 per cent and the yield on long-term corporate bonds of similar risk to that for UGG was 7.45 per cent. In late February 1997, Scotia Capital Markets estimated that the UGG's net debt (long-term debt less cash) was $161.137 million and the value of UGG's preferred shares was $21.608 million.

Scotia Capital Markets also assessed a stand-alone value for UGG using precedent transactions (see Exhibit 8) and a review of the trading information relating to the common stock of UGG and other similar public companies (see Exhibit 9). They also attempted to determine the value of potential synergies from the Alta-Man transaction and other potential combinations (see Exhibit 10).

Armed with this information, Martin and his team began their meeting. While the immediate task was to finalize the fairness opinion, Martin knew that more issues would have to be discussed. At what price would a sale to Alta-Man be acceptable for UGG management? How would UGG shareholders respond? Could viable alternatives to Alta-Man's offer be identified in a short period of time? Given the complex setting, Martin knew they were all in for a long night.

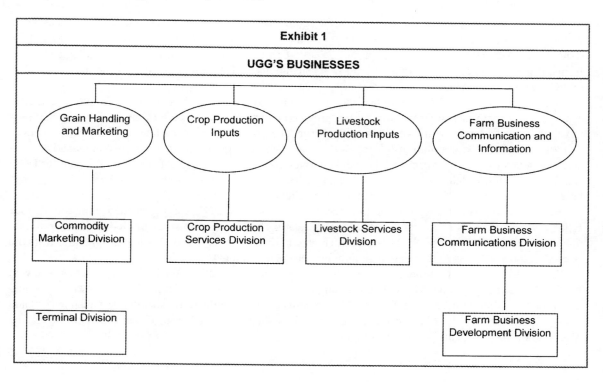

Exhibit 1

UGG'S BUSINESSES

			Exhibit 2

CAPITAL STRUCTURE OF UGG **(Cdn$ million, except share amounts)**			
	Authorized	**Outstanding 31-Mar-93 before the Reorg.**	**Outstanding 31-Mar-93 after the Reorg.**
Debt			
Current Debt:			
Bank Indebtedness.............................	200,000 shs	$ 135.87	135.87
Current Portion of Long Term Debt.........		8.35	5.19
Current Portion of Capital Leases......		0.33	0.33
		144.55	141.39
Long-term Debt:			
Promissory Notes............................		$ 21.44	21.44
Purchase Agreement......................		0.12	0.12
Debentures.................................		7.65	7.65
Capital Leases.............................		0.63	0.63
Patronage Dividend Credits...............		18.75	-
		48.58	29.83
Total Debt:		$ 193.13	171.23
Shareholders' Equity			
Share Capital:			
Class "A" Shares	2,200,000 sh	$ 24.06	-----
		(1,202,750 shs)	
Series "A" Convertible Preferred Shares [1]	1,202,750 sh	-------	$ 24.06
			(1,202,750 shs)
Class "B" (membership) Shares.........	200,000 shs	$ 0.27	
		(53,298 shs)	
Limited Voting Common Shares..........	unlimited		$ 20.51
			(6,849,029 shs)
Retained Earnings...		$ 72.05	$ 72.05
Total Shareholders' Equity................................		$ 96.37	$ 116.61
Total Capitalization..		$ 289.50	$ 287.84

[1] Convertible preferred shares pay $1 dividend per share (cumulative), are convertible on a 1:1 basis and are callable at $24.

Source: United Grain Growers Limited initial public offering prospectus, July 15, 1993.

| | | Exhibit 3 | | | |

FINANCIAL PERFORMANCE
(Cdn$ million, except share amounts)

	Year ending July 31			Six months ending January 31	
	1994	**1995**	**1996**	**1996**	**1997**
Sales & Revenue from services	$ 1,217.0	$ 1,737.0	$ 1,970.0	$ 909.5	$ 895.8
Gross Profit & Revenue from services	$ 158.1	$ 188.5	$ 203.2	$ 87.0	$ 89.4
EBITDA	$ 25.5	$ 30.6	$ 40.2	$ 9.7	$ 12.3
Net Income	$ 0.2	$ (7.4)	$ 5.9	$ (4.5)	$ (1.7)
Working Capital [1]	$ 75.0	$ 44.6	$ 71.6	$ 40.7	$ 91.9
Capital Expenditures	$ 27.7	$ 43.9	$ 26.8	$ 8.1	$ 7.9
Depreciation and Amortization	$ 12.9	$ 15.4	$ 16.1	$ 8.4	$ 8.2
Total Debt [2]	$ 269.4	$ 241.8	$ 217.7	$ 224.8	$ 280.3
Shareholders' Equity	$ 140.5	$ 130.6	$ 133.7	$ 153.7	$ 126.6
Total Assets	$ 564.0	$ 544.3	$ 531.4	$ 500.5	$ 472.3

SEGMENT INFORMATION

% of Operating Income

Grain Handling	-	49.5	72.8	929.8	301.7
Crop Inputs	-	37.9	14.5	(447.4)	(100.5)
Livestock	-	10.9	12.0	159.8	66.5
Communication & other	-	1.4	0.8	(542.2)	(167.7)

[1] Current assets minus current liabilities

[2] Bank loans plus long-term debt plus deferred income tax

Source: United Grain Growers 1996 annual report and 1997 second quarter report.

Exhibit 4

CONSOLIDATED BALANCE SHEET
(Cdn$ 000s as at January 31st)

	1997	1996
Cash	$ 64,501	5,094
Deposits - Canadian Wheat Board	3,241	7,178
Accounts receivable and prepaid expenses	95,275	77,156
Inventory	106,629	213,437
Current Assets	269,646	302,865
Capital Assets	190,660	182,997
Trade Investment and deferred charges	11,984	14,649
TOTAL ASSETS	$472,290	500,511
Bank and other loans	$ 83,338	167,901
Unpresented grain and other cheques	28,370	21,610
Accounts payable and accrued expenses	65,448	71,925
Current portion of long-term debt	598	728
Current Liabilities	177,754	262,164
Long - term debt	100,109	65,598
Deferred taxes	40,732	46,101
Shareholders' Equity -		
Series "A" Convertible Preferred Shares	24,009	24,009
Limited voting common shares	71,239	49,079
Retained Earnings	58,447	53,560
	153,695	126,648
TOTAL LIABILITIES AND SHAREHOLDERS' EQUITY	$472,290	500,511
Book Value Per Share	$ 11.22	10.94

Source: United Grain Growers 1997 second annual report.

	Exhibit 7

1997 TO 2001 FINANCIAL FORECASTS

	Forecast (Fiscal year ending July 31)				
	1998	1999	2000	2001	2002
Gross Profit & Revenue from Services	$233.49	$244.50	$270.00	$284.91	$294.92
% Change	5.5	9.4	10.4	5.5	3.5
EBITDA	$ 58.32	$ 73.96	$ 91.91	$ 99.92	$104.64
% Change	11.2	26.8	24.3	8.7	4.7
Capital Expenditures	$ 40.13	$ 27.53	$ 27.79	$ 25.82	$ 26.34
Increases (decreases) in working capital	$ 26.47	$ 24.09	$ 19.87	$ 13.67	$ 7.40
Depreciation and Amortization	$ 18.64	$ 21.51	$ 22.06	$ 22.34	$ 22.34

Source: Scotia Capital Markets.

Exhibit 8

COMPARABLE TRANSACTIONS

Transaction Description

Announce-ment Date	Target Company / Acquiring Company	Target's Business	Transaction Value (millions) [1]	Shares outstanding (millions)	Value per share	Premium Paid [2]		
						1 Day	1 Wk.	4 Wks.
	Canadian Comparables							
09-Mar-95	**Maple Leaf Foods Inc. / Castlefin** (Wallace McCain & Ontario Teachers Pension Plan Board)	Meat & poultry packer, bakery products and agri-business	$1,230.00	80.9	$15.21	5.8%	21.7%	28.1%
17-Sep-95	**Canada Malting Co. Ltd. / ConAgra Inc.**	World's largest producer of malted barley	$ 405.00	19.8	$20.50	2.5%	4.5%	0.0%
	U.S. Comparables							
12-Aug-93	**Curtice-Burns Foods / Pro-Fac Cooperative Inc.**	Produces and sells food products in the U.S. & Canada	$ 170.40	9	$19.00	34.5%	32.2%	24.6%
03-Feb-93	**Jimbo's Jumbos Inc. / JJJ Acquisition Corp.**	Buyer, miller, sheller and processor of peanuts and other nuts and nut meat products	$ 45.10	6.5	$ 6.93	42.2%	45.9%	63.1%
21-Oct-94	**Monk-Austin Inc. / Dibrell Brothers Inc.**	Purchases, processes then sells leaf tobacco to cigarette manufacturers worldwide	$ 264.90	18.1	$14.63	47.4%	51.3%	50.0%
02-Sep-92	**American Fructose Corp. / American Maize Products Co.**	Manufacturer of high fructose corn syrup, corn starch, and other corn derivative products.	$ 130.30	3.9	$33.32	-	-	-

[1] *Transaction value refers to the value of equity purchased in the currency of the target firm.*
[2] *The transaction price per share divided by the market price, subtract 1, where the market price is taken one day, one week and four weeks prior to announcement.*

Source: Scotia Capital Markets.

		**Exhibit 8 (continued)**

Target financial information [1]

Target Company / Acquiring Company	Balance Sheet Items [2]						LTM [3]			1 Year Forecast [4]	
	Cash	Invest in affiliates	Short-term debt	Long-term debt	Minority interest	Book equity	Revenues	EBITDA	Net income	Revenues	EBITDA
Canadian Comparables											
Maple Leaf Foods Inc. / Castlefin	222.1	51.9	-	38.3	61.9	1,035.0	3,185.0	185.7	75.7	3,165.0	198.0
Canada Malting Co. Ltd. / ConAgra Inc.	-	19.3	(23.5)	127.0	-	283.5	405.4	68.1	27.1	367.0	58.0
U.S. Comparables											
Curtice-Burns Foods / Pro-Fac Cooperative Inc.	6.5	-	50.6	239.1	-	75.7	878.6	64.3	11.0	-	-
Jimbo's Jumbos Inc. / JJJ Acquisition Corp.	0.9	-	15.4	0.9	-	49.1	75.0	6.0	2.3	-	-
Monk-Austin Inc. / Dibrell Brothers Inc.	8.4	15.5	243.7	34.9	-	150.8	462.8	10.4	-5.8	596.1	44.6
American Fructose Corp. / American Maize Products Co.	54.9	-	0.8	28.5	-	144.5	217.1	47.1	20.7	-	-

[1] All amounts are in millions of the currency of the target firm.

[2] Balance sheet numbers are from the most recent quarter prior to the announcement of the acquisition.

[3] LTM refers to the last 12 months leading up to the quarter which ended prior to acquisition announcement.

[4] Consensus forecast for the fiscal year ending after the acquisition announcement from IBES.

Exhibit 8 (continued)								

Ratio analysis

Target Company / Acquiring Company	Valuation Based On Transaction Terms ($)		Valuation Ratios					
	Equity Value	Total Enterprise Value (TEV) [1]	TEV / LTM Revenue	TEV / LTM EBITDA	Equity Value / LTM Net income	Equity Value / Book equity	TEV / Forecasted Revenue	TEV / Forecasted EBITDA
Canadian Comparables								
Maple Leaf Foods Inc. / Castlefin	1,230.0	1,056.2	0.33	5.69	16.25	1.19	0.33	5.33
Canada Malting Co. Ltd. / ConAgra Inc.	405.0	489.2	1.21	7.18	14.94	1.43	1.33	8.43
U.S. Comparables								
Curtice-Burns Foods / Pro-Fac Cooperative Inc.	170.4	453.6	0.52	7.05	15.49	2.25	-	-
Jimbo's Jumbos Inc. / JJJ Acquisition Corp.	45.1	60.5	0.81	10.08	19.61	0.92	-	-
Monk-Austin Inc. / Dibrell Brothers Inc.	264.9	519.6	1.12	49.96	-45.67	1.76	0.87	11.65
American Fructose Corp. / American Maize Products Co.	130.3	104.7	0.48	2.22	6.29	0.90	-	-

[1] Total enterprise value is market value of equity plus short and long-term debit plus preferred shares subtract cash and marketable securities.
Source: Scotia Capital Markets

Company	**Price ($)**	**Equity**	**Net**	**LTM** [3]			**1 Year Forecasted** [4]		
	(Mar 3, 1997)	**Market Value ($)** [1]	**Debt** [2] **($)**	**Revenues ($)**	**EBITDA ($)**	**Net Income**	**Revenues ($)**	**EBITDA ($)**	**Net Income**
United Grain Growers Limited	14.00	180.6	163.0	1,956.2	42.8	8.7	2,720.3	46.2	8.8
Canadian Comparables									
B.C. Sugar Refinery Limited	13.80	341.7	148.0	834.3	77.2	26.4	808.5	75.2	25.0
Canbra Foods Ltd.	17.40	49.5	4.5	195.0	13.1	5.6	-	-	-
Dover Industries Limited	16.50	56.6	11.3	133.9	9.8	4.5	-	-	-
Maple Leaf Foods Inc.	12.00	1,104.4	613.9	3,039.8	247.3	36.1	3,100.0	357.0	57.1
Saskatchewan Wheat Pool	18.70	553.0	507.0	4,400.1	162.6	51.1	4,259.7	161.9	50.0
United States Comparables									
Alico	19.00	133.5	8.4	44.4	20.0	9.0	-	-	-
Archer Daniels Midland Co.	18.50	10,071.6	926.2	13,582.7	1,150.9	636.4	13,185.0	1,415.0	712.0
ConAgra Inc.	53.00	13,093.2	6,364.5	24,789.7	1,684.9	502.6	26,395.0	1,817.0	620.0
Dekalb Genetics Corp.	65.25	1,123.6	122.9	404.5	58.2	19.2	427.0	55.0	20.0
Midwest Grain Products	15.25	148.9	39.5	200.6	12.8	(0.7)	207.4	35.3	10.5
Pioneer Hi-Bred Int'l. Inc.	68.13	5,611.8	(174.0)	1,719.0	430.0	223.0	1,754.7	458.0	244.9

Exhibit 9

COMPARABLE TRADING STATISTICS

[1] *Price multiplied by number of shares outstanding in millions of the currency of the firm.*
[2] *Short term plus long term debt minus cash from the most recent quarter prior to March 3, 1997.*
[3] *LTM refers to the last 12 months leading up to the most recent quarter prior to March 3, 1997.*
[4] *Consensus forecast for the fiscal year ending after March 3, 1997 from IBES.*

Source: Scotia Capital Markets.

Exhibit 9 (continued)

Company	Total Enterprise Value ($) (TEV) [1]	Valuation Multiples					Equity Value/Forecasted Net Income
		TEV / LTM Revenues	TEV / Forecast Revenues	TEV / LTM EBITDA	TEV / Forecast EBITDA	Equity value / LTM net income	
Canadian Comparables							
B.C. Sugar Refinery Limited	490.80	0.59	0.61	6.36	6.53	12.94	13.67
Canbra Foods Ltd.	54.20	0.28	-	4.14	-	8.84	-
Dover Industries Limited	68.90	0.51	-	7.03	-	12.58	-
Maple Leaf Foods Inc.	1,696.40	0.56	0.55	6.86	4.75	30.59	19.34
Saskatchewan Wheat Pool	1,036.60	0.24	0.24	6.38	6.40	10.82	11.06
United States Comparables							
Alico	141.90	3.20	-	7.10	-	14.83	-
Archer Daniels Midland Co.	10,452.50	0.77	0.79	9.08	7.39	15.83	14.15
ConAgra Inc.	19,982.70	0.81	0.76	11.86	11.00	26.05	21.12
Dekalb Genetics Corp.	1,241.90	3.07	2.91	21.34	22.58	58.52	56.18
Midwest Grain Products	188.40	0.94	0.91	14.72	5.34	(212.71)	14.18
Pioneer Hi-Bred Int'l Inc.	5,444.80	3.17	3.10	12.66	11.89	25.17	22.91

[1] Total enterprise value is market value of equity plus short- and long-term debt plus preferred shares subtract cash and marketable securities.

	Exhibit 10

SUMMARY OF POTENTIAL SYNERGIES

Potential Acquirer	EBITDA Savings (Cdn$ in millions)						One-time restructuring costs	Com-petition Risk Factor	Implemen-tation Risk Factor
	Corporate	Admin-istration	Country Elevators	Terminals	Ware-house	Total			
Alberta Wheat Pool and Manitoba Pool Elevators	11	15	9	16	5	56	31	50%	50%
Saskatchewan Wheat Pool	11	15	10	9	2	46	29	35%	35%
Pioneer Hi-Bred Int'l Inc.	11	14	1	8	-	34	18	15%	35%

Notes:

- *Full EBITDA savings are assumed to be achieved by 2000. In 1998 only one-third of the savings will be realized, and in 1999 only two-thirds will be realized. After 2000, savings should grow with inflation, which is expected to grow at two per cent per year in perpetuity.*

- *Administration refers to costs associated with the running of operations including elevators, terminals and warehouse. Corporate refers to head office expenses.*

- *One time restructuring costs will be spread equally over 1998 and 1999. These costs include severance costs of one year payroll due to layoffs and $3 million for systems upgrades.*

- *EBITDA and one-time costs are fully taxable.*

- *Competition risk factor is the probability that competition will eliminate the net synergy gains from the acquisition.*

- *Implementation risk factor is the probability that net synergy gains from the acquisition would be eliminated due to problems in implementation.*

Source: Scotia Capital Markets

THE EMPIRE COMPANY LIMITED–THE OSHAWA GROUP LIMITED PROPOSAL

INTRODUCTION

On Monday, September 8, 1998, Greg Rudka, managing director at Scotia Capital, called James Vaux, associate director, into his office. The purpose of the meeting was to discuss a story that had appeared in the newspaper that morning. The Oshawa Group Limited (Oshawa), a food retail, wholesale and distribution firm, had just announced the hiring of John Lacey as president and chief executive officer, with a mandate to enhance shareholder value. This was surprising as it meant the resignation of former president and chief operating officer, Jonathan Wolfe, a member of the family of controlling shareholders of the company. Rudka had long considered Oshawa an attractive acquisition target for the Empire Company Limited (Empire), a client interested in expanding beyond their Atlantic Canada roots. He wondered if this latest development was a signal that the Wolfe family, who controlled 100 per cent of the voting securities of the company, might consider a takeover offer. They discussed some of the key issues such as valuing Oshawa, identifying potential synergies and deal financing. Consolidation in the grocery business had been rampant in the United States and was likely to spread to Canada. They would have to act fast if Empire was to take advantage of any potential opportunity.

Richard Ivey School of Business
The University of Western Ontario

IVEY

Chris Lounds prepared this case under the supervision of Professors Tom Bates, Craig Dunbar and Steve Foerster solely to provide material for class discussion. The authors do not intend to illustrate either effective or ineffective handling of a managerial situation. The authors may have disguised certain names and other identifying information to protect confidentiality.

EMPIRE

Empire was founded in 1907 when J.W. Sobey opened a butcher shop in Stellarton, Nova Scotia. Over the years, the company grew into a diversified holding company, with interests in food distribution, real estate and corporate investment activities. The main thrust of the company was the support and operation of the Sobeys retail grocery business. Empire earned $88 million on revenues of $3.3 billion in fiscal 1998 (see Exhibits 1 and 2 for selected Empire financial data).

Food Distribution

The food distribution business, which made up 95 per cent of the company's 1998 revenue (but only 37 per cent of operating income), was composed of five operating groups: retail, wholesale, foodservice, drug and industries.

The retail group operated 112 stores under the Sobeys name. Sobeys was the largest food retail and distribution company in Atlantic Canada and had begun to expand into Ontario and Quebec. By April 1998, 34 per cent of Sobeys retail square footage was located in these two provinces. Each Sobeys location offered national and regional brand-name products, as well as private label products under the brand names Our Best and Signal. The retail group also operated corporate, franchised and associated stores under the Foodland, Lofood, Price Check Foods, Needs, Green Gables, Kwik-Way, Clover Farm and Riteway names.

The wholesale division consisted of three companies: TRA Maritimes and TRA Newfoundland in Atlantic Canada and Lumsden Brothers in Ontario. The wholesale group supplied all of the Sobeys and other stores operated by the retail division, as well as over 2,000 independent outlets, both directly and through cash and carry outlets. The wholesale division operated seven distribution outlets throughout the Atlantic provinces and one each in Ontario and Quebec.

The Sobeys Group was the largest foodservice operator in Atlantic Canada. It operated 11 distribution centres and serviced institutional clients, as well as independent and chain restaurant businesses. It also supplied fresh produce to Sobeys grocery stores in Atlantic Canada. Key operating units included The Clover Group and Judson Foods in Atlantic Canada and Burgess Wholesale in Ontario. The foodservice group also provided value-added services to clients, including access to a buying group, online ordering, menu planning and costing and nutritional education programs.

The drug group consisted of the Lawton's Drugs chain. The drug group operated both stand alone pharmacies and assisted with the development of the Sobeys combined food and drug store format.

The industry group provided ancillary services primarily to the food distribution group. The main businesses included a private label soft-drink maker (Big 8), a printing company (Eastern Sign-Print) and a video distribution business (Downeast Video).

Real Estate

The main focus of the real estate group was the acquisition, development and management of property portfolios, which supported or complemented Empire's retail operations. The group was further divided into Atlantic Shopping Centres, which consisted primarily of enclosed shopping centres and mixed-use office and retail developments, and Sobeys Leased Properties, which consisted mainly of free-standing food stores and attached shopping plazas. In total, the real estate group owned and managed 11.3 million square feet, of which 83 per cent was retail space and 17 per cent was office space.

Investments

The investments group consisted of equity investments in other companies, both long and short term. The goal of the investments group was to provide both geographic and industry diversification to Empire. Long-term investments, which comprised 76 per cent of the total investment portfolio, consisted of a 25 per cent ownership interest in Hannaford Brothers Company and a 43 per cent interest in Wajax Limited.

Hannaford

Hannaford was a U.S. based food retailer with operations in Maine, New Hampshire, Vermont, Massachusetts, New York, Virginia, North Carolina and South Carolina. The company operated 148 supermarkets under the Shop 'n Save and Hannaford names and 100 pharmacy operations within certain Hannaford locations. Earnings from continuing operations were US$84.4 million on revenues of US$3.2 billion for the year ended January 3, 1998. As of September 8, 1998, Empire's holdings of Hannaford were valued at approximately US$450 million.

Wajax Limited

Wajax was a distribution company engaged in the sale and service of mobile equipment, diesel engines and industrial components through a network of 100 distribution outlets throughout the United States and Canada. Industries served by Wajax include natural resources, construction, transportation, manufacturing, industrial processing and utilities. Wajax earned $21 million on revenues of $947 million. As of September 8, 1998, Empire's holdings of Wajax were valued at approximately $60 million.

Other

In addition to these core operations, Empire also ran Atlantic Canada's largest chain of movie theatres, with more than 100 screens under the Empire Theatre name.

Share Capital

Empire had 17.4 million Class B common shares and 19.5 million Class A non-voting shares outstanding. The Class B common shares were not publicly traded, and were held entirely by members of the Sobey family. The two share classes ranked equally, except that Class A had no voting rights, and directors could declare dividends for Class A without being obligated to declare equal or any dividends for the Class B shares. Class B shares were convertible at any time to Class A shares on a one-for-one basis. Under certain circumstances, if an offer was made to purchase the Class B shares, Class A shareholders had the right to receive a follow up offer at the highest per share price paid to Class B shareholders. This type of arrangement was known as a "coattail provision." The company also had several series of preferred shares outstanding.

OSHAWA

Oshawa was a food retail, wholesale and distribution company. It directly operated some grocery stores, but the majority (82 per cent) of their 845 stores were franchised operations. Earnings after tax from continuing operations before unusual items were $40.1 million on revenue of $6.8 billion in fiscal 1998. In 1997, after tax earnings from continuing operations were $54.6 million on revenue of $6.0 billion (see Exhibits 3 and 4 for selected Oshawa financial data).

The company was formed in 1951 when Ray Wolfe first brought the Independent Grocers Alliance to Canada. The Wolfe family remained relatively active in the operation of the company, retaining all of the voting equity in the firm, as well as occupying senior management positions and five of the 12 board seats (see Exhibit 5). The company was divided into a grocery division, Agora Food Merchants and a food service division, SERCA Foodservice.

Agora Food Merchants

Agora was Canada's second largest food retailer and was responsible for 82 per cent of Oshawa's revenues in 1998. It operated in all provinces of Canada, except British Columbia, primarily as a supplier of products and marketing programs to independent grocers under the IGA, Knechtel, Omni and Bonchoix banners.

While the majority of the stores it served were franchised operations, Agora also owned corporate stores under the IGA and Price Chopper banners.

SERCA Foodservice

SERCA Foodservice was Canada's largest foodservice business and distributed a full line of grocery and perishable products to the institutional, health care, hotel and restaurant trades. It operated in all 10 Canadian provinces, but the majority of its revenue came from the western provinces.

Oshawa Strategy

Oshawa management felt that returns on shareholder equity had traditionally been insufficient and, as a result, had recently considered various options designed to enhance shareholder value (see Exhibit 6 for the relative performance of Oshawa shares). Fiscal 1998 was a year of major restructuring which involved, among other things, the sale of non-core holdings, including the divestitures of its drug store operation (Pharma Plus), its cold storage facilities (Langs Cold Storage) and non-strategic real estate, and the expansion of its retail and foodservice businesses. During the year, Oshawa expanded its food businesses through the acquisition of Scott National, a food service distributor operating in Alberta, Saskatchewan, Manitoba and Northern Ontario, and the assets of six grocery stores in the province of Quebec. The company had previously acquired Neptune Foods of British Columbia in fiscal 1997. In fiscal 1999, Penner Foods of Manitoba was acquired.

Share Capital

The Oshawa Group had two classes of common shares outstanding, common and Class A. There were 685,504 common shares outstanding, distributed (substantially) equally amongst five members of the Wolfe family. The common shares were not publicly traded. As well, there were 37,894,905 Class A Shares outstanding. The Class A shares were non-voting, participating and entitled to a $0.10 non-cumulative annual dividend in priority to common.[1] Most importantly, there was not a coattail provision for Class A shares. This implied that, at least in theory, voting control of the company could be acquired by purchasing the common shares privately, with no obligation to make a bid for Class A shares, or in the event that a bid was made to provide the same consideration offered for the common shares. Class A shares were mostly held by a limited number of large financial institutions, although members of the Wolfe family were believed to hold, in the aggregate, approximately 10 per cent to 15 per cent of the issued Class A shares (see Exhibit 7 for a breakdown of share ownership).

THE GROCERY BUSINESS

The grocery business was a mature industry. In 1998 grocers faced increasing competition not only from other grocers, but also increasingly from various non-traditional vendors including drug stores, discount retailers, wholesale clubs and internet-based operations. On the revenue side, growth occurred primarily through horizontal merger and acquisition activity. Consolidation had increased substantially across North America in recent years for several reasons. First, it was generally cheaper to acquire a competitor than to open new stores. Acquisition also mitigated risks associated with entering a new market including lack of local knowledge, difficulty of attracting a qualified work force and the threat and intensity of competitive response. Horizontal acquisition activity also generated the economies of scale in marketing, procurement, distribution, technology, corporate overhead and private-label development.

---

[1]Participating means that if certain criteria are met, participating shareholders will receive an additional dividend payment beyond the predetermined amount.

THE COMPETITIVE LANDSCAPE

Vaux knew that in order to gauge the potential success of an acquisition, an analysis of the competitive land-scape would need to be done (see Exhibit 9 for a financial performance comparison of selected Canadian grocery store operators). It was also essential to assess the potential of rival bidders. Empire did not want to overpay for any acquisition and it was, therefore, essential that any transaction not escalate into a bidding war.

Loblaws

Loblaws was a subsidiary of George Weston Co., and was Canada's largest food retailer, with 20 per cent of the national market. In western Canada, it operated under The Real Canadian Superstore, Extra Foods, Real Canadian Wholesale Club, SuperValu, Shop Easy and Lucky Dollar banners. In the east, it operated under the Loblaws, Zehrs, Atlantic Superstore, Dominion (in Newfoundland only), Your Independent Grocer, No Frills, Fortino's and valu-mart names. Loblaws was the only company that competed on a national basis. In fiscal 1997, Loblaws earned $213 million on revenues of $11 billion.

Loblaws·was also seen as the greatest competitive risk for a rival bid for Oshawa. They had the financial capacity to make a rival bid and may have been able to capture high synergistic strategic gains. By acquir-ing Oshawa, Loblaws would be far and away the dominant player in the Canadian grocery business. The only mitigating factor in considering Loblaws as a potential competitor in an acquisition was speculation that there may be increased scrutiny from the Competition Bureau.[2]

Canada Safeway

Canada Safeway was based in Calgary and was a private, wholly-owned subsidiary of Safeway Inc. of California. Despite damaging labor disputes in 1996, Canada Safeway remained the dominant grocery store chain across Western Canada. Income before taxes and extraordinary items from Canadian operations was US$97.9 million on revenues of US$3.4 billion.

Although they had ample financial capacity to make a competing bid for Oshawa, it was not expected that they would do so. They had not yet shown any interest in expanding into the competitive Ontario mar-ket, or further east.

Metro-Richelieu

Metro-Richelieu was the largest food retailer in Quebec. It operated Metro supermarkets, Super C discount stores and Marché Richelieu neighborhood stores. It also ran an extensive wholesale distribution business. Net income in fiscal 1997 was $66.2 million on revenues of $3.4 billion.

Metro-Richelieu was seen as a potential rival for the acquisition of Oshawa. If successful, it would solid-ify their position as the largest grocer in Quebec, as well as giving them national scope.

Provigo

Provigo was the largest food distributor in Quebec and had a growing presence in Ontario. It operated under the banners Provigo, Loeb and Maxi & Co. Until 1997, it had also operated convenience store chains under its C-Corp subsidiary, but this division was sold to Alimentation Couche-Tard. Net income in fiscal 1998 was $68.7 million on revenues of $5.9 billion.

If Provigo were to acquire Oshawa, they would become the largest grocer in Quebec, improve Ontario penetration and extend their reach nationally. While Provigo also operated franchised stores, their preferred method of expansion was by building their own corporate network.

---

[2]The Competition Bureau was an agency of the Canadian Government. Part of its mandate was to review merger transactions to ensure that, if completed, they would not result in a lessening or prevention of competition in the marketplace.

Overwaitea Food Group

The Overwaitea Food Group was based in Langley, B.C. and was privately owned by the Pattison Group. It operated supermarkets under the Overwaitea and Save-On-Foods & Drug Stores and the wholesale operation Associated Grocers. The Pattison Group also operated Buy-Low Foods, a smaller chain with its own wholesale operation. Because it was a privately held company, results of operations were not known.

A potential rival bid from the Pattison Group was seen as possible. While Oshawa had only a small presence in British Columbia, the acquisition would provide national exposure.

The Great Atlantic & Pacific Company of Canada Ltd.

The Great Atlantic & Pacific Company of Canada was a private, wholly-owned subsidiary of The Great Atlantic & Pacific Tea Company of New Jersey. It operated under the A&P and Dominion banners. Income from Canadian operations was US$895,000 on sales of US$1.5 billion in fiscal 1998.

A&P was not seen as a potential rival bidder, despite the fact that the Canadian operation was outperforming the U.S. counterpart. The parent company had never before expressed any interest in expanding their Canadian operations.

CANADIAN ECONOMY

The most significant events of 1998 were the Asian and Russian economic crises. Both had resulted from defaults on corporate and government debt, which led to massive currency devaluations. These events had left the Russian and most major Asian economies in turmoil, significantly lowering world demand for most commodities and reducing Canadian corporate profit expectations.

The Bank of Canada had lowered interest rates nine times since 1996 to boost the economy and lower unemployment. The low interest rates were also having the effect of devaluing the Canadian dollar against most world currencies. By August, the Canadian dollar was worth slightly less than US$0.65. This devaluation initially helped alleviate some of the effects of the global crisis. To restore confidence in the dollar, the Bank of Canada increased the bank rate by a full percentage point on August 27, 1998. This action halted the slide of the dollar, but did not reverse it. It was currently trading at US$0.6474 compared to US$0.7207 one year before. The current yield for 91-day treasury bills was 5.6 per cent and the 10-year government bond yield was 5.8 per cent.

Real Gross Domestic Product (GDP) growth had increased substantially since 1992 and was 1.2 per cent in 1996, and 3.7 per cent in 1997. Real GDP was forecast to grow by 3.4 per cent in 1998 and 2.4 per cent in 1999. There were significant risks that, because of global economic conditions, this growth would not be achieved.

Despite the world economic crises, unemployment in Canada had actually decreased over the year. Unemployment currently stood at 8.3 per cent, as opposed to 9.0 per cent a year earlier. The decrease in unemployment had not yet had any effect on inflation. The Consumer Price Index had increased only 1.6 per cent in both 1996 and 1997. Forecasts called for inflation to slow to 1.2 per cent in 1998 and 1.3 per cent in 1999.

VALUATION OF OSHAWA

Oshawa stock was currently at $26, but had traded as high as $29.25 six weeks earlier (average price over the last 20 trading days was $26.46). With just over 38 million shares outstanding, this implied an equity market value of approximately $1 billion. Vaux knew, however, that the Wolfe family was unlikely to sell their shares unless they were offered a significant premium to market. Further, in the event that Empire wanted to make a pre-emptive offer for the company and avoid a bidding war, Vaux understood that an attractive offer would be necessary. He began by gathering information on food industry mergers that had taken place in the United States, as no similar transactions had taken place in Canada (see Exhibit 10). He also examined the relative value of comparable firms (see Exhibit 11).

In order to get a clearer picture of the value of the company, Vaux elected to do a discounted cash flow

(DCF) analysis of Oshawa. He decided to perform two separate DCF analyses. The first would be based on Oshawa as a stand-alone entity with a specific cash flows forecast five years into the future (see Exhibits 11 and 12 for some information gathered). This analysis would assist in determining the intrinsic value of Oshawa, relative to its current market value. The second would be a separate DCF of the potential synergies with Empire. Vaux knew that revenue growth, EBITDA margins and capital expenditures would be the key drivers of the analysis. Examining historical data, he saw that revenue growth had averaged approximately six per cent over the past 10 years. He believed that it would be reasonable to assume this growth was sustainable for the next five years. Beyond that, he thought that a growth rate in line with long-term GDP growth was reasonable. As of September, he estimated sales for the previous twelve months to be $7 billion. Based on discussions with Empire management, Vaux believed that EBITDA margins at Oshawa would increase over the near term to 2.6 per cent, still far below the industry average given their heavy concentration in the food service business. Recent years had seen increases in capital expenditures by Oshawa, relative to sales. Vaux believed that this was because store improvements had traditionally been low, which might mean that some of the stores would be in very poor condition and would require substantial investment. As a result, he believed that capital expenditures as a percentage of sales would remain at or near two per cent of sales for the first year following the merger, but could fall to approximately one per cent by year five.

Vaux also wanted to derive the value of any potential synergies through a separate DCF analysis. He considered two kinds of potential synergies: those related to margin enhancements and those related to cost reductions. In conversations with Empire management, he received the following "best case" information. In terms of the EBITDA margin, Empire management believed that annual EBITDA savings could be generated through stronger and more coordinated buying power. While Empire management believed that no improvement in margins were possible in the first year, they estimated that a 0.15 per cent improvement could be realized in the second year, as well as 0.25 per cent in the third year and 0.50 per cent in all subsequent years. Further cost synergies based on elimination of duplicate administration, merchandising, buying, pricing and accounting were estimated to be $39.5 million per year. Distribution and divisional management costs savings were estimated at $4.1 million per year and reflected the rationalization of direct operating and warehouse wages in Ontario and Quebec. Advertising savings were estimated at $2 million per year, based on the ability to merge retail banners. Vaux had observed that the full value of potential synergies was rarely fully realized, and that in any event, given the risk of achieving the synergies, Empire would be unwilling to pay for their full value in the transaction. Therefore, in order to be conservative, Vaux estimated that no cost synergies would occur in the first year, 37.5 per cent of potential cost synergies would occur in the second year, then 75 per cent of potential cost synergies would occur in year three and beyond.

Partially offsetting the synergy benefits, Vaux recognized that some up-front merger costs would arise. He estimated that a merger would result in one-time charges of approximately $80 million consisting of items including severance packages, and the costs associated with closing and converting existing retail spaces. All up-front merger costs were tax deductible.

DEAL FINANCING AND STRUCTURE

If the deal were to be viable, Vaux would also need to recommend a financing package. Empire carried a substantial investment portfolio, the sale of which could generate more than $1 billion at market prices and perhaps more, assuming a premium for control blocks of Hannaford and Wajax. However, the Sobey family viewed the investment portfolio, especially the long-term portion, as part of a diversified asset base essential to the long-term viability of the company.

Empire already carried a substantial debt load relative to its competitors (due in part to its extensive real estate operations) and, therefore, any additional debt could be relatively expensive and threaten their A debt rating.

Empire was a publicly traded company and, therefore, additional equity could be issued to finance an acquisition. However, the Sobey family wanted to retain control over Empire and they felt the stock was trading at a substantial discount to its true value. Another option would be to spin off the food business into a separate entity. Oshawa shareholders would receive equity in the new company as consideration in the transaction. However, if this option were to be pursued, a value needed to be determined for the new shares. Vaux believed that the easiest way to value equity in a new company would be to use trading multiples of similar companies (see Exhibit 11). This alternative posed risks as well, as the new shares would not trade publicly until after the transaction was completed. There was a chance that Oshawa shareholders would not react well to receiving something with no observable value. The advantage of the spin-off alternative was that it would create a "pure-play" stock, which would be easier for the market to understand, likely leading to a higher valuation.

Using some form of equity to (at least partially) finance the deal would be attractive to the Wolfe family, as well, as it would allow them to defer some capital gains taxes. Whatever the final structure, it was absolutely essential that Empire retain majority equity interest and voting control over all its businesses.

SUMMARY

Vaux and Rudka knew they had an enormous task ahead of them. There were many questions that needed answers and they did not feel that they had much time to find them. They had to find a way to approach the Wolfe family and secure their support. They needed to derive a value for both classes of shares that was both reasonable for Empire to pay and that would be enough to appease the Wolfe family and other Oshawa equity holders. They also had to develop a strategy that would dissuade others from entering into a bidding war. Last, but definitely not least, they needed to find a way to finance the deal. As Vaux left the office, he knew he would be busy, but was eager to get started on what was to be, at the very least, an exciting transaction.

Exhibit 1

EMPIRE COMPANY LTD FINANCIAL STATEMENTS
CONSOLIDATED BALANCE SHEET
April 30
(in thousands of dollars)

	1998	1997
Assets		
Current Assets		
Cash	$ 28,268	$ 32,185
Receivables	89,153	78,701
Inventories	197,650	194,126
Prepaid Expenses	15,319	14,100
Investments, at cost (quoted market value $246,418; 1997 $211,468)	156,388	148,746
	486,778	467,858
Investments, at equity (quoted market value $800,436; 1997 $575,133)	325,579	300,447
Current assets and marketable investments	812,357	768,305
Fixed assets	1,069,026	1,001,873
Other assets	25,850	27,193
	$ 1,907,233	$ 1,797,371
Liabilities and Shareholders' Equity		
Current Liabilities		
Bank loans and notes payable	$ 286,532	$ 239,757
Payables and accruals	338,774	298,550
Income taxes payable	9,712	11,462
Long term debts due within one year	24,222	89,702
	659,240	639,471
Long term debt	616,571	606,843
Minority interest	-	171
Deferred income taxes	73,083	71,336
	1,348,894	1,317,821
Shareholders' Equity		
Capital stock	229,889	234,130
Retained earnings	305,422	228,254
Foreign currency translation	23,028	17,166
	558,339	479,550
	$ 1,907,233	$ 1,797,371

Source: Empire Company Limited Annual Report, 1998

Exhibit 1 (continued)

CONSOLIDATED INCOME STATEMENT
April 30
(in thousands of dollars)

	1998	1997
Revenue	$ 3,320,000	$ 3,149,773
Cost of sales, selling and administrative expenses	3,127,112	2,971,925
	192,888	177,848
Depreciation	70,404	65,433
	122,484	112,415
Investment income	41,253	35,568
Operating income	163,737	147,983
Interest expense		
Long term debt	64,340	70,512
Short term debt	12,328	8,746
	76,668	79,258
	87,069	68,725
Gain on sale of investments and properties	6,524	1,447
	93,593	70,172
Gain on sale of investment in Jannock Limited	35,868	-
Share of asset impairment provision by equity accounted investment	(8,788)	-
	120,673	70,172
Income taxes		
Sale of investment in Jannock Limited	7,792	-
Other operations	25,092	16,930
	32,884	16,930
Minority interest	7	363
	$ 32,891	$ 17,293
Net earnings	$ 87,782	$ 52,879

Source: Empire Company Limited Annual Report, 1998

Exhibit 2
FIVE-YEAR STOCK PRICE OF EMPIRE

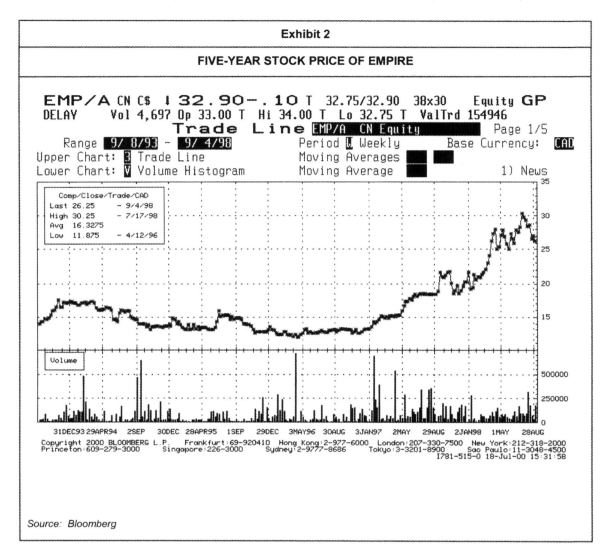

Source: Bloomberg

	Exhibit 3

OSHAWA GROUP LTD. FINANCIAL STATEMENTS

CONSOLIDATED BALANCE SHEETS
January 24, 1998 and January 25, 1997
(in millions of dollars)

	1998	1997
Assets		
Current Assets		
Cash and short-term investments	$ 65.0	$ 20.1
Accounts receivable	318.5	294.8
Income taxes receivable	5.6	0.8
Inventories	302.6	274.2
Prepaid expenses	17.4	16.9
Net assets of discontinued operations	-	99.7
	709.1	706.5
Fixed assets	501.8	509.7
Other assets	294.7	219.2
	$ 1,505.6	$ 1,435.4
Liabilities and Shareholders' Equity		
Current Liabilities		
Bank indebtedness	$ 17.1	$ 36.0
Accounts payable and accrued liabilities	429.5	379.0
	446.6	415.0
Long-term debt	128.6	120.0
Deferred income taxes	36.2	53.9
Unearned revenue	36.4	24.6
	647.8	613.5
Shareholders' equity		
Capital stock	255.9	252.9
Retained earnings	601.9	569.0
	857.8	821.9
	$ 1,505.6	$ 1,435.4

Source: Oshawa Group Limited Annual Report, 1998

Exhibit 3 (continued)

CONSOLIDATED STATEMENTS OF EARNINGS
January 24, 1998 and January 25, 1997
(in millions of dollars)

	1998	1997
Sales and other revenues - continuing operations	$6,813.1	$5,987.6
Cost of sales and expenses	6,651.7	5,837.5
Depreciation and amortization	66.2	59.7
Earnings from continuing operations	95.2	90.4
Interest	(7.9)	(6.5)
Unusual items	(20.3)	8.8
Earnings before income taxes	67.0	92.7
Income taxes	(26.9)	(38.1)
Net earnings from continuing operations	40.1	54.6
Discontinued operations	13.9	0.6
Net earnings	$ 54.0	$ 55.2

Source: Oshawa Group Limited Annual Report, 1998

Exhibit 4

FIVE YEAR STOCK PRICE OF OSHAWA

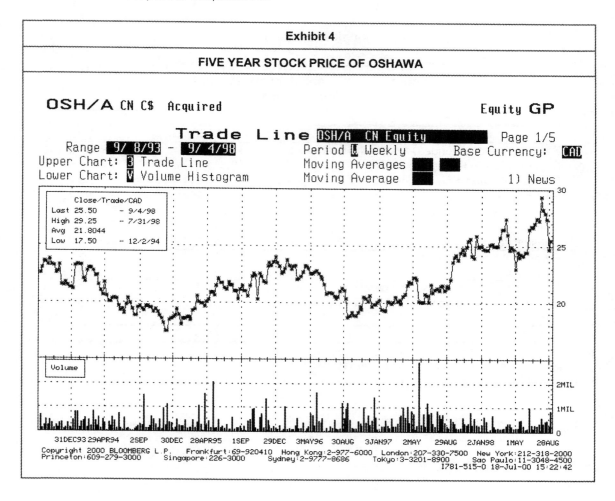

Exhibit 5

OSHAWA GROUP LIMITED BOARD OF DIRECTORS

Donald Carr, Q.C.	Partner, Goodman and Carr
Allister P. Graham	Chairman, Oshawa Group
Stanley H. Hart, O.C, Q.C.	Chairman, Salomon Brothers Canada Inc.
Peter C. Maurice	Vice-Chairman, CT Financial Services Inc.
Charles Perrault, C.M, M.Eng.	President, Schroder Investment Canada Limited
Lawrence Stevenson	President and CEO, Chapters Inc.
Charles Winograd	Deputy Chairman, RBC Dominion Securities Inc.
Harold J. Wolfe	Vice-President Real Estate, Oshawa Group Ltd.
Harvey S. Wolfe	President, Boatwright Investments Limited
Jonathon Wolfe	[Former] President and COO, Oshawa Group Ltd.
Myron J. Wolfe	Group Vice President, Foodservice and Produce, Oshawa Group Ltd.
Richard J. Wolfe	President, Codville Distributors (a division of Oshawa)

Source: Oshawa Group Limited Annual Report, 1998

Exhibit 6
SHARE PRICE APPRECIATION OF CANADIAN GROCERY COMPANIES

	1997	**Two Year**	**Three Year**	**Five Year**
TSE Food Stores Index	63.2%	32.6%	31.3%	17.6%
Empire	64.2%	29.4%	16.5%	15.7%
Loblaws	83.0%	58.6%	48.2%	31.9%
Metro-Richelieu	42.9%	26.5%	38.7%	26.2%
Provigo	55.9%	2.4%	20.1%	2.2%
Average	61.8%	29.9%	30.6%	18.7%
Oshawa	23.5%	2.1%	10.3%	1.9%

Source: Scotia Capital Markets as of December 31, 1997.

Exhibit 7
OWNERSHIP BLOCKS OF OSHAWA CLASS A SHARES

Shareholder*	**Shares Held**	**% of Total**
Trimark	6,775,300	17.9%
Templeton	4,556,159	12.0%
Investors Group	3,634,550	9.6%
		39.5%
Gryphon	1,021,822	2.7%
Caisse de Depot	853,074	2.3%
Mackenzie	600,000	1.6%
C.A. Delaney	561,600	1.5%
	18,002,505	47.5%
Total Shares Outstanding	37,894,905	

Source: Scotia Capital Markets
* It was also estimated that the Wolfe family members held approximately
15% of the outstanding Class A shares

Exhibit 8
SHARE OF GROCERY DOLLARS

(Based on 1997 Revenue, in millions of dollars)

	Sales ($)	Share
Loblaw Companies Ltd.	$ 11,008	20.5%
The Oshawa Group Ltd.	6,813	12.7%
Provigo Inc.	5,956	11.1%
Canada Safeway Ltd.	4,720	8.8%
Metro-Richelieu Inc.	3,432	6.4%
Empire Co. Ltd.*	2,978	5.6%
Great Atlantic & Pacific Co. of Canada	2,458	4.6%
Federated Co-ops Ltd.	2,411	4.5%
Southland Canada Inc.	830	1.5%
Silcorp Ltd.	743	1.4%
Calgary Co-operative Association Ltd.	592	1.1%
Alimentation Couche-Tard	390	0.7%
Interprovincial Co-op	218	0.4%
Total Industry Sales	$ 53,578	

Source: Financial Post, Canadian Grocer, Empire Company Annual Report 1998
*Food distribution revenue from Empire Company. Includes revenue
from drug and foodservice.

Exhibit 9

CANADIAN FOOD STORE COMPANY COMPARISON

(in millions of dollars)	Empire	Oshawa	Loblaws	Metro-Richelieu	Provigo
Market Value of Equity (as of 2/13/98)	776	951	6,735	850	990
Total Debt	918	135	876	77	327
Enterprise Value*	1,695	1,086	7,629	927	1,317
Revenues	3,208	7,052	10,554	3,432	5,859
EBITDA	219	165	534	155	232
EBITDA Margin	6.8%	2.4%	5.1%	4.5%	4.0%
Net Income	59	49	199	66	90
Net Margin	1.8%	0.7%	1.9%	1.9%	1.5%
Beta**	0.74	0.77	0.55	0.59	1.20
Credit Rating***	A	AA	A	n/a	BBB

Source: Bloomberg, Scotia Capital Markets

All information based on latest twelve months

* Market value of equity, plus market value of debt, less cash

** Beta based on weekly returns over two years

*** Canadian Bond Rating Service Rating of Senior Unsecured Debt

  Risk premiums over government yields were currently around 75 basis points for

  AAA-rated firms, 100 for AA and 125 for A, and 150 for BBB

Exhibit 10

HISTORICAL TRANSACTION DATA

Target	Acquiror	Announcement Date	Transaction Size			Premium to 20 Day Avg	Enterprise Value to (Latest twelve months)			Price to	
			Equity	Enterprise	Consideration		Revenue	EBITDA	EBIT	Earnings (LTM)	Book
Carr-Gottstein	Safeway Inc.	06-Aug-98	$ 113	$ 319	cash	56.3%	0.55x	6.9x	10.8x	n/a	4.4x
American Stores Co.	Albertson's	03-Aug-98	$ 8,939	$ 11,930	shares	25.8%	0.62x	9.5x	15.4x	26.8x	3.8x
Delchamps Inc.	Jitney-Jungle Stores	08-Jul-97	$ 227	$ 240	cash	0.4%	0.22x	5.8x	13.5x	26.8x	3.1x
Riser Foods	Giant Eagle	14-May-97	$ 426	$ 480	cash	15.3%	0.36x	8.5x	13.0x	17.2x	4.9x
Vons Companies	Safeway Inc.	30-Oct-96	$ 2,498	$ 3,025	shares	25.1%	0.56x	8.8x	13.7x	26.9x	0.9x
Kash n' Karry Food Stores	Food Lion	31-Oct-96	$ 126	$ 347	cash	14.5%	0.34x	6.3x	11.7x	n/a	6.5x
Stop & Shop	Royal Ahold NV	28-Mar-96	$ 1,682	$ 2,795	cash	20.6%	0.68x	8.9x	12.4x	22.3x	1.2x
National Convenience Stores	Diamond Shamrock	08-Nov-95	$ 186	$ 250	cash	9.9%	0.28x	6.8x	10.9x	19.6x	3.8x
Super Rite	Richfood Holdings	26-Jun-95	$ 212	$ 327	shares	29.4%	0.22x	6.6x	8.9x	15.9x	5.3x
Bruno's	KKR	20-Apr-95	$ 947	$ 1,167	97% cash, 3% shares	29.7%	0.41x	9.3x	15.9x	27.9x	2.2x

Source: Scotia Capital Markets

| | | Enterprise Value to EBITDA | | | Price to Earnings | |
	Year End	1997	1998E	1999E	1998E	1999E
Empire	April	9.5x	7.8x	7.1x	14.6x	11.8x
Loblaws	December	15.9x	13.6x	11.4x	31.4x	27.0x
Metro-Richelieu	September	6.5x	6.0x	5.5x	12.4x	11.4x
Provigo	January	6.0x	5.8x	5.5x	14.8x	12.3x
Oshawa	January	6.8x	6.7x	5.7x	17.9x	14.6x

Exhibit 11

TRADING RATIOS OF SELECTED CANADIAN GROCERY RETAILERS

Source: Scotia Capital Markets

Exhibit 12					
FIVE YEAR SELECTED HISTORICAL FINANCIAL INFORMATION					
	1998	**1997**	**1996**	**1995**	**1994**	**1993**

	1998	1997	1996	1995	1994	1993
Empire						
Sales	3,320.0	3,149.7	2,915.2	2,699.5	2,577.4	
Dep. & Amort.	70.4	65.4	60.0	57.5	50.7	
Working Capital	153.1	128.8	178.5	183.6	204.3	
Capital Expend.	137.5	82.7	125.7	120.1	98.1	
Oshawa						
Sales	6,813.0	5,988.0	5,765.0	5,650.0	5,305.0	
Dep. & Amort.	66.0	60.0	57.0	55.0	50.0	
Working Capital	262.0	292.0	193.0	223.0	201.0	
Capital Expend.	130.0	135.0	106.0	60.0	59.0	
Loblaws						
Sales		11,008.0	9,848.0	9,854.0	10,000.0	9,356.0
Dep. & Amort.		147.0	122.0	129.0	138.0	126.0
Working Capital		202.0	154.0	179.0	29.0	148.0
Capital Expend.		517.0	389.0	302.0	339.0	315.0
Metro-Richelieu						
Sales		3,432.3	3,266.0	3,145.6	2,909.0	2,772.7
Dep. & Amort.		39.2	37.0	38.7	40.4	37.1
Working Capital		4.6	1.0	3.8	(4.7)	(8.7)
Capital Expend.		79.1	57.1	38.0	40.5	19.5
Provigo						
Sales	5,956.2	5,832.5	5,725.2	5,542.5	5,433.4	
Dep. & Amort.	77.6	70.9	62.1	61.0	59.7	
Working Capital	(45.0)	(104.9)	(104.3)	(24.5)	(209.9)	
Capital Expend.	184.0	171.4	95.3	37.5	41.9	
Safeway						
Sales		22,483.8	17,269.0	16,397.5	15,626.6	15,214.5
Dep. & Amort.		455.8	338.5	329.7	326.4	330.2
Working Capital		n/a	n/a	n/a	n/a	n/a
Capex		829.4	620.3	503.2	352.2	290.2
A&P						
Sales		10,179.4	10,262.2	10,089.0	10,101.4	10,332.0
Dep. & Amort.		233.7	234.2	230.7	225.4	235.4
Working Capital		90.0	262.1	215.4	191.0	92.3
Capex		438.3	267.6	296.9	236.1	214.9

Source: Annual reports of listed companies